LAST OF NINE

Last of Nine

AUBREY MALONE

First published February 2021

ISBN 978-1-913144-22-7

Cover:

PENNILESS PRESS PUBLICATIONS
Website:www.pennilesspress.co.uk/books

He had come a long way to this blue lawn and his dream must have seemed to close he could hardly fail to grasp it. He did not know that it was already behind him, somewhere back in that vast obscurity beyond the city where the dark fields of the republic rolled on under the night.

Gatsby believed in the green light, the orgiastic future that year by year recedes before us. It eluded us then but that's no matter. Tomorrow we will run faster, stretch out our arms farther.

So we beat on, boats against the current, borne back ceaselessly into the past.

F. Scott Fitzgerald

Hail Glorious Saint Patrick

March 17, 1953. Dr Bourke was having trouble getting me to come out of my mother. I was staying inside just that bit too long. It was lovely and snug in there. Would he have to induce me? Perform a Caesarean section?

It was Saint Patrick's Day. I didn't want to share it with our national holy man. Why should he get the attention that should have been mine and mine alone? Why didn't he stay minding those sheep in Wales in 432 instead of sailing over to Ireland intent on stealing my thunder?

I wasn't a planned child. Was there such a thing in 1953? Family planning for Catholics in 1950s Ireland meant talking about where you were going to sit at the dinner table. The term 'surprise pregnancy' was a euphemism for 'nightmare pregnancy.'

It was three years since my mother had last given birth. That was to my sister Jacinta. She thought she'd be her last child. Little did she know what was on the way.

In the Ireland of my youth a woman's sexual choice in life was either perpetual virginity (spinsterhood) or perpetual pregnancy (marriage). If she had a big family she was either a good Catholic or a bad Protestant. It was the era between prudery and libertinism, between the chastity belt and vasectomies.

Philip Larkin wrote, 'Sexual intercourse began in 1963/Which was rather late for me/Between the end of the Chatterley ban/And the Beatles first LP.' For Irish people it began – and usually ended – with an eight letter word beginning with 'm' and ending with 'e.'

Steve Martin once joked that children were God's punishment for having sex. It wasn't so funny when pregnant mothers were told by their doctors that giving birth could endanger their health. Many Irish women died that way in the past.

There was no birth control worth speaking of in the fifties except the 'rhythm method.' It was better known as Vatican Roulette. Women were primarily seen as babymakers in those days. 'Go forth and multiply,' the Bible exhorted. The words were taken literally.

My mother was pregnant thirteen times between 1937 and 1953. Her first child, Keith, was born in 1937. I came along 16 years later. She had some miscarriages in between as well as a stillborn birth and a pair of twins who only lived a week. They were called Raymond and Mary.

When a child dies today, parents often get counselling. That wasn't available in the past. You just had to accept things. My mother was good at that. I know how traumatised she had to have been but she never talked about it. Maybe she'd even have hidden it from herself. The rest of us spoke affectionately of Raymond and Mary as we grew up but there were no photographs taken of them. We don't know anything about them so they're really just words to us. Their names are the only records of them available to us in our minds.

The nine of us that survived were Keith, Clive, June, Ruth, Hugo, Basil, Audrey, Jacinta and myself. Two boys, two girls, two more boys, two more girls and finally me. I was variously described as the runt of the litter or an afterthought. We all had nicknames. Clive was Chivers. Keith was Twitter. June was Junie. Ruth was Boots. Hugo was Mustard. Basil was Bizzy Banny. Audrey was Aunie. Jacinta was Hinty or Jin the Bin the Jelly Dee. I was Curly Top.

The boys were all given English names because my father had pro-British attitudes. They probably came from his own father. His businesses were flourishing under John Bull. My father was twelve when the 1916 Uprising took place. The most seismic event in our country's history was nothing more than a brief interruption to his schoolwork. 'A few bullets were fired from the GPO,' he said to me in later years, 'Everyone got on with their lives afterwards. It was nothing.' Maybe we all view the events of history through our own private lens. I became infected with his hibernophobia. The tricolour meant little to me during my youth. I was as happy drawing swastikas.

Two of the girls had religious names. Ruth was from the Bible. Jacinta was called after the Portuguese girl who was believed to have seen a vision of Our Lady at Fatima. Audrey probably paved the way for me. June was born on May 31. That gave my father the opportunity to say to Dr. Bourke, 'The last of May saw the first of June.'

Dr Bourke's daughter, Mary Robinson, went on to become the resident of Ireland in 1991. His first name was Aubrey. He thought I was named after him but I wasn't. I was named after Aubrey de Vere the poet. My father was reading one of his books the night before I was born.

My mother wanted me to be named Pat because of me being born on St. Patrick's Day. I wish I was. I always thought of Aubrey as a girl's name. Her own name was Patricia. My father called her Pat, a boy's name. Everything was back to front. I should have been the Pat of the family instead of her. She didn't contest the issue and he got his way. It was only right. He had, after all, impregnated her. She only had to carry me for nine months – the easy bit.

I was born on a Tuesday. 'Tuesday's child has far to go,' as the saying goes. I always felt that about myself.

Martin Heidegger coined a wonderful expression for being born: *geworfenheit*. It roughly translates as a 'thrownness into being.' That's exactly what it is.

9

You're plonked into a place where everything feels strange. Because it is.

I couldn't have been born at a better time. World War II was over. The world was on the verge of change. Ballina had started to throw off the dull grey clothes of the forties. When that decade ended it was as if the world had changed from black and white into colour. Liberation was in the air and we caught the whiff of it. Elvis was coming. So were James Dean, Muhammad Ali, John F. Kennedy and Marlon Brando. And me.

My young world had no boundaries. I didn't know who I was or where I belonged. I was like an anti-person. The sights and sounds that impinged on me were like from another planet. I felt as if I was living in a sea of ghosts. When people talked to me it was as if they were under water. Only gradually did things start to make sense to me. It was when I started walking. Afterwards everything crowded in on me like a storm - the rooms I went into, what I could see out the window, the sky and the trees and fields. It was like a sudden invasion to my senses. After that everything became expectable. It became like routine. It was as if I'd been in the world forever.

My childhood tantrums, I believe, were sights to behold. The baby of the family is usually given everything he wants. World War III is declared if he doesn't get it. I've been told I was no exception to this rule. The good news was that after my arrival my mother could relax at last. Her child-bearing days were over.

We lived on Arthur Street. It was a street you hit in a straight line when you were driving in from Foxford on the Dublin Road. It was the last in a long line of roads that went from the country to the train station. I thought of it as the first street of the actual town. You felt you were on the outskirts before you got to it. It was average in length but there was always an air of activity about it.

That was because it had so many public buildings – the cinema, the fire station, the Town Hall. When drivers got to it they started to think about what their business was. They wondered if they'd go shopping or meet people or whatever. When I was young you could park pretty much anywhere you liked because there were so few cars on the road. In later years that changed.

The font was the first thing you saw when you got to the street. Our house was on the middle on the left. It was mainly coloured yellow but there were black panels for the protruding tiles down each wall.

There were three windows upstairs and two downstairs. One was on each side of the front door. The downstairs windows had low sills. We were able to sit on them even when we were small.

If you travelled down the street in the fifties you'd probably have seen some of us playing outside. There wasn't much else to do. It was an age before leisure centres or the internet or any of the other things that keep today's children confined to their houses.

The Currans lived next door to us. I have no memory of Mr or Mrs Curran. I only remember their daughter Bridie. She had lovely fair hair. Some people said it was a wig. We heard some medical condition took her natural hair away.

The Hegartys were on the other side. I don't remember Mr or Mrs Hegarty either, just a load of children they had. They were always playing on the street like us but we didn't play together much. Next to them was Gildie Ahern. He was a strange man who had an orchard at the back of his house.

There was another neighbour we used to have called Pascal Gallagher. His family left the street before my time. I was told his favourite hobby was eating worms. I'd love to have known him. Why wasn't I born sooner?

When I was two weeks old a girl called Tina came to our house. She became our 'girl.' My mother always had a girl to help her with jobs around the house. The previous one had to go away for a few weeks. Tina was filling in for her.

She was only a teenager when she came to us. She used to see us playing on the street. We seemed to be doing that anytime she passed the house. She was only supposed to be with us until the other girl came back but my mother liked her so much she asked her to stay on. Tina was delighted and so were we.

As I grew up I spent as much time with Tina as my mother. At times I felt as if I had two mothers. Every time Tina went shopping she brought me with her on the carrier of her bike. We usually came back with my favourite purchase: a bar of chocolate. She always cut it up for me and made a sandwich from it. It's an addiction I've kept.

The main shop we went to was Geraghty's. Jimmy Geraghty owned it. His son Tommy was in Primary School with me. They lived above the shop. It was across the road from Aunt Nellie's house. They had everything from a needle to an anchor as the saying goes. It was a supermarket before the term was invented.

They sold alcohol as well as groceries. We had a book where a list of all the things we bought was written down. The price was scribbled opposite it. Every few months we paid it off. Then the process started all over again. You couldn't go down to Geraghty's without my father saying, 'Don't forget the book.' I still remember how it looked. It had a red cover with a black margin down the side.

I was five before I started school. I skipped Low First, what they call Senior Infants today.

I went to the convent first. My abiding impression of it is the railings that surrounded the building. It meant I associated school with captivity from the very beginning. I often played with marla. It was a kind of modelling clay. I used to mispronounce it as *mála,* the Irish word for 'bag.'

I was put sitting outside on the grass on the warm spring days. Nuns paraded around me with their long habits and their rattling beads. They strode purposefully about the place like an army of paratroopers. I wondered who were those strange women in black. They had something that looked like cardboard across their foreheads. It seemed to be made of the same substance as the host at Mass.

After leaving the convent I went to the Primary School. I didn't have far to travel. It was opposite Aunt Nellie's house.

It had a mixture of Christian Brothers and lay teachers. One of the lay teachers was Frank Cunningham. He taught us Irish. It was my worst subject then. It was everywhere in the classroom – on charts, diagrams, drawings on the wall. I felt intimidated by it. I thought it was Mr Cunningham who intimidated me but I realise now it was the all-pervasiveness of the Irish, not him. Every day he'd come in to the classroom with a big smile on his face. It was as if he couldn't wait to get into it. He'd slap his hands together and say, 'Anois!'

The Brothers were tough. We had our palms reddened by one of them on a daily basis for not paying attention. He used to throw the duster at us as well. He had a great aim and often hit us, even those of us sitting at the back of the class. I often thought he missed his vocation as a cricketer. He had a habit of putting chalk in his mouth as if it was a cigarette. He called us 'kneuks' if he was annoyed with us. I never found out what the word meant.

I always saw Brothers as kind of halfway priests. Some of them joined up when they were hardly into their teens. Many of them were unhappy with their lot. When they realised it wasn't for them it was often too late. There was nowhere else to go.

Maybe they took out frustration on us. We did an Irish test one day. The boy sitting next to me said to the Brother, 'Can we have our marks?' He replied, 'Where do you want them?'

Violence was hardwired into the system like a protective mechanism against its meaninglessness. It was a system geared towards the maximum amount of inconvenience. The word 'No' was on a Brother's lips almost before you asked him a question. If we asked could we go to the toilet we were told, 'You can but you may not.'

I was beaten once for getting a blot on my copybook. It was difficult to avoid. We had inkwells on our desks that we dipped our pens into. The ink often came out in blobs. I never told my parents if I was beaten. Some of the boys in the class didn't do that because they'd get another slap from their parents if they did. They'd assume they'd misbehaved. My reason was different. I knew my father would go down to complain. It would draw attention to me that I didn't want. Sometimes it was better to forget about things.

The Primary school established a pattern in my life that lasted until I left Ballina. It was that school was the unhappy part of the day and home was the happy one. You marked time until the bell went. It released you from captivity. We recited a jingle that went,

'Saturday night is my delight
and so is Sunday morning
but Sunday night gives me a fright
to think of school in the morning.'

Home was where I returned to like a sanctuary. It was my oasis of peace. It was where my 'things' were, the things I identified myself with. School was the place that took you away from them.

I spent most of my time in the kitchen. That was where most of our games and most of our talking took place. There was a loft above it. That was another sanctuary. It was dark and cobwebby but it was our place, somewhere adults weren't allowed into unless we gave them permission. Because of that I found myself turning into one when I was up there. I walked like my father and imitated his voice, barking out commands to anyone who was around. Children need places like that because so many other ones are closed off to us.

I had a teddy bear that played music when I squeezed it. It was given to me when I was very small. I never parted with it. It was dark brown in colour. It was also broken. The music box stuck out of its back. The bulge made it look like it was a hunchback. I had offers of new ones to replace it but I didn't take them. Sometimes we're more drawn to damaged things than perfect ones. Maybe we identify with them. They make us protective. Only in adulthood do we seek perfection. But of course we never find it.

A Crowded Field

Everything was already established in my environment when I came into it. That made me feel I was inheriting things from my brothers and sisters instead of finding them for myself. I inherited friends, films, books, games and places to go from them. I even inherited hand-me-down clothes. I was entering a crowded field.

Our house was called Norfolk. I always felt it was special because it had a name of its own. Most people only had numbers on their houses. Ours was big enough to justify having a name even though it opened onto the street rather than having an avenue leading up to it like fancy country houses.

There was also a big back yard with walls on two sides of it. We got into Gildie Ahern's orchard through a hole in one of them. We used to rob his apples, piling them into our jumpers and then folding them over our stomachs so they wouldn't fall out. When I started Primary School a guard came in to lecture us on crime. I wondered what he'd do if he found out we were stealing apples. Would we be locked away somewhere? Could my father defend us in court? He was a solicitor.

We didn't eat them half the time. Some of them were just crab apples. The thrill was in stealing them without being caught. It was like the forbidden fruit in the Bible. One day he chased after us with a pop gun. I'll never forget the mad look in his eyes.

I grew up thinking he was some kind of monster. His house was uncared for. It was always covered in darkness. There were curtains hanging lopsided on the windows. I never had the courage to look inside. I imagined the house having doors hanging off hinges and rats infesting it. My childish mind even conjured up images of dead bodies under the floorboards.

16

I never saw him on the street or even at his doorstep. My only memory of him was that day he chased after us. He became like a character from a horror film come to life.

The Cottrells lived across the street. We were friends with all of them. Donna was regarded as one of the town beauties. I thought Josephine was just as attractive. She had lovely dimples.

They moved to England when I was young. Their father came from there originally. We were all heartbroken. They were one of the nicest families ever to come to Ballina. Why was it that the best people always seemed to leave?

The Leonards lived a few doors away from them. They all had red hair and Irish names. One of them was called Siobhan. We pronounced it 'Shooawn.' There was a Siobhan in the Cottrells as well. That was pronounced 'Shivaun.'

Mícheál came up to our house a lot. We used to record our voices on a tape recorder Aunt Mary gave us. He was very good on the guitar. He used to play Buddy Holly's song 'Every Day.' I was only six when Holly died in a plane crash. He was dead before I began listening to him but he had a big effect on me. He wrote a huge number of songs in his short life. No doubt he'd have written many more if he lived. Don McLean immortalised him in his song 'The Day the Music Died.'

Syron's café was beside Leonards. It was a takeaway place. We used to go in there for chips. Mr Syron always gave us huge portions. His wife put them in bags for us. The chips were as big as potatoes. We drowned them in salt and vinegar. Their children would be looking on. I'd think: If I lived there I'd do nothing but eat chips all day long.

They lived above the shop. I imagined them dining on chips any time they wanted. I wondered how often they ate them. Maybe you could have too much of something if you had it all the time no matter how nice it was.

There was a one-armed bandit outside the counter. Customers played on it while they were waiting for their orders. Coins fell into a tray at the bottom if you got three cherries in a row. I didn't have enough money to play it but some of the adults who came into the shop did. Now and then you'd hear a gush of coins in the tray. You'd know they'd got the cherries. I'd think to myself: They must be rich now. They can buy hundreds of bags of chips if they want.

They say every child grows up wanting to be rich. I'm not sure I did. It made things more enjoyable if you had to save up for things. I used to see people around town in big cars but I didn't envy them. Most of them looked bored.

We didn't have a washing machine in Norfolk but what you never had you never missed. Clothes were washed by hand and put on the line to dry. If it was raining we put them on chairs inside.

We didn't have a fridge either. We bought food every day in Geraghty's. Our milk came from Arthur Wills. He lived on Convent Hill. I used to go up there with a pail and he'd ladle it in.

Convent Hill led into Garden Street. That was where most of the shops were. There was a crossroads at the end of it. It joined Knox Street, King Street and Bridge Street. People regarded this as the centre of the town. It was where the teddy boys congregated.

My father called them teddy bears. They had velvet jackets and drainpipe trousers. Some of them wore brothel creeper shoes. They flicked cigarette butts into the gutters and wolf whistled any attractive girls who passed by. They did their best to look tough but when I got to know them I found out they were often the most cowardly in a fight. They were also the least likely to make a move on a girl if she expressed an interest in them.

There was an old Primary School across the road from us. Keith and Clive had gone to it. It was closed down now. There was a place beside it that made headstones. I saw the two sides of life early on. One building gave you an education. The other one buried you.

In between birth and death there was music. I didn't grow up listening to the songs other people did, songs like 'Danny Boy' or 'I'll Take You Home Again Kathleen' or 'It's a Long Way to Tipperary' or 'When Irish Eyes Are Smiling.' I was vaguely aware of Brendan O'Dowda and Bridie Gallagher but not Sean O'Riada or any of the *sean-nós* singers. I grew up listening to pop music.

The Town Hall was only a few doors away from us. There were dances in it all the time. We had a local band fronted by Jack Ruane. His sister Phyllis played the saxophone in it. It was one of the few bands in the country at that time with a girl. I went to sleep many nights listening to him belting out old standards. They were often accompanied by trombones and guitars. I left the window open so I could hear the music better. Sometimes it seemed so close that it was going on downstairs. It was like my own band.

If I was awake when those nights were ending I used to go out to the front room and look out the window. There would be courting couples across the road. Men grabbed quick kisses - or something more intimate - before they parted. Most of them walked home. Some had bicycles locked to lamp-posts. If they were tipsy they'd wobble down the street on them.

Most of the drinking would have been done before the dances. Alcohol wasn't allowed at dance halls until many years later. A lot of the men sported pioneer pins on their lapels.

Now and then a car wheezed through the night. There were whoops and hollers from the wild ones and sometimes an altercation about a woman. Many people met the partner they'd spend their lives with on these nights, doing the jive or the twist for starters and then a slow set as the night reached a conclusion and Jack Ruane sang 'Save the Last Dance for Me' before the National anthem was played.

Some of the songs I heard from those nights still stick in my mind. They were usually love songs, or songs of faded love. One of them was called 'Eighteen Yellow Roses.' It was simple but beautiful:

> *Eighteen yellow roses came today*
> *Eighteen yellow roses in a pretty bouquet*
> *When the boy came to the door*
> *I didn't know what to say*
> *But eighteen yellow roses came today.*

I saw the images in my mind. I learned the lines off by heart. They beat the socks off the poems I was expected to learn in school. Who needed Shakespeare when you could have Jack Ruane?

'Paper Roses' was another song that got to me. It was about flowers too:

> *Paper roses, paper roses*
> *Oh how real those roses seemed to me*
> *But they're only imitation*
> *Like your imitation love for me.*

Sad songs were better than happy ones. It was more boring when someone said, 'I love you' than 'I don't love you any more.' Maybe that was because so many romances ended badly in life. Torch songs were the best of all. You could hear the pain in them. You ended up feeling it yourself.

Hank Williams gave me a lump in my throat. That was probably because he had one there himself. Could anyone have written more heart-breaking love songs than he did? He died on the first day of the year I was born. Maybe that made me feel a special connection to him. He could raise the hairs on the back of your neck with his lyrics:

I tried so hard my love
to show that you're my every dream
yet you're afraid each thing I do
is just some evil scheme.
A memory of your lonesome past
keeps us so far apart.
Why can't I free your lonesome mind
and melt your cold cold heart?

My mother liked Bobby Darin. She used to sing 'Things' when she was going around the kitchen. It seemed strange to me. I didn't associate her with pop music. She liked Judy Garland singing 'Over the Rainbow' as well. Her favourite song was 'Jerusalem.'

She was landed gentry. My father's origins were humbler. His father made his fortune in what he called 'the rag trade.' He had his fingers in other pies as well. In later life he became a Justice of the Peace and a Poor Law Guardian. He bought various properties with his money. My father told me once that his secret was knowing when to buy and when to sell.

He married three times, outliving two of his wives. My father came from the third family. I never knew much about his first two marriages. Basil was always interested in researching details about them. Anything I heard about them went in one ear and out the other. I found it difficult to retain information on people I'd never met.

My mother grew up in a house called Raheen. She came from a big family in an area of Roscommon called Mantua. Some of them moved to England afterwards. One of them was called Derek. He came back to Roscommon eventually. Another was called Tom. He lived in Coventry with his wife Beryl. Their son became a bishop.

Her sister Valerie lived with her husband in London. I met her once. She was a beautiful woman. Valerie actually introduced my mother to my father. Their first date was on a boat. It was a windy day and the water was choppy. My father became nervous when it shook. My mother was amused as he clutched the sides of it. She hadn't a nerve in her body in those days.

One of Valerie's daughters, Grace, married a man called Kevin O'Grady. Their daughter came to live with us in the sixties. Her name was Ann. In many ways she became like an extra sister to me.

The O'Gradys didn't live too far from Raheen. The school Ann went to in Mantua wasn't good. Grace felt the convent in Ballina would be better for her. Kevin did too.

He was a farmer and also ran a grocery shop. There was a post office in it too. That was often the way in the country in the old days. It reminded me of Geraghty's shop in Ballina.

Sometimes we went to them for a week or two in the summer. They lived off the main road to Dublin. Cars only passed every now and again. It was almost like an event. We'd sit for ages waiting to see one and then run back to the house with our news.

It was great living in the country. The O'Gradys had a huge house. Behind it there were acres of fields to play in. One of them had a bull we used to annoy. He was said to be cross. We used to provoke him from a safe distance. You had to get out of the way quickly if he looked like he was going to charge.

Kevin also owned a horse. I only sat on it once. I tried to get him to move but he wouldn't. Kevin said that was because he knew I wasn't used to being in the saddle. He tried to get me to milk a cow one day but that didn't happen either.

We saved the hay with them. We played in the haystacks afterwards. One year Hugo and Basil brought a tent with them and camped in a field outside the house. I'd love to have done that.

Living in the country was so different to Ballina. If we were given a message to deliver it could take all day. There was a barrel at the back of the house that caught rain water. We had to get it from a well about a half a mile away if it hadn't rained for a while and the barrel was empty.

The quietness was incredible as you walked along the road. All you could hear was the sound of birds. It was only when you heard the trickle of water you knew you were near the well. Cars only passed once in a blue moon. If we saw one we'd wave at the driver. It was as if we'd just seen an apparition.

There wasn't a doctor for miles. One day a girl got an epileptic attack in the post office. I thought she was going to die. She fell onto the floor and started convulsing. Grace put a spoon on her tongue to stop her swallowing it. That was the medical advice that was given then. I think it's changed now.

The O'Gradys had a relative who lived in America. Every so often he'd send a package to them. There was great excitement about anything coming from America in those days, even if it only contained an item of clothing or something we couldn't get in Ireland like a 'candy' bar. Its arrival was like a sacred event, something that had to be serenaded almost ritually. There was a poem about it:

A letter from America
Glory Be to God.

Go and call your mother in
But first put down the sod.

There was only six weeks in age between myself and Ann. That made us into a different kind of Irish twins than the ones in Norfolk. We were almost like 'real' ones.

We played together during the day and slept in the same room at night. I loved looking at the shadows on the ceiling as the moon drifted between the clouds outside. Sometimes we stayed awake half the night going through all the things that happened to us during the day.

We played a game that had Ann's name in it: 'O'Grady says.' It was like an Irish version of 'Simon Says.' Someone gave an order and the other person had to obey it. We thought up ridiculous commands, telling people to stand on their heads or hang off drainpipes. Usually they told us to get lost.

Ann was better at school than me. She was a quick learner and sailed through all her exams. One of the nuns took a special interest in her. Her name was Sister Assumpta. She made sure she reached her full potential.

Ann always had a healthy look about her. She never wore a coat. She was always darting down to the Fahy's to study. Mr Fahy had a mini-mart across the road from Geraghty's. Ann and Mary Fahy were around her age. My mother would be screaming out the door at her: 'Put on your coat! You'll catch pneumonia!' It was always too late. She was gone with the wind. Maybe she knew something my mother didn't. She never caught a cold. It must have been all that Roscommon air.

I could never get my head around the fact that Ann was my second cousin instead of my first one. It was Grace who was that. It had to do with the different ages people got married at. No matter how many times she explained it to me I couldn't get my head around it.

When her brother John visited us he always looked debonair. He was usually dressed in a sharp suit. Sometimes he'd be wearing a Crombie overcoat. He'd have a Windsor knot in his tie - and steel-tipped shoes. You knew he was in the house when you heard the clack of his heels on the flagstones of the kitchen floor. Or if you got the smell of chips. Cafolla's was always his first stop after getting off the bus. He'd come in eating them and regale you with some colourful stories from Mantua. He had some great expressions as well. My favourite was, 'Feck poverty, we'll kill a hen.' If he said someone was 'horrid nice' it meant he liked them.

My mother enjoyed having extra people in the house. Nine children weren't enough for her. She wouldn't rest until she'd adopted half the town – or half of Connacht. I don't know how she found beds for all everyone who stayed with us over the years but she did. There were times when you wouldn't be sure who you'd be having breakfast with.

Ann eventually got a scholarship to a convent in Belmullet. She finished her education there. Belmullet was on the edge of Mayo. Someone told me once that you could see New York from it on a clear day. I believed him. It was only 3000 miles away.

Another person I remember being in the house is Bea Melvin from Gurteens. She used to help my mother with the cooking if Tina wasn't around. She was overweight but like a lot of overweight people she was graceful in her movements. She swanned around the kitchen like a dancer.

She often moved at speed. You had to be careful not to bump into her. If you did she could get quite indignant. She was sensitive as well. If you passed even the slightest criticism of anything she did she was capable of going into a huff. We all loved Bea for her ways. She used to put on the funniest expressions if you said something to her.

I can't remember how many other people came to the house. Our door was left ajar a lot of the time. The people who lived near us were our CCTV cameras. We had our own version of Neighbourhood Watch before the term was invented.

Tinkers arrived now and again looking for work. That wasn't a derogatory term then. They did jobs like fixing tin cans. I supposed that was where they got their name from. One of them fixed a leak one time in the pail we brought up to Arthur Wills for milk. If someone was complaining about their lives not working out like they planned we had a saying: 'If 'ifs' and 'ands' were pots and pans, there'd be no need for tinkers.'

There were four bedrooms in the house. They were all the same size. There was a smaller room to the front in between them. It was like a storage room. We kept a tallboy in it as well as some of my father's papers.

The bathroom was halfway up the stairs. There was often a queue for it. With nine people in the house, eleven including my parents, that wasn't surprising. We were capable of kicking the door if someone was inside and we were in a bad way needing to get in.

Bob Hope said once, 'I come from a large family. I learned to dance waiting to get to the toilet.' I knew how he felt. There were times when we were encouraged to go out the back to prevent what were euphemistically referred to as 'accidents.'

If we weren't in a hurry we killed time by sliding down the banister. You couldn't slide all the way down because it curled at the end. You'd get stuck in it or you might hurt yourself. That would have been a different type of accident.

The small room faced out onto the street. It wasn't much bigger than the bathroom. I always thought of it as my room. It was where I felt most at home. Its smallness made it attractive to me, maybe because I was small myself. If I was bigger I thought I'd nearly be able to touch the four walls at the same time.

Ann and myself spent a lot of time in there. There was a great view of everything going on in the street. Sometimes we dropped glasses of water from the window to frighten people passing by. We even dropped metal trays. They made an almighty clatter when they hit the ground.

Children can be very cruel. We thought we were being clever ducking down on the ground after dropping the things but it had to be obvious to our victims where they were coming from. I can't remember any of them ever knocking on the door to complain. At other times we stood on opposite sides of the street holding two ends of pieces of twine tightly. Cars drove into them and snapped them with their windscreens. That was more harmless fun.

My second favourite room upstairs was the front one on the right. You could get out to the roof from it. It overlooked the back yard. We used to walk across the roof even though it was sloped. Sometimes we sat on the slates and looked across the yard at Gildie Ahern's orchard, putting our feet into the evruns to stop ourselves from falling.

There was a sycamore tree in the corner of the yard. You could get to it from the roof if you walked along the top of a broken wall that led into GildieAhern's. There was a shape like a Y in the middle of it at the top of the bark. There was only room for one person there at a time but you could still have some kind of a picnic on it. We tied a rope around one of the branches and transported food up and down in boxes.

We played golf in the yard, digging holes for a makeshift putting area. The ground only had clay on it. It must have been the only putting area without grass in Ireland. Neither was it level. The ball bobbled along as if it was drunk. Sometimes we got it into the hole after it went all around the world for sport. We'd have been experts in Augusta from our knowledge of curves.

The clothes line was in the yard as well. It used to get in our way when we were playing our shots. On a windy day you could be lining up a putt when a gust of wind came up and whacked a wet towel into your face.

We played rounders there too. It was like an Irish version of cricket. We made a wicket from sticks and threw a ball at whoever was standing in front of it. They'd have a tennis racquet or a stick or a table tennis bat. Anything would do. They hit the ball if they were able to as the thrower ran for everything they were worth into a designated spot. When the ball was located it was thrown at them to stop them. One day I hit it too hard and broke the kitchen window. Other times it went farther – into Gildie Ahern's orchard or maybe even across our roof into the street. That would be a 'home run.'

The turf shed was at the end of the yard. It didn't have a door. You just walked in. The Curran's window was above it. I was often afraid of breaking it when we played handball against the wall above the shed. Both of our houses were like L shapes. At the front of their one there was an area under the window that we both claimed as our own. It was only about an inch thick but it caused a lot of problems between us. They used to paint it their colour and then we'd paint it ours.

This went on for years. The only person to gain from it was the paint manufacturer. It was like our own Gaza Strip. It caused my father no end of frustration. For a time I thought it was going to go to court. My father told me disputes about land sometimes caused great stress among people, even small bits of land. It was all relative. He had a saying, 'An inch on a man's nose is a lot.'

There were four in his family. He had a brother called Louis and two sisters, Nellie and Mary. Aunt Nellie lived down the road from us. There seemed to be about twenty cats in her house. She wasn't married so she had lots of time to call up to us.

We had a joke about her that I never understood. Whenever any of us lost anything we'd say, 'It's in Nellie's room behind the wallpaper.' Nobody ever explained what they meant. Maybe it was better that way.

She talked a mile a minute, exploding into laughter at the slightest pretext. She nearly always had a cigarette in her mouth. Her voice was husky as a result. She spent most of her time talking to my mother. That seemed strange to me because she was my father's sister. My father usually stayed out of the way when she came to visit us. Maybe they were too similar to one another. They both had overpowering personalities. She used to fire questions at me on her visits but she rarely waited for the answer to them, swanning out the door with the same swagger as she'd entered it. She was usually dressed in a fur coat. Nothing else would have done her. It seemed to go with the cats.

We didn't have as many of them as her. One of them, Tabby, lived to a very old age. I remember her scratching the couch with her claws when it was going to rain. She knew about things like that better than the people giving the weather forecasts. Whenever we saw her scratching we muffled up well before going out the door. I've often thought cats should be employed by the Met. Office to predict the weather. They'd make a better job of it than some of

29

the so-called experts I've been listening to over the years. Anytime they say it's going to be sunny I take care to pack an umbrella.

Tabby used to go away for long periods and then suddenly re-appear. Then one time she went away and didn't come back. We didn't know if she'd been knocked down by a car or what happened to her. Maybe she went away somewhere to die. We were all heartbroken but maybe it was for the best. She'd started to lose her sight by this time. She was always bumping into things.

We had dogs too. Some of them were before my time. One was knocked down by a car and killed. Everyone cried their eyes out about that. The one I remember most was our last one, Deezer. He was a cross between a setter and a pointer. He had a brown mark over one of his eyes that made him look like he was winking at you.

We bought him from a man in Lord Edward Street who'd been mistreating him. He was so malnourished, the day we bought him down to Norfolk he jumped up on the kitchen table and ate four lamb chops my mother had cooked for our dinner. I don't know where our previous dogs came from. I imagine some of them were 'adopted the same way Deezer was. There was always room at the inn for neglected creatures in Norfolk. It didn't matter if they were on two legs or four.

Aunt Mary lived across the river. Her husband Eddie owned a flour mills in Bunree. She was frail and saintly. Like Aunt Nellie she seemed to live in another world. I rarely saw her outside the church. I don't remember her being in Norfolk much.

The Murphys had a huge house. I used to play bagatelle in it sometimes with my friend Mícheál Leonard from across the street. It was like snooker except the table was much smaller. The pockets were also in different places. There were six at the top and four others in a diamond shape in the middle of the table. There were sticks around them that looked like mushrooms. You had to pot the balls into the pockets without knocking over the sticks.

There were spacious grounds around the back of the house. There was even a tennis court. We played on it when the weather was good.

We picked strawberries if the weather permitted. We put them in the silver pail we used to bring up to Arthur Wills for the milk. When it was full we sold them to Moyletts shop in King Street.

We were allowed keep the money we got. Other people I knew delivered newspapers or mowed lawns for pocket money. I picked strawberries. I'd see them in the window of the shop and think, 'They were mine a few days ago.'

I loved going down to Moyletts. It had all sorts of food on the shelves. It was more like a supermarket than Geraghty's. Mr Moylett had a bacon slicer. He cut really thin slices of ham with it. It made a sound like the dentist did when he was drilling your teeth.

Aunt Mary died of cancer in the sixties. It was my first experience of someone dying. At that time I knew nothing of death. The only time I can remember the subject being mentioned was one day at Geraghty's corner when I heard a woman talking about someone who had a brain haemorrhage.

Losing Aunt Mary devastated my father. It took a lot out of my mother as well. They used to go down to see her during her illness. They'd say a prayer for her in the cathedral and then make their way down to Bunree.

It was the first time I heard the word cancer as well. It terrified me almost as much as the disease itself. Uncle Eddie was inconsolable after she died. He only lived six months after her.

Uncle Louis became a doctor. He married another one. They lived in Birmingham. I don't ever remember meeting him. I was very young when he moved to England.

I couldn't imagine my father ever becoming a doctor. He'd have passed out at the sight of blood. Uncle Louis was different. He was a no-nonsense type of man. I heard he walked out of the Estoria cinema one night when a film came on that he wasn't enjoying. That was a cinema across the road from us. 'I don't pay to be bored,' he said.

Another story I heard about him concerned a time when my father was spending too much of my grandfather's money. Apparently Louis squealed on him to their mother. Instead of telling my grandfather about this she went to the other extreme. She gave my father even more money afterwards, not less. She sounded like my kind of woman.

Aunt Nellie was like my father in the way that she tried to get away with things. There was a story that when she was being sent to boarding school as a young girl she did everything in her power to get out of going. When she was about to get on the train at the start of one term she cried her eyes out in front of her mother in the hope that she'd let her stay at home. She didn't get her wish.

As soon as the train pulled off she was laughing her head off with all her friends. Her good mood lasted all the way to the convent. When she got there the Reverend Mother gave her a stern look. She said to her, 'Your reputation has preceded you.' How had she heard about the crocodile tears? I never found out. The story reminded me of the one about my father and Uncle Louis. I always preferred children like that to goody-goodies.

Norfolk Novena

Because our family was large I was thrown into many situations where I was surrounded by groups of people. The four pairs of brothers and sisters that preceded me were described as Irish twins. They were close enough in age to qualify for the description. The elder one was usually kept back in school so they could be in the same class as the younger one. June and Ruth were the only exception to that.

I was only two when Keith and Clive left home so I only got to know them in later years. The same applied to June and Ruth to a lesser extent. It even applied to Hugo and Basil. I spent most of my time with Audrey and Jacinta.

June taught me reading before I started school. That was how I was able to go from Babies into Low First. I was five when I started. That was a year older than the usual starting age. When I skipped Low First it brought me back to the same age as most of my classmates.

Everyone in the family had a different personality. Keith was more nervous than Clive but Clive was more serious in other ways. Ruth was a bit more serious than June. Sometimes you could read a person's personality in their handwriting. Ruth's was long and straight. June's was smaller and more intricate. Audrey and Jacinta were similar both in their writing and their personalities.

They were very close to one another and did everything together. That made me think of them as actual twins sometimes instead of just 'Irish' ones. Their voices even sounded alike. If they were behind me I could never tell which of them was talking.

They were so much in tune with one another they even read comics together. They sat on adjoining chairs holding them at eye level in front of them.

When one of them finished a page they nodded at the other one to indicate the fact. The other one either nodded back or kept reading for a few more seconds: 'Hold on, I'm not finished!' Then they turned the page. It meant the material was entering both of their heads simultaneously. It turned reading into a process that was like watching television or listening to the radio.

Maybe Hugo and Basil were the two most different of the four pairs of 'twins.' Hugo was reflective whereas Basil was more sociable. He was probably the only one of us who didn't have the family nerves. He was academic and sporty and a good mixer as well, the whole package.

He was out of the house a lot. Everyone else seemed to think that no entertainment outside our four walls could equal what was inside it. Basil was different. He sought outside stimulation. Maybe I'm basing this idea of him on what I know of him from his later life. Memory is selective. It often plays tricks on us.

Hugo's interests veered towards the arts. He acted out plays and films with us. He had a big interest in drama and had a good way with children. It didn't surprise any of us that he became a teacher eventually.

One of the films he did with us was *West Side Story*. He must have recruited half the street for it. My mother noticed clothes going missing from various wardrobes as he kitted us out for it before she discovered what was going on.

These were our 'costumes' for the Jets and Sharks gangs. It was Arthur Street's version of New York's ghettos. After a brief period of bewilderment she accepted it. One of the songs she liked from the film was 'Cool.' It was like her philosophy of life: 'Got a rocket in your pocket/Keep cool little boy.' I clicked my fingers and swaggered down the street pretending to be Russ Tamblyn.

There was always a hive of activity around the house because of all the people coming and going. Relatives also dropped in from time to time. There were many of these. Half the time I didn't know who they were. I was familiar with my aunts and uncles and some of my cousins but there it ended.

There was a couple from the country called Bartley and Annie who visited us every now and then. Billy and Stanley Johnston called as well. They were two brothers who married two sisters. They lived on the road to Enniscrone. That was a beach eight miles from us. Afterwards they moved to Stoke Newington in England. I wasn't exactly sure where they fitted into the family tree. I was never much good at working out things like that. My father tried to give me details on who everyone was but I rarely listened to him. I was profoundly ignorant of who my relatives were.

I sat beside one of my cousins at a meal in my Aunt Florence's house one day without having a clue who he was. 'Why are you here?' I said to him as we waited for the food to arrive. 'I'm her son!' he said. He was aghast.

I was left-handed. My mother tried to get me to use my right one instead. She held my left behind my back every time she gave me a ball. I always drew it away from her at the last minute. That was something else about me. I was stubborn.

The nuns had greater success with me. They drove a tougher bargain, slapping me on the wrist with a ruler when I pursued my southpaw ways. I hated them for that but eventually I became ambidextrous so maybe I should be grateful to them after all..

Neither of my parents ever raised a hand to me or to any other member of the family. The cotton wool we were all wrapped up in made the cruelty of life harder to take for many of us in later years.

Ours was a sheltered world. We knew nothing about sexual abuse or violence or Magdalene laundries or anything of the things that would be exposed by future generations. War and murder were things that happened in other places, not Ballina. Headlines in the *Evening Press* testifying to such events might have been from another planet. They were about Korea or Russia or China. We skimmed over them as we sought out the cartoons at the back - Mutt and Jeff, Dagwood, Mickey Mouse, Woody Woodpecker, Donald Duck.

We left our toys things outside the front door at night without thinking for a second that they'd be stolen. The worst crime that was committed in those days was people cycling without a light on their bikes or cycling on the footpath instead of the road or not going to school when there was nothing wrong with them. Or begging outside the bishop's palace. My father often defended people on this charge.

The worst language we heard was 'Flip it.' We were shocked when we heard Audrey Hepburn cursing in *My Fair Lady*. She said 'Move yer bloomin' arse,' to a horse in that film. How could such a lady speak like that even if she was born in a slum? The only other bad language I remember hearing at this time was when Brendan Gaffney, one of my classmates, told me MPSI outside a chemist's shop stood for 'Monkey's Piss Sold Inside.' He also said 'P7T' - the logo for Posts and Telegraphs - stood for 'Piss Seven Times.' He seemed to have a thing about peeing.

Our parents shielded us from the worlds of crime and violence and anything else adults talked about. If there were money problems we weren't told about them. No matter how bad things became in that way my father used to joke about it.

36

One day a man he gave a loan to said to him, 'By the way, Hugh, I'm not forgetting about that money I owe you.' My father replied, 'That makes two of us!' Another day he said to me, 'Money talks. Mine said goodbye.'

He used humour to hide his financial worries but I learned about them anyway. When we won some money on the Prize Bonds one year the excitement he showed was excessive. It opened my eyes to what he'd probably been going through for years without telling me. Was it relief in disguise? A weight had been lifted.

My mother was the one who had to be negotiated if you wanted a day off school. He was easier to persuade. Usually you could wind him round your little finger. The tiniest problem was all that was necessary to persuade him to write you a sick note. You could then spend all day reading comics. Tina called him 'The Master' but nobody acted less like one.

Feminists would probably say she was chained to the kitchen sink. She definitely wasn't one of those 'ladies who lunch.' The only thing approaching make-up I ever saw her wearing was Nivea. There wasn't much feminism in Ballina in the fifties. Mary Robinson wasn't a barrister yet. In fact she was probably still in Primary School.

My mother wasn't familiar with the feminist movement. She said to me once that she believed a chair was for sitting on. If she could be one she didn't mind being used for that purpose. She didn't see herself as a doormat. She just meant being useful. We might call such an attitude being a 'people pleaser' nowadays. I never liked that expression. It sounds demeaning when all someone is doing is trying to help.

Women had their way of making their presence felt in the fifties even if it didn't look like it. My father took over a room when he was out with my mother but after they went home she was in charge. As the years went on he reverted to her for all the important decisions of his life.

He went to a lot of solicitor's functions. He was always the life and soul of the party at them. Anyone can see that from photographs that were taken at them. He'd be the person you looked at first when you saw the photographs even if he wasn't your father. He usually had a big grin on his face in them. My mother would be to the side, smiling as well but in a more subdued way.

He cut quite a dash on these nights. He'd have his pin-striped suit, his starched shirt, his Trinity tie and grey waistcoat. On cold nights the white silk scarf came out. He brought an umbrella everywhere with him even in the warmest of weathers. It was like a fashion statement. He had a tall hat for special occasions.

My mother was always at him to draw in his horns in case he said too much on these nights. That was especially the case if he had drink taken. Drink loosened his tongue. It was always pretty loose anyway.

He tipped waiters lavishly in hotels. My mother said if he kept doing that we wouldn't be able to afford to eat the following day. He admitted he always had to do 'the big,' as he called it. She was more the pragmatic farmer's daughter.

He was nearly fifty when I was born. That might have caused a distance with another kind of man but not him. He was too human. I often felt he was more like my younger brother than my father. 'A little nonsense now and then,' he said, 'is relished by the best of men.'

He played childish games with us. Sometimes at the dead of night he'd come into the bedroom holding a torch under his chin. It made him look like a ghost. It scared the daylights out of us.

He was small in stature but he had great authority. In that he was like many small men. He liked the actor Edward G. Robinson, or Edward Robinson as he called him. He modelled himself on him in the way he carried himself. Like many small men he liked the idea of power – the power of political leaders, actors, members of royalty. He told me once about a king of Spain who was so small, every time he had a problem he walked up and down under his bed trying to think of a solution for it. For years I believed someone that size could exist. He often pulled my leg with stories like that.

After we were put to bed he'd blow us kisses from the landing. He'd usually be holding a cigarette as he did that. He used to flick the ash off it by clicking his middle finger and thumb. I used to be fascinated watching him doing it. Most people just tapped it. The floor was his ash tray.

He was supposed to have smoked 100 cigarettes a day. One day I asked my mother if that was true. 'He lights 100,' she said, 'but he probably only smokes a quarter of them.'

He'd light one in the office if he was with a client. When he finished his business with him he'd forget about it. Then he'd light another one somewhere else and forget about that too. I'd see them in ash trays. They'd have long wisps of ash on them all the way down to the filters. Sometimes the cigarettes looked like perfectly formed cylinders of ash.

He smoked a brand called Boston. It was smaller than most cigarettes. Every time he bought a packet he took out about ten of them and put them into his cigarette case. It was silver with a red band across the middle to keep the cigarettes from falling out. It opened when he flicked a little switch at the side.

Most of the people I knew smoked other types. Woodbine came in a yellow packet. There were also ones called Senior Service and Craven A and Gold Flake and Peter Stuyvestant. Some people liked Players Navy Cut. There was a drawing of a sailor on the packet. My favourite ones were Consulate. They had white stems. There was a lovely menthol smell off them.

The dangers of smoking weren't talked about much in those days. A doctor might even offer a patient a cigarette to 'relax' them. In shops we bought sweets shaped like cigarettes. They had little pink tips on them. We went through the motions of smoking before we chomped into them. It was an early preparation for a habit people would curse themselves for developing years later when they got breathing problems or something worse.

We picked butts of real cigarettes out of gutters and went through the same motions. They probably had all sorts of germs on them but we didn't think about things like that. They weren't the only things we picked up from the street. Sweets were fair game too. And of course money. It was 'Finders Keepers' for that.

My mother told me once that she started smoking at the age of five. She gave up cigarettes for Lent every year. When she went back on them she usually threw up after the first one. It took a while for her system to accept the poison.

Whenever my father was finished with a box of matches he gave it to me. I collected them. They always had the word 'Friendly' written on the top of them. I didn't know why. When I had about fifty collected I used to put them standing up in the shape of a figure of 8 on the carpet. When you tipped one of them it set off a chain reaction. They were like dominos. You had to put them all the same distance apart. If they were too close they wouldn't fall. If they were too far apart it broke the chain.

My father nearly always had a cigarette in his hand when he was telling stories. That wasn't surprising. He left many of them unsmoked. That was probably how he went through so many boxes of matches.

He wore a monocle. Nobody ever knew if he needed to or not. Glasses were good enough for most people. Not him. The day an optician told him he had a weak eye he was out the door as fast as his legs could carry him. He went off looking for someone who'd sell him a monocle. It wasn't long before he found him.

He liked it from the second he put it into his eye. He thought it gave him dignity. It also gave drama to the stories he told us. It used to pop in and out at various parts of them.

A lot of them were about Trinity. As he told them you could see him going back to that time in his mind. He lived it again in the telling – a time when he was young and carefree and life held no responsibilities.

He was over ten years studying for his law degree. 'Studying' was hardly the word. He spent more time at parties than anything else. It was like an F. Scott Fitzgerald world. He sat on the bars of the college watching the pretty girls parading up and down Grafton Street.

Every year when the exam results were posted on a noticeboard he'd put in his monocle and peer at it. His friend Mido Cooligan would come up behind him. He'd say, 'What do you think you're looking at? You know you're down to hell.'

Mido would be 'down to hell' too. They'd break into a duet of 'We'll all go down together,' sung to the air of 'For he's a jolly good fellow.' My father loved telling this story against himself. He'd be laughing so much it was difficult to make out the words.

He graduated after marrying my mother. Nobody was more surprised than him that he managed to do that. It was probably desperation that caused him to knuckle down to his studies. 'The exams weren't getting any easier,' he said, 'and I wasn't getting any smarter.'

They moved into a little house in Greystones. It was called Fuschia Cottage. Keith was born there. He was the only member of the family to be born in Dublin. He boasted about it. To me that wouldn't have been a boast. I'd have hidden it. I never had any feeling for city life.

A few years later my father went back to Ballina to set up his legal practice. It was difficult making ends meet. The town only had a population of 6000. There were over a half dozen solicitors in it.

Most of his cases were small. He hated ones where there was something scientific at stake like the skid marks of a car that he had to investigate for insurance liability. He was always better when there was a human element involved. That was when his charm was called for. He had a great way with witnesses. When he was cross-examining a guard once he called him 'Inspector.' When the guard said he was far from that, my father said, 'A slight anticipation on my part.'

I don't know how he managed to support a wife nine children. How did he feed and clothe us with so much competition for business?

He lived beyond his means. If he hadn't married my mother he could have ended up on the breadline. He always had a 'Let them eat cake' attitude to life. He'd have let us live on chocolate if he could. Sensibleness was for other people.

He also enjoyed a drink. In that he was like many in the town. Someone said there were more bars *per capita* in Ballina than any other town in Ireland. They always seemed to be full.

He liked drinking with the other solicitors in the American House on the Station Road. It wasn't far from the court house. At other times he'd go to bars like Tony Crane's. That was usually at the end of the night when his defences were down. He was more relaxed with blue collar people than white collar ones. You wouldn't get him to admit that. He professed not to recognise them as his equals. He did his best to turn himself into a snob but he never quite made it.

My mother sent me out to fetch him in the bars sometimes if he was late home. I hated going to these places. If he wasn't in the American House I'd make for Tony Crane's. As soon as I got to the door I'd get the smell of alcohol and stale smoke. For a few seconds I'd feel as if I was going to pass out. Then it would go away. It became like a part of me. I didn't feel it anymore. Was this what being an adult meant?

He'd be at the counter with his monocle in. He'd usually be puffing on a cigarette and telling some humorous story. He'd have his hands clasped behind his back the way he used to when he was saying the rosary except now the cigarette would be in it instead of a rosary beads.

There'd usually be a crowd of men around him. There were no women in pubs in those days. He'd say something and wait for the reaction. He had a way of rocking back and forth on the balls of his feet when he was telling a story. They'd wobble a bit if he was tipsy. He'd stare hard at whoever he was talking to, making sure they were taking in everything he said. It was like a teacher making sure you were paying attention because he'd be asking questions afterwards. As he got towards the end of a story his eyes would widen. At that stage the monocle would fall out. I'd know it was over if they laughed.

He'd always be delighted to see me. 'That's my son!' he'd say. I'd see the pride in his eyes. He'd be high on the atmosphere as much as the drink. I'd tell

43

him my mother was waiting for him but the words wouldn't register. He'd make me stay for a mineral as he ordered another drink. I knew I wasn't supposed to be there at that hour because of my age. An exception would be made for me because of who I was.

As soon as he got me sitting down he'd launch into another story. It was as if my presence acted as a licence for it. The atmosphere was always wilder as it got towards closing time. As I sat looking at him and whoever he was talking to I'd wonder what was in the whiskey or the Guinness that made them so excited. What made them smile and laugh more? Would I one day get fed up of minerals and become like them, drinking whiskey and Guinness and telling funny stories and arguing about politics and sports?

On the mornings after such nights he'd often be quiet. It made me wonder where the magic went. If I asked him about the night he might say something like, 'What does it matter?' The lows always followed the highs.

Sometimes he brought us down the country with him. He used to have to go to farmers' houses to get affidavits signed. I once heard of a man who was so snobbish he refused to travel in the same car as his chauffeur. My father usually sat in the back of the cars he hired for these trips. Anything else was *infra dig*. There was one hackney driver he sat beside in the front. This was seen as the ultimate honour.

He told us we were superior to the people around us but it didn't feel like it. Our double-barrelled name had no follow-up because we weren't wealthy. That didn't seem to bother him. He'd have preferred to live in an exclusive house that he didn't own than a moderate one he did. The aura of faded grandeur clung to him like a drug. It didn't seem to need anything to feed it.

The fact that he wasn't good with money meant my mother had to do most of the budgeting.

44

Sometimes he spent large sums on things she didn't want. He bought her a fur coat like Aunt Nellie's because he thought it was expected of a solicitor's wife. I imagine she'd have preferred another kind. She went along with it like she went along with everything else he asked of her. This was in the days when fur coats weren't frowned on by the animal rights people.

When she married him she hadn't a care in the world. Marriage wasn't even on her mind. She was too busy dancing her way around Ireland to think about it. He pursued her vehemently after falling in love with her. Eventually she had no choice but to say yes to his proposals of marriage. 'I wore her down,' he said with a kind of grim humour.

The fact that she was from a county family impressed him. She was different. To her it didn't matter if you were born on the wrong side of the tracks or with a silver spoon in your mouth. She treated everyone the same. My father used to say she could entertain the bishop in the parlour and a binman in the pantry. She made no distinction between them.

She was working in the Irish Sweepstakes when they met. In those days women had to give up their jobs when they got married. They also had to give up their names. She wasn't Patricia Conry anymore, she was Mrs Hugh Dillon-Malone. She didn't mind leaving her job to become a housewife.

Having a big family came as a surprise to her. She told me once that she'd have been happy just to have one child.

We arrived, she said, 'like steps of a stairs.' Once she had us we became her world. She didn't visit Aunt Nellie or Aunt Mary. On her odd visits to Dublin she didn't spend much time with our cousins the O'Reillys in Sandymount or even her sister Florence in Dun Laoghaire. The mountain had to come to Muhammad.

Someone said once that women are born a thousand years old. That was the way I thought of my mother. She was like a sage who listened to everyone's problems and then gave them advice. She did it without even knowing she was doing it.

To the nine of us she was a totally unselfish person. She 'took the bitter and gave us the sweet,' to paraphrase a line from one of my father's recitations. If there's such a thing as a saint she was one. Unlike other saints I read about in books she never acted holy. She didn't look pious in church and she didn't push religion at us. Virtue was as much of a part of her DNA as breathing. It didn't need to be advertised or talked about. She was simple in the best sense of the word.

It must have been a relief to her not to have any more children after me. At last she could relax. Or did she ever relax? The only holidays she ever got were when she was giving birth.

She never stopped moving. I said to her one day, 'I'm bored. I have nothing to do.' She said, 'I wish I could be bored.' She was hoovering the floor at the time. It was the closest she ever came to a rebuke. But she still didn't ask me to help her.

I don't remember her ever sitting down to a full meal. She mainly fed herself on our leftovers. She hated us throwing things away. Sometimes I'd be scraping something into the 'brock.' That was what we called our discarded food. She'd stop me and have it herself instead. I don't know how her stomach coped with all the mixtures.

She treated us like royalty while she took on the role of slave. At times it seemed like she hadn't nine children but rather ten. My father sometimes acted like the tenth. She spoiled him the same way she spoiled us.

If he ever had a problem she'd give the day over to discussing it with him. We used to say that she came to know so much about the law she could have taken over his practice if he retired. That became even more the case when he started working from home.

He used to have an office in Bridge Street but it burned down. I don't remember it happening. I was too young. He didn't have the inclination to move to another one. I'm not sure if that was a good idea. Working from home led to him developing a streak of introversion. That was never in him before.

One of his great pleasures in life was dressing himself up. He loved leaving the house every morning in all his finery. 'I'm going down the town to give the people a thrill,' he'd say. He hadn't the same incentive when Bridge Street went. Some days he didn't bother dressing if he didn't have clients to see. Even when a client called he might see them in his dressing gown.

The dining room became his new office. He bought a safe for all his important files, a big green one that would have taken ten men to life. It was about the size of a fridge. I hid the key of it in a hole in the back yard one day. There was hell to pay until it was found. Nobody was allowed leave the house. People tell me I was like Sherlock Holmes or Poirot as I led the family out to the hole. I wasn't the last of nine that day. I was the first.

He bought a desk later. It had lots of cubicles in it. He kept anything and everything in them – pens, pencils, paper clips, even thumb tacks. In the centre of it there was a writing pad. It had a sheet of blotting paper to rub out ink stains. Beside it he kept a knife. It was an unusual one with blunt edges. He used it to open envelopes.

The desk had a roller top on it with loads of wood panels. He used to let me close it for him at the end of a work day. I rolled it up and down repeatedly for fun. It had a curl in the middle of it.

He kept some of his novels in the dining room too. Many of them were Penguin paperbacks with orange covers. I used to be fascinated looking at them. One of them was called *When the Kissing Had to Stop.* Another one was called *The Man Who Watched the Trains Go By.* When I read these books in later years I wasn't half as entranced by them as I had been by looking at their covers as a child. That's the power of imagination.

He had Christian books by Hilaire Belloc and G.K. Chesterton. Keith had been named after Chesterton – the G.K. stood for Gilbert Keith. He liked Shakespeare and George Bernard Shaw as well. Shaw never ceased to amaze him. He never put in the 'George' when he was talking about him. It was always just 'Bernard Shaw.' I didn't know anyone else who did that.

He committed a lot of Shaw's quotes to memory. They were trotted out to us at various intervals. If he wanted to make fun of someone he'd say, 'He hadn't an enemy in the world but none of his friends liked him.' That was a famous Shaw quote. Some people thought Oscar Wilde said it. That sort of thing was always going on between the two of them. It was like the debate about Shakespeare and Bacon. 'Did Bacon really write Shakespeare's plays? If that's the case, who wrote Bacon's ones?'

My father sometimes put expressions from books into the things he said to us. If you asked him a question he didn't know the answer to he'd say something like, 'That I do not know, quoth he, but 'twas a famous victory.' He had all these sayings stored up in his head. I presumed they were from the books he had in his office.

One year he had a hole drilled in the wall so cups of tea could be sent into him. It was about two feet thick and two feet high with doors at either side. We called it The Hatch. My mother used to put the cups

48

into it. Sometimes he gave him toast with it. That was in the days before toasters. She made it with a huge fork, holding it over the fire in the stove we had in the kitchen. We called it 'the range.' I never knew why. The only other range I knew was the one in cowboy films.

When I was small I was able to fit my whole body into the Hatch. That was for games of Hide and Seek. I also hid behind the shutters of windows and in wardrobes and under beds. Like many children I felt that if I put my hands over my eyes nobody could see me. Often that illusion was indulged by the people who were looking for me. The youngest of a family got away with everything.

Sometimes I'd be in a wardrobe during a game. Someone would open the door. They'd go, 'I can't see him anywhere,' even if I was right in front of them. I loved hiding in wardrobes. The smell of the fabric off coats was intoxicating.

I felt invisible a lot of the time even when we weren't playing Hide and Seek. At school I was hardly noticed. That didn't bother me. My ambition in those days was to disappear into the woodwork. If I was off school for a day I hated the attention focussed on me when I went back. The teachers would be cross and everyone else asking me why I was out. I just wanted to be left alone.

When I retired into my world I formed thoughts I didn't think anyone else shared. Only in later years did I realise many people were like me in their early years. They were 'in society' but not 'of it,' to use an expression of my father's.

I kept most of my problems to myself in those years. That wasn't because the family wouldn't have listened to them. They would. I just didn't feel inclined to share them. I escaped from them into the worlds of books and films. Only in later years did I voice them. By then it was too late to do anything about them. My character had been formed.

Being the youngest of the family I was often trotted out as an exhibit whenever visitors came to the house. I used to feel like a zoo animal being paraded for people's entertainment. 'Isn't he lovely?' they'd say, or 'Isn't he getting very big?' When children are being talked about, adults tend to forget they're in the room.

It got worse when they addressed me directly. 'And how are we today?' they'd say. They often used the plural tense like doctors. The question was rhetorical. It was usually followed by, 'What do you think you'll be when you grow up?' I never answered that one. I didn't know what I wanted to be even if I didn't grow up.

I retired more and more into myself as the years went on. That happens sometimes when a lot of people come before you in a family. The fact that my father was such a demonstrative character compounded the situation. I was so fascinated watching him I forgot about developing my own personality.

My brothers and sisters were almost as shy as I was. We were glad to see our friends coming to the house but we didn't welcome strangers. We ran under the stairs anytime the doorbell rang. It didn't matter if it was the postman or the milkman or a tinker or one of my father's clients.

Norfolk became a fortress to us, a stronghold against a vaguely threatening universe.

Out of Short Pants

Traditionally you got into your 'longers' on your Confirmation day. I can't remember if that was the way with me. All I know is that I was wearing them when I went to St. Muredach's college in 1965. I was glad to get out of my short ones. There were always getting scratches on my knees. My mother used to put iodine or TCP on them when they bled. It stung for a few seconds like when you got an injection from the dentist. Then you were fine again.

The transition from Primary to Secondary School was as much of a culture shock for me as it was to any twelve year old. I cycled down to Muredach's every morning on my crock of a bike. The brakes were practically non-existent and the chain was always coming off, especially when I was in a hurry. I hated going into class with oil on my hands but it was worse being late. You could get slapped for that. Would I stop to wash them? The choice was between dirty hands or sore ones.

Muredach's was a huge building, one of the most imposing ones in the town. It stood waiting for us at the end of a curling avenue like an imperious beast. It dipped below ground level at one point. You can see that from the photo on the back of this book. It made it look like it was built under the ground. There were steps up to the large front door. I used to get a knot in my stomach every time I climbed them.

There were no girls in Muredach's. I don't remember seeing one in the four years I spent there. It was as if they were off-limits. I don't even remember one coming in on a message or seeing one of my classmates' mothers in there. If I didn't have sisters I'd hardly have known what it was like to speak to a person of the opposite sex for any length of time. It made the sermons about temptresses like Eve and Delilah and Jezebel all the more ominous.

The priests in the college didn't like us mixing with girls. If there was one sitting on our lap we were advised to put paper between us. Girls were told to stay away from boys too. They had to avoid close dancing in the Town Hall. That was especially the case if there was drink involved. Drink reduced everyone's willpower.

Women were regarded as the strong sex in this area even if they weren't in other ones. They protected men from themselves if they saw them as sex objects. Girls were told not to wear patent leather shoes for fear boys could use them as mirrors to look up their dresses. They were told they could get pregnant from toilet seats.

They were 'occasions of sin' for boys. Their job was to stop them from kissing them or engaging in heavy petting with them. I never knew what heavy petting meant. It sounded serious. A mortal sin was going 'the whole way.' We were never told what going the whole way meant. We hardly knew what going part of the way meant.

We heard terms applied to dating situations like 'Nothing happened.' Another one was, 'He got a girl into trouble.' A relative of mine was said to have got a girl into trouble years before I was born. Afterwards he was packed off to America with a shilling. Everyone seemed to have someone like that in their family tree.

One day an unfortunate priest was delegated to tell us the facts of life in the Diocesan Hall. His face was beetroot as he approached the podium. We were pinching ourselves trying not to laugh. At last the tables were turned. We were in the ascendancy for this one day, this one moment. He fled in terror after he'd hardly begun. Afterwards someone let off a stink bomb. There was hell to pay about that for weeks afterwards. They never found out who did it.

I couldn't imagine my mother or father ever telling me the facts of life. They were too shy. Most parents were in those days. We weren't told we came from the stork like some children were. There was just a silence around the subject. We knew Dr. Bourke took us out of our mothers but we didn't know how we got in there in the first place.

Leaflets from The Catholic Truth Society were left lying around the house. They had words like 'puberty' and 'menstruation' in them. I never bothered with them. It was more enjoyable reading *The Beano* or *The Dandy* than these severe tomes. Dennis the Menace sounded like more fun than menstruation (if I ever found out what it meant). There was also Lord Snooty and Minnie the Minx and the Bash Street Kids.

The *Dandy* had Desperate Dan and Korky the cat and Keyhole Kate. Keith told me he was called Keyhole Kate because he loved looking in keyholes. Going to the pictures was a bit like that. It made us all into voyeurs.

Germany made a sex education film called *Helga* in 1967. Holy Ireland thought: It would take those filthy Jerries. Only the French and Swedes were worse. England might have been pagan but Europe was off the scale altogether when it came to stuff like that.

I still remember the names of my classmates from that all-male Muredach's world. Peter Foody, Kevin Beatty, Walter Hinds, Theo Hanley, Billy Kearney, Francis Moore, Tommy Nicholson...these and so many others.

Not all of them were locals. A few came from Bonniconlon and Crossmolina. There were farmers' sons who cycled in every morning from places like Ballycroy and Bellacorick and Cooneal and Dromore

West. Some of them came from tiny Primary Schools where they brought in turf and coal with them to light fires in the classrooms on the cold mornings.

Jerry Cowley was another country boy. He'd just moved to Ballina from a small village where he'd been up to this. We became good friends. He came up to Norfolk a lot. Sometimes we went out to the golf links on the edge of town with two clubs. We smacked balls at one another from one end of it to the other. It was more like hurling than golf. We got in through a hole in the barbed wire. That was more fun than going in the front door. We wouldn't have been admitted anyway.

Back in the college we sat in our seats like sheep and took what was doled out to us. We answered our names in Irish when the roll was called. I was after Gerard McDonnell. I'd hear his one and know I was next. It was important not to miss it. 'Gearóid Mac Domhnaill.' *'Anseo.'* 'Aubraoi O' Maoileoin.' *'Anseo.'*

It was like being in the army. The only thing that made us different from anyone else was our names. Maybe that's why we scratched them out on our desks with such enthusiasm. We wanted some record of the fact that we existed.

Others had preceded us in the same predicament. It was like the cavemen carving hieroglyphics on walls. Or maybe more appropriately, prisoners in jail cells. Kilroy was here.

On copybooks I wrote: 'Aubrey Malone, Norfolk, Arthur Street, Ballina, County Mayo, Ireland, The World, The Milky Way, The Universe, The Solar System.' If there was anything else I could have thought of I'd have added it.

We were told to cover our copies to make them last longer. I had embroidered paper on my ones. I liked feeling the texture of it when I was bored listening to the teachers. It was usually from discarded pieces of wallpaper I found in rolls under the stairs. That's where Tina put them when she was finished with them. She was great at wallpapering. If I ever tried to help her but the paper kept bubbling on me.

Irish was my least favourite subject. It was drilled into us relentlessly. If you failed it in the Leaving Cert you failed the exam no matter how well you did in other subjects. That was an indication of the insanity surrounding it. The term 'overkill' springs to mind. There was little or no emphasis on conversation. Grammar was the keynote.

We nicknamed one of our teachers Punk. He carried a bamboo cane in his soutane. It was whipped out at the slightest pretext. You got two slaps on each hand if you missed a question and more if you committed a more heinous offence. Giving cheek got you six of the best.

When we got slapped our hands burned with the pain. The best way to get rid of it was to sit on them with the palms upwards. Punk didn't like to see you doing that. He wanted the pain to last longer. Sometimes we pulled our hands away as he was about to slap us. That drove him mad. It earned you an extra slap. He'd hold you by the wrist as he gave it to you so you couldn't pull it away again.

Another teacher used to clap us on the two sides of the head at the same time. It was as if he was playing the cymbals. It made us feel as if our brains were being mashed. Maybe that was the idea.

People who say our schooldays are the happiest days of our lives are either liars or fools. This was seven hours of dread built into every day. The teachers in Muredach's were probably no better or worse than in any college in Ireland at the time. There were a handful of tough guys but most of them were okay. There were many kind Christian Brothers too. It was the system that was the problem. It told us we were there to suffer. The word 'education' came from the Latin verb *educare*. It stands for 'to educe.' That seemed to have been forgotten somewhere along the way. Implantation was more relevant.

The curriculum was about memorising facts. We learned things off by rote. If we weren't able to repeat something we were punished. Prayers and poems became indistinguishable from mathematical formulas or the counties of Ireland. Everything was part of a plan to turn us into robots. Someone said once that the only poem that meant anything to them in school was the one that began, 'Thirty days hath September' because it told them something useful. I felt a bit like that.

A lot of the poems were inane ones about birds and flowers. I was never interested in either. I thought poems like Shelley's 'Ode to a Skylark' and Wordsworth's 'The Daffodils' should only have been taught to girls.

When a great writer like Yeats appeared in our English books it was usually some trivial work like 'The Fiddler of Dooney' we got. That wasn't much more than doggerel. When I read Yeats later on in life I was blown away by him. Why weren't his masterpieces on the course instead of childish twaddle like 'The Fiddler of Dooney'? Obviously the people who drew up the curriculum thought we were lulas who wouldn't understand anything deep.

They went to the other extreme with subjects like Latin. It was totally unfathomable to me. Keith and Clive had to study Greek. That would have been even worse. What was the relevance of these subjects to real life? What was the relevance of algebra or geometry to it? We had a vague notion that there was no such thing as Latin or Greek or algebra or geometry in the actual world but we didn't think about things like that too much. We were too busy trying to avoid being hit.

Some of the poems we were made learn were also pretty depressing. They had lines like Padraig Pearse's, 'The beauty of this world has made me sad,' or Thomas Gray's, 'Can flattery soothe the dull cold ear of death.' What sadist decided on a curriculum that foisted dismal notions like these on children? We were barely into our teens.

Our leisure time became an antidote to them. We were like wild beasts when we were let out to the playground between classes. I can't remember any order to our games of chasing. Half the time I wasn't even sure who I was playing with. I just ran for the sake of it.

On the wet days we went into 'The Rec.' That was short for Recreation Room. Or more appropriately 'The Wreck.' All it had in it was a table tennis table without a net. We played push penny and tiddledywinks on it.

A packet of cigarettes was invariably produced at some stage. There were usually just a few in it. Nobody ever had enough money to buy a full pack. That didn't matter to us. There was something exciting about being offered just one cigarette. It was like getting the last Rolo. Even though I wasn't a smoker I never refused.

In the corner of the room there was a stack of old magazines. One of them was a religious one, *The Far East*. It was a missionary publication. I was rummaging through it one day when I saw a woman with her breasts exposed. She was in a tent in some African village. How did the priests miss that? They certainly wouldn't have left it there if they knew what was inside it.

It became a source of amusement to us. One of the fellows in the class tore the photo out and took great delight showing it to his friends around the town. I think he even charged them money to look at it. Here was an entrepreneur in the making. His brother had a deck of playing cards with women in naughty underwear. People were charged to have a look at these too.

We talked about forbidden books. The most well-known one was D.H.Lawrence's *Lady Chatterley's Lover*. We were led to believe it was one of the most sexual books in existence. Apparently there was a copy of it circulating somewhere in the town. Just one. Considering Ballina had a population of about 6000 people I felt it would be a while before it found its way to me.

I asked my father about it once. He said he'd been given a copy by a solicitor friend of his with all the smutty bits highlighted. That was to save people from having to wade through the rest. He said it was mostly boring. I wasn't missing anything.

I could never concentrate on what the teachers were talking about when I got back to the classroom. I'd be thinking of push penny and cigarettes and Lady Chatterley. I looked out the window at Nephin, at the handball alley, the playing fields. Such places always seemed so much more exciting when you couldn't get to them. They were the far away hills even though they weren't that far away at all.

One dull subject was followed by another. In history the emphasis was on things that happened, not why they happened. We learned dates of battles that meant nothing to us. It became something else that was taught like Maths. The numbers still stick in my head: 1014, 1066, 1798, 1815.

Science was good because it got you out of the classroom. We sat beside bunsen burners and tried to pretend we were conducting life changing experiments. In reality we were just warming our hands.

In the history class I had no interest in people like Red Hugh O'Neill or Dermot McMurrough or Patrick Sarsfield. Sometimes I used to sneak a look at the back of the book where there was a mention of 1916. Was this the 1916 my father told me wasn't important? It didn't seem to be. There were only a few pages devoted to it.

I gave up history after the Inter Cert, replacing it with French. It was just after coming in as a subject on the curriculum. All I knew about France was that Charles de Gaulle lived there. So did Brigitte Bardot. I imagined other people did as well but I couldn't swear to it.

Fr. Curry was our French teacher. We called him 'Butch' because his father was a butcher. He was learning the language just as we were. He was only a few pages ahead of us in our text book. It was called *Folens French Course*. I still remember the yellow cover. It had little dots sticking out of it like embossing. We also studied a novel, Alphonse Daudet's *Le Petit Chose*. I hadn't a clue what it was about but I grew to hate it. I resolved never to read anything by Daudet ever again and I never did.

That's what education did to you in those days. Butch taught it the same way Irish and Latin were taught, getting us to learn off the declension of verbs as if that was all there was to the language. The people preparing the courses for these subjects seemed to forget the minor fact that languages were actually spoken things, not lists of words.

Mensa, mensa, mensam, mensae, mensae, mensa. Where could you use this knowledge? Who could you speak it to if all you knew was *Chuaigh mé, chuaigh tú, chuaigh sé, chuaigh sí, chuamar, chuaigh sibh, chuaigh siad.*

In my innocence I thought French might be better. It was the language of the future, wasn't it? I thought so but after a year with Butch I began to wonder. All I could remember from it was *Je suis, tu es, il est, elle est, nous sommes, vous etes, ils ont, elles ont.*

He taught us English for a while too. He had a dry sense of humour. He gave us an essay to write on the season of spring once. Jerry Cowley wrote, 'The lambs were gambling around the fields.' He meant 'gambolling.' Butch said to him, 'What were they doing, Cowley - playing cards?'

My father wrote most of my essays for me. Sometimes they were read out in class. I don't think the teachers seriously believed I wrote them. He was trying to help but it gave me a complex. I felt I was trading off his facility with words.

There was no subject I could say I enjoyed. I was reasonably good at English but everything else was a nightmare.

The geography books had too much stuff devoted to Ireland. I didn't care if they made sugar beet in Tuam or grew barley in Dungarvan. Whenever I looked at the atlas I found my attention being drawn to countries other than Ireland, countries like Africa and Canada and America. They had exotic names like Saskatchewan, Tucson, the Yukon Valley. Being aught doing that was likely to get you a rap on the knuckles with a ruler.

A typical day in Muredach's was two hours of terror followed by three of boredom. Excitement was being allowed clean the blackboard. Anything to get out of your seat, to get away from books like *O Pheann an Phiarsaigh, Peig Sayers, Lamb's Tales from Shakespeare.*

A writer called Macaulay was supposed to be the bee's knees. I never had a clue what he was on about. Jonathan Swift wrote an essay about boiling children. We were supposed to laugh at that. Another essay on the course was about someone who discovered roast pig by accident. Was knowledge of this fact going to cause some dramatic change in our lives?

There was an American in our class called James Jamieson. One day we were learning off the Lord

Byron poem 'The Eve of Waterloo.' It began with the line, 'There was a sound of revelry by night.' He said to the teacher, 'Revelry should be in the morning.' He was thinking of 'Reveille,' the French military term. Americans pronounced it like 'revelry.'

It's strange that a comment like this comes back to me fifty years later. It's probably because so little of human interest happened in the classroom. It was rare for anyone to express even the tiniest personal reaction to anything. We weren't encouraged to have enquiring minds. It was a case of 'Ná tuig, creid' as Punk put it. ('Don't understand, believe.')

Life began when school ended. My heart lifted as I came in the door of Norfolk at four o'clock on Friday afternoons and threw my bag under the stairs. My mother would be in the kitchen cooking the dinner. I'd hate it if I got the smell of cabbage. Anything but that.

She'd ask me how school went. I'd warm my hands at the range as she put the dinner on the table. I'd eat it as I listened to the wireless. That was what radios were called then. I never knew why because they had wires on them that went into them.

I listened to programmes 'Hospital's Requests' and 'The Kennedys of Castleross.' That was a soap opera. It was written by Hugh Leonard and sponsored by Fry Cadbury. Most people in the country tuned into it. The Kennedys were like our Kardashians. We knew every detail of their lives. Marie Keane played Mrs Kennedy.

The only times my mother wouldn't be in the kitchen when I came home from school was if she had a migraine. When she got an attack she had to lie in a dark room until it passed. She never spoke about it and she'd cut you off if you asked her about it. Her problems were off limits. Only our ones were allowed to be discussed.

61

After school I usually went out into the street. Sometimes I just looked at the cars passing up and down. There weren't many of them in those days. Some of my classmates wrote their number plates down in little notebooks. They were the kind of people who went up to train stations and wrote the numbers of the trains down. I wasn't interested in doing that any more than I was in jigsaws or stamp collecting or putting ships in bottles. Most of the things other children did I found boring.

I loved listening to boxing on the wireless. One night I was allowed stay up until the middle of the night. It was when Cassius Clay beat Sonny Liston. It didn't end till about 3 a.m. That would have been about ten o'clock in American time. We were all up for Cassius Clay. My mother loved the way he said, 'I'm the greatest.' Sonny Liston was like the devil to us. Even the way he looked was scary. It was like the victory of good over evil.

I remember other fights with people like Floyd Patterson and Ingemar Johansson. There was one where Henry Cooper knocked Cassius Clay down but he got up again and beat him. The commentator made you see it all in your mind.

On Saturdays we had drill in the college. It was nearly worse than school but at least it was over by lunchtime. Afterwards I used to get a neck shave in Lowther's. We weren't allowed have your hair long at school in those days. It was short back and sides or nothing.

Mr Lowther had his shop on the edge of the lane I played in. His full name was T.V. Lowther. I thought that was strange. If you didn't know better you'd think he was a television. After asking me to sit down in his chair he draped a sheet around me to catch the hair he cut. I wasn't tall enough to see myself in the mirror so he gave me a cushion to sit on.

He had a shaver that sounded like a dentist's drill. That was for the neck. For the top of my head he used a scissors. He'd put two of his fingers together under it until some strands were visible. Then he'd clip them. I always wanted him to stop before he did. 'It won't be long now,' he'd say, 'No pun intended.' I didn't know what a pun was.

When he was finished he put a smaller mirror behind my head so I could see what he'd done. 'Happy with that?' he'd say. I'd nod my head. Then he'd shake the sheet. The hair fell onto the floor and his assistant swept it up. I think he was his son. He always looked very serious.

After I paid him he used to wink at me and say, 'See you soon.' It would be cold going home if I didn't have a scarf because of my bare neck. It was so itchy I'd keep scratching it for ages. I hated it if I met anyone I knew. They'd say something like 'Who scalped you?' It was like cowboys getting scalped by the Indians in films.

Neck shaves weren't cool. I'd have preferred to have a ducktail like Tony Curtis. Unfortunately my hair didn't grow that way. I didn't have locks either. That meant I couldn't look like Elvis. I used to slick my hair down in front of my ears with cold water to give the impression of having them. It only stayed that way for a few seconds. One time I even tried to sellotape it there. That didn't work either.

If I had a motorbike I could have been like Marlon Brando or James Dean but I was too young to have one of those. I only had a pushbike. You couldn't be cool with a pushbike. I couldn't even wear jeans like Brando or Dean. The closest I came to being cool was flicking my fingers like Russ Tamblyn when I played a Jet in Hugo's version of *West Side Story*.

When Hugo wasn't directing dramas he played soldiers with me. He used to make up scenes and act them out. He took books from the library and stood them on their sides. The pages would be spread out so they looked like mountains. I rode my soldiers through them as we created our own private Monument Valley in the front room.

Trying To Be Holy

John McGahern once said that when he was growing up he believed he knew heaven better than he did Canada or Australia. 'Religion was the weather of my youth,' he said, 'The Bible was my first book.' I felt the same way. We had a Bible in the living-room with hundreds of pictures in it. The paper was wafer-thin with gold fringes on them. It had a brown leather cover.

It was my first book too. I thought of heaven as being somewhere above the clouds. If we were good enough, the priests told us, we'd end up there one day. We'd be happy forever with God. Our lives on earth had moments of happiness in them but this wasn't the real world. It was only a preparation, a way station where you served your time before you went to your reward.

I used to wonder what being a saint meant. Did everyone who went to heaven get to be one? Would we be as good as God when we got there or would we be more like Adam and Eve, in danger of being thrown out if we got too big for our boots?

What would the ordinary day be like? Would we have any say in the running of the place? Would we be all-knowing and all-seeing like God or would we preserve bits of the way we were on earth?

Ballina had the biggest cathedral in Mayo. You couldn't avoid looking at it anytime you crossed the Moy. Even when you weren't near it you heard the bells. They pealed for Mass and the Angelus and benediction and the sodalities.

Religion was all around us when we were growing up. It was even apparent in the addresses we saw on walls. It was apparent in the places we went to play like Convent Hill or St. Patrick's Well or Marian Crescent.

That was where our friend Tom Maughan lived. His father died before he was born. My mother told me he was a 'postulant' child. She meant 'posthumous.' Her mispronunciation meant I grew up thinking Tom was some kind of priest. He actually became a doctor.

The first thing I remember about religion was the sun streaming through the stained glass windows of the cathedral. They had images of saints and other holy people on them. They all seemed to be going through some form of torment.

I watched old men and women walking up the side aisles doing the Stations of the Cross. Most of them seemed to be dressed in dark clothes. They reminded me of the black of the nuns, the Brothers, the priests of Muredach's. It seemed to emphasise the fact that life was a vale of tears. White was the colour of the resurrection. We had to die to be re-born into that.

Like everyone else I made my First Confession when I was seven. That was the age of reason. It meant you knew what sin was. I made my First Communion that year too. You had to be in the state of grace if you were going to communion. That meant you couldn't have any sin on your soul. If you were going to 'receive' you had to fast from midnight the night before.

Sometime you'd be so hungry, the 'body of Christ' would be like actual food to you when you got it. You weren't allowed chew it. It couldn't touch your teeth when the priest put it into your mouth, only your tongue. You had to keep very still. It reminded me of when Dr Igoe was taking my temperature. I had to be careful to keep the thermometer under my tongue when he did that. Everything would be spoiled if it slipped over it.

There were holy pictures all over the house. Basil had a devotion to St. Gerard Majella. He was the

66

patron saint of expectant mothers. We had a picture of him in a long thin frame. We also had ones of the Nativity and St. Anthony. St. Anthony found things for you when you lost them if you said a prayer to him. He found a comic for me once. It was under a cushion. My mother said, 'Don't forget to thank him.' That meant a second prayer.

Sometimes I wondered if she thought I'd be a priest. I was quiet. That was often seen as a sign. I thought the priests in the college expected it of me too. I didn't feel pressure from home but Muredach's was regarded as a recruitment centre for the missions. Ballina provided a lot of priests for these. Sometimes it seemed as if the town's streets were competing with one another to see which one could produce the most. As someone said once of this time, 'We grew priests like potatoes.'

I knew early on in life that the priesthood wasn't for me. I wasn't even an altar boy. That was sometimes seen as a sign too.

I thought altar boys looked like girls as they stood on the altar handing the priests cruets of wine. The only thing I envied them doing was putting out the candles. They had implements that had little triangles on the top of them. I liked watching them quenching them.

The second most important book in our house after The Bible was the Catechism. It was full of questions. We had to learn the answers to them off by heart. Some of them were easy, like 'Who made the world?' As the book went on they became more difficult. There were big words in it, words like 'transubstantiation.' That meant when the communion host was turned into the body of Christ.

Like most families in Ireland we said the rosary every night. We used to kneel on the floor and put our elbows on the seats of kitchen chairs as we prayed. My father walked in and out among the chairs threading a rosary beads through his fingers so he'd get the count right on the Hail Marys. After all the decades were said we'd have what Hugo called 'the trimmings.' That was all the extra prayers for Special Intentions. Sometimes the trimmings lasted longer than the rosary.

We usually went to bed after the rosary was finished. We said more prayers after we undressed. I always said,

Oh angel of god, my guardian dear,
To whom God's love commits me here
Ever this day be at my side
To light and guard, to rule and guide,
Amen.

Really religious people spent the whole week waiting for Sunday. That was Mass day. Many of them went to Mass on other days as well. I heard once that Aunt Mary was a daily communicant. I heard once that Uncle Eddie, her husband, gave £2000 to the church to have the bells repaired one time when they were giving trouble.

Mass was as much a social occasion as anything else. People congregated outside the cathedral before it to catch up on all the latest news, especially the ones who'd cycled in from the country. They felt out of touch.

It was noticed if you had a new coat or a new car. They might praise it to your face and rubbish it behind your back. In such ways were loyalties formed and dissensions created. Comments were made on your appearance. So little was happening in so many people's worlds, details like these were huge. In that way Ballina was like the valley of the squinting windows.

We all wore our 'Sunday best' to Mass. Most people did at that time. Like a little army we trooped down Garden Street and across the bridge to the cathedral. The crowds would already be filing in as we got to it. We blessed ourselves at the fonts inside the door. The marble on the floor would be cold as we walked up to the aisle to the top of the church. We took our place in one of the pews and started to pray. Most people prayed quietly but you could hear some of them whispering the words.

Many of the seats had 'Pray for the Donor' written on them on gold panels glued into the wood. I always wondered who that was supposed to be. Was it a person? A saint?

There was leather on the part where you knelt down. We were told not to put our bottoms against the seat behind us when we were kneeling. Sometimes we did that when we were tired.

The pulpit had gargoyles on it. It was half way down the church. The seats beside it had bits cut out of them by carpenters to make room for it. I found myself wondering how they did that than thinking of what the priest was talking about.

My family seemed lost in thought as he spoke but I was always looking around me at worldly things – the clothes people were wearing, the way they sat, how they moved. The bishop said, 'Let God into your soul.' I wasn't sure how to do that. It wasn't like food. Communion was said to be the divine food but it didn't make me feel divine. Did that make me a bad person?

Many of the women wore headscarves. Some of the men took handkerchiefs out of their pockets. They knelt on them to save their knees from the hard wood. Then the priest would come out. The Mass would begin. He spoke in Latin for a lot of the time. I didn't understand that but I knew a lot of the prayers from the epistle and the gospel. Then it would come to the time for the sermon. We'd all sit for that.

You could hear a pin drop during the sermon. Crying babies would be brought out to the sacristy. Anyone who coughed would get a stern look from the priest.

My father didn't usually sit with us. He stayed at the back of the church so he could go out for a cigarette during the sermon. The Mass seemed to go on forever. I'd find my concentration drifting to him and to my mother. Her prayer book had dozens of things in it. There were relics and special prayers and holy bookmarks. They made it twice as wide as it would have been otherwise.

After the Mass finished we used to go over to anyone we knew and chat to them. Sometimes they joined us on the walk back home. They talked of the news of the day and showed off their new fashions. When we got the Norfolk we'd already be able to smell the dinner.

My mother was an old-fashioned cook. We were a 'meat and two veg' kind of family. Marrowfat peas were my favourite vegetables. We called them 'Sunday peas' because we always had them that day. She steeped them in the pantry on Saturday nights. It was like our fridge. We kept lots of food there to prevent it going off. Jelly was steeped in there as well. Red jelly was my favourite kind and green my least. It was like with fruit gum sweets. The red ones were my favourites. I didn't like the green ones. People associated green with me because of St. Patrick's Day and because I had green eyes. They called them cat's eyes.

Custars and apple was even nicer than jelly for dessert. We had that on Sundays sometimes too for a treat. We used Gildie Ahern's apples for it. A lot of them were only good for cooking.

Sunday was the longest day of the week. If the weather was bad it seemed even longer. The shops were closed and the time crawled. Nothing was

70

capable of speeding it up. To help it along its way we played endless games of cards - Sevens, Old Maid, Picking the Pairs, Newmarket, Switch, Snap, even Patience. We'd look at our watches every so often thinking hours had passed and it would only be minutes.

If there was a football match on the radio it helped. Mícheál O'Hehir was always the commentator. He made even dull matches sound interesting. I knew his voice as well as that of anyone in my own family. Most people in the town did. There was always excitement in it. If you went for a walk on a match day, most likely you'd hear it coming through the open windows of the houses you passed or the open windows of cars. If Gay Byrne was Mr Television, he was Mr Radio.

You weren't supposed to spend too much time listening to football matches on Sunday. The priests called it 'The Sabbath.' They gave us various ways of reminding us of how holy it was.

Religion didn't only surround us on Sunday. It was there every day of the week with the pealing of the church bells for Mass and the Angelus. There were Corpus Christi processions in the streets. We stopped playing if they came through Arthur Street.

There were retreats as well, and triduums and liturgical festivals. Some priests said Mass on the top of Croagh Patrick. We called it 'The Reek.' Mission priests came to the town during Lent. They scared the living daylights out of us. Many of them seemed to have missed their vocations as leading stars in horror films.

Lent was a big deal when I was growing up. Fr Gallagher smudged ash onto our foreheads with his thumb on Ash Wednesday. It was to remind us that 'Ashes we were and to ashes we would return.'

We were expected to go around with long faces for the forty days. They had to be extra long on Good

Friday. We prayed until our jaws dropped that day. There was no diversion. We were told not to smile or play games or records. All the television programmes were morose as well. A film about the Crucifixion was about as jolly as things got.

We were told Good Friday was a particularly good day for getting souls out of Purgatory. I imagined them all huddled together like people in a burning building waiting for the fire brigade. Maybe God kept the flames low for those days.

Most of the family went off sweets for Lent. The only time we were allowed break our fast was on my birthday. I made sure I reminded people of it well in advance so they could load up on boxes of chocolates for me.

I devoured them when I got them. Some of the boxes had two rows. I used to dip into the second row for my favourite ones and replace the gaps with ones I didn't like from the first row. Hopefully someone else would eat these when I offered them to them.

We weren't allowed eat meat on Fridays. My mother liked doing the First Fridays. It meant going to Mass every Friday for nine weeks as well as on Sundays.

I went with her sometimes. I tried to look holy when I prayed. There were times when I felt it for real, like when the priest was burning incense or if the choir was singing some hymn I liked.

My favourite was 'Hail Queen of Heaven':

Hail queen of heaven, the ocean star
Guide of the wanderer here below,
Thrown on life's surge, we claim thy care
Save us from peril and from woe.

I liked it because it was protective. So many things about religion put the emphasis on fear instead. All the Commandments had 'Not' in them. They made me nervous.

The bishop made me nervous too. His name was Boyle. He was consecrated on February 25, Jacinta's birthday. He always reminded me of Pope Pius. He was called the bishop of Killala. Why wasn't he the bishop of Ballina? Aunt Nellie's house was on the Killala Road but the town itself was miles away.

His palace was beside Muredach's. It stood on high ground like a fortress in a fairytale, surrounded by luxuriant greenery. I imagined him inside sitting on a throne like some fourteenth century king, surrounded by servants who genuflected before him and kissed his ring. We had to kiss it too whenever we saw him. He was an ethereal figure to me, someone only half real. I could never imagine him doing any of the things the rest of us did, dressing himself or washing his teeth or going to the toilet.

There was a little grotto of Our Lady across the road from him. She stood there looking heavenwards in her royal blue with her arms folded in prayer. Or was she looking towards his palace? Sometimes it seemed that even she was seeking his approval.

We rarely saw him. Now and again he gave a sermon in the church. If we won a football match he came into the college and gave us a half day. Such victories were rare. They prepared me for the number of times Mayo lost crunch matches at Croke Park in the coming years when we came so close to winning 'The Sam' only to fall at the last fence. Our main bogey team was St. Jarlath's from Tuam. Whenever we played them I feared the worst. 'We need more commitment,' one of our teachers said. 'Too many players don't jump for the ball. They wait for the fella in front of him to drop it.'

We were supposed to feel holy when the bishop prayed with us but I couldn't stop thinking about the half day.

He told us we were impure. He said when we were born we already had a stain on our souls. It was original sin, the mark of Cain. So even the massacre of the innocents, those babies killed by Pontius Pilate when he was trying to find Jesus, weren't totally innocent.

The only totally innocent people were God and the Virgin Mary. Mary was born without a sin on her soul. That was the Immaculate Conception. My mother thought the Immaculate Conception meant Mary had Jesus without having sex with Joseph. She found that hard to accept. Out of all the strange things we were asked to believe in those days, this was the only one that gave her a problem.

Bishop Boyle had a particular devotion to Our Lady. He told us to strive to be as holy as she was. He said she it hurt her every time we sinned. She blushed if we said a bad word. She wanted us to be good so we could be with her in heaven.

He talked a lot about the next world. It was as if this one wasn't important. In this world, he said, we only saw things through a glass darkly. In the next one we'd see 'even as we were seen.'

He told us about hell and purgatory and limbo. Hell was a conflagration of fire where bad people went. Limbo was for unbaptised babies. Purgatory was where most of us went after we died. It was a kind of waiting room for heaven. We prayed for the souls in purgatory when we were on earth. If our prayers were genuine enough we got them into heaven. Then when we died they prayed for us in the same way. We told our sins in confession and if we were contrite enough we were forgiven. It was like putting your clothes into the laundry and having them all come out perfectly white. Your soul was like a box inside your body that you kept rubbing until it was clean.

It was worth putting up with all the bishop's talk if it resulted in a half day. As soon as I got out of the college I stopped thinking about hell and purgatory and limbo. Thoughts about them came back again on Sunday when I had to go to Mass.

My father used to say he'd like to have been a preacher. He said he'd have liked to be consigning people to hell from the pulpit. I never took him seriously when he talked like that. It was the actor coming out in him. He performed when he was doing his recitations and when he was giving a dramatic speech to a judge about a witness he was trying to get off. He was a defence counsel trying to pretend he was a prosecutor.

He often said, 'When the priests are telling the congregation they're going to hell, everyone is looking at the person opposite them in the next bench. They don't realise he's talking to them.'

My favourite priest was Fr Harte. He raced through the Mass at the rate of knots. You were usually out of the church within a half hour. He didn't bother with sermons.

We liked him for Confession too. He didn't seem to be listening half the time. That was the best type of priest to confess your sins to. There was always a big queue outside his box. Then one day I heard him shouting 'You what?' at a penitent. His voice was so loud he almost took the roof off the box. The boy was beetroot when he came out. Everyone was staring at him.

The queues outside Fr. Harte's box dwindled after that. We started going to Fr Moore instead. He was deaf so he wasn't able to hear your sins. He always gave you the same penance: an Our Father, three Hail Marys and three 'Glory Be's.' Even if you stabbed your mother to death you'd get that penance.

The last thing you wanted to be was a long time in the box. The longer you were, the worse the people waiting outside would think you were. You imagined them judging you, laughing at you, being horrified. So if you'd really stabbed your mother to death and it wasn't Fr Moore at the other side of the grill you wouldn't say you killed her. You'd only say you gave her a little nick and she survived. Brendan Gaffney said, 'Poison her. Give her arse a nick.'

Priests generally took a harder line on sex than anything else. If you told lies or cheated or stole or poached salmon from the Moy these were all understandable sins. Anything to do with women was on a different scale altogether.

You weren't supposed to have 'bad thoughts.' Bad thoughts were rarely about robbing or cheating or killing people. They were mostly about women. Voluptuous women like Hedi Lamarr from *Samson and Delilah* or Brigitte Bardot from *And God Created Woman.* You saw them in film magazines and on posters in the Estoria. You could go to hell for those kinds of thoughts.

My father had a joke about them. A man goes to confession and says he had them. The priest says, 'Did you entertain these thoughts, my child?' The man says, 'No, Father, but they sure entertained me!' Having our father tell us jokes like that helped us keep our sanity in a world that seemed to want to rob us of it.

The priests told us to read the lives of the saints to keep ourselves holy but I couldn't imagine anything more boring. I didn't want to read about lonely old men in dilapidated monasteries whispering ejaculations into the air. I didn't want to read about people like Matt Talbot lacerating themselves with chains or St Simeon spouting gobbledygook from the top of a pillar in the desert for 37 years. My favourite saint was St Jude for Hopeless Cases because I felt like one.

There were pictures of hell in the Bible. They showed sinners being cast into an inferno. Saints from heaven looked down on them. One of them showed the people in hell begging for a tiny drop of water to put on their lips. The saints didn't seem interested. They just kept staring at them disapprovingly. That picture haunted me all through my youth. I couldn't get my mind off it. It scared me more than anything I ever saw in a Dracula film.

What kind of people went to hell? Most sins were venial ones but there were some mortal ones as well. I always felt these were sexual ones, at least if you didn't murder someone. Why had religion such an obsession with it? Why did God give us sexual feelings if we weren't allowed to do anything about them? Maybe it was like going on a diet if you felt like eating. You had to deny yourself.

If you ate too much you became a glutton. People cut down on their eating during Lent. Some of the priests in Muredach's seemed to eat a lot. Some of them had fine big stomachs on them. Maybe eating was a substitute for sex. They didn't talk about food in their sermons. It was mainly 'the sins of the flesh.' The word 'flesh' always made me think of voluptuous women, the kind you saw in those pictures in the Bible or on the posters in the Estoria. Maybe that's why the priests didn't like us going to the pictures. They might have thought we'd be tempted by sins of the flesh.

Was this what Adam and Eve were guilty of? We were told Adam ate an apple in our Catechism class. Why was he thrown out of heaven for that? It seemed such an innocent thing to do, a venial sin instead of a mortal one. The apple was from the Tree of Knowledge. God had told him not to go near it. Why was wanting knowledge a bad thing?

Our Catechism teacher was called Tich. He said Adam and Eve were too curious. That's why they had to be driven out of heaven. John Milton wrote about them in a poem called *Paradise Lost*. He said they ate the apple because they wanted to be as wise as God. That was the devil's sin too, the sin of pride. The devil was called Lucifer. I liked the sound of his name even though I wasn't supposed to.

Tich told us not to question things from the Bible. We just had to accept it. It was like everything else we were told in Maths and French and History and Irish. Once again it was a question of, 'Ná tuig, creid.' If we got too curious we could end up like Adam and Eve, two people who were exiled from Paradise for eating an apple without permission.

I wondered what Gildie Ahern would have done if he caught them at it. They'd probably have settled for a few shots of his pop gun in preference to an eternity of everlasting flames.

Music, Music, Music

I tried not to think too much about religion because it brought my mood down. The things that took my mind off it were the things we did after school and outside the church – films, comics, soccer, all the card games.

Music was another escape. We had a record player that played LPs and EPs. We had so many EPs of Elvis Presley I used to think the term stood for his initials. It was years before I learned they were for Extended Play.

You had to be careful if you hit the needle. The records would scratch. If there was a scratch on a record it meant the singer sang the same line over and over again. We used to listen to them doing that for fun sometimes. I'm sure it didn't do the needle any good.

I liked the scraping sound it made for a few seconds before the record came on. Some of our records were warped. I used to lie on the carpet watching them go up and down as we played them. Warped records scratched much more than straight ones. Other ones didn't have middles. We got them from juke boxes. We made middles for them with bits of cardboard.

We had a radio as well as a record player. People would laugh if they saw it now. It was bigger than the average size of one of today's televisions. The lights shone out at us like the dashboard of a car. We sat on the floor twirling the buttons. The names of all the stations stood beside little grey rectangles.

The voices sounded funny when we were between stations. It was as if they were gargling in the bathroom. Under the names of the stations there were all the numbers: 50, 100, 150, 200. Eventually we'd get the dial up to 208. That was the number for Radio

Luxembourg. It was the first station I ever heard playing pop music. When I reached it I felt I'd found the combination of a lock. Pete Murray did The Top Twenty on it every Sunday night.

The sound was muffled sometimes but we didn't mind. We loved all the singers on it – Dusty Springfield, Johnny Mathis, Shirley Bassey, Nat King Cole, Helen Shapiro. Torch songs appealed especially to me, ones by people like Connie Francis and Peggy Lee.

For lighter listening I liked Adam Faith and Brenda Lee. Frank Ifield brought in yodelling. My attempts at that were enough to drive anyone within 100 yards to distraction.

Another thing I did that was guaranteed to drive people barmy was when putting a piece of cigarette paper over a comb and blowing through it.

Johnnie Ray cried when he sang. He was known as Mr Emotion. If someone showed that much emotion today they'd probably be put in rehab. He had a hit with 'Walkin' in the Rain.' Butch Moore came along later with 'Walking the Streets in the Rain.' It was more middle of the road. Most Irish music was. We said 'Spit on me, Dickie,' for Dickie Rock but he was soft core too. Joe Dolan got the girls going more than anyone. He sent them home sweatin' as the expression went.

Hugo had a lot of Frank Sinatra's records. He liked Tommy Sands and Marty Robbins as well. One year I remember him buying The Beatles 'White Album.' Today this is looked on almost reverentially but when it came out it was seen as just another record. Hugo was often ahead of the curve in things like that.

Basil liked Cliff Richard. Everyone talked about 'The Young Ones' but I preferred a song he sang called 'A Voice in the Wilderness.' It had an ache in it. I loved songs with an ache in them. They spoke more to me. Jim Reeves sang one called 'The Blizzard.' He was trying to reach his girlfriend, Mary Ann, but the weather stopped him. He's dying at the end of it and 'five more miles from Mary Ann.'

Elvis was like the high priest of all the singers. He had lots of imitators. People like Fabian and Ricky Nelson tried to sing like him but they didn't get there. I was too young to have heard him in 1956. That was the year he made his breakthrough with 'Heartbreak Hotel.'

In the sixties he was soft-pedalling for a lot of the time, bringing out albums on the back of many poor films. The exceptions were classic songs like 'It's Now or Never.' It was based on the Mario Lanza song 'O Sole Mio.'

Another gem was 'Are You Lonesome Tonight?' In my opinion that was his best song of all. I fell in love with it the first time I heard it. It was as if Elvis was in the room singing to me and me alone. He had a great speaking voice as well as being an incredible singer. When he said, 'Then came Act Two,' I thought he was saying, 'Then came back too.' It's strange how you can get a line wrong like that. It must have been thirty years later that I saw the words of the song written down and realised my mistake.

'It's Now or Never' was done as a kind of tribute to Lanza, one of his heroes. If Elvis was born in a previous era I often thought he'd have been an opera singer. Rock and roll wasn't his first love. Ballads were. He turned himself into a rock and roll singer because it was the 'in' thing when he was breaking into the music scene. All great singers are chameleons.

There was another Elvis song we had called 'Such a Night.' Someone gave a yelp at the end of it that wasn't edited out. I don't know how many times I played it just to hear that yelp. What simple pleasures we had in those days.

John Lennon said Elvis died the day he went into the army. Maybe it was true. His music was never as good afterwards. But he had some great hits in the seventies when he went back to live performing. Lennon should have commented on that. He should also have admitted that Brian Epstein sanitised the Beatles. They were a leather band before he cleaned them up.

Fifties music always meant more to me than anything that came out of the decade after it. They called it 'The Swinging Sixties' but all I remember swinging in it was Punk's bamboo cane. Lyrics like The Beatles' 'I Wanna Hold Your Hand' left me cold. How could they compare with someone like Roy Orbison or the Everly Brothers?

The Everlys were brilliant at harmonising. It was like listening to a person with two different voices. Almost every song they sang seemed to be a hit.

'Wake Up, Little Susie' was banned at one stage. That was the worst part of the fifties, people looking for meanings in songs and then condemning them. The same thing happened to Teresa Brewer's 'Music, Music, Music.'

How could anyone have seen anything wrong with that? Some people today think Cliff Richard's 'Livin' Doll' is sexist. The same charge has been levelled at dozens of songs we sang in the fifties without thinking of things like that. None of us can say what's good or bad in music or anything else. Often our view of morality depends on when we were born.

My mother was fond of Ray Charles. She was especially taken with his song, 'Take These Chains From My Heart.' She said it was a love song but I couldn't see it like that. I couldn't get the image of the chains out of my mind. I kept thinking of a dungeon. Years later I felt the same about Leonard Cohen's sepulchral 'Tower of Song.'

I rarely took in the meanings of songs. The imagery in them meant more to me. I listened to them for their moods rather than concentrating on what they were about. They were like poems to me.

Second Grade George Bests

The thing I liked most next to music was soccer. We played it down in Belleek. That was where the local team trained. We used to congregate at the back of the Courell's house on Convent Hill. Michael Courell organised the matches.

His father had played for Mayo back in the day. Now the 'foreign' game was coming in. We delighted to be defying the authorities in Muredach's when we played it. The ban was still in force there.

The ball we played with was a heavy leather one. It could hurt you if you got a thump of it. At times I felt we were playing with a car tyre.

There was no limit to the number of players on a team. Whoever turned up got to play. There were no subs or sending offs or even referees.

Our matches were mad affairs. Bodies flew into muck and got lashed on by rain. I always wanted to get my clothes muddy. If my mother said, 'You're as black as the ace of spades,' when I came home I knew the game had been a success. That would probably be seen as a racist phrase today.

'Just keep playing football,' Michael used to say anytime we dropped our heads. He never said anything else. It made me think: What else could we do? It became his catchphrase just like Max Bygraves' 'I Wanna Tell You a Story' or Bruce Forsythe's 'Didn't he do well.' We joked him about it for years afterwards.

He was a brilliant player himself. So was his brother Gerry. I was in awe watching them - their deft movements, how they slipped around other players or sold dummies, the way they closed in on the goal before letting fly. I imagined them playing for professional teams in the years to come, teams like

Liverpool or Manchester United that always seemed to have Irish connections.

These were the teams we were most interested in, not the national side. When England won the World Cup in 1966 it didn't mean much to us. We usually cheered against them. 1966 was also the fiftieth anniversary of the 1916 Uprising.

That gave us an extra reason not to celebrate their victory - at least those of us who didn't share our father's pro-British feelings. Arthur Street was changed to Teeling Street that year in remembrance of a republican hero but my father continued to refer to it as Arthur Street. He also refused to call Knox Street Pearse Street.

Hugo and Basil played as well. Hugo was valued for his height. He was solid in defence. Basil was a bit smaller and could move faster. He used to scurry in and out between the other players. He often scored goals. Michael had his work cut out trying to get the ball off him.

It was an era before *Match of the Day*. We were aware of the top players but we didn't try to ape them. We knew our limits and didn't try out fancy moves. The games were about getting the ball from one end of the pitch to the other as fast as you could. There were no scissors movements, no bicycle kicks over your shoulder.

There were no offside decisions either. I don't ever recall a goal being disallowed. I didn't even know there were such things then. Once the ball crossed the line, that was it. At half time we had a glass of lemonade from a bottle with a piece of newspaper stuck into the neck of it. If we finished the game with our clothes streaked in mud we knew we'd played well.

The other people I remember in Belleek were from my class - Dessie Callaghan with his tall build and distinctive red hair, Pat Curley who was equally tall,

85

Henry Wills in his green and white jersey, a testament to his affection for Glasgow Celtic.

Henry went on to become a photographer for the *Western People*. He had a twin sister. That was unusual. It was like our own Raymond and Mary, the twins who died after a week in Norfolk. The only other time I heard of a boy and girl being twins was the actor Montgomery Clift and his sister. Pat lived opposite the Courells on Convent Hill. Somebody told me my parents used to live in his house before they bought Norfolk. That was never confirmed to me. I can't believe I never found out for sure.

Pat's father had a clothing shop on Garden Street. He was one of the most prominent members of the team in Belleek. His boot scored a goal one day. It came off as he was taking a penalty. It travelled further than the ball and ended up in the back of the net.

After Hugo and Basil went to Dublin I still kept going to Belleek. I got more games then because there were less people to pick from and the standard wasn't as good. Sometimes after the games I went up a hill that was at the side of the pitch. I used to stand there looking down at the town. There was a tree there as well. It had a tyre hanging from one of the branches. I used to sit inside it and swing back and forth. Then one day the branch broke so I couldn't do that anymore.

Afterwards I climbed out as far as I could on the part of the branch that was still jutting out from the tree. You could see a lot from being on the height. It gave me a kind of spiritual feeling looking down on everything. When I read Wordsworth's poem 'The Prelude' in later years it brought that feeling back to me. It was a feeling of wildness and liberation, especially if the wind was blowing. It gave me the sense that there was something out there that I could one day be a part of if I wanted to.

When we couldn't get to Belleek we played on a makeshift pitch on Connolly Street or else I might play with my friend Mícheál Leonard in the lane behind his house. Sometimes we brought the ball out to the street. We kicked it in and out through parked cars and bicycles. These must have been the most unorthodox games in history. I don't know how many goals we scored off fenders and mudguards. One day I scored a goal off a moving car when the ball hit the side door. It ricocheted onto a wall we were using for the goal.

The daylight determined how long we played. When it got too dark to see the ball we stopped. Or maybe it burst. Sometimes our games extended into Garden Street or even the Market Square. There was more space there. Pitches were makeshift. Walls became goalposts. We put chalk marks on them to make the shapes. They'd be replaced by other walls the next day.

Soccer wasn't allowed in Muredach's in those days. It was seen as 'the pagan game' from across the water. That made me want to play it more. Maybe I inherited some of my father's pro-British attitudes. He never said whether he approved of me playing it or not. It was better for him than Gaelic for him but not as good as rugby, or 'rugger' as he called it. Muredach's didn't have rugby so he could hardly complain.

He wasn't sporty himself. Playing rugby was compulsory in Castleknock when he was at school there as a young man. It was something he couldn't abide but there was one game he played where he became an unlikely hero. A burly player from the opposing team was approaching him and he was expected to take him down.

He didn't fancy the job so he just closed his eyes and said a prayer that he wouldn't be trampled to death. The player thundered into him and they both went flying. The desired effect was achieved. He inadvertently dispossessed him and was the hero of the hour. The incident spelt the end of his sporting career.

He enjoyed telling this story against himself. If there was humour in an anecdote he didn't mind if he came off badly in it. He told these kinds of stories to his clients as well. No wonder he was so popular with them. I often saw them in stitches laughing after he'd finished his business with them. I always got the impression he was more interested in the anecdotes than the business.

After school I became his unofficial postman. I delivered letters for him to many of the solicitors in the town – Gilvarry's, Corr's, Bourke Carrig and Loftus. He had four clients that seemed like rhymes: Fottrell, Cottrell, Cox and Fox.

His envelopes were long and thin. They were usually stuffed to overflowing point with files. Sometimes he sealed documents with a red substance that he burned into them. I loved watching him doing that.

When I wasn't posting his letters I went to other places in the town – Geraghty's for groceries, Brennan's for comics and sweets, Clarke's for the ice cream he drank by the jugful, Durcan's for the *Evening Press.*

The papers used to be left in a pile outside the shop as soon as they came off the train from Dublin. I recognised them by the magenta masthead in the left hand corner. The paper on top was always tattered from the wind. Mr Durcan used to give me the one underneath it. 'Nothing but the best for Mr Malone,' he'd say.

My father regarded the *Evening Press* as a rag. That was mainly because it was associated with *Fianna Fáil.* The *Irish Independent* was slightly preferable to him. It was the paper of Fine Gael, the 'blueshirts.' *The Irish Times* was best of all. He liked being seen with it. He dumbed himself down with the trashy English papers on Sundays. In *The People* there were sensationalistic crime stories and tacky Page 3 girls.

The reason he bought it, he said, was because he liked the 'Spot the Ball' competitions. I used to do these myself too. There'd be a photograph of a football match with lots of players jumping for a ball that wasn't shown. You had to guess where it was. I tried to pick the most obvious place but it was never there.

In the *Sunday Independent* he entered a competition that gave you a sentence with a missing word. You had to choose between various options to decide what it might be. Words like 'mad,' 'bad,' or 'sad' were suggested. There didn't seem to be any logic behind how it was devised. Either of the three would usually have fitted the context. It was nonsense but he became addicted to it.

The other shops we went to were Byron's for records and Woolworth's for novelty items. There was a Wellworth's as well. It was where you went to if you couldn't get what you wanted in Woolworth's. Everything seemed to cost 19/11 in these two shops. That price always stuck with me. It would be like charging 99p for something today. Because it's less than a euro you think it's cheap.

At Christmas we got toys in the International Stores. One year I got Scalextric. My excitement was uncontainable. I still remember clipping the tracks together and sailing sports cars over them.

The best part was when they crashed. Another year I got a Batmobile. I loved the wing that stuck out at the back. John De Lorean was supposed to have pioneered things like this in the 1980s but I thought the Batmobile got there first.

Strong's clothes shop was another port of call. I always felt important going in there. The people behind the counter looked so professional. They had containers on wires above your head that they put your money into when you paid for something. When they clicked them shut they pulled a handle. The money sailed down to the other end of the shop on the wire. Someone else took it out. They sent back the change with a receipt curled inside an elastic band. Watching it rocking its way down to the cashier was like watching tiny little funiculars on ski lifts.

In the summers we cycled to Enniscrone. Deezer always wanted to come with us. We had to be stern with him to get him to stop following us. It would have been too dangerous having him on the road for all those journeys.

Some of us went by the Main Road and some of us by the Quay one. They met up about a half mile from the town. We had races to see who'd get there first.
I always got excited when I saw the sea.

Afterwards the town came into view. The first thing you'd see was the steeple of the church. It was much simpler than the one in Ballina. It was more like a Spanish church.

We played games on the beach. One of them was like a version of Hide and Seek. It involved hiding in the dunes. Various seekers followed us into them. We had to get to a designated square on the sand that was guarded by another one of the seekers. If we avoided them and got into the square we became a seeker for the next game.

We dug holes in the sand and put newspapers over them. We covered them with a sprinkling of sand so nobody knew they were there. We got a great laugh when people fell in. I don't know how some of them didn't break their necks. We never thought about things like that.

On the fine days we swam in the sea, soaking ourselves under the wild Atlantic crashers. No matter how warm the day was it was always cold in the sea, at least until you got out of pain. You could do that by splashing into the waves or more slowly by inching your way down under the water. It was like the difference between pulling a plaster off your hand or taking it off bit by bit.

We played Donkey with beach balls. If it was a windy day it was hard to keep control of it. The ball would drift away from us on the tide. My mother always told us not to follow it. A boy had drowned that way one year. It was the talk of the town.

Sometimes we went to the far end of the beach where The Valley of Diamonds was. It was where there was a dip in the dunes. The seashells that were there looked like diamonds when the sun shone on them. That's how it got its name. We glided down to the bottom of it on our stomachs.

When it rained you couldn't do much in Enniscrone. There wasn't any point going to the beach on the wet days. We went up the town instead. You'd hardly see a sinner on the streets, just the odd shopper rushing home with groceries.

The rain in Enniscrone was even worse than it was in Ballina. When there was wind it made it worse. You'd see discarded umbrellas dumped in bins and lying in gutters. You'd even see them on the sand. They looked so incongruous on a beach. I thought of Helen Shapiro's song, 'It Might As Well Rain Until September.' Sometimes it seemed as if it did.

There wasn't much to do in Enniscrone when the beach was out of bounds. There were two tennis courts behind the seaweed baths but they weren't in good condition. The tarmac had lots of bumps. The wire around the courts was torn. The balls we played with were often as bald as eggs. The colour would be gone off them. It made them look more like rubber ones.

We grabbed the odd game between showers. I had a tennis racquet that was warped from the rain. People told me I should throw it away but I didn't want to. It helped me get a curl on my serve. The high ground surrounding the court gave it a kind of stature. When we weren't playing we sat on the grass looking down at the players and felt we were in Wimbledon.

There was an amusement arcade behind the courts but it didn't have much in it. There was a machine you put money into to win a Panda bear. A silver hook appeared above the bear after you put in the money. You had to manipulate it to try and grab it. The hook always appeared to have a good grip on it but it always let it drop at the last second. I felt it was rigged to do that.

The wet days were endless. I'd keep looking at my watch wondering when the rain was going to stop. It was miserable if we had to cycle back to Ballina. It was even miserable if we went down on the bus. We'd spend our time wondering how long we had to wait for it to come. It was always late. Then when you got on you could smell the rain off everyone. We wrote messages on the windows if they were foggy: 'Goodbye, Rainy Enniscrone.'

The town became even sadder when the cinema closed down. The last film shown there was *The Magnificent Seven*. For years after it closed the manager left a poster of it in the window. The seven cowboys were riding over a hill in silhouette. It brought back the magic of the film to me.

We used to have a game where we had to name the seven of them. They were Yul Brynner, Steve McQueen, Horst Bucholz, Charles Bronson, Robert Vaughn, James Coburn and Brad Dexter.

Brad Dexter was the one people usually forgot. I used to be proud of myself if I managed to remember

Horst Bucholz. It was such a hard name to say. I was even prouder if I managed to spell it.

I was proud to be able to spell 'Vaughn' too. Robert Vaughn was a coward in the film but he found courage before he was shot in the end. He later went on to appear in *The Man From U.N.C.L.E.*

There was a man called 'Vaughan' in Ballina. That was the more common spelling. 'Vaughn' was unusual.

I liked unusual spellings. I was also able to spell Efrem Zimblast. The most complicated star name I was able to spell was Yvette Mimieux. I used to ask people to make me spell it just to show off.

I also knew how to spell 'pneumonia.' The 'p' was silent in it. My father had a joke. He asked you to spell 'Bathing.' When you did he told you that you were wrong. 'It's 'Pbathing' he'd say, 'The 'p' is silent in it.'

I was fascinated by words from a young age. It started when I saw the names of American places in my atlas. Afterwards I looked at the names of places from other countries, places like 'Chimborazo' and 'Cotopaxi.' They came up in a poem we had to learn as well.

Portugal had four rivers, the Duoro, the Tagus, the Guadiana and the Guadalquivir. I kept trying to learn how to spell them. I didn't want to see pictures of them or know where they came from or anything else about them or where they went into the sea.

We had a spelling test in Muredach's one day. Tich read out the word 'Swayed.' He asked us to spell it.

I wrote down 's-u-e-d-e.' I was the only one in the class to do that. Everyone else wrote 's-w-a-y-e-d.' He gave me a special mark for it.

I wasn't trying to be clever. I hadn't thought of the other way of spelling the word. When you did things different to other people they gave you a strange look. It was like when I wrote with my left hand.

I didn't want to be different. I wanted to fit in. That was difficult when I seemed to be on a different wavelength to most of the people I knew.

Town Life

The games we played in Ballina weren't as good as the ones in Enniscrone because we didn't have the beach. Maybe we had to try harder at them for that reason.

I don't remember playing games other people played like Charades or Kiss Chase or Spin the Bottle. My ones were more basic. I dribbled with a ball. I hopped it up and down until I was blue in the face. I passed it in and out through my legs and onto a wall. I hit it off the edge of the kerb to see if I could get it to bounce up in the air.

Another thing I liked was roller-skating. It was good on Arthur Street but even better on Convent Hill. There was a dangerous bend outside Arthur Wills' house. Ann and myself spent a lot of time going around it. You had to weave as you got to it or you'd end up in the middle of the road. God help anyone coming around the corner if we ran into them. We'd send them flying.

If there was ice on the ground we used to slide down on our stomachs like we slid down the Valley of Diamonds. That was more fun than wearing skates. We put salt on it to make it slippier. If we felt brave we'd take a run at the icy parts and skid along them, usually ending up on our bottoms. It was like slaloming without a slalom.

Audrey and Jacinta played hopscotch. When rain washed away the chalk marks they drew them again the next day. They also did skipping with Josephine Cottrell from across the road. When she was with them she held the rope. Otherwise they'd tie it to a lamp-post and just play with each another. Some skippers jumped with their two feet together. That was harder to do. It also took more out of you. It was regarded as cissyish for boys to skip in those days. It wasn't like today where you see boxers and athletes doing it for exercise.

I played a game called Queenie with them. There wasn't much to it. You stood against a wall with your back to a group of people standing behind you. You threw a ball over your shoulder and someone caught it. That made them the new thrower. If nobody caught it, someone picked it up and hid it behind their back. You had to guess who it was. You said, 'Queenie, queenie, who has the ball, Are you short or are you tall?' If you said the wrong name the person with the ball became the new thrower.

Guessing was the best part of it. It was good practice for poker. I learned to see the signs in people's faces as to who it might be. A giveaway was when they blushed. Cuter ones put on a look of boredom. That could be a giveaway too. They were protesting too much.

Musical chairs was a game that gave us endless hours of fun. It went on for ages because there were so many of us. We put the chairs back to back in the middle of the floor in the front room and trooped around them as the music played. Everyone scrambled for a seat when it stopped. The person who didn't get one was out of the game. I used to spend most of my time looking at the person beside the radio with their hand on the knob trying to figure out if they were going to turn it off or not. I often fell into the person in front of me because of not looking where I was going and we ended upon the floor laughing. Sometimes the best part of a game was something that wasn't supposed to be in it at all.

Things became interesting when it got down to the last two. If I was lucky enough to be one of them I spent even more time trying to predict when the person at the radio was going to turn it off. Sometimes they pretended they were going to so you'd throw yourself into a seat. If you did that you were disqualified. At least officially. We usually didn't bother with anything official. More often than not we made our own rules.

Table tennis was another game we played a lot. Clive was good at carpentry. He made us a table that was stored in a room behind the kitchen. Woodwork came natural to him. People's fathers usually did things like that. I can't ever recall seeing my father with a piece of wood in his hand. If he tried to make a table tennis table I dread to think how it would have turned out. One thing is for sure. We wouldn't have been playing table tennis on it.

We also played on a mahogany table that was in his office. He kept his files on it. If he wasn't busy he let us use it. We took the files off it and put them onto the shelves that lined the walls.

It was a bit thinner than the table Clive made. It had a bump on the end of it. That was to make it fold into a smaller table. If the ball hit the bump it went up in the air. It usually hung there for a second or two, giving you the opportunity to make a killer smash. It was like a 'slam dunk' in tennis. After we were finished our games we put the files back on the shelves again.

The mahogany table was also used for meals. We had these on special occasions like Easter or Christmas. My mother used to put a tablecloth on it if we were having guests. It was a white one with embroidery on it.

We played lots of board games like Ludo, Snakes and Ladders and Monopoly. We often played 'Heads or Tails' with pennies spun in the air. It was 'Doubles or Quits' if you lost. If we hadn't pennies we used ha'pennies. If we hadn't ha'pennies we used farthings.

We made up other games of our own. One of them was challenging each other to see how long we could hold our breath. We puffed our cheeks out until we almost exploded. Another one was seeing how long you could stare at someone without blinking. A lot of the games made no sense. That didn't matter. Another one was how long you could balance on one foot. We were content to engage in practices like this for up to ten or twenty minutes.

Some of our games were based on words. If we came across a new one in a comic we'd keep using it to show off. Usually we mispronounced it.

We knew a few palindromes even though we didn't know the word palindrome itself. One of them was 'Eve.' Another was 'level.' That was a special one because it sounded like what it was. Our grandfather, PJ Malone, could be made into a kind of palindrome because he was a Justice of the Peace. He was 'PJ Malone JP.' The more letters there was in the palindrome, the more points you got. We even knew sentences that were palindromes: 'Able was I ere I saw Elba.' 'Was it a car or a cat I saw?'

If we didn't want to answer a question someone asked us we'd say something stupid like, 'That's for me to know and you to find out,' or 'That'd be telling you.' I never knew what 'That'd be telling you' meant. Of course it would be telling them.

We were fascinated by the word 'Naturally.' For years we answered questions with it. It was like a fancier way of saying 'Of course.' Another one was 'Actually.' That was even posher. It paved the way for equally meaningless terms like 'Absolutely' or 'This is it' in the years to come.

Keith made up a word called 'ufungtatistical.' He never explained what it meant and we never asked him. Basil made up a colour called 'skymuggledy blossom.' That wasn't explained either.

If you asked Basil what colour something was he just said, 'Skymuggledy blossom.'

We didn't question it. It was like something being in Aunt Nellie's room behind the wallpaper. We just accepted it. Why? 'Naturally!' It was our version of 'supercalifragilisticexpialadocious.'

We played a game where you kept asking a person questions that they couldn't say 'Yes' or 'No' to. If they did they lost it. Most of us were able to last ages by just saying 'I do' or repeating the question.

'Do you go to school?'

'I do.'

'Do you like ice cream?'

'I like ice cream.'

We usually lost if the person said something quick like, 'You're very good at this game, aren't you?' We'd drop our defences and go, 'Yes!'

We rolled marbles into a hole in the wall beside our front door. If we didn't have money for marbles we played taws. They were smaller and without all the colours the marbles had. It was like a second best, the way Perri crisps were second best to Taytos and Fruit and Nut chocolate was second best to Whole Nut.

A Golly bar was second best to a Choc Ice because it had no chocolate and it was harder to peel the paper off. Flash bars were second best to macaroon bars because they almost broke your teeth when you bit into them. The best things of all to eat were walnut whirls. Some people called them walnut whips. I loved them except for the walnut. I always threw that away before starting on the chocolate. If I won a game of marbles I usually bought a gobstopper or a bar of butterscotch. I could get about a half hour's chewing out of either of these.

We also played with hula-hoops and yo-yos. Anyone could swing a yo-yo up and down but I couldn't master the hula-hoop. It was too wide around my waist. It kept falling down before I could get into a rhythm.

If we didn't have these things to play with we made up other ones. There were fruit boxes in

Lowther's Lane that we tied with ropes. We turned into sleighs and go-karts. Lynn's bicycle shop was around the corner. It had spare tyres outside the door. If they were about to be thrown out we asked Mr Lynn for them. We rolled them down Arthur Street with a stick, seeing how long we could keep them going before they toppled over. We did that for hours and hours. I remember reading a story once about a boy whose tyre was stolen one day when he went into a shop to buy an ice cream. When he saw it gone he said, 'Darn. Now I'll have to walk home.' That was how we thought about it. It was like transport.

Rolling tyres down a street was a long way from Rubik's cubes and Tamagotchi and bouncy castles and all the other things that came later. We didn't have amusement parks or leisure centres. We had to make do with hanging off lamp-posts and tumbling the wildcat for our entertainment.

We broke branches off trees and tied elastic bands onto them to make catapults. We called them 'caterpults.' My father always had loads of elastic bands for tying up his files. There was never any trouble getting strong ones. After we knotted them around the branches we put stones in them. We fired them at tin cans on the wall of Lowther's Lane. We got the cans from Mr Brogan in the Royal Café. Sometimes we fired bullets at the cans with cap guns. Mr Lowther didn't like us doing that. He said it upset his customers. One day he got annoyed with us and started using 'language.' I got a fright to see him losing his temper. He always seemed so cool when he was cutting my hair. After that we moved to a different wall.

We spent hours with Meccano sets. Some people changed to Lego when that came in but I never felt it was as good.

Plastic soldiers came in at this time as well. They replaced the ceramic ones we used to have. Parents liked plastic because it was cheap and it didn't break. In 1964 a plastics factory called Mayco opened in Ballina. It was the talk of the town for ages. We weren't used to factories of this size. A few years later in the film *The Graduate* I listened to a man advising Dustin Hoffman about what career he should go into after he left college. 'Plastics!' he shouted out. It was like a magic word.

I paid one and ninepence for a plastic soldier once. That was an astronomical sum at the time. It was about three times the size of my usual ones but it bored me. I only got it because everyone else I knew was collecting similar ones. This was long before Adidas and Nike became like religions to so many young people. Even then we were susceptible to peer pressure.

One of my favourite toys was a soccer game we had in the house. We played it with four sticks that had magnets on the ends of them. Their heads jutted out in an L shape. Two of them had red tips and the other two had blue ones. You pushed them under a table onto the magnetised feet of the players. By doing that you were able to move them towards the goals and score. Sometimes we just played with the sticks themselves. If you put the magnets from the red and blue sticks together they stuck. The two red sticks repelled one another and so did the two blue ones. It was all to do with the kind of magnets that were on them.

Subbuteo came in later. For me that was also a boring substitute. The players were motionless. You jerked their heads back to move the ball. It was about as exciting as watching paint dry. Every time something new came in I felt it wasn't as good as the thing that was being replaced. People seemed to like change for the sake of change. I wish I kept some of those old games. I'm sure they'd be worth a fortune today.

Carnivals came to the town. They were usually in summer in the Market Square. My favourite things to go on were the chair-o-planes. You sat into a seat with a chain tied around you. A man at the controls spun you all over the place at the rate of knots. You screamed at him to stop but you didn't really want him to. Today chair-o-planes would probably be looked on as high risk with all the talk about Health and Safety.

The chain was flimsy. If it came loose you'd be flung into outer space. Someone got killed one year when they fell off. We didn't dwell on things like that. We were too busy having fun.

I liked the bumpers as well. You got into a car and tried your best to crash into the drivers in the other cars. English people called them dodgems. Maybe that was the difference between our two countries. We liked physical engagement. They were more into avoidance.

I wasn't as fond of circuses as carnivals. They were boring to me. You just sat there without doing anything. Maybe subconsciously I felt sorry for all the animals that were in them. They were carted from town to town to be gawked at.

Why did I not laugh as heartily as other people at circuses? I didn't know. It bored me when clowns got their feet stuck in cans of paint. I found them scary for some reason. Maybe it was because I couldn't see their faces. Maybe I had Aunt Nellie's horror of masks without realising it.

I had other fears. I got nervous looking at the picture of the Sacred Heart that we had in the front room. I was afraid of The Boogey Man. For some reason I called him The Boody Man.

I was superstitious. I avoided cracks on the pavement when I walked down Arthur Street. I didn't walk under ladders or say the number 13. I threw salt over my left shoulder for luck if I did something that was supposed to be a bad omen. Black cats were said to bring bad luck. Why? It was never explained. People said things and you went along with them without any good reason.

It was the same with religion. Ideas were thrown at you. You were expected to accept them without question. God made the world but who made God? Why were angels always men? What did you have to do to become a saint?

These questions led to other ones. Was God behind the clouds? Where did clouds go when the sun came out? Why did mountains look blue in the distance but were green when you got to them?

I loved reading comics. There were no Irish ones. June and Ruth read *School Friend* and *Girl's Crystal*. Audrey and Jacinta read *Bunty* and *Judy*. In later years *Jackie* arrived. Sometimes they asked me to get their comics for them if I was going to Brennan's. I hated doing that. You'd never live it down if you were seen with a girl's comic on you. I used to keep *Jackie* well hidden under my other messages if I had it on me.

I mainly read *Lion* and *Tiger*. My favourite character from *Tiger* was Johnny Cougar. He had long hair and a headband. He was a wrestler. Whenever he knocked someone out, a big 'POW!' appeared on the page. Or maybe something like 'KERPLONK!' He was as strong as an ox.

Whenever people asked me why I liked him I used to say, 'Because he's a Seminole Indian.' I didn't know what that was. I just liked the word 'seminole.' It reminded me of semolina. Tina used to do desserts with that in it.

I also read the *Beezer* and the *Topper*. The first edition of the *Topper* came out just a month before I was born. If my mother was praising me for something I'd done she used to say, 'You're a topper.'

We got American comics now and again. One of them was *Superman*. I got to know everything associated with him – his girlfriend Lois Lane, his journalist friend Jimmy Olsen, his enemy Lex Luthor. There were films about him too but I preferred the comic.

If I felt like reading a book I took up something like *Biggles*. Everyone seemed to be reading that at the time. It didn't have much in it that I could identify with. Biggles was an English military figure. England had recently come through the war so the country was high on jingoism. It was ludicrous to be reading something like this after what they'd done to us for 700 years.

I didn't get into serious reading until I was in my twenties. I have no recollection of tackling any of the famous books many children seem to talk about when they're reminiscing about their youth – *Black Beauty*, *Huckleberry Finn*, *The Adventures of Tom Sawyer* or any of the other classics.

Shakespeare was a name I dreaded long before I went to secondary school. Even the sound of it was enough to put me off. Basil mentioned him to me one day when I was in Primary School. 'What kind of a name is that?' I said. He put his arm in a miming motion to indicate someone shaking a spear. I preferred when he talked to me about more modern writers he was reading, people like John Steinbeck and Boris Pasternak. He also told me the nicknames of some of the teachers he had in Muredach's: Gurks, Doc, Sprat, Dunlop. They sounded like characters from *The Beano* to me.

My life revolved around looking forward to things – trips out of town, birthday parties, events like Halloween and Christmas. Halloween wasn't like it is today where people buy elaborate pumpkins and life-like statues of witches and ghouls and where they stream cobwebs over their front gardens. I don't remember 'trick or treating.' We just hung apples from a string and tried to bite into them with our hands tied behind our backs.

The more things you have to buy from a shop, I think, the less chance there is of enjoying yourself. The only things we bought were barm bracks. The person who got the ring was expected to be the next to marry. Finding it always led to lots of giggling. We didn't express much interest in the institution of marriage at that age. Maybe we knew something adults didn't.

The magic time of the year was always Christmas. If there was snow it was even more magical. We built snowmen in the back yard or on the street. We used a carrot for the nose and marbles for the eyes. A slice of apple cut in a crescent shape usually did for the mouth. A hat completed the job. We threw snowballs at them afterwards. Trying to knock the hat off became one of our games.

Christmas began for us almost as soon as Halloween ended. That was when we started composing our letters to Santy Claus. The dark evenings came in and we started marking time. We watched the shop windows for signs of anything – toys, sleighs, candles, decorations, cribs. At last the watched kettle boiled. Christmas was coming. The geese were getting fat.

By mid-December the final drafts of our Santy letters would be ready. After we pushed them up the chimney - or the 'chimley' as we called it - we waited. I never understood the logic of putting them there. Would they not burn? And Santy had to come all the way down the chimney to find them. Then he'd have to go back up again and into his sleigh to get what was in them. Would it not have made more sense to send them to the North Pole?

The 'real' Santy was a man called Benny Walkin. He owned The International Stores. That was the place my father got all our toys. He did some legal work for him. Mr Walkin gave him a cut on the price of the toys in exchange.

On Christmas Eve we left slices of cake for Santy on a saucer. Most houses did that. Some people left mince pies as swell. If he ate things in every house he visited, I thought, no wonder he was so fat.

We were told he wouldn't come to us until we fell asleep. We also had to be good. Like God, he even saw us when we were sleeping. He was like the God of the New Testament rather than the old one. Santy was more interested in love than punishment. If you were bold you got nothing. It was like Limbo instead of Hell.

It was always harder to get to sleep when you knew you had to. How could you tell your mind to turn itself off? It was a contradiction. But eventually you'd nod off.

When we woke up on Christmas morning we'd see all the presents at the bottom of the bed. We'd be wildly excited as we ran into one another's rooms or downstairs to anyone that was already up. We'd go, 'What did you get?' 'What did you get?' to each other.

We ripped the paper off them at a hundred miles an hour. The gift-wrapping that was applied with such care a few days before – by Benny Walkin rather than Santy – was now 'flithered.' That was another one of my mother's favourite words.

The allure of the presents wore off soon afterwards. The looking forward was always the best part. In fact the allure of Christmas in general wore off as Christmas Day went on. When we played with them we pretended we were having more fun with them than we were. We looked at one another's ones and thought: 'You got a better thing than me.' It was like everything else in life, like reading a newspaper over someone else's shoulder when you had one of your own in your bag.

Mass was the next consideration. We were told it was the most special Mass of the year because it was Jesus' birthday. We trooped down to the church like soldiers in our best clothes. I tried to concentrate on it when it began but my mind kept wandering to my presents and the other treats I always got that day. The sermon was always about the Nativity. There was a crib on the side altar that was one of the best in the county. It had life size figures of Jesus and Mary and Joseph and the Three Wise Men and the shepherds and the cows and sheep. There was straw in between them and lights glowing behind them.

My mother used to put on the dinner before we went to Mass so it would be cooked by the time we got home. I hated what she had to do with the turkey the night before. She got grisly bits out called 'gizzards' or something like that. It looked as horrible as it sounded. Even so, it didn't stop me digging into it when it was cooked.

You had a licence to be a glutton on Christmas Day. Neither did you have to eat things you always hated, like cabbage or liver. It was your day off from 'good food.'

After eating too much I'd go outside and try to work it off, running around the place if it wasn't too cold. When I came in I'd listen to music. It was nearly always Bing Crosby. I never liked that sleepy voice of his. I didn't know why people went on about it so much. For me he was nothing on Elvis.

I pulled crackers and scoffed at the useless surprises that were inside them. They were like Lucky Bags in that way. You got some dull message on a piece of paper like 'Be happy' or a stupid joke you'd heard in Babies Class. Beside it would be a toy that was so small you'd nearly need a magnifying glass to see it.

The chatting began after we'd stuffed ourselves to the gills. I listened to the endless conversations that went on between my parents and my brothers and sisters. Their tongues would be going ninety to the dozen as they exchanged their news. Most of it was about people I never knew and would never know. I couldn't participate because I hadn't lived enough. They'd say to me, 'You're very quiet, is there anything wrong?'

If someone told me I was quiet it made me even quieter. What were you expected to do – start gabbing about nothing?

I yawned as the clock ticked towards bedtime. After all the preparation there was always a sense of flatness on Christmas night. I'd think of taking down the tree, of seeing the pine needles all over the carpet, of my mother making sandwiches from the leftover turkey the next day, of the snow turning to slush as the dull wet days of the end of the year approached. Then there would be the packing away of the decorations. I'd get frustrated when they didn't fold the way I wanted them to so I could hang them up again the following year. The day wasn't even over and already I was thinking of next year.

On Stephen's Day people would say, 'How did you get over the Christmas?' It was as if it was a cold or something. Why would you have to get over it if it was supposed to be so exciting? Then they'd say something like, 'It goes on too long, doesn't it?' These were usually the ones who'd been preparing for it since Halloween.

By January our toys would probably be broken. My mother would spot us in the backyard playing horse games with a sweeping brush or building a house for ourselves with the box they came in. She saw the madness of the consumer culture at first hand. Luxuries so eagerly sought for months would be thrown into a corner and discarded. Was this what my father spent all his hard-earned money on?

We weren't told the truth about Santy until we were almost in secondary school. One of my brothers was actually in Muredach's when the sad fact of his non-existence was conveyed to him. My own enlightenment on this score happened one year when I woke up in the middle of the night on Christmas Eve because of a ringing sound. I went downstairs to investigate. When I got to my father's office I saw Hugo and Basil playing with a phone. It was one of about forty toys on the mahogany table, the one we played table tennis on.

Where was Santy? The penny dropped after a minute. He was really Benny Walkin in disguise. The dream was over.

My mother's experience of seeing us discarding expensive toys for boxes had another manifestation. In the poker games we played with the Cahills and the O'Hora's she often listened to us arguing for hours about who owned a coin. Voices would be raised and games suspended until the matter was sorted. The next morning she'd find the disputed coin under the table. It wasn't the money we were interested in, it was the arguments.

We didn't play cards as much as we used to after we got television. That was in 1962. We didn't listen to the radio as much either. You couldn't use your imagination as much with TV. I once read of a girl who said she preferred radio plays to television ones. 'The scenery is nicer,' she said.

Every now and then a man called to the door to make sure you weren't a 'TV sponger.' These were people who had no licences. Some of them hid their sets inside cabinets with folding doors. Such a ruse was unlikely to fool the inspectors.

The signal was bad if you tried to get any station besides RTE. It was called TE then. People did things with aerials and rabbit's ears but they often just got static as a result.

We were condemned to one channel land but we made the best of it. It wasn't like today where everyone has dozens of stations. Even so, we still say, 'I couldn't find anything decent to watch last night.' And we're usually right.

I only saw television once before we got our own set. It was in Roscommon when I was on holidays with the O'Gradys. There was a family close to them that had one. We used to cycle miles to their house. We used to sit around it as if it was an altar. We mainly watched a programme called 'Mart and Market.' It involved looking at cows parading around a ring. Buyers shouting out strange words at them in funny voices. Nothing else ever happened. We'd have been as well off standing in one of Kevin O'Grady's fields.

In Ballina we were similarly transfixed when we got our set. We'd look at it for ages even if there was nothing worthwhile on.

I was allowed stay up late on Friday nights. There was a television programme I liked called *Arrest and Trial*. It was an hour and a half long. To me that was like a hundred hours. I never got to see all of it. My mother would usually say during a break, 'Time for bed.' Ann and myself used to try to get her out of the room when a break was coming. Once a new part began she'd let us stay up until it ended.

I also liked Jack Hedley in *The World of Tim Frazer* and Earl Holliman and Andrew Prine in *Wide Country*.

I memorised catchphrases from all the shows - Kojak's 'Who loves ya, baby,' Jack Lord's 'Book 'em, Danno,' from *Hawaii Five-O*, Maxwell Smart's 'Sorry about that, chief' from *Get Smart*.

Terry Wogan hosted a quiz show called *Jackpot*. A girl spun a wheel with lights on it. If you wanted her to stop you said 'Stop the lights.' That became another catchphrase.

Every Friday night Jack Webb appeared in *Dragnet*. He was a policeman, Joe Friday. The programme always started with the same words from him: 'This is the city. I work here. I'm a cop.'

Gay Byrne hosted *The Late Late Show* on Saturdays. People were always giving out about it. On Mondays you'd hear them on the street saying, 'Did you see *The Late Late*? Wasn't it a load of rubbish?' But they still kept tuning into it.

There was too much talk on the *Late Late* for me. Who cared about things like road tax or industry or the other things they went on about? I wanted something to fire my imagination.

Fred Flintstone played games of bowling with Barney Rubble in *The Flintstones*. That was more in my line. I never questioned the fact that people might not be bowling in the Stone Age. The rocks may not have been perfect circles but they still hit their targets. I thought there was nothing strange in it.

Neither did I think there was anything strange in the way Barbara Eden could disappear into a bottle in *I Dream of Jeannie* and come out of it a while later as a genie.

Everything we saw was normal because it was on television. That made it real. It made it even more real than our lives. It was like a magic box in the corner of the room, a visitor you didn't have to invite and could expel anytime you wanted by flicking a switch.

I was as fascinated by the advertisements as the programmes themselves. There were ads for everything. Most of them were for household products like Rinso or PG Tips tea or carpet cleaners like 1001. I remember the wording of that one: '1001, 1001, cleans a big, big carpet, for less than half a crown.'

There was a character called Jim Figgerty who was supposed to have put the figs into fig roll biscuits. He a celebrity to us. Two Arabs discussed him. 'How do Jacobs get the figs into fig rolls?' 'Who cares, Habibi, they're gorgeous.'

We shouted out the messages like mantras: 'Don't say brown, say Hovis!' 'Persil washes whiter and it shows!' 'Beanz Meanz Heinz!' 'Rael Brook Toplin, the shirt you don't iron!'

Some of them were for sweet things. 'Have a break, have a Kit-Kat.' 'Don't forget the fruit gums, Mum.' I ate fruit gums every Saturday at the Savoy. The red and black ones were the nicest. I used to save them for last.

Aspirin was advertised as being the best cure for headaches. The ad for it went, 'Nothing acts faster than Aspirin.' Some smart alec said, 'I have a headache so I'm going to take nothing.'

The best ad of all was the one for Kennedy's bread: 'K for Kennedys, E for energy, N for nice and nourishing, E for enjoyment, D for delicious, YS means you're satisfied.'

The most important Kennedy in our lives was John F. Kennedy, the president of America. He was actually greeted with that jingle when he arrived in Ireland in the summer of 1963. He must have scratched his head in bewilderment as regards what it meant.

We were all devastated when he was assassinated towards the end of the year. It was the day before Audrey's birthday. She was due to get a new pair of shoes. She was full of excitement going down to get them but then the news broke. It cast a pall over everything. There was a dismal atmosphere in the shoe shop.

I was playing in the sitting room when the bulletin came on the television. It interrupted a programme with Peter Lawford in it. I learned afterwards that he was related to the Kennedys. It was a weird coincidence.

Charles Mitchel read the news out: 'President Kennedy has been shot.' He had tears in his eyes. So had I. It was like a member of the family died. Basil had seen him in Dublin earlier that summer. He was staying with the O'Reilly's at the time. He'd injured his hand trying to fix a broken window but he was still determined to see him.

President Kennedy looked different in real life than on the television. Nobody realised he had red hair or that he was so tanned. Someone once said that politics was 'showbusiness for ugly people.' Kennedy disproved that statement. He was like a film star. He was a war hero too. The fact that he had Irish roots endeared him to us even more.

Now he was gone. It was my first exposure to the harsh world of reality. The man who shot him was called Lee Harvey Oswald. He became like the personification of evil to us, a serpent who'd entered the Garden of Eden.

I heard he went to Russia a few times. His nickname was 'Oswaldovich.' Russia was the land of communists and atheists for us. It was a place where people would shoot you as soon as look at you. When I was in the O'Grady's house in Roscommon one year I met Kevin's nephew. He told me he was going to Moscow on an educational tour. I genuinely feared for his life. If you ventured anywhere behind the Iron Curtain, I told him, you'd be tortured and killed by the secret police. Everyone knew that.

Oswald was shot a few days after he killed President Kennedy. It was by a nightclub owner called Jack Ruby. A number of conspiracy theories began to be trotted out. People said Ruby was paid to kill him in case he squealed about who put him up to the assassination.

I was too young to understand these kinds of things at the time. I just sat stunned watching the images on the television. The blood-stained garments of Jackie Kennedy. The American flag draped over the coffin. John-John saluting it. Oswald being shot as he was transferred from one jail to another.

Aunt Nellie was fascinated by it all. She had a book about the Kennedys that she kept on the table of her living-room. It was a hard-covered annual with lots of photos in it. There were little bits of text around them. I used to spend ages leafing through it whenever I was down with her. We were so obsessed with the cinema in Norfolk I'd never seen a book like that before. All our coffee table books were about film stars.

Reading it made me feel like crying. John F. Kennedy was America's first Catholic president. He was Irish as well. What a combination. Why did Oswald have to ruin it all for us by going to Russia and getting himself corrupted?

Celluloid Dreams

I can still see Satch from the Bowery Boys with his baseball cap on back to front. I see Leo Gorcey looking like someone sat on his face. I see Harold Lloyd hanging off buildings and looking almost bored. I see the bodies of semi-clad women in Busby Berkeley's films criss-crossing in and out of one another like erotic snakes. I see Old Mother Riley driving up a road on a motorbike and everyone scarpering out of her way in terror.

Or was it out of *his* way? I never really questioned the fact that she was played by a man. That was the thing about the old days. Nothing was put in boxes. We didn't think of Old Mother Riley as a drag act. She was just funny.

It was the same with Al Jolson. He wasn't 'blackface.' Blackface is regarded as racist today. So is the Lyons Tea ad we used to watch with black and white minstrels on it. I can see why someone might have that view but we didn't. If you think too much about something the enjoyment goes out of it.

People make fun of Johnny Weissmuller today because he's not seen as having been 'ethnic' enough to play Tarzan. We weren't bothered about nonsense like that. We just enjoyed watching him swinging from trees. When we listened to Elvis singing 'You're the cutest jailbird I ever did see,' In *Jailhouse Rock* we didn't think of the line having a gay code.

I went to more matinees than night films. Under-18s ones had an exotic appeal. I heard about them from my brothers and sisters or from friends who dropped in to Norfolk on their way home from them – the Cahills and the O'Hora's and the Courells. They shot the breeze with whoever was up.

That wasn't usually me. I listened to a lot of the conversations from my bed. Often I couldn't make out the words. I'd only hear voices and laughter. In some ways that was more interesting. The scenes were run through again and again over endless cups of tea. By the middle of the night the tea was so strong it was like whiskey. As the saying went, 'You could trot a mouse across it.'

Many of the O'Hora's did jobs for my father. The Courells lived around the corner on Convent Hill. That was where my parents lived when they came to Ballina from Greystones. The Cahills lived there before they moved to Arthur Street. They were our neighbours before I was born. There were four in the family: Sean, Joe, Maura and Padraic. Sean and Joe became priests. Maura was a teacher and Padraic an accountant.

Afterwards they moved to Bohernasup. They were a lovely family and all fluent Irish speakers. Fr. Joe was gone from Ballina by the time I was growing up but I got to know him later. He said to me once, 'I spent more time in your house than I did in my own.' One of the attractions for him was being able to read *The Beano* and *The Dandy* in Norfolk.

His parents had more elevated tastes than us. We watched the windows of Brennan's every week for the appearance of comics like these. Our hearts leaped when we saw them. We couldn't get in the door fast enough to drop our pennies on the counter. We read them so many times the pages fell out of them. Characters like Desperate Dan and Lord Snooty became like buddies to us. Dennis the Menace was my favourite. He was always up to some mischief with his dog Gnasher.

Fr. Joe told me he got his first kiss from June. I said he shouldn't have been kissing girls if he was thinking of becoming a priest. He claimed to have learned to play poker in our house as well. He played with Keith and Clive for money. One night he got a royal flush straight from the deal. He never got the shilling they owed him for that. They hooked off to the Estoria instead of coughing up.

He envied us the amount of time we spent at the pictures. He only got to go to the Estoria once a week. How were the Malones able to afford to go almost every night?

When other families talked politics, we talked films. As I watched the stars of them rattling their sabres or jumping off wagon trains I felt I knew them like my own family – Gary Cooper, James Stewart, Errol Flynn and dozens of others. They became oddly familiar to me as the years went on Often the films didn't live up to their reputations. I didn't mind. These were magic nights sitting in the dark with your ice cream cone and your Crunchie and your Toblerone, willing your heroes on to even more daring feats.

Flash Gordon appeared in serials. On Friday he'd be hanging off a cliff. You'd have to wait until the next week to know if he survived or not. At the back of your mind you knew he would but you didn't let yourself think that. You enjoyed the tension.

There was another cinema around the corner from us. That was the Savoy in Garden Street. I associate it with Saturday afternoons. It was bigger than the Estoria but it had less atmosphere. There was no division between the parterre and the balcony. One led into the other. You went up a side stairs in the Estoria to get to the balcony.

In the Savoy everything was in one large area. We were all lumped in together. I didn't like that as much. In the Estoria balcony you felt privileged. You were going to the Gods. Your heart started to flutter as the MGM lion roared. Then the names came down. That took forever. When you saw 'Directed by' you knew the film was about to begin. That was always the last credit.

The more I went to the cinema the better I got to know all the studio's logos apart from MGM's lion. Warner Brothers had one like a sheriff's badge. Universal had a globe. Twentieth Century Fox had their name done up in blocks like something from Mount Rushmore. Paramount had a snow-capped mountain with a circle of stars around it. The Rank Organisation had a man like Charles Atlas banging on a big orb with a gong. Republic had an eagle. Columbia had a woman like Our Lady shining a torch. I loved looking at the rays spreading out from it.

Often we didn't have to pay to get into the pictures. My father knew the manager. He used to give him free passes for us. He had a special cushion for me to sit on because I wasn't tall enough to see the screen. It was made of red velvet It reminded me of the cushion TV Lowther put me on when I was having my hair cut. It made the seat nearly twice as high.

The passes were like tickets to heaven. We saved them up for the best films. These were the ones that were retained for a week – *The Big Country, The Guns of Navarone, The Longest Day.* When I think of these blockbusters now I imagine them being in the Savoy. The Estoria was more suited to tight dramas. Epics threw themselves sprawlingly at you. The films in the Estoria had a more subdued power.

I mainly went to the Estoria at night time with my parents. Everything was quiet there. The Savoy was more rowdy. During the talking scenes we clambered over the seats. We created mayhem, banging one another on the heads with rolled-up comics. Our antics stopped during the action scenes. Sometimes we acted them out ourselves. A saloon fight could become a cinema fight.

The usher would arrive with his torch. He'd threaten to kick us out if we didn't stop the noise.

'Nobody can hear the film,' he'd say. I doubted they cared. There weren't many adults at the matinees. Nobody was interested in the dialogue of the films unless it was between two gunfighters having a showdown on Main Street.

The worlds the films created were just as real to us as our own ones. We didn't think of actors dressing up for their parts in studios or learning lines from pages of scripts. I remember going up to the screen one day to assure myself that the 'reel' world was the real one. I was disappointed that it was made of canvas, that it didn't lead into the clay of the plains, to the dust blown up by the wagon trains hurtling across the prairies.

We continued to act out the scenes on the way home from the cinema. The light hit your eyes for a few seconds after coming out. It made it hard to see after being so long in the dark.

We played cowboys and Indians. Most of my classmates wanted to be cowboys. I preferred being an Indian. I chased after people with a pretend tomahawk. I put my hand over my mouth going 'Ooowww.' I wanted to be Chief Sitting Bull more than the Durango Kid and Tonto more than The Lone Ranger.

At home I put paint on my face and a band across my forehead to continue the game. I used a hatchet for the tomahawk. One day the top flew off. I nearly decapitated a child who was playing with me. It only missed him by a whisker. After that I went back to being a cowboy. It was safer.

Cowboy films were our staple diet in those days. None of us ever thought they'd die out as a genre. Today's generation probably watch them on Turner Classic Movies and wonder why we liked them so much. To us they were celluloid gold – the cattle drives, the corrupt sheriffs, the card games in the saloons, the showdown at high noon in the last reel as the villain bit the dust.

Audie Murphy seemed to be in every second one of them. People called me Audie when they couldn't pronounce my name. At times I felt like him. There was also Joel McCrea and Jeff Chandler. Chandler was too hard for us to pronounce. We called him Jeff Challender instead. We said it like Calendar.

Jack Elam was often the bad guy. He must have got shot a hundred times in cowboy films. I used to feel sorry for him. You only had to look at his face to know he'd come to a bad end. He had scars on his cheeks and eyes like a fish. He made faces that made you think he was mad as well as bad.

'Elam' was as hard for us to say as 'Chandler.' We called him Jack Flam. Another film star whose name we mispronounced was Yul Brynner. We said 'Yule,' like Christmas.

Marilyn Monroe was 'Marlon' to us like in Marlon Brando. Joanne Woodward was Joan. I read somewhere once that Paul Newman hated it when the producer Harry Cohn called her Joan. He wouldn't have liked us much in Ballina either.

John Wayne was the biggest cowboy star of all but I never really liked him. It wasn't due to his right wing politics. I knew nothing about those kinds of things then. He was good in *Stagecoach* but that was before he became John Wayne the figurehead. I never went for figureheads. I heard a story once that my father met him when he was filming *The Quiet Man* in Cong. I never found out if it was true or not. I'd have been more interested in him meeting Maureen O'Hara.

Cowboy films in those days were uncomplicated. Heroes were heroes and villains were villains. There was no in-between. If the villain was sneaking up on the hero to shoot him we'd shout out 'Look behind you!' at him.

The heroes wore white hats and rode white horses and were clean shaven. The villains wore black hats and rode black horses and had five o'clock shadows. The only time good guys had stubbles was when they were getting on in years, like Gabby Hayes, Hopalong Cassidy's sidekick.

Cassidy broke the colour rule. He was a hero who dressed in black. Something else that was unusual about him was his white hair. It made him look older than he was meant to, like Jeff 'Challender.'

The villain's girlfriend drank too much and slept late. She'd have a low-cut dress where you could see the beginnings of cleavage. Cleavage was drawn in comics with a little line like a comma.

The hero's girlfriend often 'taught school.' The script never said, 'She taught in a school.' It was always just 'taught school' as if it was the school she taught. If they were kissing we'd hiss or go out to the shop to buy sweets. Why would people waste time locking their lips together when there were Indians to be shot?

In the last scene the hero would go off with the heroine her in a surrey with a fringe on top of it. They'd drive to a house with a white picket fence outside. They'd smile at one another and kiss again. Then 'The End' would come up. We were led to believe they lived happily ever after. In real life that's the point where problems *start*.

When we were playing cowboys in scenes that didn't involve Indians we had to decide if we wanted to be the good guy or the bad guy. It depended on whether you felt like killing or being killed. I found being killed to be more fun. You could drag out your death scene. I had some effective ones in Lowther's Lane as I fell onto waste ground after being shot down. What a pity John Ford wasn't there to film them.

The same distinctions applied to gangster films. You had a hero and a villain. The hero wore a white shirt and a black tie. The villain wore a black shirt and a white tie. Sometimes the hero was attracted to the villain's girlfriend. She was often a nightclub singer. The villain would be rough with her. After he kissed her she'd slap him but not until she'd got a good few seconds of the kiss.

She'd have blonde hair. The hero would have a brunette girlfriend somewhere in the background. She was the good one. She'd be a teacher or something like that. She'd be shy, unlike the blowsy blonde who only had sex to offer.

Women who offered sex were called fallen women. They slept with men and often got pregnant as a result. You weren't allowed say 'pregnant' then. In English films they used expressions like having 'a bun in the oven.' In Ireland we said a woman was 'in the family way.' It was as if there was something dirty about pregnancy. Women were 'churched' after they gave birth as if to cleanse them again.

The fallen women lived in dingy apartments. They didn't take much care of their appearance. They weren't young but they had good figures. The main villain in the film would visit them. They'd kiss. A fire would be blazing in the hearth. It was a symbol of passion.

The camera would cut away from the fire to the window and out to the night sky. Then there'd be a fade to the next morning. The camera would pan back into the room, maybe lingering for a moment on an unmade bed. The man would still be there. Both of them would be fully dressed. He might be putting on a tie or something like that. She might be putting on a high heel. It was the director's way of telling us they slept together. Later on in the film they'd suffer for their indiscretion.

Many films' storylines led the hero away from the bad woman (the blonde) after he'd been tempted by her. He'd go back to the 'good' one (the brunette). The blonde often got killed. It was usually by her 'bad' boyfriend. Afterwards the hero would throw himself into the arms of the brunette. He'd realise he loved her all along. I was always a bit disappointed about this. I felt he'd have had more fun with the blonde.

At the end you'd have a shoot-out between the hero and the villain like in the cowboy films. It frequently happened in a high place like a cliff or the top floor of a warehouse. The villain had a habit of running upwards when he was trying to escape from the hero. He'd keep firing bullets at him that missed the target. Guns in those days only had six bullets. After he'd used them up he'd keep clicking the trigger as if he couldn't believe they were all gone. Villains weren't any better at maths than they were at shooting.

In desperation he'd throw the empty gun at the hero. The hero would dodge it easily enough. He could shoot the villain now if he wanted but heroes didn't do things like that. It was too easy and it wasn't gallant. Instead he'd have a fist-fight with him. They'd tussle on the top of the cliff or the warehouse. The villain would get in some good early punches. We'd be worried about the hero as we crunched on our Taytos but he'd prevail finally.

The villain usually fell to his death from the great height. Before the film ended you'd hear the siren of police cars. They always arrived too late. The brunette would re-appear at this point. She'd run into the arms of the hero and kiss him. These kinds of films had to end with a kiss.

My favourite types of villains were the ones who wanted to take over the world. They'd always have a mad look in their eyes. They lived in dilapidated factories with equally mad servants. Various containers would bubble away in the background as they hatched their schemes.

They kidnapped the hero at some stage and beat him to a pulp. Then they tied him up with a rope. They spent a lot of time telling him how they were going to kill him instead of just killing him. As they did that he'd be loosening the rope. Considering they had enough equipment to blow up the world you'd have thought they'd have stronger ropes. But they didn't.

As the villain was telling the hero how he planned to blow us all to smithereens, the hero would be giving furtive glances at a gun that just happened to be beside him on the floor. After he got free of the ropes he'd run for it. He'd get the drop on the villain. He'd kill him and blow up his factory. Yippee, the world was saved.

I didn't really like war films. I used to get bored watching cities being bombed when there was no human interest. The storylines in these kinds of films were pretty standard. A guy would stand in a trench telling his friend about his sweetheart. Often he'd take out a picture of her.

When he did that you knew he was done for. After the Japs or the Germans killed him his friend would take the photo from his uniform. It would have his sweetheart's address on the back. God knows why. He should have known where she lived. She was his girlfriend.

The friend would look her up after the war ended. He'd tell her her boyfriend died a hero. That would make her feel good. Then he'd start dating her. They'd fall in love. It would be the friend's tribute to the dead hero, falling in love with his girlfriend. Yuck.

Science fiction films were better. They were scary but exciting too. I always wanted to know if there was life on other planets. Creatures only visited earth from other galaxies to destroy us in the fifties. Then Steven Spielberg came along with all his cuddly aliens. That was much later.

'The Twilight Zone' was like the gold standard of science fiction programmes. It was scary but in a way that was attractive. You got sucked into it like into an irresistible nightmare world. There was funny music when it went into its dream sequences. It made the hair stand up on the back of your neck.

Vampire films were even scarier. They had stars like Bela Lugosi and Christopher Lee. Other ones might have Peter Cushing or Lon Chaney or Boris Karloff. Most of the vampire films I saw seemed to have some of these actors in them. Put them together and you'd need a prescription for tranquillisers for the rest of your life.

I always felt brave going into these kinds of films in the daytime. Nothing was really scary at a matinee. When I came out of the cinema the sky would still be bright and I'd forget about what I saw for a few hours. If I was sent out to the turf shed that night to get some fuel for the fire it was a different story. If a cat squawked I'd jump ten feet in the air.

We went to a lot of comedies too. Charlie Chaplin was regarded as the main genius of the time but I preferred the Marx Brothers. I didn't understand a lot of the dialogue but even my young mind knew something was going on that was light years away from people like Bud Abbott and Lou Costello. Abbott and Costello banged one another over the heads with saucepan lids. That was the level of most of the comedies we saw in those years.

The Three Stooges pulled each another's noses. Laurel and Hardy got into one fine mess after another. Charlie Chaplin ate his shoes in a film.

Buster Keaton had a wall fall down around him but he wasn't hurt because there was a gap for the window. His body was under that bit. It was one of his many brilliant ideas. Next to the Marx Brothers he was my favourite. He was much more imaginative than Chaplin but he never became as big a star as him. Chaplin was mainstream. That's why he became so famous. Keaton never played the Hollywood game. He stayed on the edge of the industry.

Keith did Groucho to perfection. He flapped his eyebrows up and down and walked with his knees bent. He put a biro in his mouth to act as a cigar as he delivered his oneliners.

Beneath all the slapstick and puns the Marx Brothers were subversive. How did they come out of that simple time? They were even before it. Most of their films went back to the thirties and forties. Sometimes comedies could be before their time just like literature was. Hugo said books were usually about ten years before films in their vision.

Someone once said to Samuel Beckett that the tramps in *Waiting for Godot* spoke as if they'd been to college. He replied, 'How do you know they haven't?' People say Vladimir and Estragon were based on Laurel and Hardy but there was a lot of the Marx Brothers in there too. I wouldn't have known anything about them if it wasn't for Keith. Their films weren't shown much in the Estoria or the Savoy when I was growing up.

My father was bringing Keith and Clive to films almost as soon as they were able to walk. Keith used to scan the *Western* every Thursday to see what was coming. His week was built around looking forward to it. It made Muredach's bearable.

Keith was no fonder of the college than I was when I started going there. Clive took to it more easily. I didn't think he needed the films as much as Keith. People who are content in their world don't need to escape from it as much.

126

Maybe religion was Clive's escape. Priests would probably say it was the other way around. They'd say God was the reality and everything else an illusion. It depends where you're coming from. Martin Scorsese once said cinemas were his churches growing up. Keith was probably somewhere between Clive and Scorsese. He was the biggest film fan in the family. And remember, 'fan' is short for fanatic.

The rest of us had our favourite actors and actresses just as he had. Apart from Edward G. Robinson, my father liked Ramon Novarro and Ivor Novello. He always said the names of these two stars together: 'Ramon Novarro and Ivor Novello.' I grew up thinking they were linked in some way.

He liked Alfred Hitchcock too. Hitchcock's name on a film was usually enough to make him go to it. I often heard him saying, 'It was a Hitchcock.' It needed no other recommendation.

Hitchcock wasn't an actor, of course. He was a director. But he appeared in most of his films at some stage. The appearances rarely had anything to do with the story. You'd see him going into a shop or getting on a train. We'd jump out of our seats and go, 'There he is!' Looking for him sometimes became more interesting to us than the film itself.

There was a programme on television called *Alfred Hitchcock Presents*. He used to appear on the screen before it started and say a few words about it. He'd always have something scary in his hands like a chain or a rope. He'd give a little speech about what we were about to see. I found his programmes too scary to watch. Even though they were only a half hour long they gave me nightmares.

The scariest film he ever made was *Psycho*. I was only seven when it came to Ballina. Everyone was talking about this guy who had half his mother inside him. I was too young to be let into it. I didn't see it until years later. Anthony Perkins was the psycho. He

127

scared me half to death. When a man dressed up as a woman it was usually funny but Perkins sent a chill up my spine.

My mother liked the Thin Man films with Myrna Loy and William Powell. She pronounced Powell's name as 'Po Well.'

It wasn't the only name she pronounced different to the rest of us. She was related to James Montgomery, the film censor of the time. She pronounced his name as 'Montgumery.' I didn't know why. Maybe it was the Roscommon way of putting things.

She said other things strangely as well. If she was doing something in a hurry she'd say, 'I'll have it done before you can say Jack Robinson.' One of her favourite expressions was 'It's never too late till two and then it's too late.'

Sometimes I misunderstood her. If she got good news she always said, 'Thanks be to God.' She said it so fast I used to think she was saying, 'Thanks bit o' God.' It was as if she was talking about a part of his body.

Another actor she liked a lot was John Wayne. She liked quoting his line from *The Searchers*, 'That'll be the day.' She used to imitate his voice when she said it. ' She used to imitate Richard Widmark too. She loved him in *Kiss of Death* even though he was the bad guy in it. Her favourite line in the film was when he referred to Victor Mature as 'the big maaaan.'

Keith was the best in the family at imitating actors' voices. The ones he did most often were Humphrey Bogart and James Cagney. He was able to do Al Jolson as well. He had the voice to a T. He used to go down on his knees and hold his arms out as he sang 'Mammy.'

Jolson was one of his favourite actors. In fact I don't think I ever heard Keith saying he disliked anyone he ever saw in a film, from the main lead to the faces in a crowd. As someone said once, if he

128

looked at a poster he'd know the people whose names were so far down they looked as if they paid for the printing.

His favourite actor was Alan Ladd. He loved all his films, especially *Shane*. He talked about it so much he got us all in on it. It was shot in 1951 but it wasn't released until 1953. That was the year I was born. It gave me an extra connection to it.

We all grew up believing *Shane* was the greatest film of all time. It was even greater than *Gone with the Wind* and *Casablanca*, his two other favourites. When it was mentioned you had to stop talking about everything else. It was the ultimate film, an almost sacred phenomenon.

I didn't know much about the intricacies of the story when I saw it first. Its effect on me was mainly visual. I was entranced by the scenery and the technicolour. The mountains of Wyoming made Mayo's ones look like little hills. In later years I grew to appreciate all the things that were going on behind the scenes.

Van Heflin played Joe Starrett. Brandon de Wilde was Joey, the young boy who idolises Shane. Jean Arthur was Marian, Joe's wife. As the film goes on she starts to fall in love with Shane.

There was a lot of symbolism in it. Shane was like a saviour in many ways. George Stevenswent on to make another film about Jesus some years later. He called it *The Greatest Story Ever Told*. But we always felt *Shane* was the greatest story ever told.

Keith saw it so many times he knew all the dialogue by heart. He collected photographs from it as well. He even learned to play the theme song on his mouth organ. He acted the key scenes out so often for us we started to memorise them too.

His favourite one was the climax of the film where Shane goes into Grafton's saloon to gun down Ryker and Wilson. It was the ultimate climax to any film, the one that set the tone for everything that followed. Shane stands against the counter. He says to the villain, 'I've come to get your offer, Ryker.' Joey Starrett sits watching him under the saloon door with a stick of candy in his mouth. He crunches on it as the shooting begins.

Whenever *Shane* was showing in a cinema in later years, Keith would call us up and we'd go to it for another fix. If it was a subject on the Leaving Cert course we'd all have passed with flying colours. We were entranced by Alan Ladd's buckskin, his quiet power, the way his voice was amplified when he was talking to the bad guys. 'There never was a film like *Shane,*' Keith used to say.

Somebody once said that Ladd was a young boy's idea of a tough guy. Maybe that was true. His name even seemed to testify to the fact.

He died in 1964. It was on Hugo's birthday, the 29th of January. I still remember the headline in the *Evening Press:* '*Shane* Star Dies At 50.' There was a photograph of him beside the article. I was disappointed it wasn't from *Shane*. In later years I learned of his problems with drink and depression. It made him even more like the character who was doomed to his destiny in the film.

When Billy Wilder and William Wyler went to the funeral of the director Ernst Lubitsch, Wilder said to Wyler, 'This is terrible. No more Lubitsch.' Wyler said, 'Even worse – no more Lubitsch movies.'

That was how I felt about Ladd. I wouldn't be seeing any more of his films now. I'd seen a few of them besides *Shane* - *Whispering Smith* and *Guns of the Timberland* and some others. But of course *Shane* stood head and shoulders above them all. How were we going to replace it?

A film called *3.10 to Yuma* almost did. It was made shortly afterwards. It had Van Heflin in it again. Glenn Ford played the bad guy. He was a killer with charm like Shane. It wasn't a masterpiece but it had a big effect on me.

That was as much due to the title as the film itself. I was attracted to the names of American places. Yuma was as good as any of them. The '3.10' also got me. It wasn't three o'clock or half-three. It sounded like real time – the time a train might leave Ballina for Manulla Junction. I loved the theme song too. Frankie Laine sang it hauntingly.

Music was so important to cowboy films. *Shane* had 'The Call of the Faraway Hills.' *High Noon* had 'Do Not Forsake me Oh My Darling.' Frankie Laine sang that too.

There was a beautiful relationship between Glenn Ford and Felicia Farr in the film. It was like the one between Shane and Marian Starrett in *Shane*. It couldn't go the distance. The best relationships didn't – in films if not in life. I always thought Felicia Farr was one of the most beautiful actresses in Hollywood. She was also one of the most under-rated ones. She could convey in an expression what other actresses would take twenty pages of dialogue to get.

Another film I remember coming to the Estoria around that time was *Mutiny on the Bounty*. A big deal was made about it. There was even a programme for it. It had lots of photographs of Marlon Brando and the island of Tahiti. I was really looking forward to seeing it but when I did it didn't live up to expectations. I thought there was too much talking in it.

A few years later another Brando film was released. It was a cowboy called *Southwest to Sonora*. It was on for two nights in the Estoria. Hugo went to it on both of them. He told us about it after the second night. The way he talked about it I thought it must have been one of the greatest films ever made. Anytime Hugo saw a film that impressed him he said he didn't want to see another one for weeks. It was years before I shared that experience. As a child I just wanted more and more films regardless of their quality. He discussed the camera angles and the director's technique and the details of Brando's performance. All I wanted to know was if he died at the end. If the hero died in a cowboy film it was useless. Everyone knew that.

It was years later before I saw it. I wasn't sure if I liked Brando as much in colour as in black and white. He'd been in all these great films in the fifties. Now here he was making westerns. I preferred him on his motorbike in *The Wild One*. I remember thinking he wasn't as good a cowboy as Audie Murphy or Alan Ladd.

You were able to smoke at the pictures in those days. Couples also courted in the back seats. We were as bored looking at them as we were looking at actors and actresses kissing on the screen. We hissed them at the matinees. You couldn't do that at the night shows or the manager would probably kick you out.

Kissing scenes were excuses to go over to O'Hora's shop across the road for sweets. I usually got Foxes mints or bullseyes. I crunched on them during the fight scenes like Joey Starrett in the last scene of *Shane*.

Mr O'Hora sold us penny ice creams. They were only half the size of the usual ones. They were rock hard and had the wafer melted into them. He also sold us biscuits. If they went over the weight you asked for he broke them in half. Profits were hard come by in those days.

A new type of film started to appear as the sixties went on. *Alfie* was banned so I couldn't get into that but I was allowed into *Boccaccio 70* for some reason. It was comprised of different segments from Italian directors, each with a sexual theme. In one of them a giant poster of Anita Ekberg came to life. It caused immense frustration to a timid man who was dwarfed by it. I'll never forget his little frame sandwiched between her gigantic legs. He was trying to restore puritanical values to his village in Italy but not making a very good job of it. I couldn't believe a film like this would be shown in the Estoria.

Some great directors started to make their mark around now. People like Martin Ritt, John Schlesinger, Stanley Kubrick, Peter Bogdanovich, Mike Nichols and John Frankenheimer were all in top form.

Nichols made *The Graduate* in 1967. I was too young to be allowed into it but I saw it later in Dublin. My mother was amused at the scene where Dustin Hoffman signs himself into a hotel with his mistress, Anne Bancroft. He's also in love with Bancroft's daughter in the film. Other women of her generation would have been too prudish to enjoy a film where a man was having affairs with a mother and daughter at the same time but all she could see was the humour.

Many other seminal films were made at this time - *Bonnie and Clyde, Who's Afraid of Virginia Woolf, If, Midnight Cowboy* I admired them but I felt a pang of nostalgia as well. Two different cultures were converging. The new Hollywood was coming in but a part of me missed the old one.

Moving Out of the Bubble

Bill Haley 'invented' rock and roll with 'Rock Around the Clock' in 1955. It featured in the film *The Blackboard Jungle*. People were said to have got so excited by it in London that they ripped up cinema seats and started dancing in the aisles. That was the time everything changed in music. When Elvis came on the scene the following year he was only allowed to be filmed from the waist up on television.

Keith and Clive left Ballina to go to university in Dublin that year. Keith studied for a B. Comm and Clive became a Jesuit.

He knew he wanted to become a priest from a young age. A missionary came to Muredach's one day and gave a talk about what it entailed. He was only in his early teens at the time.

I don't remember Clive much in Ballina on account of me being so young when he left. There's a photograph of him on the cover of this book holding me in his arms when I was a child. I'm in a cowboy suit. I don't know who took it. Not many people had cameras in those days. The photograph is more valuable to me as a record of a day I don't remember than if it was taken on a day I did.

It might have been the only photograph taken that month or even that year. That's in stark contrast to today. Modern children will be able to compile a narrative of their lives from A to Z when they get to my age because of the number of photographs taken of them when they were young.

It was probably taken when Clive was on one of his rare trips home from Emo. He studied theology there. When he entered the church he was informed he'd only be allowed home once every seven years. For my mother it must have been like a life sentence hearing something like that.

134

Keith was home much more often. On some of his visits from UCD he seemed to be under pressure. He'd done two degrees together for reasons I could never understand. In some ways he burned himself out. After he graduated he went through a period when he didn't know what to do with his life.

He went to England and got a job in Wall's ice cream factory. It was one of the few times he left Ireland. Dublin never had the magic for him that Ballina had. He used to write home a lot. The letters were on big sheets of foolscap. A lot of them were about his health.

One year he got an ulcer. I didn't know what that was. He went into such detail about it I thought it must be the most terrible thing anyone could have. Years later it turned out he didn't have one at all. I remember thinking: All that foolscap wasted for nothing.

Now and then I'd see him in the kitchen laughing with my father about films or some character in the town or about the horses they backed together. My mother and Clive would be involved in some more serious discussion in the front room. Their faces would be pensive. Clive would be stroking his chin as he tried to figure out the answer to some problem. It might have been a money one or something related to my father's drinking.

Sometimes it seemed to me as if Clive was the eldest of the family rather than Keith. My mother seemed to have an almost clairvoyant relationship with him. The two of them could sit for hours without feeling the need to talk.

He was the one she always went to for advice. He was strong both in body and mind. When I looked at him I often thought of Tom Tryon from *The Cardinal*. Keith had a wiry build. He always seemed more vulnerable. He gave off the sense that life was too tough, that we should seek any avenue of escape we could from that toughness.

There's a photograph of Keith and Clive that was taken when they were two or three. They're both in sailor suits. Clive is already impossibly handsome. With his clear-eyes and his sleek straight hair he stares at the camera as if already knowing where he's going in life. Keith looks more demented. His hair is a mass of curls like Larry from The Three Stooges. Or me.

When Clive's theological training was finished he went overseas. He spent some time in England first. He was able to handle the loneliness better than the rest of us. How could he not be, having to live in faceless buildings with strangers and devote his life to prayer?

My mother was pleased that he was dedicating his life to God but she never pushed any of us in that direction. My father was delighted that he went into the Jesuits. For him that was the aristocracy of the priesthood.

Clive was as shy as the rest of us growing up but he came out of his shell in Emo. Some of the other seminarians were from posh backgrounds. He familiarised himself with subjects like classical music to be able to talk with them.

Sport was another ice-breaker. He didn't have much of an interest in football or soccer but he loved tennis and handball.

After he was ordained he went to Zambia. He became a university lecturer there. He only came home rarely. Because of that there was always a flurry of excitement around the house when he was due. My mother used to get especially excited. When he came in the door they'd fall into one another's arms crying with joy.

After he settled in he'd tell us stories about his life in Zambia. It sounded very exciting to me. One of his students was the son of the president of the country, Kenneth Kaunda.

There was political upheaval when he went there first. It was called Northern Rhodesia at that time, not Zambia. Zambia only came about when it got its independence.

He talked a lot about apartheid. I'd never heard the word before. Neither had the rest of the family. My mother called it 'apathy.' In a way she was right. There wasn't too much difference between the two things. I grew up thinking the white supremacists of Africa weren't bothered by the blacks. Only later did I realise how much they hated them.

One time when Clive came home he brought wooden carvings of the faces of primitive tribesmen with him. We hung them on the walls of the sitting room. They made it look like Halloween. I thought we must have been the only family in Ballina that had things like that in their house.

At night time they looked scary. That was especially the case if we had a fire lit. It threw shadows onto them. My mother lit the fire by putting sticks in between clumps of turf and setting a match to them. She'd put a sheet of newspaper over the grate to make it draw, holding it for as long as she could until she heard the roar of the flames going up the chimney. She'd snatch it away just in time and scrunch it into a ball before throwing it into the fire. Then she'd squeeze up other sheets of paper. She'd roll them into little packs with a kind of knot at the end. They became fuel too.

Clive often mentioned the copper mines. Zambia was rich in that mineral. He brought copper figurines to go with the masks. In other ways it was poor. The combination of the two elements made communism a very real threat. If it took root, he said, all the priests would have to leave.

My mother used to be very sad when his visits came to an end. She'd be crying for days beforehand. She never said goodbye to him on the day he was going. It would have been too emotional for her. Instead she stayed in the kitchen as he got his case. He'd slip out the door after saying goodbye to my father and anyone else who was there at the time. She'd be looking out the kitchen window with tears in her eyes. She'd blow her nose with a hankie she kept tucked into the sleeve of her cardigan. That was to try and hide them from the rest of us.

It was a cruel system that took a son away from a mother who loved him so much for so long but both of them accepted it. They got on with their lives as people did in those days. It would be a few days before she came back to herself. Thankfully there was enough going on with the rest of us to help her get her mind off her sadness.

Some of the family left home almost every year after Keith and Clive. June and Ruth were the next to go. After they did the Leaving Cert they went to Dublin. June got a job in the Irish Permanent Building Society. Ruth got one in the American Embassy. It was a very exciting job. She even shook hands with President Kennedy the summer he was in Ireland.

Both of them had done shorthand and typing courses beforehand. It was what nearly everyone did at that time if they were interested in office work. Life didn't have the possibilities for women then that it has now. The pattern was that you went into a typing pool or some dead end job where you took abuse from a male hierarchy and worked until you got married. It wasn't too different to my mother's time.

A career for women was looked on as marriage suicide. Either a ban prevented you from getting married or society thought of you as 'one of those,' i.e. a woman trying to be a man. Only one thing could

138

happen to someone like that. She'd be left 'on the shelf' – a fate worse than death.

There were only five of us left in Ballina after June and Ruth left. Hugo and Basil went to Dublin in 1964. Hugo went into All Hallows seminary to study for the priesthood. Basil did Electrical Engineering at UCD. He bought a Honda 50 to get him into the lectures. Sometimes he drove it down to Ballina during the mid-term breaks. He was young to have a motorbike. Very few people of his age owned them in those days.

It was exciting listening to his tales of university life. He was the auditor of the L&H and spoke at the debates. I'd never have had that kind of confidence. He also had poems published in university magazines like *St Stephens* and *Anvil*. He used to read them out to us if we asked him. They often had interesting titles. One of them was called 'Reincarnation of a Leaf.'

They had words in them that I couldn't understand, words that came from literature and ancient history. Sometimes he referred to the Honda as Pegasus. That was a horse from Greek mythology. Where had he picked up things like that? Hardly in the Engineering faculty.

He used modern words I didn't understand either. He said 'Blazes!' if he was surprised at something. He talked about his friends at the university being 'sloshed' at parties.' That meant drunk.

He used other words like 'gravytrain.' He said things like 'Point your boots in the flickable direction' when he wanted someone to go somewhere. All of this was exciting to me, as exciting as Clive's world in Zambia but in a different way. I wanted to say 'Blazes' and 'gravytrain' and 'sloshed' and 'Point your boots in the flickable direction' when I got to UCD despite not having a clue what these things meant.

Basil also had an interesting repertoire of songs that he sang with his friends at UCD when they were out for a night. Some of them were by The Dubliners, a group that were very popular at this time. They were a long way from the kinds of songs that were recommended to us by the priests in Muredach's, songs by Brendan O'Dowda or Sean O'Riada or the other traditionalists.

Basil talked about hits like 'Seven Drunken Nights.' It was a funny song but also vulgar. It couldn't be played in full on the radio but it made The Dubliners sensations in England. They were on 'Top of the Pops' with it. It portrayed the Irish as primarily a nation of boozers but I didn't mind that. Maybe we were.

Ronnie Drew, the lead singer of the group, held his wedding reception in O'Donoghue's bar. That was where the group mainly held court. How could you get anything more Irish than that? It's a wonder he didn't have the marriage there as well.

Every verse had the line, 'I called my wife and I said to her.' Sometimes Ronnie changed it to 'I called my wife and I said to *it*.' You'd be shot for that today. That's what's so sad about the modern world – political correctness. It sucks all the humour from it. Nobody loved women more than Ronnie Drew. He adored his wife and vice versa.

Basil also sang 'Take Me up to Monto,' another Dubliners hit. It was about Nighttown, the red light district of North Dublin that Joyce wrote about in *Ulysses*. In fact the group was named after *Dubliners*, Joyce's book of short stories. Luke Kelly was reading it around the time they were formed.

Another song Basil sang was 'Isn't It Grand, Boys.' That was a Clancy Brothers number. They were big at the time too. Bob Dylan even liked them. He slept on their sofa in New York when he was starting out and couldn't afford lodgings.

'Isn't It Grand, Boys' was the first sacrilegious song I ever heard. It had a dead person talking from the grave like in Máirtín O'Cadhain's novel *Cré na Cille*:

Look at the preacher
bloody great hypocrite.
Isn't it grand, boys
to be bloody well dead.
Let's not have a sniffle.
Let's have a bloody good cry
and always remember
the longer you live
the sooner you'll bloody well die.

This wasn't the love of death celebrated by the terrifying passages of the Old Testament. It was more like paganism. Basil put everything he had into it when he sang it.

The fact that Basil and Hugo were gone from Muredach's before I started going there meant I had no family member to share things with in the college. Audrey and Jacinta were less than a mile away in the convent but it felt like much more than that.

June and Ruth came home from Dublin at Easter and Christmas. I couldn't wait to get up to the train station to meet them. They'd be excited telling me all their news on the way down to Norfolk. I listened to their stories with equal excitement. My world was so limited in contrast to theirs. They had all of Dublin whereas I only had school and the pictures.

When we got to the house they'd go into the front room. My mother would bring in tea for them. They used to sit on a velvet bench that we called a 'form.' It was in front of the fire enclosing it on three sides. More cups of tea would come in from the Hatch as they went into the details of their adventures in the city.

Because I was the youngest in the family I thought my brothers and sisters knew everything. My ideas of life were based on what they said to me. If they expressed doubts about anything or if they had any kind of problem I was surprised. They were my barometers of behaviour.

I wanted to have a leather jacket like Basil had, the one without sleeves on it. He had a leather tie too, one of those thin black ones you saw in cowboy films. These were the kinds of hand-me-downs I wanted, not the old-fashioned things I usually got.

He even had a tiepin. And a watch with a square face. He had a diary that could only be opened with a key. I knew if I had something like that I'd really feel I'd made it in life.

Hugo had a different kind of appeal for me. He was like an artistic director. If he gave me a part in one of his plays I felt privileged. I didn't know anything about them but I still wanted to be involved in them.

They had large casts. He even put Sean McDonnell into some of them. Sean was our friend from Garden Street. He lived with us for a time even though his house was only a few hundred yards down the road. He was game for anything. When Hugo decided to act out *Batman* he made Sean into The Penguin. I was Robin.

Sean's father was an auctioneer. He had an electrical shop as well. It was beside Curley's on Garden Street. Sean wasn't interested in the auctioneering but he was good with electricity and other practical things. He could turn his hand to anything. He'd wire your house one minute and paint it the next.

One time he made a wardrobe for the father of my friend Jerry Cowley. He didn't have a car so he had to carry it by hand. He asked us to help him. It was winter and there was frost on the road. We tried our best to balance it but our feet kept sliding under us. It proved to be an impossible task. We were falling all over the place. The wardrobe ended up in bits after all Sean's work. We could only laugh about it afterwards.

Another family we were friendly with was the O'Hora's. Janey had worked for my mother's family in Roscommon when she was growing up. She had seven children. They were all boys.

Mickey did messages for my father. Sometimes he stayed with us. His brother Peter was the projectionist in the Estoria. We used to ask him to skip the boring bits of films for us. One night he told us he cut a film in half because he was rushing home to see a football match. When he said things like that you never knew if he was joking or not.

Peter was no relation to the man who sold us sweets in the shop across the road from the Estoria. One night I saw some footage of The Pathé News beamed from the cinema onto the wall of O'Hora's shop. I don't know how that came about. If it happened every night we'd never have needed to go to the pictures at all. We could have watched all our films on the wall.

Peter worked in the post office by day. It was nearby so he was always dropping in to see us. My mother had a particular affection for him. He loved her apple tarts and couldn't get enough of them. He played a lot of poker with us. He was a great bluffer. Even if you had a good hand you were slow to 'see' him. That was the expression we used when we equalled someone else's bet.

I played snooker with another one of the O'Hora's. That was in the Hibernian Hall off Bury Street. We called it The Hibs for short. His name was John. He had an interesting cue action. I remember him saying to me once, 'A cue has to be handled like a woman – delicately.' He certainly did that. He had a lovely playing style. It was simple but effective. I could never beat him.

My father didn't like me going to the Hibs. He thought it attracted the riff-raff of the town, the 'Mickey Muds and Paddy Stinks' as James Joyce called them. He'd have preferred if I went to the Moy Club instead. That was where the rich congregated. It was near his office. It had only one table. I associated it more with billiards than snooker. I imagined the players inside sipping drinks and speaking in posh accents. It was a dead environment to me, a bit like the lounge area of a public bar. The Hibs was more like a pub than a lounge. I always preferred pubs to lounges.

His advice fell on deaf ears. Thankfully he didn't push it. Maybe some people thought I was being an inverted snob going to the Hibs. That wasn't the reason I went there. It just made me feel more at home. I didn't have to perform for anyone there. I could let my hair down. I was shy with most people but even shyer with the upper-crust section of the town. I found many of them petty and patronising. It was 'the penny looking down on the ha'penny' as Sean McDonnell's brother Joe said to me once.

There were all sorts of people in the Hibs. Nearly everyone was a character. One of the players was called Ballina Town. I think his real name was Vinnie but nobody called him that. I didn't know why.

Everyone had a nickname in those days. We thought nothing of it. A lot of the players had quirks but we didn't think anything of these either. If someone had a limp or a burn on their face or a missing limb or some other form of handicap it was hardly noticed. It was an age before today's political correctness where everyone uses the 'right' words for things. But I think we were more natural with them than people are today.

There was a table in the corner of the hall. A card game called 110 was played there. It was like an extended form of 25. Nobody cared much about the games. They were more interested in the fights that took place in the course of them. We didn't say, 'A fight broke out during the game' as much as 'A game broke out during the fight.' Snooker cues were used for swordfights during some of these encounters. They were the nearest weapons ready to hand. I'm surprised more people didn't go home with concussion after these fights. Some of the cues had bits of wood missing from them as a result. You had to swivel them around to get a good bridge.

The more time I spent in The Hibs the more my father warned me against it. I often had to sneak out to it but if he found out I'd been there he didn't do anything about it. He repeated his point about it being 'a dangerous place' but that was all.

I always felt he was more like me than he realised. He told me not to play with the Hegartys too but he didn't push that either. It seemed to be enough for him to say it. By doing so he could be seen to be enforcing the *ancien regime*. As soon as he made his points we did what we wanted.

Audrey and Jacinta left Ballina before they did the Leaving Cert. Audrey went off to train for nursing in Surrey. Jacinta attended the Loreto Convent in Dublin. Afterwards she moved to London for a while. It was a wrench for her being separated from Audrey because they were so close to one another. They only met up occasionally now.

Jacinta came home to Ballina for a while after being in the convent in Dublin but Audrey didn't. My father felt she'd be away for as long as Clive. When he left her to the airport in Dublin he was crying to much a woman beside him thought she was going off to become a nun.

At that stage there was only me in Ballina. I was about to go into my last year in Muredach's when I was told we were moving to Dublin. The news came as a shock to me. I was rooted in the college by now. The discipline had become less strict.

A new priest had joined the staff the previous year. He'd come straight from Rome. Someone said he'd been at the Vatican Council. He said to us, 'I'm not going to hit any of you.' I can't remember his name or anything else about him except for the fact that he had red hair. He talked to us as if we were people instead of giving us things to learn off like the other teachers. He even asked us about the films we were going to in the Estoria. It was just my luck to be going away when some sort of sanity appeared to have appeared in the college.

Life outside Muredach's had started to change too. A youth leader came to the town that year. He was doing things with us, teaching us drama and how to play basketball. He also gave guitar lessons. I wasn't much good at things like that but I was willing to learn. Looking back now I think I was starting to break away from the womb of the family that year. I had to. They were gone from me.

The problems I had in Muredach's were minor compared to the thought of moving to Dublin. I knew I'd be replacing everything I knew with everything I didn't. I'd only been there a few times over the years. I'd stayed in Joan O'Reilly's house in Sandymount a few times and I'd also been out to Aunt Florence's guest house in Dun Laoghaire. It was in Clarinda Park with the very commanding name of Rockingham. That was only on visits. Keith stayed there all the time when he was in UCD.

She kept the guest house impeccably. There were flowery sofas all over it. The china was scrubbed to within an inch of its life. She cooked great meals but I was always afraid of saying the wrong thing or using the wrong knife or fork. One day when I was having a cup of tea I put my hand around it instead of holding it by the handle. 'My dear child!' she said, 'Is it broken?' She couldn't see the handle because it wasn't facing her. It was so different to our easygoing ways in Norfolk. There might be chips off a cup there and we'd think nothing of it.

Dun Laoghaire seemed English to me. That turned me off it. I didn't like Sandymount either. There was a strand there but no sand dunes. How could you have a beach without sand dunes? It was nothing on Enniscrone. But the O'Reillys were always very welcoming to me. That helped.

Joan gave me some fruit cocktail for dessert one day after dinner. I said, 'I hope you didn't go to too much trouble over that.' I thought she'd cut up all the fruit herself instead of getting it from a tin. I'd never seen fruit cocktail in Ballina. Paul and Derbhal, her two children, were highly amused at my ignorance.

We went into the city centre most days. Paul or Derbhal used to say to me, 'How would you like to go to town?' I didn't know why they called it 'town' when it was a city.

We always went in by bus. The buses were double decker ones with open backs. In those days you could jump onto them when they were moving unlike today with all our concerns about health and safety. I loved doing that. The faster they were going the better. I'd leap on and wrap my hands around the pole for support. The conductor would come round after a few minutes. He had a bag over his shoulder and a machine he clicked as he gave you your ticket. Some people jumped off without paying before he got to them. If he was upstairs there wasn't much he could do.

I usually sat in the front seat upstairs. It made me feel I was driving it. There was a great view from it. You could see the beach extending for miles. It was such a novelty after all the single decker buses of Ballina.

I did all the things visitors did on my trips to Dublin. I climbed Nelson's Pillar before it was blown up. (I could hardly have climbed it afterwards.) I enjoyed losing myself in the crowds. There were escalators in some of the bigger shops. It was a novelty for me going up one. You had to walk down a stairs to get back to the ground floor. Once they got you up to buy something they didn't care how you got down.

Walking down O'Connell Street sometimes a man would pop up out of nowhere with a camera and take your photograph. He was like the paparazzi today. He'd give you a little card with his details on it. If you wanted the photo you'd bring the card into his office in Middle Abbey Street a few days later. You picked it out from a large album and paid him for it. Often the definition wasn't great. The best part was looking forward to it. Even though the photos in the album were among dozens of others you still felt special when you saw yours.

One day I wandered into a snooker hall on O'Connell Street called The Cosmo. You had to go down a staircase to get to it. I gave a rap on a big steel door. A man who looked like the bad guy from a gangster film let me in. I felt as if I was going into a speakeasy from the forties.

There were dozens of tables inside. I'd seen pool halls in films like it. I'd seen *The Hustler* with Paul Newman. This made the hall in that film look like The Ritz.

Nobody seemed to be talking to one another. They played their games like robots, taking their shot and then sitting down until the other person took his. It was so different to our little hall in Ballina where everything was an excuse for a joke. I thought to myself: Was this what life in Dublin represented? Lots of space and no communication?

If someone told me then that I'd be living there for most of my life I'd have said, 'You need your head examined.'

The Big Smoke

We left Ballina in 1969. That was the year my father retired. It was a shock to the system. I always thought the town would be a part of my life long into the future. When Tina was carrying me around on her bike as a child I used to ask her where we'd park it when I went to the university. There was always the presumption that things would stay the same as they were forever. But of course nothing does.

A lot of things happened in the bigger world around that time. Christian Barnaard performed the first heart transplant in 1967. Robert Kennedy and Martin Luther King were assassinated in 1968. In San Francisco people started wearing flowers in their hair. If you put flowers in your hair in Ballina you'd have been carted off to the funny farm.

There was a rock festival in Woodstock. Neil Armstrong landed on the moon. There were riots in the Sorbonne university in Paris. The Beatles broke up. Jack Kerouac died. Sharon Tate was murdered by Charles Manson and his gang. The Concorde made its first flight. I watched it on television. It looked like a gigantic eagle in the sky with its pointed beak.

Ground-breaking films like *Easy Rider* were made. Timothy Leary told everyone to 'Tune in and drop out.' It was as if people were suddenly waking up to the fact that the sixties wasn't the dream decade we'd been led to believe.

A song came out called 'In The Year 2525.' It was about how life would be in the future. Some of the lines were scary. One of them went, 'Now man's reign is through.' It was the first time since 1962 that I started thinking about the end of the world. That was the year we were all afraid there was going to be a war between America and Russia after Russian war ships landed near Cuba.

1969 was also the year of Mary Jo Kopechne and Chappaquiddick. I never knew such a place existed before Teddy Kennedy drove his car off a bridge there. Kopechne was in the passenger seat. She drowned but he swam to safety. It was ages before he reported the incident. How could he have been so stupid? He knew the area well. Was it because he was drunk? Because he was excited by the fact that he was probably going to be sleeping with his passenger that night? Was he high on the fact that a man was shortly going to be stepping on the moon and his brother had been hugely involved in the lead-up to it?

I knew even less about Mary Jo Kopechne than I did about Chappaquiddick. Nobody knew who she was until she died. The tragedy made her a household name. It also killed off any prospect Kennedy had of becoming the next president. He was the favourite to do so before it. The sympathy generated by the assassination of his two brothers – John in 1963 and Robert the year before – would almost have been enough for him to be elected even if he wasn't such a talented senator.

I didn't think much about these events as they were taking place. My mind was too taken up with my own situation. How would I be in Dublin? Would I fit in with all the city slickers? Was there a chance I'd be able to go back to Ballina some time in the future?

That was unlikely after the house was sold. Other people I knew had family members in and around the town. It meant they had a base to operate from even if it wasn't the one they were born into. It was different for us. We'd burned our boats.

I left the town that August. Before going away I went around the town trying to imprint its details on my mind for the years I'd be out of it. I went down to the cinema, to the church, to the soccer pitch at Belleek – all the benchmarks of my days that were so precious to me now that I was losing them. There would be no more films in the Estoria, no more football games in Belleek, no more trips to Enniscrone or Rosserk or Moyne Abbey or St. Patrick's Well. There were paintings of the Stations of the Cross at St. Patrick's Well. They were more modern than the ones in the cathedral. I always felt a special connection to it because of my birthday.

The hardest thing of all was leaving Tina. I wouldn't be having my 'second mother' in my life anymore. It would have been great to bring her to Dublin with us but what would she have done there? We used to tell her she'd make a fortune if she opened up a crèche in the city but she was never interested in money.

After I packed my case I went around the house looking at everything for the last time. I went up to the landing and just stood there, positioning myself between the doors that led to the four symmetrical bedrooms. I went into the little box room, the one where Ann and myself used to drop the trays down on people and probably give them heart failure. I went out onto the roof that looked over Gildie Ahern's orchard. I thought of the kitchen below me, that incredibly large kitchen with the Rayburn where so many cups of tea were brewed and so many discussions took place into the small hours.

I went into the sitting room where we played poker and listened to Radio Luxembourg. It was also the room where my mother played the piano to relax herself when she was stressed.

I went into the dining room where we played table tennis after putting my father's files onto the shelves that lined the walls. I went into the pantry where we steeped the jelly and the Sunday peas.

I looked at the shelf with all my mother's things on it – packets of Daz and Vim and Tide, tins of Brasso, bottles of milk of Magnesia and Syrup of Figs. She

152

used to give us these for constipation. They tasted so horrible I preferred the constipation.

I opened a drawer that always contained an innumerable amount of useless objects. There were spools of thread, plasters, ball bearings, a shopping list, a broken watch, a tennis ball, a packet of pastilles, a cigarette butt, a ruler, a Brillo pad, a pair of binoculars. I saw a novena in there as well, and a pair of scapulars. Squashed behind everything was half of a Kimberley biscuit. I thought to myself: Soon all this would be gone. It would be gone just as surely as if it never existed.

How is it that I remember these details and not anything else about that day? I don't even remember saying goodbye to the people I'd known all my life. I'd probably never see many of them again. That's the nature of memory. It takes in what it wants and not what we expect it to.

I went to Dublin in a station wagon owned by a friend of my father's. As I stepped into it I felt I was going to a funeral. I thought of photographs I'd seen of people during the Famine, photos from American history books where you'd see people piling everything they owned on coaches or carts. All I had was my little case. I felt as if I'd been stripped bare. A lot of my things had gone to Dublin before me. Some more would follow. A lot had been sold in the auction in the Town Hall.

I didn't talk much on the journey. There were two other passengers in the car but I couldn't think of anything to say to them. I was too sad. The silence made the driver uncomfortable. He drove extra fast on account of that.

The towns whizzed by us as we sat there, each of us lost in our own worlds. Eventually the city came into view.

It looked horrible to me, a mass of buildings that didn't mean anything to me and never could. People on the street were roaring at one another, whether in salutation or anger I wasn't sure.

We inched our way through the traffic jams until we came to Cabra Park, a winding street in Phibsboro behind St. Peter's Church. Some red-bricked houses sat squashed together like units of an industrial estate. We stopped at number 66, a tiny house that sat at an angle between two separate rows of houses. Keith was renting it with Ruth and Basil. I rushed out of the car.

'I hope you'll be happy in your new home,' the driver said to me. I thanked him. He turned off the engine. He popped the boot. I took my case from it. The other two passengers said goodbye to me.

As he drove off I walked to my new home. There were people walking down the street speaking in Dublin accents, the kind of accents I was familiar with from *Tolka Row*.

I knocked on the door. Basil's Honda 50 was outside it. Ruth came out. She gave me a hug. I could see she'd been hoovering. There was a radio playing in the background. I heard Gene Pitney singing 'Looking Through the Eyes of Love.' She took my case and brought me into the kitchen. Keith was sitting there. He had a white shirt on him and a dark jacket.

Ruth made me tea. She asked me how I was feeling. I said too much was happening for me to be able to say. It was hard to take it all in.

The room seemed very small after the Norfolk kitchen. There was a letter holder on the table. It had a postcard from Basil in it. He was in Eindhoven on work experience. That was in Holland. He would soon be going to America to work with General Electric.

The next few days were strange. I wandered round in a daze, going in and out of rooms to try and get my bearings. In Ballina you could stand at the front door

154

looking down the street but if you did that in Cabra Park people gave you strange looks.

I tried not to think of Ballina, to tell myself there was nothing there for me now, that a house couldn't be a home without your family in it.

When Basil came back from Eindhoven he was dressed in a suit. I wondered where his leather jacket was. Was that what jobs did to you – made you have to wear suits? He was full of excitement about the work he was doing but I couldn't understand any of the technical terms he used. It was like double Dutch to me. Afterwards he talked about a party he was thinking of throwing for his friends in the engineering class. Two old biddies lived upstairs. They were in the habit of complaining about the noise. Keith said he'd have to keep it down.

Over the next few weeks I settled more into the house. Sometimes I went down to the shop on St. Peter's Road to get groceries. There was a dry cleaners there that Keith asked me to leave a shirt in for him one day.

There was also a church. One night I had a dream where it turned into St. Muredach's Cathedral. In the dream I walked down the Cabra Road expecting to be Ballina. Then I went down to Doyle's Corner. I expected it to be Moylett's corner. I searched in vain for King Street, for Bury Street, for Norfolk. You didn't have to be a genius to see where my mind was at.

I expected there to be some communication from Ballina but there weren't. It was a question of 'all quiet on the Western front.' I had no right to expect any. Why should there be? That was then and this was now.

We only spent a few months in Cabra Park. Afterwards we moved to another house in Phibsboro. We rented that too. It was in Shandon Drive. We stayed there until the house we were going to be

155

living in was ready. That was in Iona Villas in Glasnevin.

The house was semi-detached. It had a narrow passageway at the side. There was a small hallway inside the door. The sitting room was to the right and the kitchen at the end. It was only about a quarter as big our Ballina one. It was more like a galley kitchen really. There was an Aga cooker in the middle. It reminded me of the Rayburn in Ballina. I could imagine this room becoming the main talking room in the house just like the Ballina kitchen. There were three bedrooms upstairs

Iona Villas was a cul-de-sac. Our house was on a hill that curved around in a circle with a grassy area in the middle. There was no way out unless you walked up one of the lanes that led off it. The absence of traffic meant it was quiet at night.

Alice Glenn lived in the centre of the circle. She was a politician whose name I was vaguely aware of. She was very conservative. She once said about divorce, 'Any woman voting for it is like a turkey voting for Christmas.'

There was a shop called The Hillside across the road. It had anything and everything in it, a bit like Geraghtys in Ballina.

A vegetable man called every Tuesday in a ramshackle cart. He was over sixty and no beauty. Despite that we used to joke that my mother was having an affair with him. She was a great sport about things like that.

At the beginning there was only myself and my parents in the house. Then Keith and Ruth moved in. It made it more like a home.

By now Basil had gone to America. For a while he was worried he'd be sent to Vietnam. The war was raging there. People were being conscripted right, left and centre. America hadn't yet realised it was a war it couldn't win.

I'd grown up with the view of America as the greatest country in the world. Such an image was formed watching things like John Wayne riding over the hill with the Seventh Cavalry to wipe out the Indians in the Savoy when I was a child. My image of it was changing now. People said the war going on in Vietnam wasn't America's business. It had to be left to the Vietnamese themselves to sort out.

Every now and then we'd see teenagers burning their draft cards on *The News*. Some of them went so far as to cut part of their fingers off to avoid being drafted. Others went across the border to Canada in the boots of their friends' cars to escape it.

Hugo joined us after a few months. He'd left All Hallows by now and was studying for a B.A. in UCD. The freewheeling atmosphere of Belfield suited him much more than the authoritarianism he'd experienced in the seminary.

I wasn't sure if June would move in with us. She was in a flat in Haddington Road at the time and having a good social life there. She played tennis with her friend Rose in Herbert Park and went to dinner dances in the Metropole and rugby ones in Bective. She got lots of attention from boys as a result of her good looks and her personality. She was also a very good singer. She was in the Rathmines & Rathgar Musical Society. Keith was in that too. They saw each other a lot around this time.

Sometimes he acted as a gooseberry for her on dates if she wasn't interested in the man she was being asked out by. It can't have been much fun for a man going to the pictures with her and having to deal with a chaperone sitting on the other side of her. I doubt they'd have been doing much in those days besides putting their arm around her. With Keith beside her they could hardly even do that.

Keith had a good voice too. They appeared in a few shows together in the R&R. It had a high standard. People like Joan Merrigan performed in it. I'm sure they got many of their partypieces from these years.

In the end June decided to move in with us. The only family members missing now were Clive and Jacinta. Clive was ensconced in Zambia and seemed intent on staying there. Jacinta was still working in London.

My room was to the right after you climbed the stairs. It had yellow wallpaper. The first thing I did when I got into it was to sellotape a poster of Elvis onto the wall. I had one of Bob Dylan as well. He was my second favourite singer next to Elvis. It was from the cover of his album *Nashville Skyline.* He was wearing a hat in it. I cut out the hat and attached a string to it. When you lifted it up and down it made it look as if he was tipping it.

I couldn't sleep for the first few nights. It was too quiet. I tossed and turned thinking of all the things I'd left behind in Ballina. Would we ever go back there again? It was unlikely. What could we go back to? Norfolk was about to be turned into a community centre. One night I had a dream where I went back there and knew nobody. It wasn't very hard to see the symbolism. I was creating myself like Oisín in Tír na nOg.

Things always look worse at the start. People told me I'd settle into it in time. To an extent I did. I never thought of Iona Villas as home but it was a good second best to Ballina. It's like the way your eyes acclimatise to the darkness when you go into a cinema. For the first few minutes you're stumbling around the place. Then you see everything clearly. You start laughing at the other people who've come in and stumbled like you did.

It was a crazy time what with me sampling city life, the family moving all over the place and my father trying to cope with his re-location after spending most of his life in Ballina. In the middle of it all my mother had a mastectomy. She'd known she had breast cancer for some time now. She kept postponing her operation because there was so much happening. Thankfully the surgery went well but she was very weak after it. I remember looking at her in bed one night as she lay bathed in sweat. She wouldn't let you do anything for her, not even get her a glass of water. The last thing she ever wanted was to have to ask anyone for help. She preferred to suffer through it all.

After she came out of hospital she suggested I have my teeth seen to. They were in a bad state. A lot of decay had set in. The dentists in Ballina were old-fashioned. Their surgeries were almost Dickensian. If you were in the waiting room and you saw a magazine with the headline 'Titanic Just Sank' you'd hardly have been surprised.

Many of them were as rough as builders. Their drilling methods weren't much different. As I waited for the dreaded instrument to be placed in my mouth I used to feel like doing my own extraction. Dennis the Menace did it in *The Beano* once by tying the bad tooth onto a door handle with a piece of string and yanking it out by pulling the door. I doubted it could have been more painful. When my teeth fell out of their own accord as a child I put them under my pillow. The tooth fairy took them and replaced them with a gift. What a pity they didn't all come out that way.

My godmother, Feena Murphy, offered to pay whatever it cost to have them fixed. She was married to a dentist. He got in touch with a man in Phibsboro called Kevin O'Loughlin and arranged an appointment for me with him.

The first time he looked into my mouth he nearly collapsed. He said to me, 'If I let you loose in a sweetshop for a month and you ate nothing but chocolate you wouldn't have more cavities than you have.'

Over the next few months he sorted me out. He was a great dentist but like most dentists he had a habit of asking you questions just after he'd put about a dozen implements into your mouth.

Our conversations went something like this:

'Have you settled into Dublin yet?'

'Xuyzpgliochqs.'

'Very good. How long are you here now?'

'Bhkliosdfgq weeks.'

My father wasn't in favour of teeth being filled even if we didn't have to pay the bills. His view of the new breed of dentists was that they kept filling them to get more money out of you. He was from the era where they were extracted at any sign of pain. That was how things were done in Ballina. The town's surgeons had a similar philosophy. They whipped out your appendix and your tonsils at the first sign of trouble.

The brave new world of Dublin believed in preservation. My father was having none of this. For him it was 'The tooth, the whole tooth and nothing but the tooth.' As the years went on and I saw people almost having to take out second mortgages for root canals and crowns and all those sophisticated procedures. The only kind of canal we knew in Ballina was the one down by Ardnaree.

Iona Villas was a step down for us as far as he was concerned. He quoted the lines from the song, 'I dreamt I dwelt in Marble Hall, with vassals and serfs at my side.' Our house was roomy but it was no Marble Hall. We had a chandelier in the front room but that was as close to grandeur as we got.

I often thought his snobbish pronouncements were a pose. When he had a few jars in him he'd sing a 'come-all-ye' like 'The Maid of the Sweet Brown Knowe.'

I knew he'd never let go of his 'ancien regime' ideas but I caught him watching *Coronation Street* a few times when I walked into his room suddenly. It was one of his guilty pleasures. He'd always try to change the channel or say it was on without him realising it. I told him he shouldn't have been ashamed of it. Even The Queen watched *Corrie*.

His disenchantment went deeper than that. Maybe his complaints about the size of the house were a cover for something else. He'd been a commanding figure in Ballina. In Dublin he was just a retired man who sat in a back room.

Often he didn't dress. It seemed to me as if he was continuing the kind of life he'd had in Ballina after the Bridge Street office burned down. In some ways he reminded me of Aunt Valerie's husband in London. I'd visited them the year I was working there as a barman. John spent most of his days in his pyjamas too. They were living in reduced circumstances. He'd lost most of his fortune gambling.

My mother and father slept downstairs. It was to give them access to the kitchen if they needed anything in the middle of the night. My father had a bell beside his bed that he rang when he wanted tea. He spent his days reading papers and smoking his pipe. Sometimes he set the bedspread on fire.

He reminisced about the old days and mourned their passing. It was difficult for him to accept the new world, a world where, as he put it, 'Jack was as good as his master.' The tradesmen who came into the house didn't have the same respect for him as the ones who worked for him in Ballina.

He said to me one day, 'The working class is the new aristocracy.' He was astonished at the cost of labour in Dublin. He'd point to the fact that someone could charge a king's ransom to fix a pipe or put up a shelf. University graduates, in contrast, were walking the streets with their degrees under their arms. A lot of them were 'signing on' because they couldn't get jobs.

Despite all that he wanted to get me into a 'good' school in Dublin. I ended up in one of the best, at least if by 'best' you meant posh. It was the Jesuit college of Belvedere on North Great Georges Street. It was difficult to get into. That was especially the case if you were only going to be there for a year. What swung it for me was that Clive was home from Africa. It was his ordination year. He had a few words with the headmaster to get me in.

It had a Primary School attached to it. That meant some of the pupils had been there almost since the cradle. James Joyce went to it when he was six and a half - or 'half past six' as he put it. I was half past sixteen when I first walked in its doors.

Nobody gave me a hard time in Belvedere but nobody was interested in me either. In a way that was almost as bad. As my father used to say, 'Love me or hate me but don't ignore me.'

I was a fish out of water. It was a rugby college but I had no interest in that. I didn't even watch it on television. There were too many stoppages in it to get involved. Maybe the day would come when I'd end up in some educational establishment that had my game at its centre – soccer. Gaelic football was like a religion in Muredach's and rugby was like a religion in Belvedere. Academically poor pupils were sometimes 'retained' if they were winning games for the school. It held that kind of sway.

My father didn't dictate essays to me when I was in Belvedere as he'd done in Muredach's. I wrote them on my own. After years of using him as a crutch it wasn't easy. Every paragraph was like a pint of blood. Nothing more than the fear of failure drove me to finish them.

I felt self-conscious about my country accent. I had no love for the Dublin one but I was in their camp now. I felt my 'brogue' was looked down on. Anyone had only to talk to me for a few seconds to know I wasn't a Dub.

They pronounced 'medicine' as 'medcine' and 'et cetera' as 'ek cetera.' I always felt a special place in hell should be reserved for people who said 'ek cetera.'

The teachers were more easy-going than the ones in Ballina but that meant nothing to me. I didn't take to the college's progressive set-up. Too many years with my head down in Muredach's had sapped my confidence. I felt I'd been transported from a totalitarian regime to a democratic one and didn't know how to deal with it.

If I was asked for my view on anything I didn't have one to give. We were encouraged to think freely about everything, even religion. The religious class was called RE in Belvedere. That stood for Religious Education. In Muredach's it was the more forbidding Christian Doctrine.

If I was more sociable I could have fitted into the various peer groups but I wasn't. I didn't make any effort to infiltrate their world. It was boring to me. Even if it wasn't, I was too shy to make any imposition on it. I told myself I'd just get the piece of paper called the Leaving Cert and boot off as quickly as I could at the end of the year.

During the history period I sat at the back of the class gazing into space. I'd given up history in Muredach's so they didn't know what to do with me for that hour. I ended up just sitting there.

A teacher called Buddy ranted on about things like The Hundred Years War. The pupils were encouraged to join in. I couldn't imagine myself ever participating in a discussion about The Hundred Years War with a teacher. I didn't even fancy myself being able to have a discussion about the apple tarts that were served in the canteen between classes.

My head was in a jam jar for most of the year. Basil donated his Honda to me before he left for America. Some of the other pupils in Belvedere had motorbikes but I was still reluctant to bring it in with me. I preferred taking the bus. It was more anonymous.

One day as I was crossing the street at Doyle's Corner after getting off the 22A a car screeched to a halt in front of me as I was walking across the street. A man jumped out of it. He started abusing me for crossing against the lights.

Another day I found myself walking home from Belvedere towards Cabra Park instead of Iona Villas. What was I thinking? I knew I hadn't really given Dublin a chance to be my new home. Neither had I given Belvedere a chance. The other people in the class were probably fine when you got to know them but I didn't. I hung around with one or two of them but I can't say we became friends.

The person I was most fascinated by in Belvedere wasn't even in my class. His name was Adrian Hardiman. He was an amazing speaker. I used to go to debates just to hear his voice. It was so mellifluous. I was awed by his intelligence. How could someone that young know so much? He went on to become a prominent barrister and eventually a Supreme Court judge. In his later years he wrote a book about James Joyce and the legal difficulties he went through with *Ulysses*.

The things I enjoyed about the year I spent in Belvedere had very little to do with the college itself. They were things I'd always enjoyed doing - going to films and plays, reading books, playing tennis with Keith and Hugo in the Charleville Club on Whitworth Road.

I also played snooker. My main haunt was the Cosmo club in O'Connell Street. It was the place I'd first gone into on one of my trips to Joan O'Reilly in Sandymount years before. I played with men twice and three times my age, taxi drivers and other people who worked late shifts.

I used to play a game called golf with them. It was an unusual game. There were four players. Each of us had our own cue ball and object ball. You had to pot your ball in each of the six pockets, starting with the top left one and ending with the middle pocket on the right. One game could last hours. Anytime someone got near their target the other three players did their best to knock his ball around the table and make things awkward for him.

It was a wild place. One night a man pulled a fruit machine down on top of himself. Nobody passed any notice. He could have been suffocating under it and nothing would have been done. Eventually he crawled out. Another night when I was playing I heard someone snoring under the table. After a while he woke up. He sauntered out as if he'd just come out of his bedroom and was ready to face the day.

Many of the players used their wits to beat me, especially if we were playing for money. They'd do things like cough to put you off when you were lining up a shot. One night I was getting ready to pot a frame ball when my opponent reached into his pocket for the money I was about to win. The sight of that out of the side of my eye put me off and I missed it. No doubt that was his intention. It took me months to learn about ruses like that.

Despite their trickery I became fond of them. They had a street charm that was becoming anachronistic even then. Some nights I stayed there until the small hours. The late nights in Ballina had turned me into a nocturnal animal. I didn't mind going into school with the eyes falling out of my head.

I also went to a few concerts during the year. The one I remember most was Rory Gallagher. It was probably the best night of the year for me. We talk about Bono and Bob Geldof today but Gallagher was there before any of them. He was enveloped in haloes of sweat as he bellowed out his songs.

His voice was like a primal scream. You never thought of lyrics with him. It was the pulse of the music that lifted you. I imagined him getting out of bed in the morning with a guitar in his hand. What he gave you was pure music. He was Ireland's Jimi Hendrix. The Rolling Stones asked him to join them at one stage of his career but he wasn't interested. He was too much of an individual to fit into any band. Maybe you had to be stoned to appreciate him properly. What a pity he died so young. Anyone who ever met him said he was a beautiful person, someone with the humility of all great artists.

I was hardly sad when it came time to leave Belvedere. A class photo was taken. I scratched myself out of it when I saw it. I wasn't sure why. Maybe it was a symbolic removal of everything that had happened to me in the past nine months. Or rather didn't happen. I was banishing the place from my memory.

I tried my best to keep my spirits up, focusing on the fact that I was free of school now. Things were bound to get better. I was living with my family and I had lots of hobbies. Time would make me forget my old life and move on to my new one.

Nothing had really changed, I told myself. But deep down I knew everything had.

UCD

I got four Honours in the Leaving Cert despite all the hours I lost on my extra-curricular pursuits during the year. My father didn't exactly do a dance of joy when he heard the news.

'You've broken a family tradition,' he said. He was referring to the exams he'd failed in TCD. He gave me a tenner. He said it would have been double that if I failed. I loved his attitude.

My Leaving Cert results got me a grant for the university. I didn't know what I wanted to do there. someone suggested medicine. That made me laugh. If my father fainted at the sight of blood, I nearly did so upon seeing a hospital door. If there were 100 choices available to me, that would have been number 99. No. It would have been 100.

Keith thought I should do a B. Comm for job security. He was in that line himself. I agreed without thinking.

My father wanted me to go to Trinity but I preferred 'National.' That was what he called UCD. The campus used to be in Earlsfort Terrace. It was now in Belfield.

Architecturally it looked like something from Alvin Toffler's *Future Shock*. Everything was blocky. I got a fright when I saw it first but after a while I started to think it might suit me. I liked the anonymity of it. Maybe I'd have felt more threatened by the cultural overtones of Trinity. You could be your own person more in 'National.'

The first thing I noticed in the lecture halls was that all the blackboards were coloured green. Why didn't we call them 'greenboards'? I could never figure that out.

I registered for the B. Comm. There were three subjects: Commerce, Maths and Economics. One of the first books I bought was written by a man called Richard Lipsey. There were about 700 pages in it. It was simply called *Economics*. The lecturer said, 'Don't read it. Just hold it in your hands to see how heavy it is.'

I did that. It weighed a ton. I doubted I'd ever get round to reading it. Maybe if I lifted it up and down often enough I'd build up some muscles. Then I wouldn't have to go to the gym.

I met a lot of people in the first few weeks. It was like being at a bus station 24 hours a day. Some of them looked like old Belvederians. Some of them could even have been from Ballina. I didn't spend long enough with them to find out. Conversations started and stopped without notice.

I hated every minute of the course. At times it was like being back in Muredach's again. One day I was having a quiet chat with the person next to me when the lecturer, a man called Pearse Colbert, shouted up, 'Silence!' He seemed to be about half a mile away. Was this what I'd struggled through Belvedere to experience? More terrorism from a blackboard? Or a greenboard?

Our Maths teacher had wild flowing hair. His handwriting was almost illegible. He filled the blackboard with numbers that snaked all over the place. When he ran out of space he drew a squiggly arrow to a vacant spot and continued his scribblings. I had to get a grind from a man in Amiens Street to make some sense of the course.

I got a job as a barman in London that summer. I went with a friend of Hugo's called Chris Griffin. He came from Gort, a small town in Galway. It wasn't far from where W.B. Yeats lived.

It was raining the day we arrived. I'll never forget getting off the Tube at the Finsbury Park station. It looked really grotty. There was a busker playing a guitar in a tunnel at the end of it. He seemed to be on drugs. There was nobody else around.

London wasn't as lively as I expected it to be. The sixties were over. There was no Christine Keeler, no Julie Christie, no Beatles, no Rolling Stones, no Twiggy, no Marianne Faithful, no Jean Shrimpton, no George Best. Shane McGowan hadn't arrived on the music scene yet.

I was earning the grand sum of £14 per week. That included food and board. It wasn't so bad when you considered the fact that a pint of Harp at that time was only 22p. A pint of Smithwicks was only 19p.

The building I worked in was condemned. I often thought it was going to fall down on top of us. It shook sometimes when the Tube rumbled by across the road. It was called The Blackstock Hotel. 'Hotel' was something of a euphemism. It looked more like a tip.

The night after I arrived the head barman attacked the manager. He gave him two black eyes before emptying the till. Then he jumped over the counter and disappeared into the night. I heard afterwards that he was a fugitive from a psychiatric hospital in Scotland.

The customers were lively. One of them squirted a water siphon in my face one night after I'd served him a drink with a cork at the bottom of the glass. I didn't mind. I could have been sacked for something like that in another kind of pub. In another kind of pub he could also have been barred.

I put a few pounds from my salary into a drawer every week. I wasn't saving for anything in particular. It was just to have it. One day I saw a suit in the window of a clothes shop across the road that looked nice. I'd never bought a suit before. In fact I couldn't remember having ever bought any item of clothing in my life up to this. I'd gotten so many hand-me-downs over the years it became the norm.

Being the youngest of the family meant I was usually dressed in cast-offs. I'm sure there were new things bought for me over the years but I can't remember what they were. It can't have been easy for my parents buying clothes for nine children. Maybe Keith was lucky to be the first from that point of view.

Many of the cast-offs I inherited were too big for me. I was slow to grow when I was young. My father used to try and console me by saying, 'Good goods come in small parcels.' I had to double up the cuffs on jumpers if they were too long. My mother turned up pairs of trousers for me. There wasn't much you could do if an item of clothing was too wide.

In later years I developed a hatred of wearing anything that was too close to my skin. I liked my vests and pullovers and trousers to be loose. I started to sweat if a tie was tied tight. I could only breathe properly if I didn't close the top button of my shirt. I often wondered if this was a result of all the years I spent wearing clothes that I was expected to 'grow into.'

I also had claustrophobia. It hit me anytime I was in a closed space. I never knew what caused it. Maybe it went back to the time I was in my mother's womb, when I didn't want to come out because it meant sharing my birthday with St. Patrick.

The suit was pin-striped like my father's ones. It was also double breasted. I felt strange wearing it behind the bar. The manager didn't like it. He told me to take it off. When I asked him why he said he didn't want anyone mistaking me for a manager. I doubted that was likely considering I was only seventeen years of age but he still made me take it off. I put it in a wardrobe and didn't wear it again for the rest of the summer.

We didn't have too much fun after hours. All I had to entertain me was Arsenal on Saturday afternoons. I made a point of getting to see them anytime I could. Charlie George is the player I remember most from that time, charging around the place with his Jesus-like hair. Saturday was our half day but the manager always seemed to find some way of making me late for the matches. There'd be extra bottles to be collected from the tables or a barrel to be changed. I'd find myself running down the Seven Sisters Road like Ronnie Delaney trying to get to the turnstiles before the kick-off.

Every Sunday I bought the *Sunday Press*. Finsbury Park was across the road. I used to go there to read it, eating soggy chips and watching people walking their dogs. It was a huge park. There were concerts there sometimes. Irish groups that made it in England played there. I spent ages reading the paper. No matter how trivial the articles were I gobbled them up. I was hardly out of the country a wet day and already I was nostalgic for it.

We watched television after our shifts ended. Violence was breaking out nightly in the North. It was the main subject of conversation. I knew about as much about it as I did about Quantum Physics. I'd spent too many years at my father's knee hearing about Britain's great battles of yore to be aware of the latest developments. Some of the customers tipped me generously when they heard my accent and some not at all. It was an indication of where their political allegiances lay.

'Do you believe in internment?' the manager asked me one night.

I hardly knew the meaning of the word. He said he thought the population of Northern Ireland should be put into a boat and shipped off to Africa.

'It would want to be a big boat,' I said.

He wasn't amused.

'Do you think that's funny?' he said.

I said, 'Do you think it's funny having people dragged out of their beds and put into prison for having done nothing?'

I became patriotic suddenly. Why wasn't I patriotic in Ireland? I'd heard other emigrants say they only became patriotic after they left Ireland. I often wondered why. Maybe there were too many other patriots at home. We wanted to stand out.

After recovering from his wounds he continued his reign of terror in the bar. He watered down the whiskey and served Guinness slops to people too thirsty to notice. That was the overflow that went into the tray when barmen were filling pints. We were expected to do the same. When he wasn't looking at us we poured it out.

I liked talking to the customers. That bothered him. 'You're too conversant with them,' he said, 'Just get the money.'

I thought I was helping business. I told him I felt it was a good idea for people to feel comfortable when they were drinking. 'They're comfortable anyway,' he said, 'It doesn't matter if it's a robot that's serving them. Their ambition is to get drunk.' The more he talked, the less I wondered why he had two black eyes.

He worked us to the bone and paid us slave wages. It was often the way with the Irish in England. Some places even had signs outside their premises saying 'No Blacks or Irish.' I felt I was back in school. There were clearly defined rules you couldn't break.

It was my first time being in a position where someone was giving me money for doing something. That gave my boss the power to abuse me. At times I felt like telling him what to do with himself. Then I thought: If I do, not only will I be jobless but homeless as well.

We weren't encouraged to go into the city after our shifts ended. It was as if he didn't want us to have a night life. If we were out late he put a latch on the door so we couldn't get in. Someone said he thought we might bring women back from the West End and give the hotel a bad name.

'Don't shit on your own doorstep,' he used to say. We had to throw stones at the windows to get in the door if it was late and he was gone to bed. One of the other barmen used to come down and unlatch it for us.

What had he against women? He was rumoured to be gay. Maybe that was it. I hardly knew what the word meant in those days. We all knew people who were sissies. They were close to their mothers and didn't bother dating girls much. Was that the same thing?

Once or twice I remembered some of my classmates in Muredach's saying about someone that they were 'that way inclined.' They'd put on a funny voice as they said it. I'd wonder what they were talking about. In later years I read an article somewhere saying that 7% of the Irish population were gay and 7% were Protestant. For a while I thought it meant the same 7%! There was a stigma attached to both sets of people at the time. I was brought up to believe there was something odd about Protestants. In the 1940s it was a mortal sin to go into a Protestant church. Even in the fifties you could get a rollicking for going into one.

I never found out for sure if the manager was gay or not. I was always a bit nervous passing his door at night. He seemed to confirm a suspicion I had about gay men having a predatory side to them. That was another prejudice of the time.

Many of the staff were Irish. A lot of them worked on the buildings. Some weren't long off the boat. Others looked like they'd been there for decades. They wore the scars of broken lives. Many of them had drink problems. They worked to feed it. The conscientious ones sent money home to the wives and families they'd left behind. The hardened alcoholics often drank the rent money. You'd see them wandering round the park after the pub closed looking for somewhere to hang their head. They'd get a few hours sleep under some bush if it didn't rain. Then they'd head for the Tube station.

We didn't use words like 'diaspora' then. We just saw them as men anxious to get relief from their circumstances every night with the temporary thrill of the bottle.

A lot of girls came in. We used to banter with them. I expected them to say things like 'Cor blimey.' It was what I was used to from films. They didn't say that but many of them had cockney accents. They were very forward and very entertaining. They made themselves familiar with any men who happened to be in the bar when they were there. Rarely did a night pass but some match wasn't made. I watched them go off arm in arm with some other customer. Both of them were often drunk. Sometimes they asked me if we sold condoms. A lot of pubs in London had them under the counter. That would have been unheard of in Ireland at the time.

Would the girls become pregnant? Would they use precautions? I thought of all those films I'd seen growing up where women became pregnant outside marriage. It could form the cornerstone of the plot. I thought of *Room at the Top, Saturday Night and Sunday Morning, This Sporting Life*. In Ireland, we said, women conceived without sinning. In England they sinned without conceiving.

The greatest sin a girl could commit when I was growing up was being a single mother. I didn't know anything about Magdalene laundries then. None of us did. I didn't even know about women who got married for no other reason than that they were pregnant. That often led to a life of misery with a man they didn't love and who didn't love them. Someone said once of his parish church, 'There were so many shotgun marriages here we call it Winchester Cathedral.'

One night two girls started chatting to myself and Michael, one of the other barmen. They introduced themselves as Sally and Frances. They said they'd been on the razzle since early morning. Both of them were wearing mini-skirts up to their bottoms. Frances wasn't wearing a bra under her jumper. You could see her nipples. She had the jumper tucked under her skirt to make them more prominent. I'd never seen that before except once in a film. I think Joan Collins was in it.

They got merry with us. We were both on a half day that day. When we told them that they suggested we go into the West End with them. We were only too happy to do that.

We got the Tube in. I sat beside Sally. She never stopped talking the whole way in. She was like a clock. Michael sat with Frances at the other end of the carriage. He couldn't keep his eyes off her breasts. I saw them kissing at one stage.

We got to Piccadilly Circus.

'This is where all the action happens,' Sally said. There was a woman in front of us dressed in fishnet stockings and not much else. She stood at a basement railing that had a sign saying, 'Girls Downstairs.'

'Would you like a good time, darlin'?' she said to me. I felt like telling her I couldn't even afford a bad one. Sally turned my eyes away from her.

'People like that aren't good for holy Irish Catholics like you,' she said laughing.

She brought me into a bar. It wasn't like the family-run places I was used to seeing up to now. After we got seats for ourselves she made a sign at the barman. He started mixing something for her.

'You're going to pay, aren't you?' she said.

I went up to the counter. I ordered a pint of Smithwicks and some peanuts for myself and a cocktail of some sort for her. I nearly got a heart attack when the barman came over with the bill a few minutes later. It was the guts of a fiver. You'd have got drinks for a whole group of people for the night on that in the Blackstock.

'You're working in the wrong bar,' she said to me. When I told her I was only earning £11 a week she burst out laughing. 'Are you mad?' she said, 'Get out of that kip.'

She started to talk about our boss. 'He's ginger beer,' she said. She meant queer. 'Don't bend over for the soap if you're in the shower,' she said. I didn't know what she meant. I said we didn't have showers. She went into convulsions at that. She motioned Frances over to her to have a laugh. I didn't know what was so funny.

I spent most of the night feeling sorry for myself because of my poor earnings. I probably didn't give Sally the attention she deserved because of that.

I found it hard to understand the way she talked. She said things like, 'I weren't going to do that, were I?' When I went into the Gents with Michael he said, 'She's a Geordie.'

She had as many problems with my accent as I had with hers but it didn't seem to bother her. She kept saying, 'I love the Irish.' I told her to stop saying that. It put a distance between us. I didn't want to be 'the Irish.' I wanted to be me.

Michael spent most of the night with his arm around Frances. I thought she looked bored. When I said it to Sally she said, 'She always looks like that.' She kept talking all through the evening. Only rarely did I get a word in. Every now and then I looked over at Michael and Frances. It didn't seem to be going too well.

She wasn't with him when it got to closing time. I asked him where she was. 'She left early,' he said, 'She lives near Piccadilly.'

I thought there was more to it than that. He'd been coming on to her too strong for someone he'd just met. He had a big opinion of himself. That was obvious to me from the first day I met him. He thought he could get any woman he wanted.

He was quiet on the way home. When we got back to the Blackstock he went into the bar. Sally was still talking ninety to the dozen. Michael poured himself a whiskey. He did that sometimes after hours. Sally said to me, 'He's a bit grumpy, isn't he?'

I asked her if she'd like a drink but she said she was tired. We left the bar. I walked her up the Seven Sisters Road to the flat she was staying in. When we got there I didn't ask her if I could go in. I was half afraid she'd ask me in for coffee. If she did I imagined coffee would be the last thing we'd be having. 'See ya round, luv!' she said as we parted. Despite everything I think she enjoyed herself.

Michael was still sitting in the bar with his glass of whiskey when I got back. I asked him if he enjoyed the night.

'I had a great time,' he said. I doubted that.

'Their skirts didn't leave much to the imagination, did they?' he said then. It wasn't like him to be so prudish. I wondered what was up with him.

He pointed the glass at me.

'Let me give you a tip,' he said, 'Never let a woman walk outside you on the footpath.' He was slurring his words. I didn't know what he was talking about.

'Never let a woman walk outside you,' he said again. I asked him what he meant. He went into great detail about it. Apparently I'd done that with Sally after we got off the Tube. She hadn't said anything to me about it. I found it strange that he was giving out to me about something so trivial. He was the one who'd been trying to get his date into bed with him. Maybe he was trying to divert the conversation from himself.

That was one of the few nights I ventured into the city. Afterwards I confined myself to drinking in the Blackstock. It didn't matter to me if I was inside the counter or outside it. It became my social life as well as my job. Sometimes on my days off I was asked to jump over the counter and change a barrel down in the basement. That was usually if the barman on duty was too busy. Sally came in every now and again. She entertained me with her stories. I never saw Frances again.

Some of the customers had strange quirks, like the guy who wouldn't accept a drink from me unless there was a ripple in the glass it was served in, or the customer who used to order two drinks but only drink one of them. I could never understand that. Then there was the man who drank a bottle of Worthington at the exact same time every night and then vanished without saying a word to anyone.

I got to know some of these people well as the weeks went on. One man I became friendly with was running away from a bad marriage. He was now, he said, married to Arthur Guinness. From what he told me about her it seemed to be a safer option.

Another man was in trouble with the law. Both of them sought solace in the haven of the pub. This was where the real story of their lives was unleashed. It was like their confessional.

Sometimes I lowered the best part of a bottle of whisky listening to such revelations. I felt privileged they were sharing them with me but guilty the next morning if they'd said too much. They'd be awkward with me. I heard stories from the other side of the counter as well. There were as many sad cases inside it as there were outside.

On my days off I spent most of my time drinking with the customers. The more I got to know them the more I liked them. It worked the other way too.

One night after having a few too many glasses of bitter, one of them said to me, 'You don't sound like an accountant.' I asked him what he meant.

'You're a square peg in a round hole,' he said, 'or should I say a round peg in a square hole.'

When a person said something to me in a bar it always had more resonance than if they said it anywhere else. I don't know why. If someone said 'Two and two is four' to me in a pub it acquired extra meaning.

I had a long chat with him and felt I knew myself better at the end of it. Some things are so obvious when you get a bird's eye view of them or have them said to you by someone who doesn't know you, who can see you more clearly because of that. I realised I was totally on the wrong course in UCD.

I decided to leave the Commerce faculty when I got back to Dublin. It was the only option for me now. I thought of a line from *The Magnificent Seven* that Steve McQueen had. He said he knew a man once who took off all his clothes one day and jumped into a cactus bush. When he was asked why he said, 'It seemed like a good idea at the time.'

I felt the same way. I was about to jump into a different kind of cactus bush. The times they were a-changin,' and not just for Bob Dylan. I had, as my father might have put it, crossed the Rubicon.

Bohemian

I wasn't long back in the Villas before I was
informed Deezer had been put down. I couldn't take
the news in. Nobody said anything about it anytime I
was on the phone to them from London. They
probably knew I wouldn't have agreed to it. While I
was away he'd bitten a young girl under her eye. I
couldn't understand why. It was so out of character.
He wouldn't have hurt a fly but sometimes he played
with me a bit too energetically.

I heard afterwards he was in heat. My father was
afraid the family of the girl would take an action
against us. It took me ages to get over it. He was my
first dog. It was hard to believe I'd never play with
him again.

The only way to get him out of my mind was by
thinking about my future. I wasn't looking forward to
telling my father I was having second thoughts about
Commerce. The fact of Hugo leaving All Hallows and
going into First Arts was an expense he hadn't
anticipated. Now I was asking for another one.

'The Arts faculty doesn't have good job
prospects,' he said. It was unusual to hear him talking
like that. He'd been casual about money all his life. I
suspected things were getting tight that way now that
he'd been retired for a few years.

I told him figures bored me, that my real interest
lay in literature. He said, 'You can do all the reading
you like after work. That's what I did.' Everything he
said made sense but when I told him how miserable
I'd been in Commerce he said, 'All right. Do
whatever you want.' You wouldn't get that kind of
attitude from many parents.

I took English and Philosophy as my subjects. I
thought English was going to be a cakewalk until I
saw the kind of things we had to study. Woody Allen

180

once said, 'Never do any university course that makes you study *Beowulf.*' Unfortunately it was on ours. When you looked at the denseness of it, even Middle English became attractive. Picking up a text in modern English was bliss by comparison.

Everyone in the class apart from me had to do three subjects. I got an exemption in Maths from the Commerce year. It had that benefit at least.

Studying Philosophy after Commerce was like going from Auschwitz to Butlin's holiday camp. Someone once defined it as 'an invisible man going into a dark basement to look for a black cat that isn't there.' Just my kind of thing, in other words. People gave you a funny look when you said you were studying it. 'Very deep,' they'd say. I never regarded it like that. The questions philosophy asked were the questions I'd have been asking myself even if I never went to university. To me the people who didn't ask these types of questions were the unusual ones.

There was a freewheeling atmosphere in the Arts faculty. Nobody bothered too much with you. You didn't have to go to lectures if you didn't want to. Theoretically that was the way it had been in Commerce but it didn't feel like it. I became more relaxed and a bit rebellious.

I believed I held the world by the tail. For the first time I felt I was really in university rather than spending an extra year in Muredach's. It was important to be seen with *On the Road* under your arm to be hip, or to have J.D. Salinger's *The Catcher in the Rye* sticking out of your back pocket. The real trendy people had lithographs of Toulouse Lautrec in their flats in Donnybrook. They held parties for people as pretentious as themselves, people who always looked as if they were going to say something important but never did. They smoked Camel cigarettes and drank wine out of plastic cups that they used for ash trays afterwards.

I hung around the corridors doing something similar as the days stretched around me tantalisingly. Everything seemed more attractive suddenly – the campus, the students, the general routines. For some reason I wasn't as threatened by the blockiness of the architecture as I'd been in the Commerce year. to get away from the concrete I went on walks round the fields. Suddenly I felt myself infused with Paddy Dillon-Malone's agoraphilia.

Even the tennis courts looked more interesting to me. They weren't like the ones in Charleville. You had to wear all whites there. In Belfield you could dress in anything you liked. The courts themselves were different too. The surfaces were red and grey unlike the old-fashioned black and white of Charleville.

I re-invented myself in the Arts faculty. I slept later in the mornings and wore my hair longer. Some days I left notes for my mother saying things like, 'Wake me at two.'

I still got the 22A bus to the campus like I did when I was doing Commerce but everything else was different. As soon as I got off it I felt I was going into a world of irresponsibility. I was entering the beautiful lunacy of inconsequential thought. When I went into the library I pulled books from the shelves at will, books by people I'd never heard of before like Conrad Aiken and Theodore Roetke. I'd read a few sentences and then put them back again.

Afterwards I'd go over to the restaurant and drink coffee with equally dissolute souls. We'd pass knowing comments about books we'd only half read. As we looked around us we began to resent anything smacking of reality – the security guards, the cleaning staff, anyone who earned a 'regular' salary. It was as if they didn't belong in our rarefied environment of free thinking.

There were some swots in the class who did everything by the book. In Muredach's I'd been threatened by swots. They were teacher's pets there but not here. You couldn't be a teacher's pet in a university. What would be the point? It was too big. Who would you bring an apple to?

My improved state of mind spilled over onto everything else that surrounded me in the Arts faculty, even the world of nature. I'll never forget the autumn of 1971. The sun shone mostly on the cold days. It reminded me of a Van Gogh painting. It hung low in the sky but still blinded us with its rays. I couldn't stop looking at it.

The trees were equally beautiful. They were like something you'd see in a film. I liked it when the branches scraped against the windows of the bus on my journey across town. It was one of the few contacts I had with nature as I headed for the mass of concrete that was the campus. The leaves that fell from other trees would be clustered around the lake when I got there. I used to clump through them like a child.

I became friendly with a student called Harry Clifton from Blackrock. We were studying the same subjects and we also did some night security work together, spending nights in huts outside the Bank of Ireland and McCairns Motors on Alexandra Road. Chris Griffin joined us sometimes. I'd been in London with Chris when I had the bar job. Harry also knew my girlfriend Mary Mannion. They used to meet now and again for a drink in Fairview. Harry had a major interest in poetry. It was something I was pottering around with at the time but at nowhere near his level.

We also shared a fondness for the writings of Ernest Hemingway, sometimes speaking to one another in what we called 'Hemingwayese' for whole conversations. It was a language we invented that was

183

supposed to sound like the way Hemingway might have written in the early stories:

The man walked up to the door. He was not sure why he was doing this. He had not done it before and he might not do it again. He knocked on the door. It was a long time before it was answered. A woman came out. She told him to go in. He walked behind her down a long passageway. When he got to the end of it he sat down on a chair. It was not a big chair and it was not a small chair. He sat on the chair talking to the woman as the night came down.

I wandered around the corridors without any sense of purpose waiting for the lectures to begin. I left some of them half way through if I felt like it. Sometimes I wasn't even sure if I was going to the right ones. I sat in a swoon listening to lecturers rambling on about writers who'd died centuries before I was born. t was like a parallel universe.

At lunchtime there were concerts, plays, insanely passionate debates. You were allowed to heckle if you wanted. I began to feel like Basil must have in Earlsfort Terrace in the last years of the sixties. Trainee Trotskyites in badly-fitting anoraks trotted out slogans about everything from Russia during the pogroms to Tiananmen Square. They all wanted to change the world. Looking at them I thought they'd have difficulty changing their socks.

Most of the things they said were nonsensical. If someone is an idiot and you send him to university it doesn't mean he's educated. It just means he's a more verbose idiot. One man who ran for the presidency of the Student Representative Council said, 'My policy is that I have no policies.' How did that gom ever get past the door of the building?

The humour in UCD was clever in a pseudo-intellectual way. On the wall of Theatre L someone wrote, 'God is dead – Nietzsche.' Underneath it someone else put, 'Nietzsche is dead – God.'

In the bar I had fun wondering about the mysteries of existence. I said things like, 'Did I just come from a lecture or was it just in my mind?' If a lecturer fell dead off his rostrum and I wasn't there to hear him falling, would he still be dead?

Donie O'Donoghue, a friend of the family from Glenbeigh in County Kerry, told people not to talk to me because after a few minutes I'd prove to them that they didn't exist.

One of my classmates told me about a philosopher who went on holiday to Barbados. He sent a postcard home to his wife saying, 'Having a wonderful time. Why?'

He told me another story about a man who dreamt he was a mouse. He woke up the next morning wondering if that was the case or if he was a mouse who thought he was a man. 'What's your view?' he asked me. I said my view was that the man was thinking too much. Maybe he should just have invested in a mousetrap.

Was this supposed to be study? If it was I thought I could get used to it, at least if I didn't succumb to cirrhosis of the liver first.

I usually smoked in the bar. In those days you were allowed to. In fact you were hardly allowed *not* to. Cigarettes didn't do anything for me but that didn't stop me. It was important to look cool when you were discussing the meaning of life.

Most of the nicotine ended up on my fingers or up my nose instead of in my lungs. That's probably why I'm still alive today. The long wisps of ash on my father's cigarettes were caused by him leaving them in ash trays and then forgetting about them and going off to another room. The wisps on my ones stayed on my hands. They gave them a smell I enjoyed more than the inhalation of the nicotine.

There was a film society that we used to go to on Friday nights. It showed all these subtitled Norwegian films. They usually had people I never saw in them, talking gobbledygook in pregnant tones with some very dodgy camerawork playing around behind them. Everyone looked at one another meaningfully for four hours and then they all went fishing.

You could see X-rated films there that weren't shown in the ordinary cinemas. A lot of people outside the university regarded them as unadulterated filth. We were above all that. To us they were 'artistic,' even when the love scenes consisted of the characters appearing to be doing gynaecological examinations of one another's nether regions in seedy boudoirs.

I didn't like all the philosophers I studied. Plato I found to be a bore, for instance, and Socrates wasn't much better. I agreed with what Lord Macaulay said about him: 'The more I read of him, the less I wondered why they poisoned him.'

Everyone went on about Sartre. He was the big guy in the seventies. He was a novelist as well as a philosopher. He'd even been in the French Resistance during World War II. He shared many of his ideas with another left-wing thinker of the time, Albert Camus.

Camus had written *The Outsider*. Hugo was the first person who mentioned that book to me. Reading it changed my life. It shook me to my foundations in a way no other book ever could. Someone described it as 'Sartre written by Hemingway.'

Sartre's masterpiece was a book called *Being and Nothingness*. It was about as big as the Bible. A lot of pages were devoted to his theory about people being made up of two parts, the In-Itself and the For-Itself. Don't ask me what they mean now. I hardly even knew then, despite spending hours trying to work out the difference between them.

If you knew your In-Itself from your For-Itself you had street cred. Being spotted with a copy of *Being and Nothingness* under your arm also increased your chances of getting off with the pretty girl sitting opposite you in Theatre L who tried to conceal her acne under a pair of oversized glasses. If you read the novels it was even better – as long as you said, 'But of course Camus is more *cerebral*.'

Sartre was the guy who said 'Man is condemned to be free.' Coming out with stuff like that was also a good way of getting off with the girl sitting opposite you with the big glasses. It certainly beat 'Do you come here often?'

Sartre also said, 'Hell is other people.' That didn't sound quite as good. Philip Larkin amended this to 'Hull is other people.' That's where he came from. He didn't sound like much fun. Neither did Sartre but you weren't supposed to say that.

There were tutorials on certain days after the lectures. They took place in tiny rooms on an upstairs floor. Photocopies of poems by writers like Ezra Pound and Theodore Roethke were left on our chairs before we went in.

I tried to say something about them fast to get it out of the way. If you waited for others to speak it got harder and harder. Everything would be said and you'd feel like a dummy sitting there with the poem in your hand.

We pretended we understood them, trying to say something about them that no one else thought of. The word became more important than the world. Millions of people were dying of starvation all over the world as we sat in our comfortable chairs discussing iambic pentameters and free verse.

We treated the lectures as preludes to the night's revelry. In the bar we imbibed lavishly. We conducted debates on issues like how many angels could dance on the head of a pin. We gazed into the middle distance with deep frowns on our faces as we discussed angst-laden existential tracts. Then we slumped home to our comfortable suburban beds to sleep off the effects of badly-brewed beer.

There were nights when we solved the world's problems over a few pints. The next morning we'd wake up with nothing more on our minds than whether we had the bus fare to the campus.

We thought we were superior to everyone we met because we'd read Sartre and Camus. The cockier ones among us studied thinkers like Schopenhauer and Heraclitus. The more syllables there were in a person's name the better a philosopher he was. If the names were hard to pronounce it made him even better.

After boring everyone with the people on the course we proceeded to lecture them on every other subject we could think of – politics, the salvation of the planet, even what songs they should listen to.

I'd conveniently forgotten singers like Bobby Darin and Hank Locklin by now. They were too lowbrow. I started talking about rock bands instead, even though I secretly detested most of them. I was never into Led Zeppelin or Cream or even the Rolling Stones. Even Elvis bit the dust for a while.

Instead I learned off lyrics of 'important' songs like 'A Whiter Shade of Pale': 'Your multi-lingual business friend/Has packed her bag and fled/Leaving ash-filled ashtrays/And the lipsticked unmade bed.' It was from someone called Procul Harum. Was that a singer or a group? I didn't know and I didn't care. All that mattered was that it sounded significant.

It was a bit different to the songs I remembered dancing to in Ballina – 'Hang down your head Tom Dooley,' 'There's a hole in the bucket dear Henry, dear Henry.' These seemed so childish now. How could I have once sung 'How Much is that Doggie in the Window?'

How could I have got excited singing, 'Keep your eyes on your drivin'/Keep your hands on the wheel/ And keep your filthy eyes on the road ahead/ We'll have fun/ Sitting' in the back seat/ Kissin' and a-huggin with Fred'?'

There were dizzy days and dizzy nights. I fell into bed at all hours and got up at all hours. Nothing had any pattern. I enveloped myself in the lives of people from books, people that became more real to me than the ones I knew. I wrote essays with titles like 'The Adventures of Being' as if Being was a person. Meanwhile the real world went on around me with its poverty and unemployment. I became oblivious to things like that, oblivious to murder, broken marriages, broken down cars, traffic jams, strikes, rain, shoelaces that wouldn't close, malfunctioning cisterns…at least unless I was reading about them in books.

Ordinary people meant nothing to me. I wanted to read about Umberto D, Ivan Denisovich, Arturo Ui. When I saw Commerce students in the bar I wondered how I'd ever been one of them. I imagined them discussing the Ftse Index. Arts students were more inclined to be *playing* footsie.

They didn't seem to have any sense of fun. In three years, I thought, they'd be articled. Spending their time writing figures down the left hand side of a page and other figures down the right hand side and making sure they matched. That kind of life was unimaginable to me now.

Some of the philosophy lecturers were priests. It was the last thing I expected. There wasn't the same kind of deference to them that there was in Muredach's. One day I remember a Fr Chisholm giving us a lecture on Ethics. Half way through it a student called David McKenna stopped him in mid-flow.

'I don't accept your thesis,' he said, 'you're arguing from the normal to the moral.' It was Game On.

One of the people in the class was a seminarian from Clonliffe College. He was very devout. If any of us was talking to him and he heard a bell for The Angelus he'd stop in mid-sentence and launch into prayer. This usually caused an outbreak of laughter among us. We were all so cool then, so anti-establishment. And yet most of us would be propping up that same establishment in a few years.

We had some brilliant lecturers – Denis Donoghue, Seamus Deane, Jim O'Malley, Jerusha McCormack. Seamus Heaney was there as well but we didn't have him.

A man called Terry Dolan lectured us about etymology. He came across as someone who'd stay awake all night worrying about the misplacement of a semi-colon. He was English. Andrew Carpenter was another Englishman. He looked like a cricketer. All he was missing was the peaked cap.

'What do you think of Wordsworth?' he said to us, 'Is he over-rated?' He advised us to try and write poetry ourselves, to imagine ourselves lazing under hot suns in shimmering meadows.

Jim O'Malley was the most intense one of them all. He never looked like he was telling us things because it was his job. It was more like an enchantment for him. He was capable of going through a half pack of cigarettes during a lecture. You'd see the butts clustered around the rostrum after he was finished like remnants of his adrenalin. He had a particular fascination for Pirandello and *commedia dell'arte.*

Eva Thornley was another one of our lecturers. She was the sister of the Labour politican David Thornley. Not too many people went to her lectures. That must have been embarrassing for her. I used to go to them just to fill the theatre up a bit. She was a sweet lady. She rambled a bit but she was always praising writers. Sometimes I thought that came against her. People often sounded more knowledgeable if they were knocking someone.

I had a crush on Jerusha McCormack. I was forever going up to her room with questions. After a while she must have realised I wasn't quite as concerned about the Platonic sub-themes in Wordsworth's 'The Prelude' as I made out.

Denis Donoghue was often in the room when I went up to her. He towered over her little frame. It was funny seeing them together. She was about five feet nothing and he looked twice that. He almost had to bend himself double to even get in the door.

He was married with a large family. His daughter Emma would go on to become a famous novelist. He met T.S. Eliot one time. When Eliot heard how many children he had he said, 'I didn't know you were Catholic.'

Donoghue was like the godfather of lecturers to us. It wasn't just his height or his voice. We wondered if his feet touched the ground as he entered Theatre L. None of us had a clue what he was talking about half the time. We stroked our chins pensively as he rambled on about sprung rhythm in Gerard Manley Hopkins or the abstruse hermeneutics of F.R. Leavis and R.P. Blackmur. He rattled off the names of literary critics I'd never heard before and haven't heard much of since either – Roland Barthes, Natalie Sarraute, Alain Robbe-Grillet.

He could have been spouting the greatest nonsense since the dawn of civilisation and got away with it. 'The only function of a student at a lecture,' he said once, 'is to be present when a great mind communes with itself.' As I looked at him I thought of Oscar Wilde's comment, 'Are *Hamlet's* critics mad or are they only pretending to be?'

191

There were some unusual people in the class. One of them was a girl called Barbara Allen. She had jet black hair and dressed totally in black as well. She only turned up at the lectures once in a blue moon. She used to go down to the front row and sit alone. She never took notes. After the lecture finished she'd disappear as mysteriously as she arrived.

She only said one thing to me during the term: '*The Great Gatsby* is the best book of all time.' I'd never heard of it. I bought it later that day. I was always intrigued by people like Barbara. Anytime I heard Bob Dylan singing the song 'Barbara Allen' afterwards I thought of her.

I went to the theatre a lot during the term. One of the people in Hugo's class, Shelagh Jennings, had recently been engaged to Siobhan McKenna's son, Donnacha O'Dea. Donnacha swam in the Olympics for Ireland and he was a professional poker player as well. Chris Griffin knew Shelagh. Chris was the guy I'd worked with in the bar in London. He brought me round to Siobhan's house one night with Shelagh. It was like meeting royalty. We sat at her feet as she pontificated about the state of art. She reminded me of an Irish version of Katharine Hepburn.

Shelagh was a beautiful girl both inside and out. She was well got but you'd never think it. She always seemed to me to be in a dream world. She'd look up at you with those big eyes and that irresistible smile. I could never imagine her studying or worrying about anything.

She'd listen to you forever even if you were talking nonsense, which I was most of the time I was with her. Beautiful women had that effect on me. I used to go into lectures sometimes just to sit beside her even though she wasn't in my year. She'd have been great as Daisy Buchanan in *The Great Gatsby*. She had that devil-may-care aura about her.

I often wonder what happened to her. So many people drifted in and out of my life in UCD that I never saw again. She used to come round to the Villas now and then if we were having a shindig.

She had a crush on Hugo. I heard Josephine Cottrell had a crush on him when we were in Ballina. He was as handsome as Clive. Basil used to say, 'How is it that the two best-looking boys in the family went into seminaries?' Of course Hugo was out now. He could look at women again without feeling guilty. I don't know if a relationship between him and Shelagh would have worked. He was a bit of a dreamer too. Two dreamers together sometimes spelt disaster. He often said he needed an anchor in a woman.

He put Shelagh into one of his home movies, *The Distance Between Us.* He had a Fuji camera by now. It was like the seventies equivalent of a camcorder except for the fact that he had to send the footage away to Holland to be developed. Shelagh's face was made for the camera. It fell in love with her just like we all did.

Winter came early that year. I didn't go to the lectures after the nights started to close in. The short days gave us an excuse to light fires in the Villas. We huddled around them exchanging our news every night.

Hugo and myself usually talked about films. Marlon Brando was his god. I had yet to discover Robert de Niro. His favourite actresses were Maria Schell and Genevieve Bujold. I liked Lauren Hutton and Katharine Ross.

My mother buzzed around us giving us meals and cups of tea. I listened to titbits from June about the Irish Permanent and Ruth about the Embassy.

My conversation about books can't have held much interest for them. I talked mainly about people they'd never heard of, people I hadn't heard of myself until a few months before. They'd listen politely before getting onto their own stuff about things that had happened in their own days.

After our talk was exhausted we'd turn on the television. I hadn't much time for it now. There were programmes like *Upstairs Downstairs* and *The Forsyte Saga* that did little for me. I was too full up of myself to involve myself in such lowbrow fare. After suffering them for a while I'd waltz off to bed with some dreary Russian novel under my arm.

As Christmas approached I became like the child I'd been in Ballina. There was no Santy Claus now - or even Benny Walkin - but I still caught a whiff of the old magic. We put up a tree and decorated it with every old ornament we could find under the stairs. We stuffed ourselves with all the chocolates you could fit into your stomach (even the ones from the second row).

I got a job as a supply postman for the two weeks leading up to Christmas Day. A lot of students used to do that every year. It was to soak up the extra mail that always accumulated at that time of year. I can't remember how much I got. Anything was better than nothing to people like us who were on lean budgets. It was relaxing roaming around the streets with a bag in my hand. It reminded me of the days delivering letters for my father in Ballina – Cottrell, Fottrell, Cox and Fox. The only thing you had to worry about was dogs nipping at your heels.

When the new year came in I bought myself a polo neck jumper and a pair of bell bottom trousers. Everyone was wearing things like that at the time. I didn't usually fall into trends but I did that year. Another studenty thing I did was grow a goatee. I don't know why. Maybe I wanted to look like a poet. I shaved it off when I realised it made me look stupid. Ruth said I looked like the bad guy in a cowboy film. Was she talking about Jack Elam? Or Jack Flam?

My social life got a bit wild. I gatecrashed parties thrown by people I didn't know. Being Irish, I always enjoyed going to ones I hadn't been invited to than ones I had. I stayed overnight in strangers' houses, falling asleep in rooms I'd never been in before. If I drank too much Stag cider or Southern Comfort (my two favourite beverages of the time) I'd think to myself: I'm turning into my father in Tony Crane's bar.

The next morning I'd wake up with my head feeling like a nest of bats were in it. I'd think: How did I get here? Then I'd crawl down to the kitchen. A few similarly bewildered souls would be there nursing their hangovers and recalling the events of the night. Who got drunk? Who got off with who? What kind of fools did we think we were?

They'd say things to me like, 'You're still alive. Well done. For a while we thought you were going to throw yourself off the balcony.' And I'd think: what balcony?

I'd get some tea and toast into myself to try and burn out the hangover and then I'm stumble home from whatever corner of the city I was in. As I sat on the bus I'd dredge my mind for the events of the night just gone - girls I'd danced with, cigarettes I'd smoked, music I'd listened to.

There would have been discussions about books where I acted the know-all, boring the pants off people who'd probably have paid good money to get away from me. I'd day to myself, 'Never again' but by the evening I'd be rearing to go again.

At that age I was able for it. My system regenerated itself. I was able to withstand the pummelling I was giving my body. There might have even been another party the following night. They were always erupting without notice. There would be more booze, more arrogance, another opportunity to disgrace myself either with misbehaviour or the feeling of omnipotence. Or both.

My favourite kinds of parties were the ones that went on all night. I didn't need to kip down in someone else's house on these occasions. Instead I watched the sun come up over the horizon as I made my way home. The sky was always a strange colour with the half light that was in it. There'd be clouds with shapes I never saw before and maybe a brooding moon scudding through them. There'd be nobody on the roads and no cars, just birds squawking and maybe a seagull foraging through a bin somewhere. There was a strange beauty in the silence.

The lectures became denser as the year progressed. Denis Donoghue started talking a lot about the Modernist movement in literature. T.S. Eliot was listed as one of its prime exponents. Most of the articles I'd read by Eliot up to now were about Jacobean tragedies. A lot of the imagery in his poetry seem to be drawn from that era as well. 'How can Eliot be called modern?' I said to Professor Donoghue after one of his lectures. I don't know how I had the courage even to address this deity.

He almost went through the floor. 'Eliot is a *post-modernist*,' he said. I didn't know what that meant. Could you be more modern than modern? Did it mean he wasn't really modern? What was the difference between being modern and modern-*ist*?

As the months rolled on I became more careful in what I said. You could come across as an idiot if you said anything spontaneous. It was important to play the game by the lecturers' rules. And by their vocabularies.

I later learned Donoghue had grown up in an RUC barracks. It seemed to make him very prosaic suddenly. When I went to his lectures at first I thought of him as having been born on some alien

196

planet and being spirited down to us to impart his wisdom. That didn't sit too well with the idea of him growing up in a dull barracks in Warrenpoint.

Seamus Deane had a more muted appeal. He was one of my tutors as well as a lecturer. In his little room on the first floor he recommended books to us that weren't on the course – Norman Mailer's *Armies of the Night*, Malcolm Lowry's *Under the Volcano*, William Faulkner's *A Light in August*. When I look back at that year now, these are the books I remember rather than the official ones.

I also read Harper Lee's *To Kill a Mockingbird*. The character of Boo Radley resonated with me more than any of the others. He's a recluse who's a figure of fear for the children in the book until they realise he performs acts of goodness by stealth. He reminded me of Gildie Ahern in Ballina. By now I'd learned that this man who struck terror into me every time I passed his door was in reality a gentle soul who'd been let down by various people in his life. No doubt we compounded his misery by our casual acts of vandalism on his property.

Deane talked about playwrights I knew little about at the time – Genet, Bertolt Brecht, Antonin Artaud. Inspired by them I started doing some creative writing of my own.

I felt it was only right. Imagine if you were studying carpentry and you were never given a hammer and nails? Or if you were doing a course on plumbing and never saw a pipe? That was how I felt about the way English was taught. People who couldn't string two words of a story together set themselves up as authorities about other writers' work.

I wrote a few stories to try and justify myself. Some of them were printed in David Marcus' *New Writing* page in the *Irish Press*. Marcus gave me a lot of exposure but I'm not sure it was good for me to have it this early. It made me write for the buzz of seeing my work in print rather than for quality. When I look at these early scribblings now I realise how contrived they were.

Samuel Beckett originally wrote *Waiting for Godot* in French. He did that because his French was no more than basic and he was searching for a simple style for it. If only I could have had that kind of insight.

Gus Martin started lecturing us now. His background as a secondary teacher came against him as far as some of the students were concerned. They said that was where he should have stayed. I thought that was a narrow-minded attitude. Because his lectures were understandable they were deemed to be too ordinary. People preferred being bewildered by Denis Donoghue's abstruse flights of fancy. I was reminded of Oscar Wilde's dictum, 'I live in terror of being understood.'

The exam I did at the end of the year was a breeze. I approached all the ones I'd done in the past with fear. My early years in Ballina were spoiled by the spectre of The Primary Cert. I believed my life would be over if I failed that. It was the first Day of Judgment in your education. It was done away with a few years after I did it. If I was born later than I was I'd have been saved about 1000 hours of worry.

In Muredach's the terror of the Primary was replaced by that of the Leaving Cert. The Commerce exam I did was only slightly less stressful. The First Arts one was a doddle by comparison. I wrote a few essays on things I'd been talking about in the bar. I don't even remember getting the results.

People said things to me like, 'I got a 2.2,' or 'I got a 2.1.' I congratulated them even though I didn't know what these terms meant. Sometimes I felt like saying, 'You think that's something? I got a 1.1.' There was probably no such thing.

One guy in the class who got a 2.1. asked me what I planned to do for a living. He'd just got himself a job in the Civil Service. I told him I was thinking of going to a desert island to become a chess grandmaster. He looked at me with his mouth agape. I loved shaking up smug people like that.

Anything to do with numbers brought me back to the Commerce year. I felt some of my classmates would have been happier in that faculty with their 2.1s and their 2.2s. The way they talked about literature reminded me of the vivisection of frogs in a laboratory.

Outside...It's America

I went to Connecticut that summer. The spirit of liberation was everywhere. I'd just seen *Jesus Christ Superstar,* a film that was like an explosion in my mind. It kicked everything I'd ever been told about religion out of the ballpark. Jesus was more like a hippie in it than the severe character from my Ballina Bible. Mary Magdalene sang a love song to him at one stage. She was portrayed more as a passionate person than a sinful one. Even Judas was a sympathetic figure.

I'd seen *Last Tango in Paris* by this time as well. That was revolutionary in a different way. What would have been seen as underground pornography in former times became mainstream because of the presence of Marlon Brando. The renaissance in his career that he'd started with *The Godfather* was continued here. *Last Tango* shredded our taboos about sex in the same way as *Jesus Christ Superstar* shredded the ones we had about religion.

I went with a guy called Dom Hackett. He was in UCD but in a different faculty to me. He'd been in Belvedere with me too but I didn't get to know him there. It was easier to relate in the university.

I was on Cloud 9 as I flew to America – literally. There's nothing to compare to your first time on a plane. It's as if you're levitating when it takes off. You feel there's nothing under you. It reminded me of the sensation I used to get in my stomach in Ballina when we'd be going over hills with my father in the hackney cars he hired. The exhilaration of being in the clouds was tempered by the fear of crashing. I was advised to take a tranquilliser or a glass of whiskey to soothe my nerves. I took both.

Dom sat beside me at the window. The man sitting on the other side of me was one of those bores who said, 'Did you know it's actually statistically safer to fly than drive?'

'Really?' I said in a bored voice.

'Yes,' he said, 'I'd prefer to take my chances here than on *terra firma*. You could be knocked down by a bus'

Why did these sorts of people always blame buses? I said to him, 'I didn't know buses knocked down that many people.'

I can't remember getting off the plane or travelling from New York to Connecticut. My head was in a daze from all the excitement.

We stayed with Basil in a rambling house on the outskirts of a town called Stratford. It was like an American version of Stratford-on-Avon. That was where my old friend Shakespeare was from in England. The local theatre had Shakespeare plays on all the time. I knew how fascinated Americans were with English culture from some of the people in my Arts class in Belfield. They were fascinated with Irish culture too. Like most young countries they longed to have more traditions of their own and embraced any they could find. Why else would they name places 'New England' and 'New York'?

The first thing I saw when I got into the house was a painting of a flamenco dancer. It was finished except for the face. It hadn't been coloured in. Basil said the man who did it was a previous tenant. He had to leave in a hurry because he owed a lot of debts. I asked him why he didn't put the painting away since it wasn't finished.

'It's a great conversation piece,' he said, 'People keep asking me the same question you just asked. It gives me an excuse to talk about him.'

I was so tired from all the travelling I went to bed almost immediately. I don't know how many dreams I had that night but it seemed to be about a hundred. So many things had happened so quickly.

I woke up the next morning not knowing where I was for a few seconds. Someone was cooking bacon in the kitchen. Birds were singing in the trees. It was only when I heard a strange voice on the landing that the penny dropped. I was in America. It wasn't like being on a holiday in Ireland or even in London or Europe. This was The Big One.

There were three other lodgers in the house besides Basil. Getting to know them was like a culture shock. They were different to anyone I'd ever met before. All of them seemed very knowledgeable. They spoke intelligently about every subject that came up. I felt totally out of my depth as I listened to them. If I said anything at all it was only a sentence or two.

My opinions were usually naïve but they seemed interested in them. I thought it might have been my accent they liked. A lot of people had been intrigued by it when I worked in the bar in London. Maybe it was the same in America. If I had a penny for every time I heard someone saying, 'I'd love to go to Ireland,' over the next few days I'd have been rich enough to buy the country.

There were a lot of things going on in politics at the time. George McGovern was running for president against Richard Nixon. He was every liberal's dream but there was a question mark over Thomas Eagleton, his running mate.

They spoke a lot about sports too. American football was like a national obsession. I knew nothing about that. It bored me as much as rugby did and for the same reason – there were too many stoppages in it.

I was more interested in chess. Bobby Fischer was playing a world championship match against Boris Spassky in Reykjavik. Spassky was Russian. It was like the Cold War crystallised onto a board.

Everything that happened to me in Connecticut was like a heightened form of experience. It wasn't so much like being in a different country as being on a different planet. The America I thought I knew from films and books was nothing like the real thing. Dom and myself loaded something into every minute and fell asleep every night as soon as our heads hit the pillow.

I started sleeping on a water bed with Basil. It rocked every time you moved. I kept thinking there was going to be a leak somewhere and that the water would all spill out. The electrical sockets were close to the floor so we'd both have been toast if that happened.

The landlady of the house was a woman called Stella Lesneski. She didn't know Dom and myself were staying in it. Anytime she knocked on the door we had to hide in a wardrobe.

Some other people often stayed overnight. Or 'crashed,' as the Americans put it. One morning there were about six cars in the driveway when she dropped in unexpectedly. She was dumbfounded.

'What's going on?' she said to Basil. He told her he was having some friends around for breakfast. I don't think Dom and myself had time to get into the wardrobe. She must have thought Basil was very popular. The open house policy of Norfolk had extended all the way to Connecticut.

One of the official lodgers was an army man called Paul. His favourite book was John Barth's *Giles' Goat Boy*. He never stopped talking about it. 'It's America's forgotten masterpiece,' he said. I tried to read it but I couldn't get past Page Two. It seemed to be longer than the Bible.

Paul wasn't a graduate of charm school. Every time I asked him a question he said, 'What's your fucking problem?' The conversation usually ended there. That was a pity because he was an interesting man.

He was always disappearing on these mysterious trips to Philadelphia. That was where his family lived. He was alienated from them. He seemed to be alienated from everyone. He reminded me of Jack Nicholson from *Five Easy Pieces*.

I drove him mad playing Bob Dylan records all the time. 'He can't sing,' he used to say.

The second lodger was a person we called Captain America. I can't remember his real name. He wore trousers with stars and stripes on them like the American flag. I used to be fascinated looking at him. He was like a cartoon character.

Every time he saw me he said, 'What's happenin', man?' He didn't wait for an answer. If he saw you five minutes later he'd say the same thing again. What could have happened in five minutes? Another expression he had was 'far out.' It was his way of saying 'Amazing.' He'd say 'Far out' even if you told him you'd just had a cup of tea.

He gave me a joint one night. I'd never smoked one before. I didn't know anything about drugs at that time. The Irish singer Big Tom was in a band called The Mainliners. Some Americans thought they were making a statement about injecting yourself with drugs. Nothing could have been farther from the truth. The most dangerous thing Big Tom was likely to do was have a pint of Guinness.

'Pot should be legalised,' Captain America said to me one night. He wanted nicotine put on the banned list instead. He said marijuana was harmless, that nicotine was the killer. His point seemed to make sense. I knew at first hand what it did to people. It was responsible for my mother's mastectomy. My father was always terrified of 'the bug.' That was his term for cancer.

Every time he handed me a joint I felt like I was sitting beside Peter Fonda and Dennis Hopper in the campfire scene in *Easy Rider* where Jack Nicholson says, 'This used to be a helluva country once.' His pronouncements were like papal encyclicals. I listened to them with the same enthusiasm as I did the customers in the Blackstock. Having a joint in your hand made you sound as authoritative as if you were holding a pint of beer.

The third lodger was bisexual. I hardly knew what that word meant at the time. How could a man be interested in both men and women sexually? He'd been married and had children. Now he was dating a tennis instructor from Idaho – a male one.

I hadn't met a gay man since my time in the hotel in London. My sheltered life continued after I went back to Dublin. I was confirmed in my belief that gay people only existed in England and America. Ireland was still the island of saints and scholars. And heterosexual males.

Basil was a great host. He took us everywhere – to a football game in Yale university, to a Neil Diamond concert in Saratoga Springs, to New York to capture that city's wild electricity. At night sometimes we played pool in a bar called Esther's Hacienda. It was as exotic as it sounded.

Paul Newman lived in the next town. We were told if you passed by his house on Saturday mornings you could see him mowing his lawn. I loved Paul Newman but I had better things to do with my Saturday mornings. I spent them looking out at the water sprinklers on the lawns, at the wind blowing the cherry blossoms over the road like confetti.

It was a magic summer. For the first few weeks we couldn't get work. Instead we just slept late and took showers. They were a great novelty to me. We only had a bath in the house in Dublin. It was over ten years since Janet Leigh had her unfortunate experience with Anthony Perkins in *Psycho*. I felt I'd be safe enough.

We watched a lot of television. There were an incredible number of films on. (Not *Psycho*, thankfully.) You'd be lucky if you got one a week in Ireland. The only problem was the ads. They came on every five or ten minutes. It made me want to throw the set out the window. They stopped you being able to get involved in the stories.

Some days we treated ourselves to six packs of beer. I wasn't served in the off-licence because I didn't look old enough. 'I'd lose my job if I served you,' the man behind the counter used to say to me. Dom had a stubble so he didn't have a problem getting served. In those days they didn't ask for ID cards.

We spent a lot of time listening to music. Basil had loads of records. He had a great sound system as well. I think he called it quadraphonic. It was probably like what we'd call 'Sensurround' today. He had records by people like Join Mitchell, Tom Rush, The Kinks. The one I played more than any other was Bob Dylan's double album, *More of Bob Dylan's Greatest Hits*. I played it until I almost wore the needle out. Maybe that was what annoyed Paul so much.

The only thing I didn't like about Connecticut was the weather. It was humid most of the time. The air seemed to suck oxygen out of you instead of the opposite. I wasn't able to deal with it. It sapped my energy and made my clothes stick to me. I was delighted one day when it rained. All the other lodgers were glum. It was like they'd never seen it before.

'It's rain,' I explained to Captain America, 'It comes from the sky sometimes when the sun isn't shining.' Rain was in my DNA. It made me feel alive. The following day the sun shone again and they were back to themselves as they lazed in the sun in their shorts and bare chests.

There was a car at the back of the house that Dom and myself drove around in. It wasn't much more than a wreck. Basil told us not to go out on the road in it in case it broke down. One day the steering wheel spun out of control on me when I was doing a reverse turn. The car went around in a circle. There was a drop at the end of the garden. It must have been twenty feet deep. If I went over it I'd probably have been killed. Luckily the chassis got stuck on the edge of it. The car was left perched on it with one of the wheels hanging in mid-air. We were supposed to get a company called U-Haul to cart it away but we never did. For all I know it's still hanging there.

Hugo joined us in the middle of July. I was walking along the road near the house one night when Basil honked a horn from a car and he was inside. Clive was in the seat beside him. He was studying in Fordham University at the time.

Ruth and Jacinta were also in America that year. Ruth had married a man from New Jersey. Jacinta was working in the Irish Embassy in Washington. It was hard to believe six of the family were 'stateside' at the same time. The world was becoming a small place. It was so different to the previous generation. I don't think either of my parents ever stepped on a plane. My father had a phobia about flying. It meant he missed Uncle Louis' funeral after he died in Birmingham. The time was too short for him to get the boat. He always felt Louis' widow had delayed telling him deliberately. they hadn't got on.

Hugo loved America. He associated it with the future. The bright clothes people wore was like a liberation from the dull greys and blacks we saw so often in Ireland. He liked American people too. One thing that annoyed me about them was the fact that they talked so loud. 'That's because the rooms are bigger,' he said, 'Everyone is far away.' It seemed to make sense when I thought about it like that.

Dom and myself eventually got work. Two jobs materialised at the same time. It was always the way in life, a feast or a famine. One of mine was a busboy in a restaurant. The other was labour with a construction firm. They couldn't have been more different. I had to be ultra-clean for the busboy. On the building sites I was the opposite.

I came in from the construction site every day with a ton of cement on my hands. I had to shower so that I'd look like someone who could serve a fresh fruit salad to a customer in the restaurant without turning his stomach with my dirty fingernails.

After a few weeks it got too hard living a double life. I decided to give in my notice in the restaurant. The boss knew I was a student. She was a nice woman who'd spent a lot of time trying to teach me how to hold a tray over my head with one hand. I could never do it. One night when I tried to I sent about fifty glasses flying dangerously in the direction of an octogenarian golfer digging into a lobster.

'I failed my exams,' I said to her, 'I have to go back to Ireland.' It was the best lie I could come up with at short notice.

'That's funny,' she said, 'I heard you got another job.'

Ouch. Cue mush stammering and stuttering and a hasty exit.

Who ratted on me? Was Stratford really that gossipy? As gossipy as Ballina? Were all small towns the same no matter what side of the Atlantic they were on?

One of our bosses at the building site was a man called Eddie. He drove a Corvette sports car. There was only room for one person in it besides himself. Dom usually sat beside him. I ended up curled in the back like an embryo. There was no back seat as such.

There was more of me in the window than anywhere else.

Eddie couldn't understand how we drove what he called 'stickshift' cars in Ireland. Or how we drank warm beer. What I couldn't understand was how Eddie managed to drive at about a hundred miles an hour without killing the three of us. My legs were always blocking his view out the back window.

We mainly worked for a man called Skil. He drove a pick-up truck. We often moved furniture from place to place on it. One day Skil had a passenger in the seat beside him so we had to sit on the furniture. There were dozens of chairs piled on top of one another and we were in the middle of them. The faster he drove, the more they started to move.

At one stage we were hanging on for our lives. I thought we were going to be flung off the truck onto the motorway. There was nowhere to grab onto for support because they weren't tied down. We were roaring at Skil to stop driving but he had the radio on so he couldn't hear us. Eventually he stopped at a red light so we were able to get his attention. That was one of the scariest experiences of my life.

Skil was a ferocious alcoholic. If we ever wanted a break, all we had to do was suggest a drink. He'd down tools and head for the nearest 'gin mill.'

He used to drink in a place called Steak and Brew. They gave you unlimited food and drink for a set price. They had to change that policy after Skil started patronising it.

One night he slammed the door of his truck shut when his leg was hanging out of it. He was too drunk to notice. He didn't feel the pain until the next morning. When he went to his doctor he was told he'd broken it.

For the rest of the summer he hobbled around the place in a cast. We called him Hopalong Cassidy. Even so, there was nobody quicker than him to paint a wall. I suppose that was why he was called Skil. If it wasn't for his drinking problem he'd probably have owned the company. When I was leaving I gave him a bottle of whiskey. Anything else wouldn't have made sense. 'Don't break the other leg,' I said as I put it in the cabin of his truck. He was already guzzling from it as he waved goodbye to me.

For the last part of the summer we decided to just chill out. We hung around Stratford feasting our eyes on all the young women passing by us in their skimpy summer gear. Some of them didn't seem to have more material on them than you'd get in a handkerchief. Not that I was complaining. They were all very attractive with their hourglass figures and their hair parted in the middle.

That was one of my prerequisites for a girl. I was going through my Ali MacGraw phase at the time. I'd seen *Love Story*. The term 'Six Kleenex film' seemed to have been invented for it. For me she was the ideal woman. Perfect features, perfect figure and that parting in the middle of her hair. Why did she have to get cancer? What sick-minded individual dreamt that plotline up?

We sleepwalked our way through the days. At night we sat around listening to the grasshoppers and button-hopping TV channels. News bulletins came in every few seconds.

In America something dramatic was always happening but 1972 was extra special that way.

Fischer beat Spassky in his chess game after accusing him of trying to hypnotise him. George McGovern relinquished his bid for the presidency. It came out that Thomas Eagleton, his running mate, had received electric shock treatment in the past. What if he was shot and Eagleton proved to be unbalanced? Why didn't interesting things like this happen in Ireland?

It's only when I look back at that summer that I realise how little of life I'd seen before I went to America. I don't think I'd even seen a radio in a car in Dublin at the time. I used to be amazed when Skil turned the ignition and music came on. There were so many things I took for granted, so many little adventures happening each day to make everything so special.

The only blemish on it was the fact that I didn't get to see Elvis in Las Vegas. I had plans to see him in Las Vegas where he was performing at the time. 'Go west, young man!' Captain America said when I told him of my plan. I was hoping to go there with three other lads but everything fell apart at the last minute. One of them was my friend Jerry Cowley from Muredach's. He was stacking shelves in a supermarket Philadelphia that summer. We tried our best to make it happen but it got too complicated in the end so we had to drop it.

I wasn't too disappointed. So many other things worked for me that year. Everything was heightened - the smell of grass, of petrol, of the air itself. Even sitting around the house was special. It was so different to anything I'd known in Ireland. Small things became important, even if it was only going into Stratford to buy a hamburger or having Basil drive myself and Dom to one of the neighbouring towns to do some shopping.

I went to a disco one night in New Haven with my cousin George Caulfield. He was the son of Valerie, Grace O'Grady's sister. We were in separate cars for some reason. He was swigging grape wine with his friends. We were side by side on the motorway. Everyone was making faces at one another. He really looked handsome that night. He had no trouble getting women at the disco. I remember being envious of him. I spent most of the night just listening to the music. The band was called

211

Dead Brandy Dog. How does a name like that stick in my head fifty years later?

George died young. Valerie was devastated. She'd given her whole life to him. I often wonder if his death was related to a car accident he'd had in New Jersey some time before. A man crashed into him in the small hours after robbing a store. Bizarrely, the man afterwards sued George afterwards for dangerous diving. Only in America, as they say.

Eventually the summer ended. I was distraught. It should have gone on forever. I knew I'd never be the same in Ireland. I was an adult now, blooded into the ways of the world.

I came home vowing to myself that I had to have three things to make me feel fulfilled after all my adventures: a shower, an Easy Rider motorbike and a girlfriend as beautiful as Ali MacGraw who parted her hair in the middle.

I got the shower.

Back in College

I started Second Arts in an upbeat frame of mind. We were finished with Old and Middle English now and could get stuck into the modern writers. There was a great atmosphere around the university. Everyone seemed to be doing their own thing.

When the lectures ended there was often a play reading in Theatre L. I saw Hugo there one day in *Who's Afraid of Virginia Woolf?* He was also in *King Lear*. He'd been preparing for that when he was in Stratford. I used to see him with a copy of it in his hand whenever I went into town for a pizza.

The great thing about readings was that you didn't have to memorise the texts. You just read them out. Plays could be prepared and staged in a matter of days. The actors didn't bother about costumes either. *King Lear* was performed in modern dress.

Some of the readings were experimental. At one of them I was dragged up on stage to be a part of the cast. I nearly floored the guy who pulled me out of my seat. I wasn't a fan of interactive theatre any more than I was of Buddy's history interchanges in Belvedere.

Hugo was also in a production of *Oedipus Rex* that year. It was with Dramsoc, UCD's dramatic society. That was done in modern dress too. It was directed by Jim Sheridan. Sheridan went on to become one of Ireland's most famous film directors. 'This is a play that tells everyone to fuck off,' he announced. It certainly did that. His recreation of Thebes was like Gardiner Street on acid.

The following summer I went to Washington D.C. Audrey and Jacinta were in an apartment there. By now Audrey was a nurse. Jacinta was still working in the Irish Embassy. They said they'd be delighted to have me stay with them. The apartment was in a huge complex with thirteen floors. The numbers went from 12 to 14 because of people's superstitions about the number 13. We were in C311.

They spoiled me rotten. Like Basil they worked hard and played hard. They were both capable of putting in their forty hours at work and then throwing parties for twenty people without a thought.

Audrey was also instrumental in getting me a job as a janitor in the building. The wife of the owner had broken her arm. Audrey helped her with the dressings when she came out of hospital.

Jacinta was going out with a man called Dan. He was a male nurse in Walter Reed Military Hospital. He was a big man, a gentle giant from Texas with a twinkle in his eye. Audrey was dating his room-mate. He worked in the hospital too.

The doorman of the apartment complex was a man called Miguel. He was from Brazil. He told me he had cancer but he couldn't tell anyone. It would have meant giving up the job and he couldn't afford to do that. He had a wife and children that he was sending money to in Rio de Janeiro. They were in very poor circumstances.

He was polite to everyone. They all had a word for him. He told me he made more on tips than on his basic salary.

He brought me into his room one day. It was where he changed into his uniform in the mornings. He kept it in a casket. When he put on the trousers I thought they looked too big. He tightened them with a belt. He said they used to fit him before he got the cancer. 'I lost 30 pounds,' he said. I tried to work out what that was in stones. People said everything in pounds in America.

I told him he needed to go to a doctor. 'If I did that,' he said, 'I couldn't afford to live.' I told him he couldn't afford to die either. He laughed at that.

Every day I saw him afterwards he gave me a big wave anytime he saw me. Then one day he wasn't there anymore. He was replaced by a burly-looking man from Detroit. He wasn't friendly. When I asked him what happened to Miguel he just shrugged his shoulders.

As janitor I was tasked with menial chores like changing bulbs and reporting problems in the apartments to someone who could fix them. I also had to shovel garbage. The boss didn't know I was staying in the building. It was like the previous year in Connecticut. By now I was getting good at being a secret lodger.

I told him I was staying across town. He was amazed how punctual I was getting in to work every morning with the problems of crosstown traffic in such a big city. Needless to say I didn't tell him all I had to do was come down the elevator.

One of the worst parts of the job was shovelling the garbage. I had to do it from a steel ramp in a basement. People from the various floors threw what they didn't want down chutes that were on the corridors of each one. I had to shovel it into a machine. When I pressed a button it squeezed it into a rectangle. When I pressed another button a wire came out to secure it. Finally a pulley hoisted it up onto the street to be brought to the city dump.

People threw all sorts of things down. I had to be careful with anything made of glass. If it hit the steel and shattered it could knock your eye out. That nearly happened a few times. I preferred to delay my shovelling until a lot of stuff was on the ramp. It acted as a buffer for the glass. There were also beetles everywhere, so many I almost got on first name terms with them. The smell was desperate. I was advised to wear a mask but the space was so cramped I could hardly breathe with one on.

I often dropped into the apartment for a cup of tea during the day. One day I almost got sacked when I was in there and someone's sink started to spout water. They were almost drowned and the janitor was nowhere to be found.

Where was he? Watching *Bonnie and Clyde* on TV with Audrey and Jacinta.

Sometimes we went out for drinks at night. They met their friends Mary Reilly and Monica Murphy at an Irish pub called The Four Ps. I knew Monica from Ballina. She was in Audrey and Jacinta's class in the Convent of Mercy. Mary trained to be a nurse with Audrey in Surrey. Marian, a cousin of hers, was also staying in the apartment. I was surrounded by as many women as I had been in Norfolk when I was growing up. If Connecticut was like a men's club for me, Washington was like a women's one.

Most of the talk that year was about Richard Nixon. He'd bugged the Democratic headquarters the summer before. Two *Washington Post* journalists, Bob Woodward and Carl Bernstein, had written a series of articles exposing him. The Watergate scandal took on the proportions of a global catastrophe as the months wore on.

One of the people I worked with said to me that it was no big deal, that politicians had been bugging one another since the dawn of time. He said even John F. Kennedy, my knight in shining armour, did it. Of course Nixon's main problem was covering it up. It eventually led to his resignation.

When I got back to Dublin I found I had a lump on the back of my neck. It turned out to be TB. For the next six months I was on streptomycin and injections. In a previous era I could have been dead. Thank God for Noel Browne. Almost single-handedly he eradicated the TB scourge from Ireland.

Anytime I came back from America it took me ages to re-orient myself to the slow pace of life in

Ireland. My head was all over the place at the university. The last thing on my mind was the course. I discussed books more in the pub than in the lecture halls. If I could only have committed my bar conversations to paper I felt I'd have sailed through all the exams.

I started to enjoy the company of girls more in the Arts faculty than when I was doing Commerce. I was always awkward with them growing up. An age of segregated education made it hard for me to relate to them. I was able to be myself more with them when I was in England and America. Foreign ones were easier to talk to for some reason. Maybe it was the fact that they were more forward. I experienced that in first when I was in England. American girls were even more forward than English ones. They seemed to like my shyness. In Ireland it wasn't as appealing because the girls were shy there too. Opposites attracted.

The girls I met in the university were more confident than the ones I knew in Ballina. The fact that we had something in common to talk about helped. It wasn't like meeting strangers in a pub or a club. They were in my tutorial groups and at the lectures. I was surprised to see so many of them in my Commerce year. I grew up with the chauvinist notion that women weren't good at things like Maths. There were even more of them in the Arts faculty than the Commerce one.

Outside the university the only place you could meet girls was at dances. The system was primeval. It was humiliating for a man to have to walk back across a floor to his friends if he'd been refused a dance. Neither was it much fun for women to have to stand like cows at a fair and be looked up and down by sozzled lechers.

I usually smothered myself in Old Spice before hitting a dance hall. That was the extent of my

217

preparation for a 'Me Tarzan, You Jane' scenario. It was what men did before feminism emasculated us. Afterwards we started putting more substances on our faces than the women.

I wasn't much good at dancing. If I grew up in the era of the waltz or the foxtrot I might have been able to learn the moves but when I started going to dances people didn't do these things. They just jumped all over the place. The best dancer was the person who could do the most energetic epileptic fit. I'd probably have been happier in the showband era but I only experienced that at second hand from my bedroom in Ballina listening to Jack Ruane and all the other bands in the Town Hall.

I hated the mechanics of what you had to do to get to know a girl. If I asked one to dance and she said yes I found my tongue glued to the roof of my mouth as we took the floor. One night I was dancing with a girl when she suddenly turned away from me and started dancing with another girl. Then they started kissing. I was a long way from Ballina.

Conversation was difficult. A familiar opener was, 'Do you come here often?' The classic response was, 'Only when there's a dance.' Paddy Cole said to a girl once when he was trying to get off with her, 'Do you feel like an orange?' She replied, 'No. Do I look like one?'

Anytime I asked a girl what she did for a living she tended to yawn. If I asked her was she enjoying herself she might say 'Yes' in an equally bored way. It was impossible to get anything going with the music blaring away behind you. I found myself roaring platitudes at women. They'd roar other ones back. You could have a decent conversation during a slow waltz at the end of the night or if you were able to have a coffee away from the noise. Other than that it was as if you were having an argument with someone.

At the Revolution disco one night I met a girl who looked like Ali MacGraw. When I told her I was studying English in UCD she started talking about how James Joyce had to leave Ireland to fulfil himself. I felt an immediate connection with her.

She was left wing in her politics and was also a strong republican. This was a world that was totally alien to me. I didn't mention her to my father. It would have been like a red rag to a bull to him.

She opened my eyes to some of the horrors that had been perpetrated in Ireland when we were under England's tyranny. It was a long way from the history lessons I'd been given in Muredach's.

I didn't think much about Ballina now. There was a lot of activity in the Villas. People were always coming and going. In many ways it was just as much of a buzz as Norfolk with all the chats and sing-songs. Heated discussions went on into the middle of the night over cups of tea and burnt toast.

There was a lot of activity outside the house too. You didn't always have to go into town for entertainment. I went to films in the State cinema. They showed European ones sometimes. The Bohemian was around the corner from it. We called it 'The Boh' or, more usually, 'The Fleapit.' It was more commercial.

There was also a snooker hall nearby that saved me going into the Cosmo. It was at the Cross Guns bridge just down the road from us in Phibsboro.

In time it became my Dublin Hibs just like the Villas became my Dublin Norfolk. Maybe we all make these adjustments in our lives, transforming the place we've come to into the one we've left. In that way we delude ourselves that things can still be like they used to be. The need is fulfilled in the new environment even if it's in a muted form. We accept it as a consolation prize for our inability to return to the original Eden.

I drank with Keith and Hugo in the Addison Lodge. It was a family-run pub near the Botanic Gardens that had an old world atmosphere about it. Hugo was living on the south side of the city but he spent a good bit of time in the Villas. He'd married a nurse called Kathleen and got a job teaching in Blackrock. He always had a strong bond with Keith. One day when he was young he was almost electrocuted by a faulty plug. Keith pulled him clear of it.

I spent most of my time out of the house. My mother wanted me to stay in more but she didn't push the issue. She wasn't the type to. When I was out she transferred her attention to the other members of the family. She lived for visits from the ones who weren't living at home, either in Cork like Audrey or the three who were married in America.

I remember the first time Basil came home after getting his job in General Electric. He had something called an integrated circuit with him. It wasn't much bigger than a cigarette packet. He said it contained innumerable pieces of data. My mother was mesmerised looking at it. I suppose it would be the equivalent of a microchip today. It was my first experience of a world where things were becoming so small as to be almost invisible. Up to now people boasted about things being big. It started in the schoolyard: 'My father is bigger than yours.' Then you went out and got a job and said, 'My car is bigger than yours.' In the new world that was all being turned on its head. Big wasn't beautiful anymore. Small was.

We had some great nights in the Villas during these years. They weren't so much parties as nights that turned into them. Our Glenbeigh friend Donie O'Donoghue said to me one day, 'That was a great party at your place the other night.' I said, 'What are you talking about? We didn't have one.' It was a different way of looking at things. Norfolk had been like an endless party. We continued that in Dublin in many ways.

People weren't issued with invitations. They just appeared at the door and we admitted them. They drifted in and out of our lives and brought great richness to them. I remember them now in images that come back to me in snatches. So much of it was taken for granted. I see them sitting on the carpet or the edges of chair or sofas as sing-songs began, trying to balance tea cups on their laps or munch a sandwich or smoke a cigarette or drink a beer as they came and went.

There are nearly too many of them to mention. Tom and John Wills were equally kind and loyal. Liam Hogan sounded a lot like his hero William Holden when he spoke in that fathoms-deep voice. He liked to sing a ballad about the labour leader Joe hill. Like him, his loyalties were always to the poor. The three of them were teachers. Liam had originally worked in the B&I. He put himself through night school to become one.

Liam's brother Michael was quieter but equally deep. Like Liam he was a great listener and fascinated by dozens of subjects. There was also Ray O'Toole. Ray worked in the post office but like Liam and Michael he had a great interest in the arts. He loved Bing Crosby and entertained us all with his songs. He was also fascinated by George Eliot's novel *Middlemarch*. He could talk about it for hours. 'A much admired but little read book,' he'd say before going into a dissertation about it. His girlfriend, Sybil, eventually became his wife. Sybil had an old world quality about her that touched everyone. She was a lady to her fingertips.

Then there was Muiris, a lovable scoundrel with a history of pulling every scam in the book and then a few more. He looked like butter wouldn't melt in his mouth but you knew there were always a hundred things going on in his mind, none of which he was going to tell you. He passed every question off with a laugh. Someone should have written a novel about him. He was a bit of a ladykiller too. One of his chat-up lines was, 'Your nearness is driving me crazy.' Anyone else would have been laughed off the stage with that one but with Muiris it seemed to work.

A man called Clint was another charming rogue. He went back to the Shandon Drive days. I only met him once but I heard lots of stories about his exploits. He was a notorious sponger when it came to food. He gobbled up anything he could find that was lying around the house but he rarely bought anything himself.

June told me he bought a cake once and stored it in a corner if the fridge. There was a piece of paper on top of it with 'Hands Off!' scrawled on it.

June's friend Myra came to a lot of our nights too. She had a sunny disposition. She was also something of an eccentric. She liked telling stories that went all went all over the place. She was so girlish I could see her still being the same at ninety.

Marius, our next door neighbour, was also in the habit of dropping in. She looked so cool with a cigarette in her hand. Myrna Loy and Lauren Bacall sprang to mind. She'd take long drags and look into the middle distance as she analysed her love life. Every now and then she'd go up to The Maples with June to have a chinwag about men. She'd usually have to check in with her parents first. Her father was fussy. My mother used to be amused watching him mowing the lawn. If he missed even one blade of grass, she used to say, he'd have to cut the whole lawn again to get them all the same size.

The O'Gradys were often with us as well. They brought back the magical summers we spent in their home. John O'Grady used to have friendly arguments with Hugo about politics. John was a diehard Fianna Fáiler. Hugo was equally passionate about Fine Gael. Their discussions usually boiled down to the contrast between 'Champagne Charlie' (Charlie Haughey) and 'Garret the Good' (Garret Fitzgerald.)

Polly Sheil came out to see us occasionally. She was Aunt Florence's daughter. She was always asking us out to Rockingham. I preferred when she called to us rather than the other way round. Going out to the south side of the city was never much fun for me. I still felt I was in England when I was in Dun Laoghaire. Wasn't it called Kingstown once?

Tina joined us on some of the nights. She'd got a job with a family in Boyle after we left Ballina but she hadn't really settled there. A number of other jobs had come up in the meantime. One of them only lasted a day. She said nothing could ever compare to Norfolk. Her mind was always on it no matter where she was.

The people in Boyle had lovely children. That was the main reason she stayed. The man she worked for was a solicitor. It seemed she was destined to end up with solicitors.

When her parents died she inherited the family home in Ballina. She was able to buy a house in Boyle with the proceeds. It reminded me of 'the little house on the prairie.' It was beside a railroad track. I never understood how anyone would be able to sleep at night with trains rattling along outside. 'You don't hear them after a while,' she said.

She still went down to Ballina anytime she could. She either went on the train or on a Wisp motorbike she'd bought. She hadn't changed a bit since she was with us. I knew she wouldn't have. She had the same girlish charm as she always had. It made her fit in easily with everyone she met at the Villas.

Our own bunch at the get-togethers most often consisted of couples. Hugo and Kathleen would nearly always be there. Kathleen sometimes brought Mary Reilly with her. She was a relative of hers from Westmeath as well as having trained to be a nurse with Audrey in Surrey.

June would be with Pat, her boyfriend. He was a lecturer in Bolton Street. Keith would be with Jacqueline. She was a quiet girl he'd been dating for a few years. Her mother ran a guest house in Bray. They got married in 1970. He was 33 at the time. 'The age of JC when he died,' as he put it. Speaking of marriage and Jesus' crucifixion in the same sentence didn't really sound like he was approaching the institution with optimism but Jacqueline knew him well enough himself to take the comment in good part.

I'd usually be with Mary, my girlfriend from Galway. June had worked with her father, Tom Mannion, for a time in the Irish Permanent. She fitted in as easily as anyone. It was no time at all until she became part of the family. She was quiet in her personality like Jacqueline but full of fun when she got going.

She worked in a solicitor's firm in Clare Street. I'd known her from the seventies. She grew up in Galway. Her father was from Cork and her mother from Glenamaddy. They were both lovely people, gentle and kind and very easy to get on with, the salt of the earth. I could see where she came from. The apple didn't fall far from the tree.

She got on great with both of my parents and all my brothers and sisters. She knew more about my family tree than I did from conversations with my father. If she hadn't been a solicitor's secretary she could have had a career as the presenter of *Long Lost Families* or *Who Do you Think You Are?*

Audrey was back in Ireland now. She'd had a car accident in Washington after I left. She developed whiplash as a result. After a painful recovery process in hospital she decided America wasn't for her. She was going out with an accountant from Cork called Bobby. She got a job nursing in the Mater.

Afterwards she did a course in midwifery. She worked in a psychiatric hospital for a while as well. Her hours were crazy. I don't think she got much sleep on the nights Hugo and myself stayed up half the night talking about films or singing Bob Dylan songs. We ate burnt toast and drank endless cups of tea as we discussed things that were as inconsequential as the discussions over poker games in Ballina but just as important to us at the time. It can't have been much fun for Audrey going into work the next morning with the eyes falling out of her head, especially if she was on 'earlies.'

Jacinta married Dan. He was the man she'd been dating when she was in Washington. They moved to Florida after they got married. She came home to Dublin with him anytime she could.

Basil was home a lot too. He acted as Master of Ceremonies alongside Hugo. There was a friendly rivalry between the two of them about who could hold the floor longest. Hugo could do a medley of a dozen songs without blinking an eye. Basil could tell a heap of stories about the countries he'd visited in his job as a sales engineer. He seemed to have been around the world more often than the moon. The proudest moment of his life was writing on a backboard used by his hero Einstein once when he was giving a presentation. In later years he moved into the area of Cable TV. He met loads of celebrities from the film world there. In his capacity as a Joycean scholar he became friendly with the Chinese translator of *Ulysses*.

My mother was a quiet presence on these nights. She'd usually have some child on her knee that she was minding. She preferred listening to other people rather than doing anything herself. We tried to get her to sing 'Jerusalem' on many occasions but she rarely did. Performing wasn't her thing.

My father did his recitations. He put a huge amount of drama into them, especially 'The Green Eye of the little Yellow God.' 'Lasca' and 'Babette' were two other ones he did. They were more moving. He also liked to recite 'Dangerous Dan McGrew,' a more well-known one.

'I didn't do it well,' he'd say sometimes. No matter how much we praised him it wouldn't work. He'd tap his foot on the ground and puff his cigarette extra fast. That was how he showed his nerves. It showed how much it meant to him. Other times he'd know he did the recitations well. He could draw tears to your eyes with 'Lasca' and to his ones as well. He'd have been a great actor if he ever went in that direction. The performer in him came out on these nights now that he had no law courts to showcase his personality anymore.

Keith and Hugo did impersonations. Keith liked doing the classic film stars, - Bogie, Cagney and countless others. Hugo did Elvis and the modern ones. Pat played some rousing numbers on the accordion that got us all tapping our feet.

Bobby was too shy to sing but he'd usually have some witticism to entertain us. He chuckled merrily when Audrey took the floor. She was a great mimic and took us all off.

Jacqueline made the window panes vibrate with her voice. She liked to sing 'One Kiss, One Man.' Keith glowed with pride as he listened to her. As someone said of Ethel Merman, she could hold a note longer than the Chase Manhattan Bank.

Mary had a range of funny Irish songs and recitations. Her favourite partypiece was 'My Husband's Flannel Shirt,' a song she picked up at her mother's knee. It always got a great laugh. She had a few recitations too, or she might tell a funny story from real life. If there were children in the room she'd entrance them with fairytales.

Basil did songs like 'Big Strong Man' and 'The Parting Glass.' He liked 'Scarlet Ribbons' and 'The Dawning of the Day' as well. June sang 'Lovin' Dat Man' and 'I Used to Dream That I Would Discover.' She sang them just as well as the singers in the films of *Showboat* and *Oklahoma*. Ruth was seldom home but we remembered her in our mind's eye and our mind's ear. Her laughter was infectious.

Jacinta sang Hayley Mills songs. She duetted with Audrey on Eurovision classics like 'No No L'Eta' and 'Poupée de Cire Poupée de Son' from the sixties. They were able to sing both songs right the way through. I don't know if they understood the words or not. Maybe it made them more entrancing if they didn't.

I played the occasional song on my guitar: 'Bright Eyes' and 'Only Our Rivers Run Free' are two I learned the chords to. I really only knew three chords: C, F and G7. Occasionally I'd learn a fourth or fifth one if I really liked a song but it was such an ordeal trying to manipulate my fingers on the frets I lost the continuity of the music. The strings were sore on my fingers unless I played every day. After a while they developed calluses but if you stopped they got soft again. It was like everything else. You had to keep at it. My basic problem was that I lacked rhythm.

Hugo taught me 'Four Strong Winds.' Jacqueline's brother Paul taught me the chords for 'The House of the Rising Sun.' It was the first song most people learned on the guitar. I also knew a few Dean Martin ones. Sometimes I tried to imitate his voice.

The main song I did was Kris Kristofferson's 'Sunday Mornin' Comin' Down,' the best song he ever wrote in my opinion. Nobody captured Sunday better than he did in it. I always found something cathartic in the beautiful desolation of his lyrics there.

We've all been that person who went for a walk on a deserted Sunday morning to clear our head from the night before. Kristofferson invested the situation with so many resonances it took on the quality of an epiphany. I loved the line where he said of the church bell, 'It echoed through the canyons like the disappearing dreams of yesterday.'

The problem with sing-songs in your living-room is the fact that the applause generated is excessive for those of us who only sound good in the shower. Buoyed up by the praise of my family I started to think I had a voice. At one point I even embarked on a practice of inflicting myself on audiences in the singing pubs of Dublin.

My poor timing became a bugbear. There'd be a band behind me making me sound much better than I was but I never knew when to start a new verse. They'd be playing riffs and I'd be wondering at what point to come in. You can't teach someone something like that. You either have it or you don't. When Elvis was asked why he moved so much to his music he said, 'I don't know. It just happens.' Hugo had a theory that music was often created by mathematical formulas.

On Sunday nights in the Drake Inn in Finglas you were allowed up on stage to sing with the resident band. All you had to do was leave your name at the door on the way in. One Sunday I went there with Keith and Hugo. We all gave our names to the barman. He said, 'What's this, the Von Trapp family?'

Hugo sang Josef Locke's 'Goodbye' when his name was called. Keith did 'The Impossible Dream.' Both of them got big rounds of applause. Then it came to my turn. I decided to do Elton John's 'Goodbye Yellow Brick Road.' I don't know where I got the idea that I had a falsetto voice. I was only a few lines into it before I realised I was a key too high for my range. I should have stopped there and then but I didn't. My enthusiasm was bolstered by a man in the front row who was ossified. He kept clapping frantically.

I got to the second verse before my voice went. It had been hovering between octaves like a laughing hyena up to this point. Now it went totally dry. A few seconds later I was ushered from the stage by the barman. By now he'd realised the Von Trapp family had a rogue member. I apologised to the congregation as I stepped down. I thought they were going to boo me but instead they cheered, especially the ossified man in the front row. People who are ossified, I learned, tended to prefer bad singers to good ones. Maybe they can identify with them.

That night ended my career as a singer. Karaoke came in afterwards. The population of Finglas were able to breathe freely once again.

Graduate

I got my M.A. in 1975. I wasn't into graduation ceremonies so I avoided the official one. Instead I went down to the Botanic Gardens. Someone stuck a parchment in my hand and took a photograph of me. I put on my best Intellectual Scholar expression in honour of the occasion but I wasn't really thinking about anything more profound than whether we'd make it to the Addison Lodge for a pint before the Holy hour.

I didn't think I deserved any congratulations for what I'd got. The real people who needed to be congratulated on days like that were the parents who paid for their little brats to doss their lives away on campuses. They were the ones who should have got the mortarboards.

I tried to remember what I'd learned in the four years. Not much except some big words to describe books. Hopefully I'd forget them now and get on with my life.

I did my best to avoid the people I knew from university after I left it. Some of them became drop-outs and acted quite superior about it. Others drifted into boring jobs. The worst propped up an establishment they pretended to revolt against when they were in UCD. I always expected that to happen. I hoped it wouldn't happen to me.

Does university educate us? I'm not sure. It opened my eyes to the existence of some writers I didn't know about but I'd probably have found out about them anyway. I'm talking about the creative writers, not the academics. I thought it would be a good idea to put all the literary critics I'd been reading for the past four years up against a wall and shoot them. Then maybe real education could begin.

It was time to think about what career I might take up. Nothing was jumping out at me. Would I pound the streets trying to sell encyclopaedias to people who slammed the door on my face? Could I become a fulltime night watchman who slept on the job?

I flirted with the idea of doing law for a while despite my father telling me it was the last refuge of a scoundrel. I even registered for a course on it. Strangely enough it involved a lot of Irish. That put me off straight away. I felt I could have got through the academic side of it but I wasn't sure if I'd have the stomach for what came afterwards. It would have been easier if my father still had his practice. The fact that he hadn't meant I'd have to start from scratch. I'd probably have ended up in a dusty office in the sticks taking orders from some gobdaw who hadn't two brain cells to rub together.

I hated jobs where you had to serve an apprenticeship. It was one of the reasons I dropped out of the Commerce faculty. Our next door neighbour in the Villas had offered to 'article' me when I was studying for my B. Comm some years before. He said I'd only be earning a fiver a week for the first few months. The salary would increase as I worked my way up the ladder. I said thanks but no thanks.

In the end I plumped for primary teaching. The Minister for Education, John Wilson, was responsible for this. He initiated a scheme where university graduates could qualify to be teachers if we did a year in St. Pat's Training College. It was three for everyone else. He was trying to get lazyboneses like me off out arses and give us pensionable jobs in the process.

It was an offer I couldn't refuse even though teachers as a breed never held any huge appeal for me. I thought of them as boring sods who drove Volkswagens and wore second hand duffel coats with sticks of chalk hanging out of them. My father wasn't over the moon either. He wanted me to be a secondary teacher. 'NT stands for National Tramp,' he said.

Going into Pat's was like returning to secondary school. The students didn't talk about Sartre or Camus or Bob Dylan or Marlon Brando. They talked about Piaget. They didn't have straggly hair or lounge around corridors in scruffy clothes. The dissolutes among us had to lose our long faces and act as if we were put on the earth to make children happy.

How were we going to recover the decadence of UCD? One way was by drinking in the Cat and Cage, or 'The Cat' as we called it. It was a pub across the road from the college. We didn't talk much about the course when we were there.

The lectures were boring. The people who gave them spent too much time stating the obvious. My philosophy of teaching was that you were either good at it or you weren't. All the lecturing in the world couldn't change that. One of the lecturers was Michael Jordan, the father of Neil. I thought he'd be interesting but he turned out to be one of the most old-fashioned of the lot of them.

The fact that The Cat was so close to the college made it uncomfortable for us. The lecturers rambled in now and again for a drink. We could never enjoy ourselves when they were there. It was like drinking beside a priest or a parent. They'd say things like, 'Enjoying ourselves, are we?'

Our nights only began after they left. That was when we could let our hair down and remember that we were still young. One of the guys in our group kept singing a song I'd never heard before. It was about a person who left a steady job to become a singer. The key line in it was: 'I gave it up for music and the Free Electric Band.' I never found out what 'it' was. Presumably the job. I couldn't see him lasting long at teaching with that attitude.

In the middle of the year we were sent down to a Gaeltacht in Kerry to learn Irish. We shared a hostel and got to know one another pretty well. We were all in nearby quarters, both the girls and boys. I found it liberating after the segregation of Muredach's. It was even more liberating than UCD. Neither did it have any of the university's pretentiousness. We went to lectures in the mornings and played football in the afternoons.

We were told we'd be sent home if we were caught speaking English. Threats like that brought me back to the ethos of Muredach's. It sucked the love of Irish out of me. Would it not have been better to say, 'We're sending you down to Kerry to make you fall in love with the language'?

A girl from the class put a mouse in my bed one night for a prank. It was a live one. She didn't realise how paranoid I was about things like that. I felt something warm at my feet. It was as if someone was tickling me. I almost hit the ceiling when I saw it.

The lectures were as boring as the ones in Pat's but the drinking scenes were lively. There's nowhere like a pub to get to know someone. People I saw every day at the lectures in Drumcondra without speaking to them suddenly became like long lost brothers and sisters to me under the influence.

We practically drank Kerry dry. The hangovers in the mornings were horrendous. My mother always said it was the last drink of the night that did the damage. She was right but how could you finish on the second last one?

Glasses of water were placed on tables of the hostel every morning as the breakfasts were being cooked. We emptied them at the rate of knots for the dehydration. Some mornings the waitress had to refill them about a dozen times. She got good exercise from us going in and out of the kitchen.

Getting to know people well had its downside. A lot of slagging went on in the pub. Some of it related to my writing. The pieces I had in *New Irish Writing* came to the notice of one of the other people in the class. He was a fellow called Paddy Langan.

I hated it when something like that happened. I'd had experiences in the past where people changed their attitude to me when they found out about them. Some of them thought you were getting above yourself. Others feared you might use them for raw material.

It was an impossible situation for me to be in. I wrote things because I wanted them to be read and yet I didn't want anyone in my social circle to see them. How could you have one and not the other? Someone once defined writing as a self-invasion of privacy. It was like having a skeleton in the cupboard and taking it out to dance.

One night when we were in the pub Paddy said to me after a few jars, 'You're not a short story writer. You're just someone who writes short stories.' How can you react to something like that? It was a meaningless comment.

Later in the night he jumped up on a table saturated with beer and launched into 'The Green Fields of France.' I'd never heard the song before. It blew my mind, especially the line about the man getting his arse blown over his head after a bomb hit him. How did Paddy remember all the verses? It also blew my mind how he didn't fall off the table as he slithered around the place with the beer all over his shoes.

'You're not a short story writer. You're just someone who writes short stories.' Forty years later I still haven't figured out what he meant by that.

After we got back to Dublin one of the lecturers asked Paddy what he'd learned in Kerry. He said, '*Faic.*' That was the Irish for 'Nothing.' The lecturer said, 'So you learned nothing.' Paddy said, 'No. I learned the word *faic.*' What a crazy character.

Most of us tried to build on what Irish we'd picked up down there. Many nights after the lectures finished I went into the Conradh na Gaeilge club on Stephen's Green. It served beer into the small hours. That was an incentive to break into Gaelic. If someone was offering me alcohol in the middle of the night I'd speak to them in Swahili.

The Conradh was different to Muredach's in the sense that the people there didn't care too much about grammar. Many of them had grown up speaking it in their homes. Their interest was in chatting to one another rather than the finer points of irregular verbs. If they made a mistake on a technicality it didn't stop them jabbering on.

It was a joy to listen to them. Before going to the Conradh I was always inhibited when I spoke Irish. That was gone now. I threw myself into conversations and somehow fumbled my way through them. That was because the fear factor was gone. someone said once that the English beat the Irish language out of us for 700 years and then our own people felt obliged to beat it back in again. Such insanity seemed to summarise our history.

Teaching the language, unfortunately, wasn't as much fun as speaking it outside the school. I always felt teaching could never fulfil me in the long term but if I had other things going on I thought I might be able to stick it out for a few years, especially if I combined it with writing. I'd kept in touch with editors I'd worked with over the years so I knew I'd be able to do the odd articles for them.

I did some book reviews for *Books Ireland*. The editor was Bernard Share. He used to arrive at the door at dawn with some pretty substantial tomes. I was rarely up at that time. My mother used to take them in. One day I happened to see him pulling up outside the door. When I opened it he ran up to me with the books. 'I can't stay,' he said, 'I'm going to China in an hour.' I thought to myself: I'd love to have his kind of life.

Jeremy Addis replaced him after a few years. He stayed on as editor for most of my time with the magazine. I still remember his first phone call to me, 'My name is Addis – nothing to do with the toothbrushes.'

He let me choose what I wanted to review. I often went to his house to browse the shelves for books. It was enjoyable picking and choosing what I liked. He always had a huge selection. The house was also where his Christmas parties were held. We all drank too much punch at them. We enjoyed bitching about writers who were more successful than ourselves. Then we went back to our little enclaves, content in the knowledge that we were much better than them even if we were nobodies.

Alan Titley was the Irish editor of the magazine. He'd been one of my lecturers in Pat's. I was doing an exam one day that he was supervising. He tapped me on the shoulder and said he'd seen a story of mine that day in the *Irish Press*. It was a small world.

Because *Books Ireland* was a trade magazine you were expected to adopt a restrained style of writing in it. Sometimes it bordered on the obsequious. I tried to break out of it whenever I could. That was a dangerous line to tread as the publishers of the books I was reviewing often advertised in its pages. One time a publisher rang Jeremy in an apoplectic rage about something I'd written. He even threatened to withdraw his advertising from the magazine if I wasn't removed from its pages.

What I'd said was that Alice Taylor, one of his writers, was 'Literature's answer to Daniel O'Donnell.' Poor Alice. I hadn't meant to offend her. She was very successful so I felt she'd be able to take it.

She was but he wasn't. Jeremy explained to him that he wasn't responsible for what his writers wrote. Neither were their views necessarily shared by him. He died the following year. I hoped I wasn't a contributory factor.

I was also doing some reviews for a paper called *Hibernia* at that time. Every few months I'd go into their office in Beresford Place. The editor, Nuala O'Farrell, used to come down the stairs with a box full of novels. Some of them had up to 700 pages in them. I covered about a dozen books per column. I was only allowed write a few paragraphs about each one. A person could have spent their life on a novel and I'd be dealing with it in a sentence or two. It didn't make sense.

People sometimes wrote in complaining if I appeared dismissive about a book. I didn't concern myself too much about their sensitivities. Once you put yourself out there you had to contend with the brickbats as well as the bouquets.

One day I got a letter from a woman called Jennifer Lash thanking me for something I said about a novel she wrote. I thought nothing of it and stuffed it into a drawer. Years later I learned she was the mother of the actor Ralph Fiennes.

I was trying to write my own stuff now as well. It was the usual juvenilia. Adolescent scribblings that I thought would win me the Booker. I sent them off to various publications. One or two were accepted for publication the odd time but most of them came back. Sometimes in the same post as the rejected item I'd get a book to review from the same publisher. It was like getting a 'Dear John' in the same post as an invitation to a date. I put such review books into the bin on days like that.

Reviewing books often spoiled the experience of reading them. I was always wondering what I'd say. It was as if you were watching yourself reading.

The same applied to film reviews. I'd started doing these for a magazine in TCD when I was in UCD. UCD didn't have one. It was called *TCD Miscellany*. that was my first experience of going to press shows. I stood in a mouldy little room with the other reviewers before the films began. We were given cold tea and stale ham sandwiches as we exchanged cliches about the latest releases. I knew that was never going to work for me in the long term.

Press shows freaked me out. For one thing I liked to eat when I was watching a film. It was the way I'd grown up. I got my bag of Taytos in O'Hora's before going into the Estoria.

There was an almost reverential silence at these shows. If you put a Tayto into your mouth at one of them you couldn't bite on it until there was a noisy scene. It was like being at Mass and being afraid the Holy Communion wafer was going to melt in your mouth and make you commit a mortal sin by touching your teeth.

I didn't mind being quiet if I was at a film by some intellectual director like Ingmar Bergman. That was acceptable but at press shows you were meant to sit like a church-mouse even if you were watching Benny Hill looking up women's dresses.I also had a problem with the 'groupthink' atmosphere at them. You couldn't make up your mind about what you saw.

There were certain films you were allowed to like and certain ones you weren't. It depended on the director. If someone made a successful film last year it didn't matter if this year's one was junk. The goodwill carried over. Everyone liked and disliked the same films. They were afraid to step away from the pack in case they came across as philistines. It was like The Emperor's New Clothes.

I was expected to give good reviews to what we call 'feelgood' films today. Feelgood films almost invariably made me feel bad.

I preferred edgier material. there was a lot of that too. Hollywood had changed since I left Ballina. Crime films had become more violent. Intellectual ones were more incomprehensible. Romances weren't just 'Boy meets girl' anymore. sometimes they were 'Boy meets boy.' (Or in the case of *Equus*, boy meets horse.)

I found film critics to be a strange breed. Some of them didn't seem to know whether they enjoyed a film or not until they read what other people said about it. They also lacked humour. I read somewhere that Billy Wilder almost had a breakdown after showing the first cut of *Some like It Hot* to a group of them. Nobody laughed. 'Have we a dud on our hands?' he said to the man who ran the projector. The man said, 'Don't worry. This is an audience of critics. Critics don't laugh.' The film turned out to be one of the most successful comedies of all time.

I wrote for a lot of small magazines at this time. I rarely got paid for them but it was a buzz seeing my name in print. It didn't matter to me who I wrote for. One magazine I contributed to was said to be run by the IRA. I was told that if I sought payment for my articles I'd be kneecapped. I kept writing for nothing and held on to my knees.

The Lion in Winter

My father got me a job writing film reviews for a coffee table magazine called *Image* in 1977. It was edited by Anne Reihill. She'd been married to my cousin, Paddy Dillon-Malone. He was the son of Uncle Louis, my father's brother. I was glad to get the job. Maybe now, I thought, I'd be able to gush out all the thoughts about films that I'd had in the Estoria and the Savoy back in the fifties and sixties.

I only met Paddy once. He had a charismatic presence about him. 'Renaissance man' was a term that applied to him. He spoke five languages fluently. His other interests ranged from rugby to ballet. He said once, 'I may be the only ballet dancer ever to play for the London-Irish First Fifteen.' He sang the occasional come-all-ye at parties if the mood took him. That would have been something to hear. He had such a posh voice it would probably have been like listening to Prince Philip singing one. Or my father. Inside all these so-called elitists I always felt there was a common man trying to get out.

My father said to him once that the people of Ballina sometimes tried to pull him down by saying his father was only a ragman. The fact that he made his name from the drapery trade led to the slur. 'There's only one way to deal with people like that,' Paddy said, 'Tell them he rode into Ballina on an ass and cart.' My father loved his use of reverse psychology.

Paddy was only 40 when he died. He reminded me of John Milton's Lycidas, a noble soul cut down in his prime. He'd been educated at Stonyhurst. Afterwards he went into business. His brother Stephen told me once that he thought he'd have been more suited to the life of an academic.

He wrote a book about marketing that was widely praised. In the course of it he coined the term 'agoraphilia.' It was the opposite of agoraphobia. It meant a love of open spaces. Paddy died on one of his marketing expeditions to Paris. It seemed appropriate for an agoraphiliac.

He had three children with Anne: Patrick, Louise and Hugo. Hugo was tragically killed as a young man when a tree fell on his car during a thunderstorm. A person I knew thought it was our own Hugo who'd been killed when he heard the news on the radio. He knew him from me. He looked up his number in the phone book and dialled the Hugo who'd died by mistake. He got his answering machine. He said it was a very scary experience.

Anne's maiden name was McCoy. After Paddy died she married to a coal manufacturer called John Reihill. We were now able to say that she was 'the Reihill McCoy' - as in the expression 'the Real McCoy.'

My father met her in the Shelbourne Hotel one day to ask her if I could do film reviews for the magazine. She immediately said yes. That was how business was done in Ireland in those days. Maybe it still is. I was reminded of how Clive got me into Belvedere.

I was surprised he thought of it. He'd never expressed much interest in my film reviews. Had he heard me saying I wasn't that keen on being a teacher? He always said he wanted to have all his children set up before he died. Was he thinking he didn't have much time left to do that with his youngest?

He'd been losing his zest for life for a few years now. Towards the end of his time in Ballina he kept saying he couldn't wait to get out of it but at the end of the day it was his world. Now he became nostalgic for it, saying things like, 'Memory is the only friend that grief can call its own.'

It was a bit like my transition from Muredach's to Belvedere. I complained about Muredach's but at the back of it all I had a feeling for the place. It was also where my friends were.

My father had had a few falling-outs with the people he knew in Ballina over the years but they could have been remedied. The loneliness of Dublin was much worse. He always said he only wanted a back room to grow old in but as the years went on that back room became too uneventful for such a sociable man.

My mother tried to cheer him up when he felt down but she couldn't. It was like when she tried to get him to drink less. His determination was too much for her.

He was like a lion in winter as he sat in his bed gazing into space wondering where the world was going. She tried to get him to think of people worse off than him but he wouldn't be swayed. 'If someone across the road has cancer,' he'd say, 'it doesn't make my toothache feel any better.'

His grim moods weren't only caused by his own situation. He worried about the world in general as well. It was 'in a state of chassis,' as Sean O'Casey put it.

One day I listened to him talking about an article he read in the paper. It was about all the wheat that was burned every year in America to keep the price down. 'Why don't they just give it to the poor?' he said.

He believed the world was built on lies. He told me he read somewhere that a man invented a table tennis ball that didn't burst and his boss sacked him as a result. The company had been making most of their profits on the burst balls. It was the same with women's stockings. If someone found a way to make ladderless ones he'd lose his job too.

'Business is based on things breaking down,' he said. Or things not being used. He read in another book that salt manufacturers made more from what was left on people's plates than what was eaten. The oil they put in sardines, he said, was more valuable than the sardines. That's why the manufacturers put so many sardines in a can. It certainly wasn't out of generosity.

I was always interested in hearing these kinds of anecdotes but they made me sad too. They testified to a kind of cynicism about life. I felt he'd have been better off reading the novels by Sexton Blake and G.K. Chesterton and Hilaire Belloc that had carried him through so many years in Ballina, the ones that Sean McDonnell sold for £1 each that night in 1969 when he held the auction in the Town Hall. Who was reading them now?

He was depressed about the way religion was going as well. He didn't like Vatican II. Priests were strumming guitars on altars. They were wearing 'mufti' so they could blend in with lay people. Nuns were tumbling the wildcat up and down the aisles. He wanted the Latin Mass back.

I was with him on that. I preferred it when the priest had his back to us. I didn't think religion should be accessible. Vatican II made it prosaic. I wanted it to be mysterious. Wasn't that what religion was about? Weren't the decades of the rosary called Mysteries? There were things beyond understanding - like faith.

His main hobby was backing horses. He knew nothing about them. He'd put money on them if he liked their name. He usually put a few shillings each way on a massive number of them.

There was one horse he backed religiously. It was called Uncle Whiskers. Uncle Whiskers never won a race in his life. We had a joke about him: 'I backed Uncle Whiskers last week at twenty to one and he came in at half four.'

He was often last in races but my father still couldn't stop betting on him. 'I can't let him go now,' he'd say, 'If he won I'd never forgive myself.'

He was able to laugh about things like that when he was in good form but when he was feeling low he'd say things like, 'We kill time and then times kills us.' He liked quoting a passage from Omar Khayyam: 'The moving finger writes, and having writ moves on. Nor all thy piety nor wit can lure it back to cancel half a line, nor all thy tears wash out a word of it.'

He spent many of his days taking files out of a box and then putting them back in again. They'd be in exactly the same order when he was finished. It was like something out of Beckett.

The best fun you could have in life, he said, was hitting yourself on the head with a hammer: 'It's lovely when you stop.' He'd laugh uproariously when he said things like that. It was funny but there was a blackness in it too.

I wished he could have had more hobbies but he was never the type for them. Even his love for films dwindled when he came to Dublin. Like Keith he didn't have much time for the modern ones. The realist movement spelt the end of star power as far as he was concerned. There were no 'Edward Robinsons' anymore, no more Bogarts or Cagneys. Alfred Hitchcock had even gone flat.

One of the few films I remember seeing with him in Dublin was a routine thriller with Barry Newman called *The Vanishing Point*. I enjoyed it but it left him cold. In retrospect maybe the title was significant.

We went into the Royal Dublin Hotel for some sandwiches afterwards. He started to feel unwell before he ate them so we decided to go home. He dismissed it as indigestion but maybe it was something more. He took a Rennies tablet and passed it off.

There was a queue for taxis so I suggested getting on a bus. There was one outside the door. He wouldn't hear of it. I remembered Robert Morley saying once, 'Anyone seen on a bus after 30 is a failure in life.' He felt that way too. One of his favourite jokes concerned an aristocrat who falls on hard times in London. He hails a bus and says to the driver, 'Do you stop at the Dorchester?' The driver replies, 'What – on my salary?' I didn't get it at first. ('Stop' also means 'Stay' in England.)

He was nervous in the taxi. I knew that because of the way he kept tapping his foot. He always did that when he was worried about something. He tried to pass it off by talking about the film. When we got home he went to bed. He told my mother it was just indigestion.

After that night he didn't go into town much. He spent most of his time reading. He didn't read as many books as he had in Ballina. Newspapers were more to his taste now. They seemed to underline his belief that the world was going to hell. 'Good news is no news,' he said.

He watched a lot of television now even though he was bored by it more often than not. He found most of the programmes to be 'humbug' or 'Not worth a curse.' If he watched *Perry Mason* he got upset if the courtroom scenes were done wrong. There'd be hysterical outpourings of witnesses, sensationalistic climaxes, sudden revelations in testimony that weren't presented to the attorneys before the cases started. He didn't mind these sorts of indulgences in other genres but not the legal one. He'd spent too much of his life adjudicating cases. To see them falsified like this cut him 'to the quick.'

He said he was looking forward to seeing God. He wanted to put him in the witness box for all the misery he'd caused by making the world. 'I'll sue him,' he'd say, 'Let's see how he defends himself in the dock.' Most people who think about the afterlife have a fear of meeting their maker. I read once that Winston Churchill said, 'I'm not afraid of meeting God. He should be afraid of meeting *me*.' I thought of my father in the same light.

He died the month after he got me the *Image* job. He got a massive coronary. There hadn't been any symptoms.

He'd brought me breakfast in bed that morning. I told him I was going to town later in the day. He asked me to buy a book about Hitler that had just come out. He was fascinated by him as he was by all dictators. I inherited some of that fascination. World War II was well over before I was born. I hadn't experienced the horrific nature of his behaviour at first hand. Russia and China were bigger fears to mewhen I was growing up than Germany.

I was at a film when he got his attack. It was called *The Omen*. As I was watching it I got a premonition about him. There have only been a few times in my life that I got premonitions. That was the most frightening one.

As soon as I got home I knew something was wrong. There was a silence in the house. I went into his room to give him the Hitler book but he wasn't there. The clothes on his bed were tousled. There was a Super Ser heater in the middle of the floor. His dressing gown was on top of it.

I went into the kitchen. My mother was sitting there crying. Audrey was beside her. She was crying too. Where was my father? They didn't need to say anything. Their faces said it all but I couldn't take it in. It was too sudden. He couldn't have died. He was my father. All our fathers are immortal.

'We did our best to save him,' my mother said. The doctor was called but it was too late. He kept

246

doing CPR on his chest. She wouldn't let him stop even when it was clear he wasn't going to respond. Then the ambulance came and took him off.

I was in shock but also numb. I didn't know what to feel. We sat there saying nothing as a clock ticked on the wall. Was he really dead? I believed it and I didn't believe it. Sometimes you think you're taking something in when you're not.

They told me the details of what happened. It was an argument with some coalmen that brought on the attack. He thought they under-counted the bags they delivered and they got aggressive with him when he confronted them about it. I knew he wouldn't have been able to deal with that.

I imagined him being intimidated by them, his blood pressure rising and his foot tapping the way it did when he got worked up. He would have been puffing his pipe fast too. That was another sign.

The coronary wasn't surprising to me. A life of smoking and drinking ensured that. His bad diet and sedentary lifestyle made him an accident waiting to happen even if he'd never taken a drink or a cigarette in his life.

We were relieved he died fast. He wouldn't have been able to cope with a hospital or a nursing home. We were also relieved he died before my mother. If she went first, he often said, he'd have drunk himself to death.

By the time he died he wasn't drinking much. I used to smuggle him in the odd six-pack of Guinness when my mother wasn't looking. She accepted his passing as she accepted everything else life threw at her. I heard her crying in her room in the nights afterwards. It was so low as to be almost inaudible. She was never demonstrative in her emotions.

She didn't like talking about him. It brought it all back too much. All she said was, 'Thank God he didn't suffer.'

Aunt Florence thought she'd had a hard life with him. If she did she was able for it. Fate brings people together for a reason. She'd have been bored by a more straightforward man. Her kindness would have been wasted if there was nobody to use it on. As she said, a chair was for sitting on.

My father indulged his appetites instead of living a life of austerity. People gave toasts to him after he died. They said things like, 'May he be in heaven a half hour before the devil knows he's dead.' Because he sucked on the pap of life, as the expression went, it was as if he'd have to sneak in the Pearly Gates when St. Peter wasn't looking.

I never went for that line of thinking. I didn't like goody-goodies who never walked on the grass or ran a red light or looked left and right before crossing their legs. He was a full-blooded human being who threw himself into life 100%. I couldn't think of God disapproving of that. He wasn't a spoilsport. He didn't create us as spirits.

The words of 'The Parting Glass' came back to me:

Of all the money that e'er I had
I spent it in good company
And all the harm I've ever done
Alas it was to none but me.

He often talked about heaven. He was curious about what age he'd be in it. Would he be a baby? A young boy? An old man?

'I might end up in the other place,' he laughed, 'with Mido Cooligan.' It might have been more fun. Heaven for the climate, hell for the company.

I found it hard to believe in heaven. How could there be a place where you were happy all the time? Almost every good day of my life so far was followed by a bad one and every bad day by a good one. That was the way things worked for most people. I found it difficult to conceive of a state of permanent happiness. I wasn't even sure I'd want it. Most feelings, I thought, was that much stronger for not being there all the time. It was like my father's point about hitting yourself over the head with a hammer. It was lovely when you stopped.

I said that to a priest once. He said, 'You're thinking about it in earthly terms.' But what other way could I think of it? I was born on earth.

My father donated his body to the science department in TCD. 'If you're ever in Trinity,' he used to joke, 'Go in and see me dangling there.' It was where he spent so many years failing all those exams. Now he'd be there forever. It seemed appropriate.

Basil wrote a tribute to him that was printed in the *Western People*. He wrote it in the form of a poem. He'd done some of his essays in Muredach's that way as well. It was very moving. He called *Primrose Hill*. We used to be brought walking there anytime he was visiting the family vault in Leigue Cemetery.

I didn't remember these walks like Basil did. I probably wasn't long out of the cradle when we took them. The opening line of the poem mentions Kathmandu, the location for my father's favourite recitation, *The Green Eye of the Little Yellow God:*

Though never been to Kathmandu,
more east than Lake Lausanne
I saw a vast frontier from Primrose Hill.
My father's disquisitions
altercations, recitations
entranced me
as we slowly walked along.

I was probably better acquainted with Kathmandu than Crossmolina or Bonniconlon when I was growing up. That was as a result of hearing him recite *The Green Eye of the Little Yellow God* so many times. He invested such drama in it you couldn't fail to be moved.

In the next verse Basil wrote:

> '*A monologue for every lip*
> *to mimic and expound,*
> *his monocle contracted with remorse*
> *dilated with emotion,*
> *pain and fear – his repertoire*
> *flamboyant, debonair.*
> *We often sauntered up this path,*
> *attended to his tale and stave.*
> *We loved him*
> *for the way he gave himself*
> *on Primrose Hill*
> *walking by the ditch*
> *outside the sheltered towns*
> *and down by Attymas.*'

Lines like those made me feel part of something that took place when I was too young to remember it. 'Nine little ducklings,' Basil wrote, 'trekking, tripping up the road/intent to hear adage and anecdote/ in veneration of his spell.'

The students in the training college were supportive to me at this time. A person from the class had died some months before. He was a clerical student who'd gone to Brazil for a holiday. He drowned while swimming. He was a strong swimmer but he'd gone into a bay that had a deceptive shelf in the water. Everyone was shocked.

It was only weeks after my father died that I realised how much in shock I was about my own bereavement. It hit me for six then.

Delayed reactions are always worse than immediate ones. The energy drained itself from my system. I brooded about him the way he told me he'd brooded about his own father when he died. He'd been very close to him. He got a heart attack saying the rosary one night. My father was 24 at the time. He left a huge gap in his life. My father left a huge one in mine too. History was repeating itself.

Everyone becomes a child when a parent dies. In another way his death hardened me. On teaching practice I became more relaxed in front of the pupils. I wasn't shy with them suddenly. I became like the other students in Pat's, the confident ones who had 'ink in their blood.'

But I couldn't stop thinking of him. He was gone from us like Lasca, like Babette. No longer would the kitchen resound with his laughter. No longer would he write letters to the *Irish Times* bemoaning the end of civilisation as we knew it. No longer would he toss matches from his pipe into the fire. No longer would he bring me tea and toast in the mornings in his pyjamas, the blue ones with the white cord. No longer would the tea drip onto the toast as it teetered at the side of the plate.

He'd been taken from us quickly and without warning. It was the vengeance of the little yellow God.

The King and I

Anne Reihill asked me if I wanted to take a break from my reviews on account of my father having died. I told her there was no need for me to do that, that writing was therapy for me. I hoped she didn't think that sounded cold-blooded.

A few weeks later she asked me if I'd like to do an interview for her. It was with the singer Geraldine Branagan. She would later marry Phil Coulter. I didn't know a thing about either of them at the time. Anne told me she'd come fifth in the Eurovision Song Contest some years before. 'I think she'll be big,' she said.

I drove out to her house in Castleknock. She talked to me for a few hours. I had no tape recorder in those days and I didn't take notes. After our conversation finished I went out to my motorbike and thought: I'm not going to be able to remember anything she said. I drove to a bar and asked the barman for a coffee and a few sheets of paper.

As I guzzled the coffee I started to write. I'd never learned shorthand but I had my own form of it. I abbreviated a lot of words. 'Function' was 'fn.' 'Point' was 'pt.' I used mathematical symbols for some words. A plus sign meant 'and' or 'with.' A triangle meant 'change.' It was something I'd dredged up from my memory from doing Maths in the Commerce year at UCD.

After a few minutes everything started to flood out of me. I got energy from somewhere. Maybe it was what had been drained out of me after my father's death.

It wasn't the first time I managed to absorb information in some compartment of my brain and regurgitate it when I needed to. I'd done it for the

Leaving Cert as well. I had no long term memory worth speaking of but a good short term one.

I remembered reading about an interview that Truman Capote had done with Marlon Brando once. He got him drunk and Brando opened up to him about intimate details in his personal life. Capote had a photographic memory. He wrote down everything Brando said after he went back to his apartment. Then he had it printed. Brando never forgave him. I hoped Geraldine wouldn't have been as upset with me. I doubted she would be. She hadn't said anything off the record to me.

There was another fatality that year – Elvis Presley. August 16th 1977 imprinted itself on my mind almost as much as February 11th, the day my father died. First a father and now a brother. Or a soulmate. That's what it felt like. Elvis went out like a light too. Both of them lived hard and died easy. They shared a quicksilver temperament as well as a devilish charm. Maybe it was fitting that they died within a few months of one another.

I went up to my room and looked at the poster I had of Elvis on my wall. He was in a blue jumpsuit in it. The sweat was dripping off him. I imagined it was from the early seventies when he went back to live performing in Las Vegas. It was the first thing I'd put on the wall when we moved into the Villas.

Beside it was the poster of Bob Dylan from *Nashville Skyline*. A newspaper I read a few days later said Dylan locked himself in a room when he heard Elvis died. He couldn't talk to anyone. I knew how much it meant to Dylan that Elvis recorded his song 'Tomorrow is Such a Long Time.' He said he'd never sing it himself again after that. He'd just heard the definitive version.

'The first time I heard Elvis,' he said, 'It was like bustin' out of jail.' Elvis had problems with Dylan's ideas on politics just as Dylan had with Elvis' ones but music over-rode things like that. They never met. I wondered what would have happened if they did. Probably similar to what happened when Elvis met the Beatles – nothing till they started jamming.

I wrote a tribute to him in the *Western People*. At one stage I compared him to Mickey Mouse and Coca-Cola in his iconic status for Americans. I quoted a line I'd read in one of his biographies, 'In the fifties, Elvis rebelled against the establishment. In the sixties he joined the establishment. In the seventies he *was* the establishment.'

It never bothered me that he went downhill in the sixties. He got it back with the live concerts. But it was these that killed him. He'd still have been alive if he kept making those stupid films he did in the sixties.

That was the sad thing about concerts. Robbie Robertson said in *The Last Waltz:* 'The road took so many of the people we loved.' It was a good way of putting it. 'The Road.' It was as if it was a human thing that claimed them. It reminded me of when someone drowns in Ireland and we say, 'The sea took them.' Maybe 'the road' is an urban manifestation of that prhenomenon.

Most of the singers who died 'on the road' were in their twenties. Elvis was different. He was 42. To many of his critics he was a joke when he died. Not me. The weight he put on made him even more impressive in my view. It made him look like an opera singer. He had such a powerful voice, if he was born in a previous era he might have become one.

The T Rex guitarist Marc Bolan died a month after Elvis in a car crash but people hardly noticed. There were so many headlines devoted to Elvis it was as if he didn't matter. That was always the way it was in show business. Bette Davis was in hospital once when there was an industrial dispute in the printing world. She was asked if she thought she might have died.

''During a newspaper strike?' she said, 'You must be joking.' We were living in an age where death wasn't as important as the size of one's obituary.

Bolan wasn't the only other person to die at this time. An unknown pedestrian was knocked down by one of the many cars that congregated around Graceland for Elvis' funeral. He didn't get many headlines either. How must his family have felt? At times it seemed like our celebrity culture was going out of control. At the end of the day a life was a life. As Elvis himself said when people called him The King, 'There's only one King.' He was referring to Jesus. That was another thing I loved about him – his humility.

He died the day before he was due to start a new tour. It was going to be his first time facing the public since his bodyguards wrote their book about him, the Judas one that exposed his wild habits and his drug-taking. He was nervous of how it would be received. John Lennon said, 'It's always the courtiers who kill the king.'

Some months before he'd gone on a rant on stage saying that he never took anything but prescription drugs. For Elvis that made everything all right but the public thought differently. To the public drugs were drugs, period. They were right. It was drugs that killed him.

After he died, the 'Elvis industry' began. People who'd dismissed him as a has-been couldn't wait to buy his records fast enough now. Everyone started writing books about him, from his dentist to his gardener and all the women who said they were his secret lovers. He became a franchise.

Near-broke when he died, he was now a multi-million dollar earner. On television there were retrospectives commending him for his genius, for pushing back the barriers of music, for being a pioneer and an inspiration. As I listened to them I thought of a comment a friend of Brendan Behan's made after he died. Like Elvis, he'd largely been discarded by people in his last years but his funeral drew a huge crowd. The friend said, 'It's a pity they didn't give him the flowers when he could still smell them.'

Paul Brady wrote a song some years later called 'Nobody Knows.' It starts off with the lines, ''Nobody knows why Elvis threw it all away. Nobody knows what Ruby had to hide.' Ruby was Jack Ruby, the man who shot Lee Harvey Oswald. I had no problem with that line but I objected to him saying Elvis threw it all away. He was a drug addict. His first drug was music and his second one prescription pills. One caused the other. Brady is one of my favourite singers but he's off target in this song.

Elvis was an icon. If Brady was one he might be aware of the pressures that brings. Elvis was once asked how he felt about his image. He replied, 'It's very hard to live up to an image. Let me put it like that.' Trying to do so cost him his life. The same thing happened to countless other icons. Would Brady say Jimi Hendrix 'threw it all away'? Or Jim Morrison? Or Janis Joplin? Or Kurt Cobain? Elvis will be remembered long after Paul Brady is forgotten even if he lives to be 100. Singers who live to great ages are often middle of the road. There are exceptions, of course, like Bob Dylan, but when someone is touched by greatness we should expect them to have a flaw somewhere as well. Such a flaw can make the greatness blossom and then blow itself out. Like Icarus, they fly too close to the sun.

Genius and self-destruction often go hand in hand. The intensity that pushes people towards the pursuit of excellence often pushes them towards death as well. We can see that in people like Vincent van Gogh and some other artists. Very few of us outside the artistic field experience such intensity.

There's no way Elvis could have stayed on the road for the eight years between 1969 and 1977 without some form of artificial stimulation. Colonel arker had him doing two shows a day for many of those years. His unnatural life led to his unnatural death. He was the loser in that scenario. His fans are the winners because we have a record of those years – no pun intended. Paul Brady should realise that considering he's in the same business himself.

Elvis' bodyguard Sonny West tried to get him off the pills once. Elvis refused. He said to West, 'I need 'em, man, I need 'em.' He couldn't have put it more plainly than that.

One of the venues on the tour he was planning when he got his heart attack was Syracuse. That was where Basil was living. He'd booked a ticket to go to the concert. He wasn't as big a fan of Elvis as I was but he was still shocked about him dying. So near and yet so far.

Basil was married by now. So were Ruth and Jacinta. June and Audrey were engaged. It seemed to be a pattern in families that people married after a parent died. Was it a kind of line they drew in the sand now that their figurehead was gone?

I thought of those films I used to see as a child in the Estoria where cowboys were being attacked by Indians. If they shot the chief the Indians always turned back. Maybe it was the same with families. The father was dead and the unity was gone. It was like the principle of entropy. Things fell apart, as Yeats said. The centre couldn't hold.

June got married to her boyfriend Pat shortly after Elvis died. It was a quiet wedding, at least until Donie O'Donoghue arrived. He was our friend from Kerry. After everyone finished their meal he jumped up on the wedding table and started doing an Elvis impression.

He had the movements to perfection. He even looked like him. His pout helped him tilt his lip up exactly the way Elvis did. It was nice to know someone was remembering him. Even though Donie was an accountant by profession - and later on a barrister - music was his real passion.

Before we went home he told me about a night Bruce Springsteen tried to get to see Elvis by climbing over the fence at Graceland. It was at the beginning of his career, during the *Born to Run* tour. It was 3 a.m. and he was passing by in a cab. He saw lights on. He'd just been on the cover of *Time* and *Newsweek* and was feeling good about himself. He wanted to show the magazines to Elvis, to tell him how much his career was influenced by him. Unfortunately Elvis wasn't home at the time.

Bruce was regarded as an intruder. He was almost arrested. 'I just wanted to see the guy,' he kept saying to Elvis' Uncle Vester. Vester was guarding the gate that night.

The Boss was escorted back to his cab. He often thought back to that night in later years, becoming depressed at never having had the chance to meet his hero. I knew exactly how he felt.

Talk and Chalk

The minor problem of getting a job reared its head after I left Pat's. I applied to everything I saw in the papers. There wasn't much available. I didn't want an office job. Spending my day with people my own age wouldn't have worked for me because I wasn't sociable.

The way I looked at it I could only work with children or on my own. That meant becoming a teacher or a writer. Becoming a writer in 1977 would have netted me about £10 a week. In teaching you got paid good money for saying things like 'Two and two is four' or 'Don't walk on the grass.' In writing you got paid buttons for spending hours sweating over how a line looked.

I interviewed for a job in a small school in Clonsilla. I had references from some of the UCD priests. One of them was from Desmond Connell. He went on to become Archbishop of Dublin. The clergy were much more involved in Primary Education at that time than they are now. When I was told I got the job I wondered how much that reference helped.

Like the women in the cowboy films, I 'taught school.' It was great to be getting a salary. I never had much pocket money in the past. Now suddenly I had more than I knew what to do with.

As soon as I cashed my first pay cheque I threw all the notes into a drawer and took them out as I needed them. Most of them went into pub tills.

On Fridays I used to drink with some of the teachers from another school down the road. We usually had a game of basketball in their gym first. 'You have to earn your pints,' one of them liked to say. He had a Mars bar after each drink. He said it stopped them going to his head.

One day during a game I watched a player fall awkwardly. Someone else fell on top of him and he let out a screech. When I looked at him I saw his foot was at right angles to his leg. It was a horrific sight. A few minutes later one of the other players said he could fix it but it would be painful. After taking a deep breath he twisted it back into shape. It must have been agonising for the player. I can't imagine it being much fun for the man who fixed it either. I wasn't able to play basketball for a while after that.

Our drinking sessions often lasted well into the evening. I used to drive home afterwards. The attitude to driving with drink on you was casual in those days. I was often stopped by guards and waved on even if I was smelling strongly of it.

There were eight classes in the school. Girls and boys were mixed in them. I envied them that. It made getting to know the opposite sex so much easier than it had been in my time.

'The girls mollify the boys,' I said to one of the other teachers. 'I agree,' he said, 'They turn them into mollies.'

Country kids were generally more obedient than city ones. In my early days behind the rostrum I didn't have any discipline problems.

The principal had been in the Christian Brothers for a while before he got married. He was a nice man but I never fully relaxed with him. If the children in my class were behaving themselves he'd say with a grin, 'Enjoy it while it lasts.' There was always the idea of a threat around the corner.

The Clonsilla community was closely-knit. The downside was that you felt on display because everyone knew everyone. The lollipop lady's son was in my class. So was the footballer trainer's one, and the principal's daughter.

I became friendly with a lot of the parents. They liked my easygoing ways. Maybe they expected me to be different because of my writing background. At parent-teacher meetings sometimes they looked at me intensely and asked me what their children should be reading. I always gave them the same answer: 'The Cornflakes packet.' From my experience, I said, it had more appeal than some prize-winning novels.

We chatted about things that had nothing to do with teaching. For a time my life in Clonsilla became as important to me as my one in the Villas. The job consumed me. I went to sports events, dramas, social occasions where I interacted with people as if I'd known them all my life. For a time I saw myself spending my life in this world, becoming almost like a surrogate parent to the children in my charge.

My classroom was a prefab with a little cloakroom off it. The principal called it 'The Horsebox.' It wasn't quite that small but I felt a bad wind could have blown it over. Field mice trotted in every now and then, causing hysteria to the nervous children. Birds sometimes flew into the cloakroom if the door was left open. There was no window in there so it was hard to get them out. The principal used to wrap them in a sheet and carry it outside. I didn't trust myself to do that. I'd probably have smothered them.

I often came in early to draw pictures on the blackboard. They were usually scenes from books that the pupils transcribed into their copies. They were quiet when they were drawing. It meant I was in charge when they came in. That was their noisiest time. The first half hour of the day, I learned, was the most important. If I controlled that I controlled the rest of it as well.

Having a job grounds you. You stop thinking about philosophy when you're worried about getting into work on time. All my life up to now had been escapism – films, books, even school. We studied subjects like science and geometry in Muredach's as if they contained the secret of eternal life. I wasn't convinced.

Isaac Newton was said to have discovered something called gravity when an apple fell onto his head from a tree. I could never understand the fuss about that. What kind of an idiot would think it could fall upwards? If I got bonked on the head by an apple falling from a tree I'd be too busy cursing to think of anything like gravity. If it happened in Gildie Ahern's orchard I'd have been more concerned about doing the 100-yard dash back to the safety of our back yard than contemplating scientific principles.

A man called Pythagoras proved that the square on the hypotenuse of an equilateral triangle was equal to the sum of the squares on the other two sides. I thought Pythagoras should have got out more.

Someone called Archimedes discovered that when you got into the bath you displaced you own weight in water. He got so excited about this that he ran down the street in the nude shouting 'Eureka!' He needed to get out more too. But maybe there weren't that many places to go in Greece 2000 years ago. If you weren't inventing things, all you could do was look at the scenery.

I wondered what the point of Latin and Greek were too. And even literature. How could D.H. Lawrence help me with an 11-year old haemophiliac? Could William Carlos Williams help me communicate with a boy whose mother was shooting up? Could he help me communicate with one whose father was doing 'hard time' in Mountjoy jail?

I became real in a ramshackle pre-fab in the wilds of North Dublin. I taught the children fairytales but their lives were far more cerebral than mine. I learned from them instead of them learning from me. I learned from their parents too – the butcher, the baker and the candlestick maker. All life was here from the lollipop lady up.

I took a special interest in art. I hadn't done it as a subject in Muredach's. Now it became an obsession with me. Some of the other teachers used their art class to get the pupils to do still lifes of flowers. I was more interested in craft than art. I'd never been encouraged to use my hands as a child. My father filled the house with books. Clive and Basil were fairly good at fixing things but the rest of the boys weren't.

My parents never encouraged me to use my hands. That's probably why I had an ambition to go to the Tech. we all want to be our opposites. I'm sure a lot of people who went to the Tech would have loved to have the opportunity to go to Muredach's.

I indulged my technical side in a small way in the art classes. I got the kids to make rocking chairs with clothes pegs and windmills with lollipop sticks. For the clumsier ones I ended up doing most of the construction myself. The important thing was to give them something to bring home.

I read a book once called *Medals for Everyone*. It was about our new education system. Children got awards regardless of whether they deserved them or not. It was an attempt to create a feeling of well-being in pupils, especially insecure ones.

I never got a medal in Ballina, not even on sports day when we had three-legged races and egg and spoon ones.

The 'medals for everyone' culture is the same one that produced fathers who keep hugging their daughters and calling them 'Princess.' It's the one that produced mothers who tell their children they love them fifty times a day.

My parents never told me they loved me but I knew they did. The more times the word 'love' is used in the world, it seems to me, the less it's practised. The huggers and medal-givers often produce monsters. Sometimes they tell their children they love them when they aren't sure if they do or not. Why is it that the 'I love you' society has resulted in more hatred and dysfunctionality than any one preceding it?

I had to do a diploma for the first two years in Clonsilla. That meant having an inspector in the room for a whole day in each of those years. He went through my notes and looked at how I dealt with the pupils for every second of five continuous hours. I didn't think that's a fair system. A child could have been acting up that day and wrecked your lesson. It wouldn't have been a fair reflection of your general work.

Some children went out of their way to create trouble if there was an inspector in the room. I remember a trouble-maker saying to me one day, 'Is he here for you or for us?' I wouldn't have thought of saying something like that in a million years when I was his age. I automatically assumed the inspectors of my childhood were for us.

After the freewheeling atmosphere of UCD it was a culture shock to have to listen to an inspector telling me I needed to brush up on my discipline. I read a story by the writer John McGahern that impressed me. It was about an upper class man from the forties who went into Primary Teaching much against his will. He only did so because his family came down in the world and he had to make a living. One day an inspector came into his class and read him the Riot Act about his teaching methods.

The man wasn't used to being talked down to by someone from the lower orders so he decided to take action. He went home and got a rifle. That afternoon he came back to the school and gave the inspector both barrels. I didn't go quite that far.

Sometimes I patronised the pupils. 'We're not children,' they'd say if they thought I was talking down to them. The girls were particularly indignant about this. They wanted to be older. They were like children who walked around the place in their mother's high heels, their feet barely fitting half way down. Sometimes they added years to their ages in their wish to be older. In later years, I thought, they'd probably take them off.

It was the way with everything. I often saw boys behind the pre-fabs swapping cigarette butts. Cigarettes were like holy grails then. Some years down the road that would change. They'd curse themselves for the day they started smoking if they got health problems. Why did people always want one thing and then its opposite?

'Act your age and not your shoe size,' I'd say to them. They hated that too. It reminded them of their parents. I was supposed to be *in loco parentis*. So the handbooks said. I never tried to assume that role. I'd have preferred to be plain *loco*.

The other teachers were friendly. They made me feel at home immediately. We had great chats between the classes.

The principal was a nice man but he was very conservative. He left the room in anger one day when we were discussing the subject of rape. The next day a note was left on the table saying, 'Rabhadh – no sensitive subjects to be discussed.' ('Rabhadh' was Irish for 'Warning.')

I felt strongly about the subject. I'd recently been a juror on a rape case. I felt the guy on the stand was guilty. So did most of the other jurors but the judge directed us to enter an innocent plea due to lack of evidence. My heart went out to the girl who'd been raped. It was a tremendous ordeal for her to have to testify.

She was given the third degree by the defence counsel. He asked her a lot of intimate questions that seemed irrelevant to me. Meanwhile the accused man sat listening to it all with a grin on his face. She knew him. He'd raped her in her own bedroom and he still got off. Meanwhile she was traumatised. I was shocked by the whole experience. It was as if women who were raped and reported it went through more pain than those accused of the crime. We had a robust discussion of the subject in the staff-room that day but because of the principal's 'rabhadh' it was never brought up again.

At times I felt like a pupil of his rather than a colleague. 'You're too soft on the pupils,' he used to say to me. I knew he was right but I wasn't sure if I could change or even if I wanted to. Everyone had their own style of teaching. Usually it was based on their personalities.

Some of the pupils in my glass came from rough homes. I thought they needed a break. 'Don't be led on by them,' he said, 'At the end of the day it's them or you.' Another one of his admonitions was, 'Don't smile before Christmas.'

The other teachers thought I was too soft as well. If I ever said a pupil was disturbed they'd say something like, 'He isn't disturbed, he's just disturbing.' I thought this kind of thinking was unfair. Children who came from broken homes couldn't be seen as bold. They didn't know what they were doing half the time.

In those days we didn't use terms like ADHD. I noticed some of them couldn't concentrate for any length of time. It was something I empathised with. Why should they be interested in listening to me blabbing on about Irish verbs when they had their Arnold Schwarzenegger films or Teenage Mutant Ninja Turtles to busy themselves with?

I suffered from it myself. It was one of the things that made it hard for me to review films. Sitting in a seat for 100 minutes was an endurance test. I was like a cat on a hot tin roof. I'd have to get out of it every so often to stretch my legs.

I still got invitations to attend press shows. Most of them ended up in the bin. The same tension prevailed at them as in the days I'd started reviewing for *TCD Miscellany*. In the cinemas I watched them with my grub in my mouth and my feet up on the seat in front of me if there was nobody around. If I wasn't enjoying something I walked out in the middle of it. Like Uncle Louis I didn't pay to be bored.

Patience was never one of my virtues. It wasn't one of my father's either. I remember him being on the phone one day when he was put on Hold by a secretary. She was ages coming back to him. When she finally came back he said to her, 'Did you enjoy your holidays?'

I tended to give better reviews to short films than long ones because of my patience problem. It was the same with books. I could only read a few pages at a time without getting restless. I probably inherited that habit from my father. I'd pick up a book and then drop it and pick another one up. Then I'd drop that.

I didn't care too much about storylines. I was always looking for an image or a turn of phrase to stimulate me. I felt I was soaking up different styles of different people that way. It was like litmus paper. I felt they'd percolate into me. I'd get into the mood of a film the same way. It kept my concentration going.

Norman Mailer said once that if he was on the phone to someone and another person was talking to him in the room where he was phoning from he didn't cut them off. He preferred to keep the two conversations going. He said he was able to absorb 60% of both conversations. That was a net total of 120%. It beat devoting himself to either one by 20%. It was the Andy Warhol way of looking at life, grabbing at everything in a skittish way. Maybe this was what T.S. Eliot meant when he said modern man suffered from a 'dissociation of sensibility.'

One day in 1980 I wandered into the Savoy in O'Connell Street. Martin Scorsese's film *Raging Bull* was showing. The scene that was on when I went in was the one where Joe Pesci is trying to adjust the reception on a television for Robert de Niro. The acting between them was unbelievable. It got even better in later scenes. I watched the film to the end and then sat through it again. You could do that in those days. I got even more out of it the second time. Things often meant more the second time you saw them. The film went on to become my favourite of all time.

Or rather my second favourite. My favourite was another Robert De Niro one, *The Deer Hunter*. I went to it one night a few years previously with Harry Clifton, my friend from UCD. We'd been drinking in Doheny & Nesbitts beforehand. It was a late night movie. I was so sleepy from the drink I fell asleep half way through it. When I woke up I had the feeling I'd seen something special. How had I not been able to stay awake for it?

The next night I dragged Keith and Hugo along to it. I said to them, 'This is either the greatest film ever made or one that'll put you to sleep.' It turned out to be the greatest film ever made. Even *Shane* had to take a back seat to it. Keith liked it. That was saying something as he rarely watched modern films.

Hugo was almost as impressed by it as I was. We still shared a lot of the same ideas about things even if we had our own special favourites. He talked a lot about Wim Wenders' film *Paris, Texas* when it came out. It had as hypnotic an effect on him as *The Deer Hunter* had on me.

By now he was making more and more films with his Fuji camera. He wrote scripts for us and we acted them out. He put me in one of them where I had a dramatic death scene as an IRA man getting gunned down off the Iona Road. It was a development from clicking my fingers to songs from *West Side Story* as the Ballina equivalent of Russ Tamblyn.

I was more of a watcher than a doer when it came to films. I wouldn't have had the patience for all the hard work being a director entailed. When videos came in I was able to indulge my impatience more by fast forwarding through the parts I didn't like. You could watch them any way you liked unless there was someone else with you who didn't share your tastes. Soren Kierkegaard said once, 'We can only understand our lives backwards but we have to live them forward.' Not if you have a remote control, Soren. It's a pity we can't use it in real life when people are telling us things that bore us.

You couldn't watch films back to front before videos came in but you could always read books that way. I often started in the middle of them and worked my way to the end. If I was impressed I'd go back to the beginning afterwards. I'd read what J.D. Salinger called 'the David Copperfield crap.'

I don't know how many times I watched *Raging Bull* over the years. It must have run into double figures. I even got Keith to sit through it one day. That was some achievement on my part. He regarded it as heresy to watch anything made after 1959.

I was still reviewing films for *Image* and some other places at this time. I felt the principal thought I was more interested in that side of my life than the teaching. Maybe he was right. It made me feel like the weak link in the teaching staff sometimes.

My soft approach to the pupils led to other kinds of problems. They moved around my classroom much more than the ones in the other classes. That didn't go down well with the principal either.

'We're not progressive here,' he said, 'This is a Three Rs school.'

I was never much for the Three Rs. I liked Dennis Miller's quote, 'You know there's a problem with the

269

education system when you realize that out of the three Rs, only one of them begins with R.'

To be a successful teacher, I learned, I was expected to get a nervous breakdown if a pupil dropped their pen on the floor or came in without their lessons done. I was only able to have such breakdowns when I was in a bad mood. When I was in a good one I had to try and fabricate anger. It wasn't easy unless you were a very good actor. I wasn't in Robert de Niro's class.

My favourite children were the ones who gave me the most problems. I hated what they were doing to me in the classroom but they were my best friends outside it. The swots made my life easy in the classroom but I had nothing to say to them after the bell went. Maybe that's why I should never have become a teacher.

I felt like a juvenile delinquent in the classroom sometimes. I hadn't had a chance to misbehave in my youth. Now I was trying to do it vicariously through the new generation. I was like a prison warden who bonded with his Death Row inmates, a kidnapper who wanted to bond with his hostages. Was this what people meant by the Stockholm Syndrome? How were the parents going to take it?

Parent-Teacher meetings became the bane of my life. I tried to sound impressive at them but I didn't make a very good job of it. They asked me about my plans for their little darlings and I muttered some mumbo-jumbo about behavioural psychology to impress them. The reality was that I was just winging it, trying to get from day to day without falling on my face.

The pupils liked that about me. They knew we were all in this idiotic charade together. I told them education was important, that it would change their lives, but deep down I felt we were all just there because we had to be.

I was there to earn money and they were there to avoid being arrested for truancy. That was the situation in a nutshell. It would have been better for all of us if we could have admitted it. I was being paid to tell them that if they got good grades they'd end up in good jobs and eventually make them realise all their dreams. I doubted that was going to happen. All it would do was get them a job in Daddy's office or a spot in a dole queue.

As the years went on I found a gap growing between myself and the other teachers. They talked intensely about child development as I contemplated Robert De Niro's latest film or what was on television that night. They'd be talking about Eileen Whelan's inability to grasp the finer points of irregular Irish verbs and I'd be thinking about my next game of snooker. Or my next pint.

Now and again they asked me about my writing. That was my least favourite subject. I tried to keep a low profile about it. It was hard to do that if the subject of films came up. Everyone knew I did a column for *Image*. I hated the silence that descended on the room if people were talking about films. I felt I was expected to come out with something extra special because I was a reviewer. Why was that? Who came up with the idea that reviewers knew more about films than anyone else? In my view they probably know less.

If I was asked for my view of a film I'd come out with something like, 'I'd prefer to have lighted matchsticks put under my fingernails than watch it.' A comment like that tended to cut the conversations short. That relieved me.

I used to enjoy going home from work on the first day of every month. That was the day *Image* came out. I always got off the bus to buy it. There was a shop at Doyle's corner in Phibsboro that sold it. It was my first time being in a glossy. I used to get a buzz seeing my name at the top of the page even if what I was writing was rubbish.

The secret of becoming a respected film critic, I learned in time, was to be as negative as you could. That made you sound more intelligent than if you praised something. Even if you enjoyed a film you had to pretend you didn't. You had to find some fault with it to justify your existence. There was a joke I heard once that made the point.

How many film critics does it take to change a light bulb? Two. One to change the bulb and the other to say, 'I could have done it better.'

Travel Bug

Getting to work on time became a problem. Basil's Honda had been great for my first few years in Dublin. Afterwards I graduated to a Yamaha twin. It wasn't exactly a Harley Davidson but it had 100ccs and a centre saddle. Unlike the Honda you had to throw your leg over it. That was more macho.

When I got fed up being exposed to the elements I started to look at cars. I came off the Yamaha a few times in the bad weather. Some of the roads on the way to Clonsilla were treacherous in winter.

I bought an Austin. The door was hanging off it and the choke only worked when you stuck a penny in it but I didn't mind. At least I was in out of the weather.

I failed the driving test. In the middle of it I nearly knocked down a cyclist coming out of a driveway. I didn't need a crystal ball to know what the upshot would be. Someone told me a joke about a guy who was asked by his friend if he got the test. He replied, 'I won't know until the instructor comes out of hospital.' That was close to the truth in my case.

I failed other tests afterwards. Maybe I'd never have passed the car one. An insurmountable backlog in the numbers of people being tested caused me to slip through the net. A letter came in through the door one day saying they were giving an automatic licence to people like me who were in the queue. I imagined a nation of road hogs getting such letters and dancing around the place in glee. Imagine if half-blind bozos like Colonel Blink from *The Beezer* got one. Ireland would have been a vehicular Pamplona.

Having a car meant I was able to go on long journeys. Now and again I drove down to Audrey's house in Cork. On one journey I forgot to check the radiator. It was only when I saw smoke hissing out from under the bonnet that I knew I was in trouble. Another time I forgot to put oil into the car and the engine seized up. I thought it was going to be a write-off but I managed to get a reconditioned one.

The more I travelled the more I wanted to. The big advantage of the job was the long holidays. Someone said once that the two best things about Primary Teaching were the months of July and August. The vacation element beat the vocation one. If you had hobbies it was a job made for you.

I was a Piscean so I was always searching for new things. I never saw a plane in the sky but I wanted to be on it. I did something special most summers.

In 1979 I went on a fly-drive holiday to Europe. I went with three other people who'd been with me in Pat's, John Moynihan, Dermot Dunne and Don Conway. John and Dermot had become a bit disenchanted with teaching by now. John was eyeing up a legal career. Dermot was thinking of going into the IDA. I wasn't sure how long I'd stay at it. Don seemed to be the only really committed one among us. He was a special John of Gods school in Islandbridge. Anyone teaching in a special school, I always thought, was really into the vocation aspect of the job.

I wasn't originally inked in for the trip. The fourth person who was supposed to go on it dropped out at the last minute. I filled in for him.

A lot of things that happened in my life came about as a result of me filling in for people. Hugo was supposed to take the bar job in London in 1970 but he couldn't make it. I wasn't the first choice for the teaching job in Clonsilla either. The man the principal wanted did a second interview the same day. When he was offered that he took it. I only got the call afterwards. Now I was acting as a stand-in for the third time.

The trip started off on a high. We got merry in the airport lounge over a few beers. Dermot had just bought a money belt. He started showing it off to us. It had lots of pouches in it where you could put your money.

'Why didn't you just buy a wallet?' I said.

Our first stop was Barcelona. A Fiat was part of the package. We picked it up from a company called Europcar. The plan was to drive to Athens in it. Along the way we intended to make various pit-stops, wining and dining ourselves and hitting all the tourist spots.

Things didn't work out quite like that. We were robbed twice, first in St. Tropez and then a few nights later in Milan. In the first robbery our money was taken. We got so excited seeing the beach we rushed out of the car without locking the car. Dermot's precious money belt was taken. It was an obvious target because it was visible in the back seat. The rest of us had wallets snatched from the pockets of coats that were in the boot.

The second robbery saw us stripped of all our luggage. We were tempted to throw our hat at the trip and go home but I didn't want to do that. 'Things can't get any worse,' I said, 'Let's stick it out.' It's always dangerous to make predictions like that.

The next day the car started to over-heat and we had to go into the Milan branch of Europcar to get a different one. By now we were all in a daze.

The only thing I remember about the Europcar office is that everything in it was orange – the walls, the furniture, even the ash trays. When the mechanic came out to see us I almost expected him to have his face painted orange.

We contacted a broker who had good English. At first he thought we were Dutch. When people asked us where we were from and we said 'Ireland' they often heard it as 'Holland.'

I gave him the number of my bank in Phibsboro. He rang it and arranged for money to be transferred over to us. Things were starting to look up.

There was now the problem of where we were going to stay. We weren't exactly flush even with the Phibsboro money. Dermot had contact details for a man who used to play soccer for Bohemians. He was living in a fishing port called Livorno so we made for there.

When we tracked him down he was all friendship. He said he was happy to let us stay in his apartment for a few days. That suited us down to the ground. For the first time in a while we started to relax.

We had fun traipsing around Livorno on our meagre resources. 'Maybe the worst is over,' I said to the lads. It's always dangerous to make pronouncements like that.

One day I forgot my key and had to get in through the window. A police officer saw me. He thought I was trying to break in. Try explaining to an Italian police officer that you're living in an apartment that doesn't belong to you in a foreign city without having the language. He brought me down to the station and made me fill in a form. Then he read it out to me – in Italian. I still remember the wording: 'Aubrey Dillono Malono, *nato a* Mayo…' I don't know how I got out of there.

We drove out of Livorno with a sense of relief. Over the next few days we saw a lot of different towns. We slept in the car many nights because we didn't have enough money for hotels or even camp sites. I was usually delegated to drive. In the mornings I'd wake up aching everywhere as a result of being cramped over the steering wheel for so many hours.

We visited a concentration camp in Dachau one day. A sign outside it said, 'Plus jamais' – 'Never again.' A tour guide showed us around. It was mainly photographs. There was a chapel beside the camp where we heard nuns praying. When we asked the guide about them he said they spent hours there every day doing nothing but that.

We wandered around the camp in a state of numbness. There was nothing to say. Anything we'd suffered in our lives wasn't even a millionth of the horrors the concentration camp victims went through. At least it stopped us complaining for a while.

John took over the driving afterwards. I was glad of the break. One day he tried to overtake a tractor on a hairpin bend. A car was speeding towards us in the fast lane. He had to swing away from it to avoid a collision. We ploughed into a ditch.

After that I was back behind the wheel again. I don't know if I was any safer than he was. Sometimes I found myself almost falling asleep. The only thing that kept me awake was bonking my head off the wheel – not always intentionally.

Our next stop was Trieste. It was a city I'd always wanted to visit. I was hoping to see some places associated with James Joyce. When we got to it we were stopped by a Gestapo-style guard. After looking at my passport he told me it was four years out of date.

Four years? I couldn't believe it. God knows how many borders we'd crossed by that stage without it being noticed. He told me I'd have to go to the Irish Embassy in Rome to have it updated.

We drove back to Rome but it was a Saturday so the embassy was closed. By now we were starting to think there was a curse over the holiday. First the robberies and now this. Again the discussions started about whether we should think about calling it a day. This time I was almost tempted to do that. We decided to see what happened at the embassy. Whether we went home or not I still had to have the passport updated.

We binged out on pizzas for the weekend. We were too fed up to do anything else. Here we were in one of the most famous cities in the world and it meant nothing to us. We might as well have been in Donnycarney. Even the colosseum meant nothing to us.

I got the passport updated on the Monday. By now I was being called 'The Traitor of Trieste.' It would have made a good film title. At times I felt I really *was* in a film. Could anything else go wrong?

Instead of making the journey back to Trieste again we decided to go down through the boot of Italy and get the ferry from Brindisi to Igoumenitsa in Greece. From there it was only a short journey to Athens.

Once again the plan came a-cropper. When we got to Brindisi we were told there was a two-week queue for the ferry. Brilliant. 'The Traitor of Trieste' was blamed for that too.

We stayed in a campsite that night. Round about midnight the heavens opened. You've never seen rain like Italian rain. The top of the tent came down in the middle of the night. We were grabbing pieces of tarpaulin and wrapping them around us to try and keep dry.

Two days later we were back in Rome again. We drove to Trieste without stopping for food. Keeping the car topped up with petrol was the priority. Our thinking was, 'Feed the engine, not ourselves.'

When we got there the same guard was at the border. For a minute I thought he was going to stop me again.

Yugoslavia was our next port of call. We had a meal in a place called Split that we couldn't afford to pay for. We made a run for it after gobbling it down. I think it was me who suggested it. 'Let's do a split in Split,' I said. It seemed appropriate.

I can still see the waiter chasing after us through the town's square before giving up the ghost. There's nothing like the fear of being arrested for putting a spring in your step. I don't know how I didn't throw up the meal.

The next day we did a detour through Albania. John wanted the border stamp of the country on his passport. He didn't care about seeing it. He just wanted the stamp. I don't know how many borders we'd crossed at this stage. The pages of our passport books were so black you could hardly see them.

We didn't spend long in Albania. I can't remember much about it except a turnstile at the border going in and another one coming out. I'm sure there's more to the country than that but I can't say for sure.

We eventually got to Athens. I thought things were going to look up there but we were too drained to enjoy it properly. It was like Rome all over again.

We looked at the Parthenon and the Acropolis and went, 'So what?' Some people might have spent their lives saving to go somewhere like that but we were just bored. After taking a few photographs and wandering around the markets for a few days we headed back to Barcelona.

I don't think I was ever happier to see the back of a city. As we got on the plane I thought: all we need now is for it to go down in the Atlantic. Thankfully it didn't. As we sat in the Arrivals area waiting for our luggage we felt we'd been pummelled solid for a month. If that was meant to be a holiday, give me work every time.

After about an hour waiting for the luggage I saw a bottle of shampoo wobbling its way towards me on the conveyor belt. I recognised it immediately as mine. It must have fallen out of my case. What amazed me was that it was standing upright on the rollers. It was as if it was calling to me to claim it. When I pointed it out to the other guys, for some

279

reason we all burst out laughing. It was as if the tension of the month gone by had a chance to finally release itself.

To this day my abiding memory of that trip wasn't Rome or Greece or Italy or any of the beautiful scenery we saw but a half-fitted bottle of shampoo waddling its way towards me on a conveyor belt like a child looking for its Mammy.

I went to America again the following summer. My first stop was Graceland, Elvis Presley's home in Memphis. I'd always wanted to see it. Unfortunately it didn't live up to expectations any more than the fly-drive trip to Athens. That was mainly because Elvis wasn't there.

You weren't allowed inside the house in those days. You could only wander around outside looking at his grave or buy memorabilia from the shops. That was a disappointment to me but I still got something from standing outside the building that was so close to his heart.

Over the course of the next few days I met some people who knew him personally – his mother's hairdresser and one of his cousins who stood on the lawn outside Graceland every day giving little speeches about him. I also met a local guy one night at a laundermat. He said he used to see Elvis now and again on his motorbike late at night when all the fans were gone home. 'Imagine that,' he said to me, 'Coming out the back gate and zooming down the road just like the rest of us.'

Afterwards I went to Denver. I got a job working for a carpenter there. His name was Tiko. He put me up as well.

When he picked me up at the bus station he said, 'Let's go for a Mexican.' He meant for a Mexican meal. I told him I wasn't used to anything more exotic than potatoes. I don't know what we ate but it burned me so much I thought I was going to die.

That night he gave me a Margarita. I'd never had one of these before either. It was a cocktail with tequila in it. It almost blew my head off. There was salt on the edge of the glass. I brushed it off. 'Don't do that,' he said, 'It's part of it.' No wonder I didn't try for a job making cocktails in the West End when I was in London.

He told me he was from a posh family. He'd dropped out of college to see how the other half lived. So had a friend of his called Don. Don worked with him. He built a food stand from which he sold enchiladas. This was run as a kind of sideshow to the carpentry business.

Tiko lived in a rambling house on the outskirts of the city. He had sunflowers that reached high into the sky. It took him over an hour to water them. You were only allowed do that every second day because of the shortage of water. If you were caught using it on the restricted days you could be fined or even arrested. The humidity was so strong I could see it killing the flowers. It nearly killed me too.

Tiko reminded me of a hippie. He walked around the house all day in his shorts singing songs. There was no pattern to his behaviour. He spent a lot of time on the phone to people. He even brought it into the bath with him. In the days before mobiles he managed to talk on the move by using a long cord. It went around corners and under doors as he rambled around the place nattering. It must have been over thirty feet long.

He had a dog that suffered from granuloma. I was tasked with giving him his pills but he bit me every time I tried to do that. Eventually I left the job to Tiko. He had a way of putting his fingers down the dog's throat that stopped him biting him. In the evenings he brought him for a walk. He did it the lazy man's way, driving his truck beside him as he galloped through the streets.

Tiko gave me lots of time off. I went travelling to places I never thought I'd see. One weekend I went to the Grand Canyon. That and Niagara Falls are probably the two most impressive sights I've ever seen in my life. They stay with you forever. I won't even try to describe the Grand Canyon. Let's just say it was a bit bigger than the Valley of Diamonds in Enniscrone.

Another weekend I went to Cheyenne to a Merle Haggard concert. It was in a big field. He had cowboys and Indians on the stage with him. Afterwards there was a rodeo. The cowboys and Indians staged a shoot-out. It was like watching a film. They fell off their horses and pretended to be injured.

On the way out of the show a man handed me a form. It was for a competition. The prize was a trip to Las Vegas. I filled it in. A few days later I got a letter to say I'd won. My first thought was whether I'd be able to see Elvis but unfortunately he wasn't appearing there at the time.

When I got there I discovered the so-called prize was a scam. It was nothing more than a collection of food vouchers that you could only cash in after midnight. The idea was that you'd stay up half the night losing all your money in the casinos.

You got free beer when you were gambling. You were expected to tip the cocktail waitresses about four times what an average beer would cost. I underestimated how much I was supposed to give them until their frowns alerted me to the fact. Someone said, 'I love gambling in Las Vegas. I don't mind losing a hundred grand. The drinks are free so it evens out.' Maybe I should have given all my chips to the waitresses and forgot about the gambling.

I started playing blackjack. Before long I was hooked on it. And on the cocktail waitresses.

One of them showed me what she called The Frank Sinatra Room. It was more like a cubicle. She said he went in there once in a while with a very large number of chips and came out with a very small number. It was nothing for him to lose $100, 000 in a night.

Tom Parker was also a visitor. He'd been Elvis' manager. I suppose he needed some way to spend all the millions he'd earned from his 'boy.' He'd caused his death after all. Why not continue to spend his money now that he was six feet under? I hoped the cocktail waitresses got their money's worth out of him. I never had him down as a big tipper.

I got on a winning streak one night. My chips kept increasing. Then I lost them all again. It was the old story. The high I experienced as I saw them building up in front of me made me understand those people I saw in films who blew every penny they ever owned. With my addictive personality I could easily have been that soldier. I lost over $1000 in ten minutes. I didn't feel it was money because it didn't look like it.

Towards the end of the summer I met a girl called Dede Banks. The reason I remember her last name is because she worked in a bank. It was the only boring thing about her. She was a real free spirit. We got on so well she asked me to spend a few days with her in her trailer in Aspen. It was parked in a field in the middle of nowhere. We didn't have a romantic relationship but sometimes a friendship is better for that.

You can learn more about some people in a weekend than you can about others in a lifetime. That's the way it was with Dede and me. We had some great chats in the moonlight outside her trailer drinking Coors beer as we watched the sun go down over the mountains. She said she loved Ireland from what she'd heard about it. Before I left she told me the one thing she'd always wanted was an Aran sweater. I told her I'd mail one to her when I got home.

Another person I met in Boulder towards the end of the summer was a New York jeweller. He told me he spent six months in The Big Apple doing business and the other six ski-ing in Aspen. He was like Gordon Gekko and John Denver rolled into one. To me it was the ideal mix. You worked for half the year because you had to and played for the other half because you wanted to.

All of these people personified the American spirit for me. On the surface they were different but they shared one thing in common – the quality of wanting to live in the moment. I envied them that because I was always making plans – most of which went disastrously wrong.

I was sad to leave Denver. Tiko had been so good to me. I appreciated his kindness all the more because he didn't know a thing about me before I arrived on his doorstep. It was like leaving home having him drive me to the airport on the last day. The memories of all the things I'd done swirled around in my head all the way back to Dublin.

I didn't tell anyone when I was coming home. I knew they'd want to meet me at the airport. I hated the fuss of that. Anytime I went away I liked to arrive back without notice. That might sound odd. Maybe it was a reaction to the emotion of the rest of the family, or of my parents.

I remembered how cut up my mother used to be when Clive was going away or how my father was when Audrey was going off to Surrey to become a nurse. It might also have been a reaction to all the attention I got as a child on account of being the youngest.

After a few weeks I bought the sweater Dede asked me for and mailed it to her. She wrote back immediately. She said she was so touched to get it she said she cried 'a wee bit.' She said she'd left the bank. A person had lied to her about a loan and when she gave out about him to a third party it got back to her boss. She was going to be placed on probation for three months as a punishment. She said she couldn't abide the idea of that. She decided to give in her notice instead.

'I hate being lied to,' she said. She was teaching reflexology now and moonlighting in a health food store. She'd also been at a lecture given by Uri Geller. I thought bending spoons suited her personality much more than counting people's money.

She said a 46 year old man called Emmanuel had just moved into the trailer with her. He brought two snapping turtles with him and a German Shepherd dog. He was originally from Czechoslovakia and gave attacking instructions to the dog in Czech.

I read her letter over and over. It was so simple and yet so poetic, especially when she was describing the world of nature that surrounded her in Boulder. 'The leaves have all fallen,' she wrote, 'and turned to a brilliant gold. The hills are covered with evergreens and aspens. I wish you could see them. The fall is so pretty up here. We got our first snowfall a couple of days ago. The weather is cold and dreary with low-hanging clouds and lots of slush on the ground. In just a few days most of the snow melted from my end of the valley.'

I also got a letter from my friend Harry Clifton. He was teaching in Nigeria now. Harry's letters were like extended poems. I'd recently written to him in our 'Hemingwayese' lingo. His reply was more Maileresque:

'Listen Malone,
Apologies for absence of recent Ernesto shit. I have a lot of it on hand but haven't had time to organise it into a rejoinder worthy of the Old Sea-

Dog. Things are busy here and I'm too tired to compose elaborate letters outside work hours. We're coming into the hot season. The heat varies from balmy in the morning to fucking unbearable most of the rest of the time.

If you get a chance, fill me in on the wretchedness of your scene, the utter physical and mental degeneracy of the Dublin *shebeens* you're slowly dying in, the nightmare of the National School classroom, your daily terror. Make me glad, in other words, to be alive. Fill my heart, Malone, with light musical laughter at the spectacle of your foundering hopes.

Let there be Chris Griffin, loping on an Oedipal clubfoot between the loneliness of the Bank of Ireland and the loneliness of McCairns Alexandria. Let there be Mary Mannion, a metaphysical question-mark in a belted gabardine. Let there be the inanimate peace of a half-drained pint on a table at The Longshoreman in Fairview. Bring it all in, Malone, the whole Homeric cast of characters as they make their odysseys through the Dublin lanes. I will understand it. It will speak to my heart, the profound poetry of the individual soul in the chaos of contemporary life.

Yours ever in constancy,

The Wandering Rock.'

Back to Porridge

I found it hard to settle back into the teaching that year. My mind was miles from what I was doing. It always was every time I came back from America or wherever else I'd been.

All the plans I'd made during the summer to be more patient with the pupils who were doing my head in usually came unstuck by about September 2.

I'm sure the kids didn't know what to make of me. They'd be asking me questions about fractions and long division and wondering why I wasn't answering them. I'd be thinking about cocktail waitresses and Frank Sinatra's gambling room in Las Vegas and Dede Banks and her aspens and Harry Clifton trying to compose lyrics between classes in the jungles of Nigeria.

The summers created a thirst for adventure in me that came to a shuddering halt at the end of every August. Every September I had to face the fact that it would be nine months before I got off the leash again. Jacinta always said that if she had something to look forward to it made the week work for her. It was the same for me. I tried to give myself treats like a book or a film I wanted to see. Things like that got me through the dull days.

Books got me away from them as well. I decided I wanted to get away from reviewing them and start writing some instead.

My first foray into that area was a set of study guides. I did them for a company called School and College Services. They were targeted towards students studying for the Inter and Leaving. I did one on *Silas Marner* and then one on *Macbeth*. The following year Gill and Macmillan asked me to write a guide to Henry James' *Portrait of a Lady*.

The editor was my former lecturer Gus Martin. He remembered me from UCD. I asked him what he thought of the book. He said, 'It's one of the best *bildungsromans* I've ever read.'

I said, 'I beg your pardon?' I'd never heard the word before. When the guide sold well he said to me, 'I made you famous.'

He was joking of course. It was very much a niche market. I was sad when Gus died some years later. He was still a relatively young man.

In 1980 I published a book of short stories called *Flight*. It was made up of some of the ones I'd had in David Marcus' page in the *Irish Press*.

I went down to Listowel to launch it. They had a Writer's Week there every year. I thought I'd fit in but I soon discovered I was punching above my weight. I was totally out of my depth with icons like Bryan MacMahon and Brendan Kennelly.

The book wasn't good. It was full of the amateurishness of anyone's first attempt at trying to string different ideas together into a makeshift unit. As Philip Larkin might have said, it had a beginning, a muddle and an end.

I had to say a few words about it from a podium. Most people's first book is regarded as an autobiography in disguise. I was conscious of that. Was I expected to do an emotional striptease?

I went into a pub beforehand to get the dutch courage to help me through it. John B. Keane spotted me coming out. I should have known he'd be around somewhere. He was a publican himself.

'You have a fine stink of porther off you,' he said to me, 'You'll obviously make a good writer.'

His comment relaxed me. John B. always spoke humorously about alcohol. He said to a fellow Kerryman once, 'Your father was a great man but he was never as drunk as my father.' Kennelly was an alcoholic. MacMahon used to say, 'I can get drunk on the smell of a printer's ink.'

I went to see Bob Dylan in Earl's Court in London the following year. The death of Elvis meant I needed a new idol to replace him. As Don McLean put it in *America Pie,* 'When the king was looking down, the jester stole his thorny crown.' MacLean said he saw Dylan appearing at Washington Square Park one year. He was lighting a cigarette at the time. When he threw away the match a fan picked it up and put it in his pocket. That's fame.

Earl's Court was an unbelievable experience. The auditorium was as big as a football pitch. Dylan seemed to be miles away.

I went up as close as I could to the stage. I wanted to wave to him but the bodyguards pushed me back. I let his voice deafen me. The vibe that came from the crowd was like idolatry. I told myself I'd never miss any of his concerts when he came to Ireland.

I decided to do the H. Dip. It was to give myself the option of becoming a secondary teacher if I wanted. I was allowed to do the teaching part of the course in my class in Clonsilla but I had to go to Belfield for the lectures. It was a nightmare trying to beat the traffic across the city after school.

I got invited to an *Image* party towards the end of the year. It was in Deepwell, Anne Reihill's house in Blackrock.

I spent most of it standing in front of a roaring fire being burned to a cinder. Anyone who was anyone was there. I listened to the chattering classes of South Dublin emote on all the issues of the day.

A group of film buffs collared me. They asked me what I thought of the old movies. It was always the way. People could only see one side to you. I wrote film reviews so therefore that was the only thing I could talk about. I soon became bored and decided to leave. Anne was surprised to see me going. What excuse could I come up with?

'I have a lecture in UCD,' I told her.

'Are you attending it or giving it?' she said.

The 'Dip' became more and more of an ordeal for me as time went on. After a few months of risking high blood pressure to-ing and fro-ing across the city I asked a friend to sign my name for me when the roll call was taken.

This was discovered after a few weeks and I got a dressing down from the authorities. It probably resulted in me failing the course. I was one of the few people in the country to do that. I thought I did well at the exams. It had to be the memory of my failure to turn up at the lectures that did it.

Nobody could believe I failed it. I don't think I ever failed an exam before in my life. In a way it was a novelty. It became like a boast to me. I started telling people I was the only person in history who ever failed the Dip. I said things like, 'Any idiot an pass that exam. It takes a particular type of genius to fail it.' My father would have been delighted.

I ran the Dublin City Marathon that year, a journey of over 26 miles. I didn't train for it. Some of my pupils turned out to watch me in the Phoenix Park. I put on an extra burst when I saw them. That was a mistake. I was drawing on resources I didn't have. Such bravado might have worked in a sprint but not in a marathon. It took its toll on me.

After about fifteen miles my legs gave out. I'd reached what they call 'the wall' – the point where your body gives up on you. I walked the rest of the way. Or should I say hobbled. I think I came in last.

It was after tea when I crossed the finish line. My shoes were stuck to my feet when I got home. I thought I was going to have to soak them in hot water to get them off.

For the next few days my legs wouldn't do what I told them. They were in protest. It was my last year doing the marathon. You had to know your limits in life, I told myself. Drinking in The Clonsilla Inn was much more enjoyable.

Transitions

Teaching became more of a drain on me as the years went on. Did my enthusiasm trail off or did the routine get to me? I wasn't sure but when I took my foot off the gas the children copped it.

Nobody is a better psychologist than a child. They began to play up on me, doing their best to wreck my head. I said to a pupil one day when he was gazing into space, 'Do something educational.' He started picking his nose.

Some of them were comedians. When they said something funny I was entertained but I couldn't admit it. My position meant I had to take the high moral ground.

I sent him to the principal's office. It wasn't really a punishment. Anytime I sent a pupil there he put them drawing pictures. It became like a free class for them more than anything else. I only did it so the other pupils would see it was unacceptable to give smart answers to me. Unfortunately it didn't have that effect.

A witty pupil always beat the boring teacher in the smart answer department. You lost unless you came up with a smarter one. You lost with the pupil in question and also with the other pupils. You even lost with the principal because you'd exported the problem to him. If you did it too often you were regarded as the person with the problem rather than the pupil.

Children kept me young in some ways and aged me in others. Teaching was the only job I knew where your energy level had to be maintained in top gear as the years went on. You got older but the pupils didn't. They pushed you as hard at 60 as they had at 20.

Corporal punishment was done away with in 1981. After that the children got more and more in the ascendancy. I was never in favour of hitting them but it was reassuring to know you could threaten them if things got out of hand. Now you couldn't threaten them with anything.

They knew that too. I put my hand on a child's shoulder one day to usher him into a seat and he jumped away from me. 'That's assault!' he said. He'd obviously been watching too much television. I wondered if we'd see the day when a pupil would sue a teacher on some ridiculous pretext like that. Or shoot him down with a Kalashnikov like in Bob Geldof's song 'I Don't Like Mondays.'

By now I'd started to agree with the other teachers that some kids were just plain bold. Benjamin Spock wouldn't have been too pleased with me. Or would he? Maybe he'd have changed his tune if he spent a few weeks in my classroom. It was kill or be killed. 'Them or you' as the principal had said to me years before. Why hadn't I listened to him?

Once the fun went out of teaching I lost a lot of my motivation for it. I began to prepare less classes and to correct less exercises. Eventually I turned into the thing the lecturers in Pat's told us never to become: a clock-watcher.

The pupils looked up at me sometimes with an expression that said, 'I know you don't want to be here and I know you don't either. Why don't we call it a day?' If one of them said that to me I'd have had no answer for him. We were all prisoners of our lot, either because of government stipulations or the need to earn a living.

Around this time one of my neighbours in the Villas, a girl called Paula, said she was going to become a teacher. She was high on the idea of getting into Pat's. I hadn't the heart to tell her the place had been like a prison to me a lot of the time.

She asked me for advice about teaching. What was it like? How did I deal with the kids? I did my best to answer her questions but I felt like the least equipped person to do so. I gave her some books I'd kept from the training course but I couldn't give her the encouragement she expected. The words wouldn't come out of my mouth even if she was going to be brilliant at it. I'd suffered too much.

There was a lot of talk in the staff-room about falling numbers now, about the importance of us all pulling together to keep the ship afloat. There were frequent conversations about trying to haul children in from the surrounding estates to increase our catchment area. I wasn't in favour of this ploy. My preferred one would have been to get rid of a few of them. I'd nearly have viewed houses for any parents who were contemplating moving to hurry them along their way.

Sometimes I used to drive out to Howth to clear my head after school. It was a distance of about twenty miles. I played pool there in a pub called The Pier House. During the day I scratched words on a blackboard in a classroom to develop the minds of the next generation. At night I took a different stick of chalk and wrote my initials on a blackboard to join the queue for games.

If I lost I walked the pier. It was beautiful if the sun was going down and the sails of the boats in the harbour were tinkling. I used to sit on a bench and look across at the hill above the pub glowering like a human thing. In the other direction was Ireland's Eye. Now and then I'd see a ship making its way to some other country. At times like that my old restlessness kicked in. I'd tell myself I should have been on it, regardless of where it was going. Maybe it was the journey I craved rather than the destination.

One night when I was driving home with a few pints on me I skidded on some ice and ended up on the far side of the road. If there was something coming the other way I'd probably have been killed.

Experiences like that made me think it was time for me to give up drink. Or pool.

I ran into Phil Lynott another night in the Pier House. He was just sitting there gazing into space. Nobody was paying any attention to him. He was looking the worse for wear. I asked him if he had a coin for the table. 'There you go,' he said as he handed it to me. Then he said, 'Would you like a pint?' I said no. I was too immersed in my game at the time.

A few months later he was dead. I'd turned down a pint with a rock legend for a game of pool. Anytime I think of that incident now I can't believe it happened. The things we do on the spur of the moment without realising it. I sometimes wonder what he was 'on' that night. He'd been so full of life not so long before. It was like another Elvis.

When I wasn't playing pool I used to go to dances. Like most men in Ireland I was usually well tanked up with beer when I went to them. It was almost a law for Irish people. You went to the pub and then the disco. The crutch of drink was no way to get to know someone but it made it easier at the beginning. It loosened your inhibitions for that walk across the floor when you asked someone if they'd like to dance. Women didn't seem to need such crutches as much as men. Was that because they didn't have to do the asking? Maybe they were just naturally more sure of themselves.

I didn't want to marry yet even though I was getting close to thirty. I liked going out with women who didn't have designs on me. After I came back from the fly-drive I took Dermot Dunne's sister out for a drink. I also went out with Harry Clifton's sister. Hugo used to say women felt comfortable with you if they knew someone you knew. It worked that way with me as well.

Around this time I started going out with one of the other teachers from the school. I used to visit her in her house in Rialto. It was really bohemian.

She had a lot of style in the way she carried herself. There was a quiet authority about her. The first thing I noticed about her when she came to the school was that she didn't shave her legs. I saw that as a kind of feminist statement. Neither did she wear make-up. She was very good-looking. I was reminded of my mother. She didn't care about things like that either. Maybe people who are good-looking don't have to.

My mother was the farthest thing from a feminist I could imagine. Growing up in that environment I developed attitudes I wasn't always conscious of. It led to some conflicts between us when we went out. I was grateful to her for opening me up to a world I'd hardly known existed before.

We were opposites in other ways as well. She was practical and I was all over the place. I brought her to Tom Murphy's play *The Gigli Concert* in the Abbey one night. After the first act we went for a coffee. Before we finished it I said, 'I'm bored, let's get out of here.' She couldn't understand that someone would buy tickets for a play and not wait for the end of it. It was one of Murphy's most ambitious ones but I couldn't sit through it. I found it unwieldy.

She said she didn't want to get married. That made me feel relaxed in her company. She often quoted Gloria Steinem's line, 'A woman needs a man like a fish needs a bicycle.' I didn't see myself as the marrying kind either. Could I be with anyone for any length of time? I wasn't sure. I really enjoyed her company but I thought I was too restless to settle down with any one person forever.

I acted the idiot a lot of the time when I was with her. She became impatient with that. I was drinking on many of these occasions. She didn't need drink to enjoy herself. She often told me I was childish. I didn't argue with that. Acting the idiot, I often thought, was a much under-rated activity. If we don't do it when we're young we may regret it later on in life when we become sensible – if we ever do.

My drinking caught up with me one day in 1982. I'd been having a session with some of the other teachers in a pub in in The Strawberry Beds. There was going to be a party that night in The Meeting Place. That was another pub I liked going to. I should have driven home and got a taxi to the party but I hung on in the Strawberry Beds. I decided to drive straight to The Meeting Place to save time.

It started to rain when I was outside the Phoenix Park. A car pulled up suddenly in front of me when the traffic lights went red and I crashed into it. It was only a slight scrape but the woman in the car was furious. She jumped out of the car and started roaring at me. She said she was phoning the guards. I knew I was over the drink limit so I didn't know what to do. I pleaded with her to let us settle things between ourselves but she wasn't interested.

In a panic I made a run for it, jumping over the gates of the park and darting across the grass. I didn't know what this would achieve as my car was still in the middle of the road. A few minutes later I found myself being rugby-tackled to the ground by a garda. He brought me to a police station on the Navan Road and said he was going to give me a breathalyser test. I refused. That meant I automatically failed it.

When I went to walk out of the station he stopped me.

'Where are you going?' he said.

'To a party in The Meeting Place,' I replied.

'No you're not,' he said, 'You'll stay here till you sober up.'

I continued to walk to the door. He grabbed me by the shoulder and I foolishly threw a punch at him. A few minutes later I found myself in a cell. That was the last place I wanted to be because of the tendency I had towards claustrophobia. It went with the feeling of not wanting clothes close to my skin, the one that went back to my thing about wearing hand-me-down clothes.

That night I didn't care about claustrophobia or tight clothes. I didn't even care about losing my licences. All I cared about was missing the party in The Meeting Place.

Donie O'Donoghue defended me on the drink-drive charge when it came to court. He got me off on the 'fleeing the scene' part of it but I had to pay a fine for the rest of it.

I was put off the road for six months. It meant I had to get two buses into work every day. Donie was more amused by the episode than anything else. He liked his drink too so he understood me.

William Faulkner said once, 'A man shouldn't fool with booze until he's fifty. Then he's a damn fool if he doesn't.' I thought the opposite. If you don't fool with booze before fifty it's a mistake and if you don't stop fooling with it after that it's a bigger one. I don't know if Faulkner ever stopped fooling with it but he wrote some fine books. That's another part of it. Acting the idiot sometimes helps us tap into our creative side. You can't finish a good book drunk but maybe you can't start a good one sober either.

My mother died in 1985. It was a deeper shock for me to absorb than the death of my father eight years before. I hadn't prepared for it and I wasn't ready for it. I spent my life apart from her even though we lived under the same roof. I was the spoiled son, the irresponsible reprobate. I didn't listen to her when she asked me to drink less or stay in more. Now I was going to be punished. I took her for granted like we all did, imagining she'd be there forever.

She clutched her side sometimes in pain. I'd ask her if she was all right and she'd brush it off. When she was diagnosed with cancer I went into denial. When the doctor told us she mightn't survive I put on my poker face. To him it was just another day at the office. Meanwhile we crumbled inside. A world without her was impossible to contemplate. She was the glue that held us all together.

She didn't speak about how sick she was. Her focus was on us instead. How were things at home? Were we eating right? Meanwhile we arranged shifts to go in and see her. The 'steps of the stairs' were suddenly behaving like orderlies on shifts.

That whole time is a blur to me now – getting the news from the doctor that she was bad, her having an operation that didn't work, the endless hours of sitting around her bed in Jervis Street hospital afterwards hoping for a miracle, then finally the phone call we'd been expecting for months. It said she wasn't expected to last the night.

We got a taxi in to her and said the rosary on the way. We weren't kneeling on the kitchen floor now with our elbows on the chairs as our father threaded his way through us with the beads dangling from his fingers. We'd lived a lifetime since those days but we were still the same children at heart.

When we got to the hospital she was unconscious. The night nurse brought us chairs so we could sit by her bed.

She seemed to be smiling with her eyes. After all the months of pain she was finally free of it. The worry lines were gone from her face.

I tried to imagine her when she was young. It was a world I knew nothing about. I never knew her as a young married woman. I never knew her with black hair. For me her life began when she became a mother. She was now at the end of that life and I wasn't able to ask her any questions about it, questions I could have asked her over thirty years but didn't. Why didn't I? We only want things when they're going away from us.

Religious people pray for a happy death. I don't know what she prayed for. I only heard her talking about dying once. She used the phrase 'When my time comes.'

Her time had come. It wasn't dramatic like in the movies, just a slow slipping away. She went 'over the rainbow' like in Judy Garland's song.

She donated her body to science as my father had. I didn't go to her commemoration service. I couldn't face the prospect of listening to the endless re-telling of fond stories about her. They were pointless now that she was gone. They only compounded the tragedy.

As time went on I started to talk to people about her in a way I hadn't done before. It was good for me to express vulnerability because I wasn't usually the type of person to do that. Maybe we all do it when someone close to us dies. Maybe we do it more if we didn't know how much they meant to us when they were alive.

One day I found a sheet of paper in the pantry with details of a doctor's appointment on it. It was one of the many appointments she failed to keep, one of the appointments that could have saved her life. Looking at it brought me back to the time in 1969 when she kept postponing her mastectomy because she was too busy with the move from Ballina.

Hugo said to me, 'Let her rest in peace. She's gone to a better place.' I said, 'Maybe she's in a better place but I'm not.' I started to talk about all my memories of her, all the things I took for granted that I could never have back now. He said, 'Why didn't you tell her these things during all the years you were with her?' I had no answer for that. Of course I should have but who ever does what they should?

We embrace death in Ireland in a way we can never embrace life. It's even apparent in our language. Words like 'wake' conjure up images of celebration. At the other end of the scale we indulge in endless eulogies for people we ignored when they were among us. Ireland has always been in love with the backward glance.

I wrote a poem for her. I didn't want to publish it anywhere. I found it recently in a drawer. I called it 'Speak not'

Speak *not of pain that sounds like you*
or suns that promise more.
The sea receding in the main,
not here,
whole swamps of where
you were healing,
or were you?
The sea swelled in the reaches
of your heart,
curling like a release.
The shore furled into the sea.
I walked under it.
The grass swept you away
to your birth
your hearth
the freedom days of Raheen,
life opening like a flower
as we watched from the shore.

How did you shelve that storm,
the moon shivering in your
early radiance, wreathed now
in weeds, the undergrowth,
every memory I ever had?
You knew it. You were me.
The tide brought you back
like a mermaid.

Speak not of pain that sounds like you.
You're the sun that promised more.

When the pain of her passing went away I came to think she died at the right time. It was like my father. She'd gone through some bouts of depression in the years after he died. She told me once that she didn't understand the condition when he had it, only after she developed it herself.

It was partly caused by grief over his death and partly by the fact that she didn't have him to take care of anymore. She needed to be needed. After he died I became her job, her mission. Sometimes she seemed to see motherhood as a religious calling, like Clive being on the missions. When I grew up she thought of entering a nunnery.

She was happiest when she was doing things for people, first him and then her nine children. She sometimes spoke jokingly of him being a tenth one. My Aunt Florence had been of that view. She held it mainly because of his fondness for the bottle. My mother never judged him for this. When Dr Igoe told her it was an illness rather than a failing it gave her great solace. That was just before we left Ballina.

He recommended Valium for her to help her though the stress it brought into her life. That was in the sixties. She never abused it but it was like a panacea to her, the pill that cured all ills. Whenever I had a problem in teaching or anything else she popped one into my mouth.

In the seventies in Ireland everyone was taking Valiums. They were like Smarties. It was only in later years we woke up to the addictive quality of this tranquilliser. Today they're rationed severely by doctors. They're sold on the black market for people who get high by combining them with more toxic substances. Maybe I should have stored up a stash of them. They'd have been nice little earners.

My mother encouraged me to buy a house in 1981. She said it would be a good investment for me. I was squandering most of my salary from teaching at the time so it seemed to make sense.

I bought an artisan dwelling in a place called Viking Road. That was a little terraced street in Dublin 7. It wasn't in great condition when I bought it but it had 'potential,' as the real estate agents liked to say. After doing it up I started renting it out.

It had two bedrooms and an outside toilet. Over the next few years I painted and wallpapered it. I did all the things landlords did. A few years before I'd have thought there was more chance of me flying to the moon than becoming a landlord. Life has a strange way of making us acclimatise to things.

I preferred doing jobs myself rather than getting other people to do them. That was a surprise too as I wasn't particularly handy. There were always streaks on the paint and bubbles in the wallpaper. My skills in that department hadn't improved much since the days with Tina in Ballina. That didn't bother me. As the man said, 'Anything worth doing is worth doing badly.'

I fixed a staircase when a step came loose. I went in under the stairs and hammered a beam onto it. I don't think the Health and Safety brigade would have been too impressed with that. I had nightmares of it coming loose again. It could have sent the tenants into ICU units if they fell through it. I converted the small bedroom into a bathroom so people wouldn't have to go outside to the toilet if they were short-taken in the middle of the night. I thought of living in the house now and again but in the end decided against it.

I stayed in the Villas for a year after my mother died. Keith's son David was with me for a lot of the time. He was addicted to computer games and he got me addicted too. I developed calluses in my hands from playing Pacman. At one stage I considered buying a machine.

Every Wednesday we played snooker in a club called Breaks in Drumcondra There was a flier there that night. We also watched a lot of videos. I ate junk food and drank beer when I was watching them. David ate junk food and guzzled fizzy drinks. He was capable of lowering a litre of Coca-Cola during a Sylvester Stallone film. I could knock back a six-pack in that time. It was like hog heaven.

On Sunday mornings we entered a pool competition in a place called Caesar's Palace in Phibsboro. In the afternoon sometimes we went to see a rock group The Business in Slattery's of Capel Street. I always found Sundays hard to kill. I'd be thinking of the following day at work. It was like when and said,

> *Saturday night is my delight*
> *and so is Sunday morning,*
> *but Sunday night gives me a fright*
> *to think of school in the morning.*

I was a teacher now instead of a pupil but the dread of school was still there. I thought of the old joke about the person who doesn't want to go. His mother comes in to him one morning when he's malingering and says, 'You have to.' He says, 'Why?' She says, 'Because you're the teacher.'

In my last months in the Villas the floorboards were dug up. The new owners were having the house re-wired. Some walls were being knocked down too. I picked my steps in a fog of dust over broken boards to get from one side of rooms to the other. Sean McDonnell was doing the work. I helped him sometimes. It was like helping someone to amputate one of your arms.

The house looked like a building site. That made me feel good in one way and bad in another. It eased the nostalgia but also created a sense of defilement in me. Most people who buy houses like to put their stamp on them. Those who are selling them don't usually see that happening but I did.

Leaving the original Norfolk happened too fast for me. Leaving the Iona Villas one was too drawn out. Nothing in life is ever as you want it. But I was better able to handle the day itself. As Rod Stewart said, 'The first cut is the deepest.' After that you get inured. It's like iron in the soul.

I was sixteen years in the Villas. It was the same amount of time as I'd been in Ballina but it felt like about half that. It didn't register with me because I was that much older. I can't even remember our phone number in the Villas but I'll never forget our Ballina one. It's the early memories that count.

Where would I go next? I wasn't sure. Maybe it didn't matter. I looked up ads for places to rent and found one soon enough. It was in Claremont Court, only spitting distance away from the Villas. I enjoyed the independence of it. It was my first experience of living on my own for an extended period of time.

It was a bed-sitting room with a small bedroom off it. Everything was within reach – the cooker, the television, the furniture. When I got out of bed I only had to take a few steps to get anything I wanted. All the nooks and crannies of the two Norfolks were things of the past now. I was in the modern world with all the 'mod cons' at my fingertips.

I thought I could happily spend my future in this compact world. The only problem was that the phone was in the hallway so my conversations could be heard by the tenants in the other flats. That made me self-conscious. One of them, to my amazement, turned out to be from Ballina. He even knew my father. That made me even more self-conscious when

I was on it. I ended up talking as low as I could. People kept saying, 'Speak up, I can't hear you.' I couldn't tell them why I was whispering in case he was listening. He probably had no interest in my life but once I got an idea into my head I could never get it out of it.

Hugo visited me one day. We sat listening to Mary Black singing 'Song for Ireland.' I'd always loved her voice. One night when I was at a concert in the National Stadium I left a tape recorder in the back seat with one of her cassettes in it. The door was unlocked and someone stole it. I was in the Baggot Inn one day when I saw her with some other people. I went up to her and told her the story. I said, 'I missed your cassette more than the recorder.' She was touched.

Hugo and myself got into a discussion about teaching. I told him I was losing my zest for it. He loved it himself. He put his pupils into debates and won a lot of Chamber of Commerce awards. He also put them into plays. He was as busy outside the school as inside it. I used to be like that once too, at the beginning. I envied him his energy.

June and Audrey came over another day. Anytime I was in their houses they fed me like a king. I was sorry I couldn't return the compliment. They were lucky if they got a cup of tea and a biscuit. It felt strange being in the position of being a host. I wasn't a very good one. Up to now I'd always been going to other people's houses. I never had the experience of having a family member knock on my door, not even in the year I spent in the Villas after my mother died. They still had their keys for it whether they used them or not.

I also got a visit from Jerry Cowley. He was a doctor now. I remembered the day he said he wanted to be one in Muredach's. Most of us were surprised. He was pretty wild in those days. We hadn't realised how much of an idealist he was. He said he couldn't live with himself if he saw someone bleeding on the street and couldn't do anything for them.

I told him it would have been my last choice of profession. 'Each to his own,' he said. Maybe I was more like my father than I realised.

We swapped stories about the old days. Life was so simple then. We laughed about the day Sean McDonnell asked us to help him carry the wardrobe he'd made for his father up to Connolly Street, how we'd ended up falling on the ice and breaking it into smithereens.

Sean stayed with me sometimes. Claremont Court was like a base for him when he was in Dublin. He was married now and living in Louth. I was glad to see he'd settled down. Since we left Ballina he'd tried his hand at anything and everything in the job line. I imagined it would have been the same with women, that he'd have brief relationships with them that wouldn't go anywhere. He reminded me of a cowboy roaming from town to town. Maybe he was a bit like Alan Ladd in *Shane*. He lost the woman in his life too.

I remembered a night in Ballina when I was in Sean's car with him. He was leaving a girl home from a dance. She was sitting beside him in the passenger seat but they weren't talking to one another. They looked awkward together. A few other people were in the back seat with me. We'd all been at the dance together. It could have been in the Moyland.

We seemed to be driving for an eternity and still getting no nearer to her house. Eventually we reached a tiny *boreen*. It had grass growing in the middle of it. It was so narrow, both sides of the car were touching the bushes growing at the edges of it. They were scratching the windows. Sean looked fit to be tied. I was waiting for him to explode.

Eventually he couldn't take it anymore. He looked over at the girl and said, 'Have we far more to go, Margaret?' For some reason we all exploded with laughter at that. It was probably because he said it in such a quiet voice.

After a while more we got to her house. It was a little cottage by the sea. I felt we were going to drive off a cliff or something. Sean got out of the car with her. He lifted up the bonnet. He was giving her a goodnight kiss and didn't want us to see him.

He was quiet the whole way home. None of us said anything to him. We were still trying to keep in the laughing. My sides were sore trying to hold it in. I'll never forget the way he said, 'Have we far more to go, Margaret?' We used to quote that line for years afterwards. We burst out laughing every time we said it. I often wondered what happened to her.

Sean spent a lot of time working in the city. I never knew who he was working for. It seemed to change with the day. He was like a masochist. When a job was going well he'd get bored with it and leave. It was like he used to be with the women.

He was always looking for things to do around the flat. I wasn't handy so he was a good help to me that way. If there was a problem with the electricity or if a press was hanging off the wall there was no better man to fix it.

One day I went out to my car only to find all four tyres were punctured. There was a child from a troubled background living nearby. I suspected he'd done it. Sean took them off one by one and drove down to a garage to have them fixed. It took him four journeys but they were all repaired within the hour. I couldn't believe he got everything done so fast. If he stuck to one thing I was sure he could have gone to the top but he could never too that. His mind was always consumed with new ideas.

A days later he arrived at the flat on foot. He'd lost his car. He never said how. It was just one more piece of drama in his life. After that he used to take off for Louth every Friday with an empty can of petrol in his hand. He said it helped when he was hitching. He held it out to passing motorists as if he'd just run out of petrol.

There was a pub down the road from the flat where I went most nights. I played pool there. A band member from a rock group, Aslan, used to play there as well. He was called Joe. The band weren't big yet. They soon would be. Joe was a *citeóg* like myself. We were around the same standard so it suited us to play together. As long as I was winning I held the table. When I lost I went out to the snug and corrected copies or made a stab at a poem.

I was doing more writing now. There was a magazine called *In Dublin* that I started sending articles to. It was like an Irish version of *Time Out*. It was edited by John Waters. He'd recently written a book about the Irish political scene called *Jiving at the Crossroads*. The title was a play on De Valera's famous comment about his vision of Irish womanhood being comely maidens dancing at crossroads. John said Ireland had now become taken over by the jiving generation.

He was from Roscommon, my mother's county. He seemed to be outside the mainstream, to be someone who'd look at what you wrote and make his decision on whether to print it on that basis rather than the fact that you were a friend of his or someone he owed a favour to. That was a novelty for me. Up until now I felt journalism was little more than 'jobs for the boys.'

The first article I sent him was on snooker. I put my phone number on the top of the page. He rang me the next day. The first thing he said to me was, 'Who are you?' It reminded me of the title of a book the journalist Nuala O'Faoláin wrote, *Are You Somebody?* A boy said that to her in the street one day. He 'sort of' knew her face.

That was the usual way things were with writers. They weren't celebrities. They were just 'sort of' known. When I started writing I often got looks on the street by people who seemed to know me. They might have been contributors to publications I wrote for or people who wrote for them. They never went further than giving you that knowing look.

After the snooker article I did some more pieces for John. In later years I learned that his father was friends with my cousins the O'Gradys. John's father was a postmaster like Kevin O'Grady.

After he left *In Dublin,* another John took over, John Doyle. I continued sending pieces into him. One of them was a profile of the actor Donal McCann. I'd met him one day in The Gravediggers Pub in Glasnevin. I wasn't sure it was him at first.

'Are you Donal McCann?' I said.

'I used to be,' be replied.

We got talking. He asked me what I did for a living. I told him I was a teacher. He said he thought teachers were underpaid.

He was in his cups at the time. He had a major problem with drink but he was great company. He used to come out with statements like, 'Those whom the Gods wish to punish they make mad – or actors.' He'd been in *Strumpet City* not too long before. It was a TV adaptation of James Plunkett's epic novel.

'You look like you wanted to kill someone in it,' I said to him. 'Maybe it was myself I wanted to kill,' he said.

He'd also been in *The Dead*, John Huston's majestic adaptation of the James Joyce short story – which is anything but short. One night when we were in The Gravediggers he quoted the moving final lines of it to me. They were the ones where his character

310

Gabriel Conroy thinks about the snow falling on the graveyard of his wife's first love, Michael Furey. The way he delivered it almost reduced me to tears.

Huston died a few months after filming finished. I knew how deeply the death would have affected him as they'd built up a strong friendship on the set.

I went up to his house to see how he was. When he answered the door I hardly recognised him. He had a big gash on his forehead. He said he fell into the fire the night before - presumably as a result of the effects of drink.

He died not long afterwards. What was it about the film world that took so many people before their time? Not Huston – he was elderly – but McCann and so many of his contemporaries.

As well as *In Dublin* I was writing for a good few other publications at that time – *The Sunday Press, The Sunday Independent, U* magazine and some others. I also did reviews for *The Sunday Tribune*, another paper from the *Independent* group.

Two *Independent* journalists, Kevin Marron and John Feeney, were killed in a plane crash in 1984. They'd been on the way to France to launch the first bottle of Beaujolais Nouveau. The plane they were travelling on went down in Eastbourne. It was the result of a structural defect. Marron was a very witty man. He once said, 'I left the *Irish Press* to go into journalism.' John had interviewed me for *Flight*, my book of short stories from 1980. Its title seemed ominous in retrospect.

I knew I couldn't combine teaching and writing forever. Sooner or later I was going to have to give up one or other of them. They were getting in one another's way and stopping me from doing both the way I wanted to.

The teaching got harder as the years went on. One year we got a grant to build a new school. That made things even worse for me. It meant I was moved out of the prefab I'd been in since 1978. There was always noise in my room but when I was in the prefab it didn't bother anyone because I was out in a field. In the new school I was much closer to the other teachers. I didn't think they'd have as good a threshold for it as me. They were better disciplinarians and they weren't used to it. I was so used to it myself I almost didn't hear it after a certain point.

The walls between the rooms were thick but I still felt it wasn't fair to them. The more I told the kids to keep quiet the louder they got. I said to a teacher one day after they'd all gone home, 'This would be a great job if it wasn't for the pupils.' He laughed but I didn't really mean it as a joke. Their energy was getting under my skin.

In the staff-room there were conversations about how best to stimulate them. My ambition was to try and *de*-stimulate them. I was tempted to put tranquillisers into their fruit drinks so they wouldn't be so noisy.

My policy of bringing shy children out of themselves worked too well. There were no shy people in my class. They'd all become assertive under my tutelage. The parents didn't like it. They said things to me at parent-teacher meetings like 'What's happened to Tommy? I don't know him these days.' I usually knew what happened to Tommy. I'd given him an overdose of self-confidence. Now he was a monster.

I devoted more time to trying to keep the children quiet than to teaching them. I didn't know what to do with the headbangers and the space cadets.

One day at the tea-break I told the other teachers I thought I had a solution to the discipline problem. I suggested employing a bouncer who was built like Arnold Schwarzenegger. The idea was that we'd put them all into a room with him for a few days. They'd engage in a few wrestling matches together. It would be survival of the fittest. The last man standing would emerge to a round of applause. Everyone thought I was joking and they laughed heartily. I knew it sounded crazy but sometimes crazy schemes worked best. They laughed at Marconi too.

At the end of the school day my room would be like a bomb site. After it was vacated I used to go down on all fours to sort out the mess. If any of the other teachers saw me they'd say, 'That's the cleaning lady's job.' They were right, but I couldn't leave it to her. She'd have run out of the place screaming.

Now and again I decided to become Mr Angry. On days like that the floor was so clean you could eat your dinner off it. Nothing was dropped. But nothing was taught either. It was too time-consuming being a disciplinarian.

The kids knew it wasn't my style to swing the lead. Whenever I tried it they looked at me with an expression on their faces that said, 'Come on, sir.' Children always know when you're not being yourself. After a while I went back to my old way of letting them do what they wanted. Now you could eat your dinner off the floor for a different reason. There was food all over it.

The new school had a gym. No longer could I have games of football as my P.E. class. I had to give formal ones with exercises. They involved activities like running on the spot, swinging on ropes and performing elaborate manoeuvres on climbing frames. It was almost impossible to supervise them at these activities. It would have been easier to mind mice at a crossroads.

A lot of the time they ran riot. I kept thinking they'd injure themselves and the school would be sued. God be with the days I could just throw a ball at them in the field behind the old school and say, 'Kick that around the place until you get tired.'

313

The P.E. classes in Muredach's consisted of jumping up and down like an idiot for a half hour on Saturday mornings. If I'm honest I'll say we got more fun out of that than the kids did in our post-Montessori era of fulfilment.

Between my time in Ballina and Clonsilla the parameters of Primary Teaching went through something of a sea-change. Fifties teachers sat you in a seat and mouthed words at you. Seventies ones were meant to be everything – parent, babysitter, psychologist, policeman, traffic warden and general dogsbody. As my father put it, National Tramp. We were jack of all trades and master of none.

We were meant to be doctors as well. If a pupil had an accident at the break the principal used to say, 'Get up on the operating table' as he was tending them. After he was finished he'd say, 'You'll be better before you're married.'

I knew how to put on a plaster on a cut but that was about it. If a chicken bone got stuck in someone's throat I wasn't sure if I'd be able to perform the Heimlich Manoeuvre to get it out.

I was more comfortable with some aspects of the job than others. I liked teaching English and Maths, for instance. I probably spent more time on these subjects than others for that reason. Every teacher had his comfort zones. There were other subjects I wasn't too keen on. An antipathy towards Irish had been hardwired into me from the Muredach's days. My later experiences in Conradh na Gaeilge and the Gaeltacht hadn't entirely eradicated it.

As someone who spent most of his life studying Irish I got frustrated sometimes when the pupils couldn't grasp even the simplest sentences. One day someone said to me, 'Just think about the fact that, Irish makes as much sense to them as Chinese would to you.' The remark stuck with me.

I felt unequipped to teach subjects like Art and Civics as well. That was probably because I hadn't studied them as a pupil. Music was another challenge. My expertise in this area didn't extend far beyond do-re-mi. I tried to teach the pupils the tin whistle one year but it turned out disastrously. The main problem was the fact that they weren't able to cover the holes with their fingers. When they played they sounded like a bunch of popinjays blowing wind out of their rear ends.

Different kinds of problems came from activities outside the classroom. Every Friday I used to take them for a swimming class in the secondary school down the road. There was a lifeguard there to keep an eye on them but with my over-active imagination I always thought one of them was going to drown the second he had his back turned. There was also the danger they'd crack their heads on the hard tiles at the pool's edge. One day that nearly happened. A pupil was showing off how well she could dive when she slipped on a pool of water someone spilled at the edge of the pool. Luckily she fell into the pool instead of onto the hard surface. Things could have been so different if she hadn't.

Would I have been able to do that thing where you pumped someone's chest and blew into their mouth to get the water out? I wasn't a doctor and I wasn't a lifeguard. I hardly even knew First Aid. I stood rooted to the spot in terror as I looked at her going down for the third time in my mind's eye.

A New Decade

Mary and myself got married at the end of the eighties. We'd been seeing one another on and off since the seventies. We started going out again when I moved to Claremont Court. Everyone said we were destined to be together. We were alike in our personalities. We also had a lot of other things in common like our love of the west and the fact that both of our mothers were from Roscommon.

She was born on Christmas Day. That meant we both came into the world on national holidays. Neither of us had to work on our birthdays either. The disadvantage of that was that we never had the experience of getting a birthday card or a gift in the post.

People usually went wild on my birthday. That wasn't on account of me but rather St. Patrick. (I was still resentful of him stealing my thunder.) They took great delight in drowning the shamrock. Some of them painted their bums green in his honour. I don't know if he'd have appreciated that.

He was said to have driven the snakes out of Ireland. Brendan Behan said they swam to America and joined the police force. From my experience I thought he left a good few behind.

The job kept getting worse. Mary advised me to stick at it when I told her I was having problems. She probably prolonged my time at it. Anytime I told her I was thinking of leaving she said, 'The devil you know is better than the devil you don't.'

It was good advice but I never felt I was going to stay in teaching forever. I enjoyed it for the first few years but after that it took too much of a toll on me. It was doing my head in and I was coming down with a lot of bugs from it as well. No amount of encouragement could compete with that.

As the youngest of a family it was a novelty for me to have children dependent on me during the first few years at it. They cried and got sick. They needed help with their emotions and their work.

It fulfilled me for a time to attend to these dependencies. Maybe I fulfilled them too much. Sometimes I thought I almost became one of them. Maybe I was trying to improve on my life as a pupil in Muredach's through them. That was never going to work in the long term.

I left the job at the start of the nineties. By then I felt I was ready to be signed into Grangegorman if I didn't bale out. The kids were getting bolder and I was getting older. I'd lost the ability to teach them and they'd lost the desire to learn from me.

Keith was going through the same kind of stress in his job at this time. He left his job too. We were the only two boys in the family to succumb to work stress. Clive was going a bomb in Africa and Basil in America. Hugo couldn't wait to get into his class in the morning in Blackrock.

I probably stayed at it a few years too long. The honeymoon had ended for me in the early eighties. After that I was really just marking time. Maybe my destiny was never being able to stay at anything forever. I was a Piscean after all. Pisceans were said to be in love with change.

I wondered what the new decade was going to bring. Even when you leave something you're not happy with it's still a wrench. I felt a lump in my throat as I walked out of the classroom for the last time. It brought so many happy experiences into my life that I'd never forget. Maybe in time the good memories would outweigh the bad ones.

My new life started with me doing some humorous pieces for the *Evening Press*. I did some celebrity profiles as well, and the occasional feature.

I liked writing what were called 'think pieces.' These were usually commissioned. At other times I sent things in on spec. A lot of journalists did that. We flew on the wing, grabbing onto flotsam and jetsam as the mood took us.

There were many sexual scandals in the headlines in the early nineties. I wrote articles about some of them. In 1992 it came out that Bishop Eamon Casey had fathered a child by an American divorcee, Annie Murphy. It gave a whole new meaning to the expression, 'It could happen to a bishop.'

Nobody blamed Casey for falling in love. They blamed him for living a double life, for misappropriating diocesan funds and hypocritically speaking from the altar about the evils of sex.

At least in his case the sex was consensual. He was an angel in comparison to some of the clerical paedophiliacs who came after him, like Brendan Smyth. It was bad enough to hear about priests abusing altar boys but the cover-up was worse. Most of the boys were silenced and most of the priests sent to other parishes to re-abuse when their cases came to light. Canon Law was conveniently quoted to avoid full disclosures.

I tried not to tar them all with the same brush. I'd known some great priests in my childhood. I had my problems with some of the ones in Muredach's but there were also many I liked – Padraig Loftus, Martin Halloran and others. Then there were the family friends – Gerry Courell, Joe Cahill and his brother Sean.

Things were different now. People were angry. God-fearing Catholics who'd spent their lives obeying the rules now saw those at the top flouting them. Desmond Connell didn't exactly cover himself in clover either when it came to calling priests to task. I wondered how much my reference from him would be worth if I used it at a job interview now. Maybe it would even have come against me.

Sinead O'Connor tore up a photograph of the Pope on television. We needed a new type of priest, she said. She went on to become one.

She was also a Rastafarian and into Kabbalah. This was a mixed grill approach to religion, an *a la carte* version of Catholicism. It was a long way from De Valera's dancing at the crossroads. It was even a long way from John Waters' jiving at them. Sinead once had a relationship with John. They even had a child together. It sent out a message to Ireland. The era of 'Dev' – the Devil Era - was over.

I was doing film reviews for the *Irish Catholic* at this time. It wasn't a big seller. *Playboy* had just gone on sale in Ireland for the first time. That drew more interest from the public. I said to my editor, 'In the old days we hid *Playboy* inside our copy of the *Irish Catholic*. Now we're hiding the *Irish Catholic* inside copies of *Playboy*.'

Ireland was becoming trendy. We were throwing out all the old cows. The old-fashioned things we once revered were now being laughed at. A joke started going the rounds: 'I bought some condoms in Virgin Megastore yesterday because I was too embarrassed to buy a Daniel O'Donnell record.' There was something strange about a shop called Virgin selling condoms.

Religion was dying all over the country. Maybe it had been for a long time. Dylan Moran said, 'It was what we used to have before TV.' One of my friends from UCD said to me, 'May the last parish priest be strangled with the garter of the last centrefold.' I thought that was a bit harsh. I was never a Holy Joe but I didn't like the anti-clerical aggressiveness that was coming into the country under the guise of liberalism. I rebelled against religion when everyone was obsessed with it. Now that it was being trashed on a daily basis I felt less negative about it.

A culture of sanctimoniousness prevailed when I was growing up. It was a culture that lauded miraculous medals and plenary indulgences and all of those things that subsequently came to be seen as outmoded superstitions. At its worst it reminded me of why Martin Luther started Protestantism. I thought of Frank Sinatra at the end of his life trying to get confession from the Pope. He was willing to offer him $1 million for it. There was a crazy kind of logic to it. He'd bought everything else in life, hadn't he? Why not Paradise as well?

An organisation called 'I Am Not A Catholic' started up. This was shortly after the scandals broke. I thought it was superfluous. If you weren't one, why did you need to say it? Could you not just stop practising? James Joyce once said you could never stop being a Catholic. You could be anti-Catholic or a lapsed Catholic or a failed one but never un-Catholic. It was like the IRA. If they got you they had you for life. When you turned against the church in that kind of way in my view you were showing your Catholic credentials all the more.

The organisation seemed to be fuelled by rage. But rage isn't theological. You can't be angry with a God that isn't there. That was the problem with the 'I Am Not a Catholic' brigade. They wanted to revile God and also deny that he existed.

Why, I wondered, did Protestants never have that kind of anger? Why were there no lapsed Protestants? Why no Protestant *Fr Ted*? On the surface that was a comedy show but there was a lot of anger there too. If you were in any doubt about that you had only to read interviews conducted by its writers, Graham Linehan and Arthur Mathews.

Sex was behind most of the anger. Jesus said the Ten Commandments could be reduced to two: Love

God and love your neighbour. The Catholic hierarchy of yesteryear misread these to be the sixth and the ninth. Sexual sins were now catching up on the church. There was a grim irony about it. He who lives by the sword dies by the sword.

I thought back to the posters of voluptuous women I'd seen in the Estoria growing up. They were often from Biblical films. They'd be dressed in loose-fitting robes that showed all their curves. I remember looking at a poster of a Biblical film once with my father that had a woman who looked more sexual in her burlap than if she was in the nude. 'It hints at what it hides,' he said. He was always giving out about women in mini-skirts. 'They spent most of their time pulling them down over their knees,' he used to say, 'If they wore them a bit longer they'd save themselves a lot of time.'

Many of these films were directed by Cecil B. De Mille. He sold sex under the auspices of God. As long as the sinners were punished at the end you could get away with any kind of debauchery. Eve, Salomé, Delilah - it was always the women who were the tempters.

The priests in Muredach's used to say that if you had 'bad thoughts' about women you shouldn't go to Communion without having been to Confession first. If you had them every Sunday at Mass that meant you could never go. One of the laws of the church was that you had to go once a year. I remember thinking: If it was the last Sunday of the church year and you hadn't received Communion all year it meant you'd be committing a mortal sin whether you went or not. What should you do? Had Joyce ever explored that conundrum? It was a Jesuitical one. Maybe Clive had the answer to it.

Now that the church was embattled, the sermons tended to be more and more about forgiveness. I was amused. In my youth they were all about hellfire and damnation. Now the focus was on making allowances for sinners. It was like, 'Would you hit me now with the child in my arms?'

Hell wasn't fire anymore, it was loneliness. The absence of God. Heat as a punishment became replaced by coldness. The temperature of the hereafter was significantly reduced. Many people stopped believing in hell even if they continued to believe in heaven. Limbo was officially done away with but purgatory was still hanging in there.

I found it difficult to re-evaluate my theology. The Old Testament deity of anger, the one who'd destroyed Sodom and Gomorrah, was too deeply ingrained in me. I couldn't understand this new sweetness and light figure who wanted to wrap us all in cotton wool and carry us with him to an eternal life of bliss in the clouds. My father had the same problem when Vatican II came in.

I returned to prayer when I had problems. Maybe we all do when we reach a certain age. It was the old Push Button attitude to religion, the one beloved of all bad Catholics. I remembered Basil doing his speech from the film *Judgment at Nuremberg,* the one where Burt Lancaster says about one of his former Nazi colleagues, 'He's an old man now, crying into his Bible.'

Would I turn into him? Maybe I'd be like W.C. Fields. He once claimed to be reading the Good Book 'for loopholes.' So many people lived one kind of life and then jettisoned it for another one. The first time I ever saw that happening was when the actress Dolores Hart became a nun. She was Elvis Presley's co-star in *Loving You.* I could never understand the idea of an actress going into a convent. It seemed too incongruous.

Years later I had an email correspondence with one of Elvis' girlfriends, Barbara Leigh. She was an actress who dated him at the same time as she was dating Steve McQueen. On her own admission she played them off against one another. She was even dating a third man at the time, an executive called Jim Aubrey. He was the president of the CBS TV network.

When I started communicating with her she talked a lot about God. I didn't doubt her commitment but people who lived a hedonistic existence and then became overly-religious always seemed to me to want to have their cake and eat it. 'Women give themselves to God,' Sophie Arnould said, 'when the devil wants no more to do with them.' Maybe that was a cynical way to look at it but as far as I was concerned it was what was going on.

Religion always gave rise to extreme attitudes. Maybe they were more prevalent in Ireland. Piety was held in high regard here before the backlash caused its opposite.

When I was working for the building firm in Connecticut in 1972 we spent a week doing up a church. A guy I was working with found some unconsecrated hosts one day and started munching into them. I read somewhere that Gabriel Byrne engaged in a similar practice before he became an actor. He'd been in to be a priest once. Was it a rebellion against that?

Maybe it was an act of rebellion against the way religion was presented to us. When we were growing up we were told it was a mortal sin if the host touched your teeth. Mortal sins meant you went to hell for all eternity. How long was eternity? Punk used to say that if a bird flew to Enniscrone one day every thousand years and took away a grain of sand with him in his beak, eternity would be only beginning by the time he'd removed it all.

I never properly grasped the concept of eternity from my Maths teacher in Muredach's. He gave it as the figure eight turned sideways. Punk's depiction was much more graphic.

Fear was the common thread between teaching and theology in those days. If you didn't know your lessons you'd be slapped and if you didn't obey God you'd burn in hell. Scary stories about hell, of course, didn't prove it existed. All they proved was that fire was hot. If it had been portrayed as a cold place in the Bible we'd have been inundated on Sundays with sermons about frostbite. Modern theologians were softer. They portrayed hell as the absence of God rather than anything more grisly. For me this was more like limbo than hell.

Limbo disappeared as a concept somewhere along the line. In that it was like St. Philomena. Adam and Eve also went for their tea at a certain stage. Was it due to the influence of Darwinism? There always seemed to be a disparaging attitude to evolution among Catholic theologians.

Darwin created a lot of atheists. I never understood why. Whether we came from monkeys or not it didn't have any impact on my ideas about faith. I held to the belief of 'Ex nihilo nihil' – Nothing comes from nothing. Somebody had to create the monkey, didn't they? The world was too miraculous to have emanated from a Big Bang. There had to be somebody behind the bang. Otherwise how did it happen? Even the thought of nothing is a thing. I suspect this is what Descartes was getting at with his 'cogito.' He put it a bit better than me.

The Catechism told us God made the world. Bertrand Russell said: 'Who made God?' Christian theology told us he made himself. If that was so, was it not equally reasonable to argue that the world made itself? Therefore the world is God. We're getting into linguistics here – or pantheism.

Stephen Fry said on a religion programme with Gay Byrne that there couldn't be a God in a world that permitted children to get cancer. This is an understandable viewpoint but I don't agree with it. If we accept the fact that we can get a pain in our little finger there has to be a lead-on to that. Not even God can stop at trivial pain. Or trivial anything else.

I like Norman Mailer's idea of the Almighty: 'He makes it up as he goes along.' Sometimes I think there has to be a God and sometimes I think it's the most absurd idea imaginable. I have as little time for Thomas Aquinas, who 'proved' God existed, as I do for Richard Dawkins, who, with alarming frequency, 'proves' he doesn't.

The idea of religious worship was always a bugbear with me. I never felt God's ego would be so fragile as to need us to go down on our knees every Sunday to adore him. That's one of the reasons I stopped going to Mass in 1970. It was when I was working as a barman in London. I expected my mother to be shocked. At that time it was unusual, unlike today, but she took it in her stride. Like me she felt religion was in the heart. 'Somewhere below the left nipple,' as Martin Luther put it. I grew up in an Ireland where you were socially ostracised if you didn't go to Mass. Today you're almost socially ostracised if you do. That makes me want to go more. I hate conformity.

I've never been comfortable in crowded churches. I like going into empty ones to reflect sometimes. I don't know if that could be called prayer. Gabriel Byrne said the church is like the Mafia: 'They get you young and they have you for life.' Religion will always be ingrained in me as it is in the rest of the family but I'm different from the other eight in the sense that I don't think its practice is important. To me the institution of the church is something that sprung up like a comglomerate. It has very little to do with 'the shoes of the fisherman.'

Some of those shoes are made by Gucci today, if we're to believe reports that come online from Vatican watchers. That doesn't bother me any more than it would have bothered me to see a priest driving around Ballina in a fancy car or dining out in a posh restaurant. I always saw a difference between the ideological dimension of religion and its practice by fallible people, even if those people were members of the cloth.

Keith used to say it was easy for Jesus to be crucified on a cross because he knew he was going to heaven. The rest of us could only hope we were. I said to him, 'What if he was deluded? What if he was wrong about his belief in God?' He said, 'That's nonsense. Not only did he believe in God. He was him.'

Keith didn't question religion like I did. To him it was another part of the Dream Factory of life like Hollywood. In that he was like everyone else in the family except me. They believe fervently too. Clive became a Jesuit. Ruth never questioned her faith for a second. Hugo gives out Communion. Basil reads frequently from the altar as a lector. June and Audrey are constantly saying novenas. Jacinta is in the Legion of Mary.

No member of my family shares my doubts about God. Their faith is almost scientific. I see doubt as an endemic part of faith. Without it we're talking about knowledge. Most of my family would say this knowledge has come to them from personal experience of God communicating with them. I've never had that. Clive tells me I have to 'let God in.' I'm not conscious of trying to keep him out. Clive would probably regard me as a logical positivist. I don't know what I am. I don't like labels.

The rational side of me tells me the idea of God is absurd. It tells me that he exists because we invented him. It's like when someone says to you, 'Don't think of a pink elephant.' When they say that, the first thing you think of is the elephant.

God is a bit like that. The idea of him has been implanted in us since birth but if we lived in a communist country the idea of his non-existence would have been implanted the same way. We'd have grown up as non-believers.

From that point of view he's a sociological phenomenon rather than a religious one. We learned off the Catechism in Muredach's by rote. It became as much as part of us as the colour of our eyes or the way we walked. That's why it was important for me to go against the grain in 1970. It wasn't pagan England that caused me to do so. I'd been bored by Mass long before that. It stopped meaning anything for me.

Keith's son David often visited me on Sunday mornings when I lived in Claremont Court. He was supposed to be at Mass at the time. He said he couldn't tell Keith he'd stopped going. I said that was sad, that my mother had been more understanding of me in the same situation when I was his age.

Keith was more insistent. That created a problem with David. He bridled against everything religion represented as a result. This was fifteen years after me coming back from London. The religious landscape of Ireland had changed markedly in the meantime. There was a heave against the church after the sexual scandals and, by extension, a heave against religion. It saw priests topple from their thrones and some of them even being spat at on the street.

I was never part of that heave. I always thought the two things should be kept separate. When the politician Jim Kemmy was dying he was offered the Last Rites but he refused them. 'I think I'll take my chances,' he said. Another person I heard about refused the Last Rites for a different reason. 'I don't need you to comfort me,' he said, 'I'm on the way to see your boss.' From this point of view priests are little more than middlemen. For atheists they're middlemen on the way to nothing.

Maybe Keith's point about Jesus having an easier time than the rest of us could be extended to God. He didn't have to do anything special to be omnipotent. He was born lucky, as it were. If we're to believe Catholic ideology he was always there. He made the world because he was lonely. It didn't take any great effort on his part to create it.

The Bible says it took him six days but he could have done it in six seconds, or six milliseconds. Neither did he need to rest on the seventh day. These are fairytale scenarios we're fed to give us pictorial representations of creation. Like the goodness of God and his immense powers of forgiveness for our failings they give us solace in times of trouble.

That's the other aspect of religion we need to look at – the fire insurance angle. Some people develop passionate ideas about it towards the end of their lives from fear of the afterlife. They feel they're 'coming up the straight,' as my father used to put it. They want to settle their affairs. I don't think God would have much time for this attempt to cleanse our souls because we think we're going to die. Deathbed repentances are about as useless as people cramming for a school exam after spending most of the term dossing. Any audit of our lives should be compiled on its totality rather than its final phase.

In a recent programme on religion on RTE the actor Colin Farrell was asked what he'd say to God if he met him at the Pearly Gates. 'I wouldn't say anything,' he said, 'because he'd be able to read my mind.' It was an interesting answer. In the same way I've often wondered why God – if there is a God – bothered to create the world at all. He knew what each of us was going to do at any given moment. What was the point?

People say the point is our free will but this could have been conceptualised in God's mind as well. He didn't need to physically create us for us to exercise it. That's where most discussions of religion break down. They create a theology that operates from a human perspective instead of a divine one. In such discussions we always end up where we began, at the 'Eye hath not seen nor ear heard' end of things. That's why I feel my mother was as well off with her penny catechism.

It's often been said that religion came about from man's need for a protective figure. That's what Karl Marx was alluding to when he called it the opium of the people. He meant poor people. They created God in their image instead of vice versa. It was like the difference between the Ptolemaic view of the world and the Galilean one.

No matter how much you suffer in this life, religion tells us, it will be made up to us in the next one. Such an ideology went down well with repressive governments. It meant they could practise the most gross injustices without fear of revolt.

Sin was another concept that kept people from revolting. Religion loves sinners just as much as sinners love religion. Mary Magdalene is as central a figure in Catholic iconography as the Virgin Mary. My father's sense of sin fortified his faith against every rational thought he ever had. It made him take the pledge when he drank too much and go down on his knees in supplication.

We sinned and then we made restitution. That was the deal. He loved the word 'restitution.' It took place when you went to confession. You poured your soul out to a man on the other side of a grill and left the box feeling cleansed. Cleansed to sin and repent again in an unending cycle. Liturgical Persil washed whiter and it showed.

Edmond de Goncourt once told a funny story about a man who went fishing with an atheist friend of his. After a while they dredged up a stone with some words carved on it. They said, 'I do not exist. Signed: God.' The atheist said to his friend, 'What did I tell you?'

Equally ludicrous arguments are posited by theists. Like for instance when there's some natural disaster like an earthquake and 59 people die from the 60 that were injured. Why did the sixtieth one survive? 'God intervened, they say. Then there's another one where the whole sixty die. Why is that? 'God has His reasons.'

When you explain everything you explain nothing. The only people I'm interested in talking to about religion are the ones who say they haven't a clue either way. As for the question of where we go when we die, I like Rabelais' expression 'The Great Perhaps.'

When people ask me if I have faith I say I have hope. It's like faith 'lite.' Being a Catholic I can never let go of it no matter how many times I tell myself it doesn't make sense.

The decline of faith in the world, to my mind, is theologically unsound. A lot of it results from suffering. We blame a God we don't believe in for mucking things up. It's like Beckett's line, 'The bastard! He doesn't exist.'

Atheism has often resulted in people acting like Gods. Because they're not answerable to anyone they engage in reckless and immoral behaviour. It goes back to Shakespeare's phrase in *Hamlet*, 'Conscience doth make cowards of us all.' The fact that capital punishment has been abolished in so many countries means they aren't answerable for crimes against the state either – at least in the way they once were. They don't have to worry about the ultimate punishment in this life (the death penalty) or the next (eternal damnation.) This creates something of a global irresponsibility, except, of course, for those who have an innate moral sense not based on eschatological concerns, or who believe virtue is its own reward.

Many people today believe in heaven but not hell. I hate to put a damper on such cuddly optimism but can you have one without the other? If we're all going to heaven, why did God bother creating us in the first place? Was it because, as someone once suggested, this world itself is hell and if we come through it unscathed we 'inherit' heaven by proxy.

Tommy Tiernan said once that if he dies and gets up to the Pearly Gates and St. Peter refuses to let him in, 'I'm going to go for the fucker.' Here we have Tiernan's typical irreverence but also a very relevant example of the prevailing theology among those who believe the fact of being born into this miserable world in and of itself gives us a right to eternal happiness.

The greatest enemies of religion are often the religious themselves. By digging their heels in about science they create a dichotomy that snowballs back on them every time science makes a discovery they can't deny. Or when people make a laugh of the Adam and Eve version of evolution.

I know pious people who won't buy a side of bacon from their local butcher because they think he's trying to fob off inferior meat on them. They have no proof of this and yet they distrust him with some ingrained sense of suspicion. And yet these same people blithely swallow the poppycock we were fed as children about a man in a white beard living somewhere behind the clouds as 'gospel' – no pun intended. I'm not saying faith has to be logical but it would be nice if creationists accepted the fact that their beliefs were based on the absence of this. That way, maybe we could all have a sensible discussion of the issue.

'Never discuss sex, politics or religion,' my father advised. He was right, needless to say. People have been killed as a result of all three. Meanwhile God laughs – 'if there is a God.' That was another of his expressions.

He was always my role model in matters like this. At the end of his life he concluded that the Almighty was a sadist. I don't think God would necessarily mind this definition of him in view of the destruction he's caused on the planet over the millennia since he made it.

Sex continues to be a bugbear for the pious among us whether they're proponents of Darwin or not. It wasn't the apple on the tree that created original sin, it was the pair on the ground. David Norris has a different slant on things. 'I'm sure God has more on his mind than wondering what I do with my plumbing,' he says of his homosexuality.

If the church could get over its hang-ups about sex it would have many more adherents. It also needs to get rid of celibacy. The actor Gabriel Byrne said once, 'Seminaries are breeding grounds for perversion.' If sexual urges aren't allowed natural outlets, he believes, they'll go in other directions.

It's strange that he has almost the same name as our recently deceased national broadcaster Gay Byrne. Gay was short for Gabriel. Both of them were named after the Angel Gabriel. When Gay was thinking of emigrating to America some years ago, the people who were about to employ him suggested he change his name.

'Gay,' they said, 'has overtones of homosexuality. Have you any other name?' 'Yes,' he replied, 'Mary.' They said, 'Let's stick with Gay.' Mary was a common name for boys of my generation. Keith and Clive both had it as Communion names.

Gay suffered under the Christian Brothers like Gabriel but he wasn't as bitter as he was about it. He had an old-fashioned loyalty to traditional values but he was still credited with starting a sexual revolution in Ireland. 'There was no sex in the country before Gay Byrne,' a man called Oliver Flanagan pronounced in the sixties. It made you wonder where he himself came from.

Gay unwrapped a condom on *The Late Late Show* one night to show people how to use it. It was when AIDS had started to become rampant. Some viewers were shocked. They called him degenerate.

He was, of course, the farthest thing from that possible. Though liberal in many of his views, his lifestyle was almost monk-like. Contrast that to someone like Charlie Haughey. Haughey had a decade-long extra-marital affair with the journalist Terry Keane and yet was against divorce. Garret Fitzgerald was in favour of it and never looked at another woman in his life besides his wife, even after she became stricken down with elephantitis.

The church and state continued to cross swords with one another. No longer was fear of 'a belt of the crozier' enough to make people silent. Vocations dried up. A lot of our priests started coming from overseas. In the next generation, I thought, maybe we'd have black priests ministering to us.

When I was young we sent people like Clive to places like Zambia to convert the pagans. Now they were coming over to us to do the same thing. Ardal O'Hanlon had a joke about it: 'I remember giving money to the Black Babies as a kid. I never thought they'd come back to thank me personally.'

I continued to write about religion in the *Press*. As the years went on I branched out into other kinds of writing for it - book reviews, celebrity profiles, general journalistic pieces.

Aunt Florence's daughter Polly said to me one day, 'You should do more news stories.' She wanted me to be a roving reporter like RTE's Charlie Bird. I thought about what she said. Now and again I rang up the news departments of papers with ideas for articles about current affairs but they rarely picked up on them. They saw me more as a features writer than a news one. An editor said to me once, 'I'm looking for some hard reporting.' I told him I was more into the soft stuff.

I typed fast. On a good day I was able to keep up with the speed of a newsreader on the television. I'd never done a typing course. Neither had my father. I probably inherited my two-finger technique from him. As a child I used to be amazed listening to his speed. You really had to pound the keys on these old machines, especially if you were using carbon paper to take a copy. He hit them so hard he bored holes in the carbon paper.

Sometimes he'd be typing in anger. If he was annoyed with somebody he'd lash out at them in a letter. I'd often be delegated to post it but my mother would tell me not to. He'd usually regret having written such letters the next day. We could never tell him they hadn't been posted. If we did he'd have insisted on going out to the letterbox with the next one himself.

When people asked me where certain letters were on the keyboard I couldn't tell them. It was like the story about a centipede being asked how he walked. He wasn't able to explain it. Only his feet knew. My fingers were the same.

I was forced to join the NUJ in 1994 because I was doing so much writing in the *Evening Press*. The following year the paper closed down. It was always the way things worked in life. It was like the guarantee on your washing machine running out the day after the machine broke down. Murphy's Law, in other words.

I wanted to leave the union but I hesitated. Now that I'd come to their attention I knew they'd be looking out for my name anywhere it might appear. I decided to stay for the time being. The union sub wasn't much but I resented paying it when I wasn't getting any work on the strength of it. My understanding of unions was that they helped you get work. The NUJ didn't do that, at least for me.

The loss of earnings from the *Press* meant I was more dependent on the rent from Viking Road to make ends meet. It was great to have it for security but I never borrowed on the strength of it. I didn't want to get into that habit. I knew if I did the money would walk. I'd become irresponsible. It would be like the night in Las Vegas where I lost $1000 in ten minutes.

If I got a book contract I treated myself to a holiday. Otherwise I tried to live moderately. Viking Road ticked away in the background.

By now I'd put an extension onto it. It was difficult to let with just one bedroom. I got a builder to pull down the outside toilet. He built an extension there instead. He put in a toilet and a shower area and also a little utility room. It had two bedrooms again now. After all the years of chopping and changing it was finally beginning to look like a real house. The only problem was that people still had to go downstairs to go to the toilet. There didn't seem to be any way around that.

I kept writing the light-hearted books but without much conviction. It was soul-destroying work gnawing away at the same old bones. A lot of them were quotation anthologies. I kept buying these kinds of books done by other people so I'd have more material to draw on. After a few years I amassed a few hundred of them. If a publisher put an idea to me I was able to take some quotes from them and add some more from biographies I'd been reading.

One of my best-selling books of this type was *Football Wit*. There were a huge number of anthologies built around this theme that I was able to draw on.

Ireland was gripped by soccer fever at this time. We'd started to do well under the stewardship of Jack Charlton. He knew our limitations and played to them. As a result of him our world ranking grew. We were coming out of the era where FAI stood for 'Find An Irishman.' Nell McCafferty put it well when she said, 'I knew the face of Irish soccer had changed when I heard my coalman talking about Gelsenkirchen.'

That was the location of a famous match. We were now talking about soccer venues in the way our history teachers had talked about pitched battles. Footballer players were the new gladiators. 'Who fears to speak of '98?' could now be seen as a reference to 1998 rather than 1798. Gelsenkirchen was the new Waterloo, Landsdowne Road the new Boolavogue. When we spoke of the 'BC' era we meant 'Before Charlton.' We were never prolific scorers but if we nicked a goal thanks to one of Jack's famous 'long balls' we were good at parking a bus in the defence to protect it.

He'd taken on the job in 1986. His style helped us 'beat' England 1-all in the quarter finals of the World Cup four years later. (Yes, that was how we thought of it.) That was the year we got to the quarter finals. The Pope even ended up praying for us to win. Against Italy of all places. Unfortunately God wasn't interested. A player called Salvatore Schillaci scored the goal that killed our dream.

Charlton was replaced as manager ten years after he got the job. In retirement he bought a house outside (where else) Ballina. He went there to indulge his favourite hobby - fishing.

He was criticised for his style of management but the team didn't achieve much in the years following. We paid megabucks for managers like Giovanni

Trapattoni but they didn't really do much for us. He sounded sophisticated but what was in a name? what was in an accent? Behind all the glitz he had much the same defence strategy as Charlton.

He shared something else with him as well – his inability to remember the players' names. In his case there was an excuse. English was his second language. Was it Jack's? There are those who would say Geordies spoke a version of it only they could understand.

I loved the sense of excitement the games brought to Dublin. You'd see flags flying out of every second window in those years. If we won a match it was like winning the World Cup itself. Small nations celebrate more than big ones. That's probably because they don't have the chance to do so too often. Eamon Dunphy said our fans enjoyed celebrating more when we lost than when we won. Maybe he was right. I could never tell the difference. Anything is an excuse for a piss-up if you're Irish.

You weren't regarded as a real fan if you didn't go to the matches but I preferred watching them on the television. You saw more of the action that way. Con Houlihan said, 'I missed the World Cup one year for an unusual reason. I was at it.'

Life in the Fast Lane

I started writing for a publication called *Modern Woman* in the nineties. It was like a substitute to me for the *Evening Press*. Margot Davis was the editor. She thought I was a woman when I contacted her first. I'd written to her asking her if she'd be interested in me being a contributor. My name sounded like a woman's one to her. The name of her publication also suggested only women would write to her.

When I spoke to her on the phone she got a fright. 'You're a man!' she said. I said, 'I hope so or I'll have problems with my wife.'

We became good friends over the years. She was a very warm person and great fun as well. I wasn't used to editors being so human. Up till now they were mainly faceless creatures to me. I rarely met the ones I worked for. My conversations with them on the phone didn't range much beyond asking how long they wanted articles to be or when they needed them for. The fact that Margot wasn't from Dublin helped too. It was like the situation with John Waters. Us culchies stuck together. 'The Dublin media don't take me seriously,' she said to me one day. I told her I didn't think they took me seriously either.

I ended up writing a fair amount of *Modern Woman* every month, often up to 5000 words an issue. I wrote articles on everything from women selling their babies to having sex changes. I also did film reviews for it and the occasional interview. I even interviewed John Bruton for her when he was Taoiseach. He was a friend of Margot's. It was my first time being in The Dáil. I called the piece 'Et Tu Bruton,' one of my typically bad puns. I don't know if she got it. She preferred 'The Real John Bruton.' I don't think I got that.

Writing for *Modern Woman* was never predictable. There were times she'd ring me coming up to midnight with a suggestion. She'd be having a glass of wine out on her porch in Navan when she'd get an idea. Would I be able to drum up a few thousand words on it?

Anything put to me around midnight got me going. I'd work into the small hours feeling like Woodward & Bernstein during Watergate. I faxed my articles to her the next morning. She was always amazed at my turnaround. So was I. It was as if someone else was writing them. I tended to go off the point a lot but she didn't mind. In fact she liked me doing that. My style led her to ask me to do another column called 'Aubrey's Ramblings.' That got me an extra page. I was encouraged to indulge my various eccentricities. I didn't need much encouragement.

Every few months she came up to Dublin for some social event she'd been asked to cover. We'd go to that and then somewhere else afterwards. We blagged our way into art exhibitions and fashion shows and whatnot, anywhere there was free booze. She'd take a few photographs and put them in the paper. We'd roll out of the venues at all hours. She'd have pieces of paper hanging out of her pockets. Her handbag would be stuffed with notes, beauty products, goody bags. She could take or leave all these. They weren't half as important to her as having a good time.

Her sister Carmel was often with us. She did a social column for the paper, 'On the Prowl.' She lived in Dun Laoghaire and knew my Aunt Florence. She'd met Keith once in Rockingham. When she came to a party one night in the Villas they didn't seem to remember one another. Maybe too many years had elapsed.

There was another writer called Tom Locklin who wrote for 'The Woman' as well. He did the music page. I think his real name was Loughlin. He spelt it the other way because of Hank Locklin. I always enjoyed his columns. He told me he had to be careful not to be too critical of albums because he was getting them for nothing from the musical companies. If he rubbished them, that would be the end of the freebies. Thankfully I didn't have that problem with the films I went to. By now I'd stopped going to press shows. I could be as corrosive as I liked because I was paying to get into them into the cinemas. Tom and myself were the only two men writing for the paper.

The nights out with Margot often went on until well after midnight. By that time the buses would have stopped running. Margot usually had some friend or other drive her back to Navan. They'd arrive mysteriously like private chauffeurs. Carmel would get a taxi back to Dun Laoghaire. I never knew how Tom got home. He lived in a remote part of the country. I was glad I didn't have to negotiate a trip like that in the small hours. Sometimes I walked home. If I felt lazy I got a taxi. That was usually a bad idea. Walking helped you work off the effects of the drink. If I succumbed to the taxi I'd often wake up the next morning with the mother and father of all hangovers. I'd clutch my head in pain and say to myself, 'Never again.'

Sometimes I went down to Navan for events instead of Margot coming to Dublin. She organised a lot of benefits for mental health. Mary and myself used to go down to them. We usually stayed in the Ardboyne Hotel. There was always a buzz around these nights.

Tommy Tiernan said Navan sounded the same backwards because it was a backward town. That was a good joke but it didn't correspond to my experience of it. I got to know a lot of local people through Margot. Most of them were progressive in their thinking.

She paid me well but it wasn't enough to live on. Writing never was. I tried not to think of the financial aspect of it. I knew very few journalists who were making a living from it. It was doubtful I'd prove to be an exception to that rule. It was great as a nixer but it didn't put much bread on the table.

I got a job as a courier while I tried to figure out what to do with the rest of my life. It was easy to get that kind of a job. There were loads of them featured in the 'Situations Vacant' page of the *Evening Herald* every day. You didn't need qualifications but the pay wasn't great unless you worked yourself into the ground.

I rang the number given on an ad one day and was asked to come in that afternoon for an interview. It consisted of just two questions from a man called Kieran: 'Have you a bike?' and 'Do you know Dublin?'

I was in. I had to buy a motorbike but that was it. No other qualification was needed. I got a second hand one cheap enough.

Bopping around town with a bunch of parcels reminded me of when I did the Christmas post when I was in First Arts. I was on foot in those days. It also reminded me of when I was wandering around Ballina with my father's letters as a child. He'd have turned in his grave if he saw me now. He'd have been wondering was this why he sent me to Belvedere and UCD.

My attitude was a bit more upbeat. I was back in my comfort zone again, in the Hibs instead of the Moy Club. I was with all my working class heroes, the Lord Edward Street people instead of the swanky ones from Bunree or Bohernasup.

Some of the other couriers never had another job in their lives. Some of them had been involved in accidents and were waiting for insurance claims to come up in court. If they worked in their favour they thought they'd be able to retire young. The longed-for case would be their holy grail. All they had to do was fabricate a whiplash injury and get a few letters from a physiotherapist. These would be their ticket to Easy Street.

I introduced myself to them as Peter. Kieran adapted it to Yayther. It was a Dublinisation of it. The work was physically hard. Sometimes I'd have over a dozen packages on the back of the bike. If there wasn't enough room for them there I'd have to hold a few of them up front. If I was on a hill I'd be cradling them in my elbows and trying to change gears at the same time.

I rarely stopped moving but there was no mental pressure in the job. To be free of that was everything for me. It was bliss coming home in the evening and not having to worry about a misbehaving child or a parent coming up to you complaining about something you did or an inspector going through your work with a fine toothcomb or a priest on the Board of Management telling you how to teach. If I had a problem with a pupil in the school on a Friday it was a long weekend wondering if it would be regurgitated on Monday morning by some aggressive parent coming in to me in the classroom. I never had to worry about things like that in the courier job. My weekends were my own.

The conversation in the office revolved mainly around drink and motorbikes. Nothing else seemed to be allowed. I was expected to get 'slaughtered' every night in the pub with Kieran and then get up the next morning bright-eyed and bushy-tailed for more deliveries.

The worst part of the job was when it rained. At such times I had to put all the gear on: a thick coat, a balaclava, a pair of leggings, a pair of elbow-length gloves. I probably looked like the Michelin Man at times like that.

On one particularly wet day, who should I see coming out of the Shelbourne Hotel but Billy Connolly. He'd always been my favourite stand-up comedian. I went over to him.

'I'm a journalist,' I said, 'I'd like to interview you.'

I was speaking to him with a balaclava on me and all the rain gear. He must have either thought I was insane or having him on.

'Ye don't look like one!' he said in his Glaswegian lilt. That was the extent of our conversation. He went off laughing merrily.

I spotted other famous people rambling around Dublin in subsequent weeks. One day Terry Venables went into a limo on Stephen's Green. Van Morrison came out of the Shelbourne Hotel with Sinead O'Connor. Kim Basinger arrived into the Norseman bar one night. It was just down the road from our base. Kim is a few months older than me but she looks an awful lot better.

I felt like the poor boy at the feast looking at all these celebrities. As I watched Morrison coming out of the Shelbourne I remembered the day my father met Ann Reihill there. It was when he asked her about getting me a job in *Image*. Now I was just a courier. But I was much happier.

There was no pattern to my days. I never knew where I'd find myself sent to. I could be given a hair-drier at 9 a.m. to go to someone and still have it in my bag at 5.30. There were that many changes of plan. It made nonsense of the idea that a courier firm guaranteed speed in delivery. Sometimes I felt the customers would have been better off posting their packages in the conventional way. The U-turns were where the money was made.

My life as Peter got a jolt one day when I got a parking ticket. I asked Kieran sort it out. I forgot that it would lead to my name coming up. He came back

343

to me the next day and said, 'Who the fuck is Aubrey Malone?' I had to make up some excuse about the documents for the vehicle not being updated since I bought it.

He used to drink with Donie O'Donoghue in the Norseman. He was always telling me yarns about their binges together. I couldn't tell him I knew Donie because of my name problem. I used to look into space when he mentioned him as if I didn't know who he was talking about.

Donie was always getting into trouble with his wife Mary for being late home. He'd usually have been with Kieran on these occasions. One night he said to him, 'I got the hot tongue and the cold shoulder when I went home last night.' Kieran said, 'Poor you.' Donie said, 'I didn't mind. When you're hungry you'll eat anything.'

I often had to deliver packages to newspapers. I was writing for some of them at the time. It was demeaning having to hand Jiffy bags to editors I knew and wait for them to sign for them. They looked at me with pity as if I'd fallen on hard times. After a while I decided I'd have to do something about it.

I got an idea. Whenever I got a package for a newspaper I stood outside the office waiting for other couriers to come by. When they did I gave my package to them. I paid them a fee to deliver it for me, making up some excuse for why I couldn't go in myself.

This ploy didn't work if there was a rush on some 'screamer.' That was the term Kieran used to describe urgent deliveries. He'd be sending up smoke signals wondering where I was. I'd have my walkie-talkie turned off as I stood in the foyer of some newspaper office praying that another courier would arrive sometime soon. Afterwards I'd say I got a puncture or something. It would be miraculously repaired as I awaited my next assignment.

The courier work gave me more of an interest in playing snooker in the evenings. I'd done that when I was teaching but I was usually too wired up to enjoy it properly then. Now it was different. My mind was free.

It was like being in The Hibs all over again. The flipping of coins over a cloth, the abstract tussle with a stranger, the spectral quiet of a back alley at midnight. You chalked your cue and feathered the ball, willing it on that extra inch to make it fall into the pocket, spinning the white around the cushions as if it was on a string.

Sometimes I was happy to practise on my own. I put the reds in a triangle and smashed them up, clearing the table in however long it took and then starting off all over again, picking them off like a sniper.

When I felt I'd worked myself up to a certain standard I started playing for the leagues for a team based in Drumcondra. I had to use a lot of strategy in these matches. They took me away from how I knew the game should have been played, the way it was played by my heroes. Often I had to turn myself from Jimmy White into Steve Davis to win. Every ball was a pint of blood.

At their worst these matches became wars of attrition, a process of wearing the other man down. You had to train yourself to hate him even if he was your friend. You went for the jugular when you saw him weakening because you knew he'd do the same to you. We were like two weasels in a hole, vying with each other to climb up to the light. After the game was over we'd share a pint.

My standard was mostly mediocre but I managed to carve out the odd result if things went my way. I felt I could climb up the ladder a bit more if I got a cue that suited me. The one I had was so insensitive to what I wanted it to do I might as well have been using a battering ram.

I liked thin cues. Some people in the club said to me, 'What you need is a fishing rod.' They weren't far wrong. The problem with thin cues was that I couldn't play screw shots with them. They weren't powerful enough. My bridge hand also tended to slide up and down the rail.

One night I was playing in the Janelle Shopping Centre when I saw a cue with streaks of green paint down the side of it. I took it up more in amusement than anything else but once I started playing with it I found it had exactly what I wanted. It was thin but because of the paint my hand didn't slip on the rail. The only thing wrong with it was that it wasn't a two-piece. I hated walking down the street with a one-piece cue because everyone knew where you were going. You could be much less conspicuous with a two-piece.

When I finished my game that night I went up to the man behind the counter. 'I'd like to buy this cue from you,' I said. After looking at the paint on it he laughed.

'Take it away with you,' he said, 'Just don't let the manager see you.' I went off with it.

Over the next few weeks my form started to improve. I won a few matches comfortably with some decent-sized breaks. My confidence grew as a result. I knew snooker was all about that. A frame of snooker was also a frame of mind. The most important space was the one between your two ears. When you were on song you felt you couldn't miss but if you weren't you could fluff a shot your granny would get.

One day I went down to a place on the Malahide road that turned one-piece cues into two-pieces. 'I'll have it for you tomorrow,' he said. When I went down to collect it the following day he said, 'I did you

346

a favour. I took the paint off. There's no extra charge.'

I felt like punching him. I could never play with it afterwards because my hand kept slipping along the rim. Maybe the moral of the story is that crime doesn't pay. I should have asked the manager of the Janelle for permission to take it with me.

I stopped playing snooker for a while and concentrated on the courier work. The main problem with it was the fact that the motorbike seemed to own me. I felt if I was in a car I'd have more control over how I spent my time between drops. I'd be able to read books for one thing. The weather was often brutally cold on two wheels as well.

I told Kieran I was going to buy a van.

'Your earnings will be halved,' he said. I didn't care.

A bigger problem was the fact that I wasn't able to negotiate traffic jams easily anymore. Neither could I do U-turns when he asked me to change direction. The van was fine if I was given a provincial run but I only remember getting one of these. He kept them for his inner circle.

As an outsider I was relegated to the graveyard shifts. I did a lot of drops to a company called Stone Developments in Enniskerry. I had to lift heavy pieces of rock into the van when I was down there. They were for a statue that was being built at a roundabout near Dublin Airport. Sometimes I had so many of them in the storage area of the van the view out the back window was practically non-existent. Their weight was a problem too. I lived in perpetual fear of punctures.

'Don't have your dinner until you've made the delivery,' Kieran used to advise. That could have been the tipping point.

Stone Developments was one of my favourite places to be sent to. There were never any distractions on that journey. I was able to turn the walkie-talkie off and listen to the car radio. I always kept it tuned to *The Gerry Ryan Show*. He was on for three hours every morning. I'd speed through all the hairpin bends listening to him, feeling like Ayrton Senna as I clipped the heads off the flowers on the ditches at breakneck speed.

Gerry would be talking about something stupid like the cream on the biscuit his assistant had just presented him with. He was capable of going on for ten minutes about something like that. One day he asked someone if they could fart the National Anthem. I loved his sense of irresponsibility. It reminded me of my first days in Belfield when we were all full of a beautiful sense of escapism. That was taken away from me in all the years I'd spent teaching. Now I had it back.

Even though the courier work was tiring I never saw it as a real job. It was more like bunking off school to me. The fact that I'd spent nearly forty years in one educational establishment or another gave me the feeling these were the only places I could ever be. There was a certain satisfaction in knowing that not to be the case.

They were also the places that made me suffer the most. It didn't matter what side of the rostrum I was on. I went through the doldrums first as a pupil and then as a teacher. What was the difference? Not as much as people thought. I liked the old joke about the person who doesn't want to go to school. His mother comes in to him and says, 'You have to go.' He says, 'Why, Mammy?' She says, 'Because you're the principal!'

I came home in the evenings feeling burned out in a different way than I was when I was teaching. There was always the worry of a parking ticket or being clamped as you ran up a staircase at a hundred miles an hour to dump a parcel on someone's desk and get a signature before the traffic attendant saw your vehicle. They often hid so you wouldn't see them. I knew they got more money every time they wrote a ticket. They purported to be there to help the flow of traffic but from what I could see they were more interested in their commissions.

I only earned buttons in the van. If I got a ticket that was two-thirds of my weekly wage gone there and then. Push bike couriers earned more than any of us. They did most of their drops within a short radius. They could get in and out of places in the blink of an eye.

Neither did they have to worry about tickets. They could nearly bring their bikes into offices with them. I envied them. They also got to stretch their legs more. Sometimes I dumped the van into a parking zone and went off walking with a few parcels if the addresses were near one another. I could never admit I did that to Kieran. He'd have gone mad. I'd turn off the radio to avoid having to tell him white lies about where I was. That made him madder than ever. I'd have to say it malfunctioned to avoid a dressing down. He was never able to understand that I was more interested in the exercise than in what I was earning.

Money became a struggle. I lost my paypacket one Friday and panicked. It fell out of my pocket as I was going into a Spar shop. A few days later I saw a notice behind the counter: 'Sum of money found. Enquire inside.' A baker from Swords found it and handed it in. There were still some honest people out there. He only accepted a small reward from me when I went out to him.

One advantage of the van was that I was able to read books in it. Most of the other couriers were happy with the newspapers. If I was seen with a highbrow book it became a source of great merriment to everyone.

Kieran's definition of an intellectual was anyone who could listen to the William Tell overture without thinking of Robin Hood. Doing the Cryptic crossword in *The Sun* instead of the Simplex one was even seen as pretentious.

I kept my books out of sight when the other couriers were around. If I ran into them I talked about the kind of things I thought they'd be interested in – spark plugs and insurance claims and overhead campshafts. After they were gone I'd get stuck into biographies of people like Alain Robbe-Grillet or Charles de Foucould. Then I'd go back to the office and look at Page Three girls with their boobs hanging out.

The World of Words

I gave up the courier work when it became a drain on me. It was starting to take its toll on my health in the same way teaching had. I saw a pattern developing in my work life. It seemed I could only do something for a while before it got in on me. Maybe my threshold of stress was low. Teaching and courier work were regarded as high stress jobs. Was there any one that wasn't?

I didn't know where to turn next. Mary suggested I look for a job in a newspaper. I didn't fancy that. I couldn't imagine myself in an office all day trying to make conversation with people. It would have been torture. I was never staffer material.

I decided to write books instead. The idea had been kicking around in my head ever since the *Evening Press* closed down. I knew from other writers how difficult it was to have them accepted. The first step was to get myself an agent. I bought a book called *The Writer's and Artist's Yearbook* and took down the names of a few. One called Chelsey Fox said she'd take me on.

Chelsey organised two book deals for me, one from Guinness Publishing and one from Pan Macmillan. The Guinness book was a collection of humorous anecdotes that I was asked to compile about Irish people. My editor was a man called Richard Milbank. Richard was a very refined gentleman. He flew over from London to talk to me about the book. We met for coffee in Bewley's in Grafton Street. It turned out to be the longest cup of coffee I ever drank.

He knew much more about Ireland than I did. He had a fascination with Oliver St. John Gogarty. I knew nothing about Gogarty at the time.

Richard said it might be an idea to write to some people who were household names and ask them to contribute anecdotes. After selecting about a hundred of them I wrote a 'round robin' letter to them. Only about a half dozen replied. I couldn't believe it. One of them was John Bruton, the man I'd interviewed not long before in the Dáil. He said, 'My anecdote is that I don't have one.' He said politicians were too dull to have humorous anecdotes. At least he replied.

John Banville said he strenuously objected to being in the book in any shape or form. I suppose I should have known better than to ask him. It was a bit like asking God to be in the *Beano*.

Brendan O'Carroll also replied to me. He went on to become famous as the brains behind *Mrs Browns Boys* – if brains is the word.

He asked me what kind of anecdotes I wanted. I said any kind as long as they weren't 'blue.' I knew the language he used in his stand-up gigs wouldn't have been accepted by an old-fashioned firm like Guinness. I told him he could use poetic licence to embellish the stories if he wanted to.

He replied to my letter with the following: 'Dear Aubrey, I have received your letter. I must admit to be not very happy with the content of it. For instance I don't do 'blue' material. That's a sixties term and refers to comics who did stag shows. It's not me. You also say in your letter that I may take some liberty with the truth. That means I'm not to say 'Fuck' but it's okay to lie. Unfortunately I do it the other way round. I do say 'Fuck' but I don't lie. Based on these guidelines I'm afraid I must decline the invitation to contribute to your dome.'

He took such care to make his points I was surprised he didn't correct the typo in the last word. I was also surprised that a man who came across as so funny on television could have such a cranky side to him.

My next 'dome' was another book brokered by Chelsey. It was a collection of women's quotes from Macmillan. They were intending to call it *Women on Women*. 'Would that not sound like a book on lesbianism?' I said to Chelsey.

I wanted to change it to *Women's Writes* but that was regarded as too confrontational. My pun on Women's Rights wasn't appreciated. They were looking for a lighter touch.

I wasn't allowed put my Christian name on the book. Macmillan didn't think a man should be compiling anthologies of women's quotes. They just put my initial on it. It came out as being written by A.Dillon-Malone. The idea was to make readers think I was a woman.

I thought that was sexist. Women had compiled books of men's quotes and nobody said anything to them. There seemed to be a double standard in writing. I'd seen it in other places over the years as well. I often saw short story competitions advertised solely for women. If you advertised one solely for men you'd be seen as a chauvinist.

I wasn't allowed put my name on my next book either. Michael O'Mara asked me to ghost a book for the actor Richard Wilson. He was in the TV series *One Foot in the Grave*. His trademark line was 'I don't believe it.' I was asked to compile a list of 'unbelievable' facts and feats. For the next few months I devoted myself to collecting them and cobbled the book together.

Wilson's name went on it instead of mine. 'Why can't I use my one?' I said to the editor. 'Because then readers will know you wrote it,' he said.

Michael O'Mara now asked me to do a book of politically incorrect jokes. They gave me a £1000 advance for it. I compiled a strong collection but it proved too much for W.H. Smith, the distributors. They refused to stock it because they said it was too offensive. I said to my editor, 'I thought that was the idea.'

I felt let down because I'd done everything they asked me. It was a hard lesson to learn. Even when you obeyed orders you could get screwed. Writers were collateral damage for the bad judgment of editors. The book still awaits a publisher. The world has changed a lot since I was asked to do it. Today it would probably be rejected for being too tame.

I asked Chelsey if she had anything else on the horizon. She said she was sending out some floaters on my behalf but I'd have to be patient. Patience was never one of my virtues so I started to approach publishers without her help. Word got back to her eventually.

'I see you've been doing the rounds,' she said. I told her I wasn't able to sit around waiting six months for someone to say yes to an idea I had – or no.

'I'm afraid that's the way the business works,' she said.

'Not for me,' I said. We parted company shortly after that.

I decided to collect my humorous articles from the *Evening Press* and put them into a book. I called it *It's an Awful World, Thank God.* Dylan Thomas used that expression once. I knew what he meant. We were all stuck in this mess called life and expected to be grateful for it.

The sales of the *Evening Press* had been high. Those of the book didn't follow suit. I should have expected that. I thought it was funny when I wrote it but then we're usually amused by our own jokes. The public don't always agree. It's like the star of a soap opera who gets too big for his boots. He embarks on a solo career only to find nobody is interested in his acting. What they were interested in was his character in the soap, not himself. It was a sobering lesson for me to learn that people bought the *Evening Press* not for me but for all the other articles that were in it. Maturity means realising that you're not the most entertaining person on the planet after all.

Hollyweird, was also published by Michael O'Mara. It was about the insanity of Hollywood – the wasted lives, the early deaths, the crazy things they said and the even crazier things they got up to.

I loved reading titbits about their lives, the things they got up to, what they said. I enjoyed it when they were self-deprecating, like Victor Mature when he was told the golf club he wanted to join didn't take actors. 'I'm no actor,' he declared, 'and I have 64 films to prove it.'

Another story in the book told of an actor who was trying to get into Warner Brothers studio one night. He was stopped by a guard at the gate and asked to prove his identity. He said to him, 'Did you see *Quick Before It Melts*? The guard said, 'See it? I directed it.'

A third story I read concerned a man who doubled for Mel Gibson when he was playing nude scenes. That was all he did. I wondered what he'd have put on his passport under 'Career.' Probably 'Mel Gibson's Bum.'

In the old days people honed their craft and then they became stars. In our one they became stars first. Then they tried to act.

I saw articles in film magazines entitled, 'Ten Things You Probably Didn't Know About...' followed by a photograph of somebody. And I'd think: The first thing I didn't know about him was that he existed.

Anyone could become a celebrity I they were in the right place at the right time. Lana Turner was discovered at a soda fountain. What if she stayed home that day? Would we have missed her? I don't think she ever gave what might be termed a performance in a film. A director said of her once,

'No matter where you put her, she always looks as if she's lying on a pillow.'

Lana summed up the craziness of the film world when she said, 'I grew up wanting one husband and seven children. It turned out the other way round.' She also had a good attitude to wedding dresses: 'I don't believe in spending too much money on something you're only going to be wearing six or seven times.'

The publisher sent me to London to do some interviews for the book. Every day I went in to a little studio in the BBC and put a pair of headphones on. Disc jockeys with plummy voices from places like Rotherham or Lincolnshire would come on the line. They always started with the same question: 'Is it true that Melanie Griffith has a pear tattoo on her left buttock?'

It flummoxed me. I had a vague notion that she had but I wasn't sure. I figured it was in the book somewhere. Interviewers laboured under the misapprehension that authors remembered everything that was in their books. As soon as I finished something I tried my best to forget it and go on to the next thing. That wasn't a very good philosophy heading into interviews.

It was only after I came home that I found out why everyone was so fascinated by Melanie Griffith's buttock tattoo. It was mentioned on the publisher's press release. Most of my interviewers probably hadn't read the book at all, just the press release. They were probably better off.

Hollyweird got me some attention in media circles because it focused on the underbelly of Hollywood. That was always of more interest to people than the happy-clappy stories.

Keith was different. 'Why are you always looking at the dark side of films?' he said to me. He wanted the Dream Factory. It was the Dream Factory that made films worthwhile for him. It took him away from his worries and catapulted him to the Gods on a celluloid chariot. Realism was boring by comparison. For him all romances ended with a kiss and all adventures ended with the hero beating the villain. He didn't want any truck with anti-heroes or revisionist parables.

One of the first films I ever went to with him in Dublin was *Butch Cassidy and the Sundance Kid* in 1970. He booked almost a whole row of seats in the Carlton for us. Looking back on it now, that film signalled the end of cowboy films as we knew them. The freeze-frame in the last reel with Paul Newman and Robert Redford blasting their way out of the corral was classic. It was almost as if the director was afraid to show us them being shot. He was killing a genre as well as seeing off his two main leads.

Little did I know then that it would be one of the last old-fashioned westerns Hollywood ever made. It was the end of an era for Hollywood just like leaving Ballina was the end of one for me. Afterwards we got films that debunked our old heroes. Frank Perry's *Doc* made Wyatt Earp and Doc Holliday into unsavoury characters in 1971. *Dirty Little Billy* demythologised Billy the Kid the year after.

Dublin was changing too. Many of the cinemas I used to go to were closing down – the Capitol, the Metropole, the Astor, the Corinthian. The Plaza went too. I'd seen Stanley Kubrick's mind-blowing *2001: A Space Odyssey* there. It was now The Dublin Wax Museum.

I shared Keith's fascination with old films but I didn't let it stop me watching modern ones. Neither did I let it stop me seeing Hollywood as a sewer. Films sugar-coated their themes to give audiences the escapism they craved from lives that weren't quite as cheesy as those of their idols.

He didn't see it that way. Most of the films he liked were anathema to me. When he had showings in his house I found it difficult to work up the energy to go to them. He knew they were endurance tests for me so he didn't impose them on me much. When he did it was like Jesus in the Garden of Gethsemane: 'Would you watch one hour with me?'

I must have inherited my restlessness from Uncle Louis. I always remembered the story of him leaving the Estoria one night saying, 'I don't pay to be bored.' My favourite part of the remote was the Fast Forward button.

Keith's favourite genres were musicals and cowboy films. These were what he watched most in Ballina as a boy and what he continued to watch in his showings in Dublin. You had to observe a sacred silence at them. It was like being at Mass. Clive said Mas sometimes in Iona Villas. There was the same kind of silence in Keith's house during a film. Maybe cinemas were Keith's cathedrals. Maybe cathedrals were Clive's cinemas. We all need something reverential in our lives.

One of the people I featured in *Hollyweird* was Peter O'Toole. I also had him in the book of humorous anecdotes I did for Guinness. When he published the second volume of his autobiography in 1997 I went to his signing. I brought my own books with me to give him.

When he signed his book for me I told him I'd mentioned him in some of my own ones. I thought he might be interested but he wasn't. His daughter was behind him. When I handed my two books to him he roared out, 'Kate!' as he threw them at her. I got the impression they were headed for the waste paper basket.

Afterwards I did two books as marketing experiments. They were pocket-sized volumes about the making of the films *Ryan's Daughter* and *Michael*

Collins. I did them as part of a series of books called 'Movies Made in Ireland.' It didn't take long to write them.

I knew the illustrations would be too expensive if I got them from the studio. To avoid that I went looking for an individual collector who might have some. I eventually found a man called Peter Vollebregt who had a picture stills agency. I told him what I wanted and he said he might be able to help me. We met for coffee in the Café-en-Seine in Dawson Street. He had a lot of stills from the film but he didn't own the rights to them. I asked him if he'd let me have them. I offered him £100 for them. He was delighted with that because he had no job at the time.

When I got home I wrote a begging letter to Ted Turner . He was married to Jane Fonda at the time. He owned the rights to the film. In the letter I told him I had no money. I must have got him in a good mood because he let me use all Peter's stills for a nominal fee. It wasn't much more than $100 if I remember correctly.

Afterwards I tried to get photographs from *Michael Collins*. It had been directed by Neil Jordan. He used to live around the corner from me in Clontarf. He was now living near Ardmore Studios in Bray. I'd met him one night at a party some years before. I didn't know him but I still went up to him. I said, 'Your father lectured me in Pat's Training College.' He gave me that killer Neil Jordan look. 'Not another fucking teacher,' he said.

When I started writing short stories he was a member of the Irish Writers Co-Op. They'd produced some fine books from writers like himself and Des Hogan. I ran a few of my stories by him to see what he thought of them. I didn't think they were anywhere in his league so I didn't hold out any great hope. He'd recently published a book called *A Night in Tunisia*. It got a puff from no less a luminary than Sean O'Faoláin. When I read it I felt as if two different eras had suddenly merged.

Jordan was polite about my stories but he didn't make me any offers. I wondered if I'd have better luck with him this time around. I wasn't asking him to publish anything, just to help with the visuals.

I faxed him to Ardmore Studios and told him what I wanted. The answer came back a few days later. It was just one word: 'Sorry.'

I rang Warner Brothers to London. It was their film. They said the fee would be £500 for any image I used. I said, 'That's my budget for the whole job,' I said.

It looked like the project was dead in the water unless I did the book without illustrations. I rang a printer in Dublin but his quotation was outlandish. Then I went into the company in Pearse Street that had done the other books in the 'Movies Made in Ireland' series. The director of it was a man named Pat Neville, told me the previous ones had been printed in Budapest. He gave me the number of a man to ring.

His name was Istvan Lukacs. He only had broken English but I got the gist of what he said. He gave me a brilliant quotation. His fee for the whole book was the same as the Irish printer was charging for the cover.

My only problem now was to get images for *Michael Collins*. I was reading *The Star* newspaper one day when I saw some photographs that had been taken during the shooting of the film. Most of them had a mixture of the cast and crew. They had stars from the film in period costume and in the background some people in modern dress, the photographers and crew members and some fans watching on. I got an idea. If I could use these photographs I wouldn't have to pay Warner Brothers.

360

They would be the property of the person who took them.

I went out to the offices of *The Star* in Rathmines and met him. He said he'd be more than happy to give me all his photos. There were about thirty of them. I asked him how much he wanted for them. I expected him to say at least £1000. He said, 'There's a newsagent's across the road. Buy me three packets of fags and they're yours.' I almost embraced him.

After the books came out I got a rep to take them around Ireland with him. He brought them into gift shops as well and they sold quite well there. A few months later I was down in Kerry on a holiday. I wandered into a shop. It was on Inch Beach. That was where *Ryan's Daughter* was filmed. I hadn't been thinking of that when I went in.

The shop was run by an Iranian man. He spoke with a Cork accent. His name was Sammy. He said he'd buy a few thousand copies of the books from me. He wanted them for half nothing. I didn't care. This was still good news. I rang Istvan and asked him to do another print run. By now his English had improved considerably. He was able to say 'Yes' in a way I understood perfectly. Wonders never ceased.

After finishing the two film books I decided to bring out a collection of Brendan Behan's sayings. It was another business opportunity. I wouldn't have to do any writing except for a brief introduction. It could be another moneyspinner.

That was the theory but nothing is ever simple in writing. It was easy to collect a bunch of quotes but was I going to be allowed use them? That was the crunch.

The Behan estate was represented by the Tessa Sayle Agency in London. It was presided over by an Italian lady. At this point I had a Russian agent, Vernon Futerman. He didn't get me any contracts but he vetted the ones I got myself. He was a real gentleman but he was in his seventies at this time and only working now and again.

He set up a meeting with the lady from the Tessa Sayle Agency. A Russian was meeting an Italian in London to talk about an Irishman. It was a cosmopolitan brew. Eventually the deal was struck. The book came out but I didn't make much money from it. There were too many people involved.

One night when I was wondering where to go for my next project I saw Brendan's brother Brian being interviewed on *The Pat Kenny Show* on television. Being a Behan I expected him to be cantankerous but he wasn't. He was very human and also very funny. I rang RTE and found out the name of the hotel he was staying in. I visited it the next morning and ambushed him at breakfast. I always believed in cutting to the chase in situations like that. When he asked me what I wanted I said, 'I'd like to write your biography.' Amazingly he said he was interested so we took it from there.

He'd lived a hard life but was never bitter. He'd been put in the Artane Boys School for petty theft as a boy. It was where a lot of children were sent to if they committed minor misdemeanours or if they were from broken homes. The Christian Brothers ran it with a rod of iron. He moved to England when he became an adult.

He started co-writing the book with me by sending me pieces of text or by phoning me from his home in Brighton. I found him very entertaining.

He played up the stage-Irish image he had there. 'What's wrong with it?' he'd say, 'It's a talent like any other.' He preferred it to the high seriousness of people like Yeats. He called him 'Silly Willie.' Beckett in his view was nothing more than 'a long string of misery.'

Unlike some people I found Beckett to be a very funny writer. I thought he played up his depression just like Brian played up his stage-Irishry. I liked the story someone told of being with him one day when a glorious sun was shining. He said to him, 'Sam, this is the kind of day that makes you feel good to be alive.' Beckett thought for a second before replying, 'I wouldn't go that far.'

When Brian came over to Ireland I met him a lot. He told me about how he'd struggled to fit into the world as a young boy. The school where he'd been put was just down the road from where I lived. Anytime we passed it he averted his eyes. He was beaten there almost on a daily basis. One day I asked him if he'd been sexually abused.

'No,' he said, 'I mustn't have been attractive enough. I was offended.' He was always able to turn bad experiences into jokes.

On one of his visits over here he brought his wife with him. She was an artist called Sally. I drove them down to Enniskerry to see the Sally Gap. It seemed appropriate.

I was in my courier van at the time. Mary was in the passenger seat. There were no seats in the back. Brian had to stretch his long legs over the storage area. He seemed more able for this than Sally even though she was 25 years younger than him.

He was a treasure trove of anecdotes. He boasted of having met Stalin and Mao Tse-Tung. He enjoyed rattling cages. 'I comfort the afflicted,' he said, 'and afflict the comfortable.' He once set up a society for the abolition of marriage. It had 300 paid-up members.

He was also against organised religion. In fact he was against nearly everything official. He was even thrown out of the Anarchist Party. I didn't know that could happen. How could you be thrown out of a party that believed in nothing?

Funerals weren't high on his list of priorities either. 'In fact I may not even go to my own one,' he declared.

He lived on a houseboat in Shoreham for much of the 1970s. It was actually a converted torpedo boat. Here he set up a refuge for distressed woman.

'If they weren't distressed coming in,' his mother said, 'They certainly were going out.' Five shots were fired at it one day. He wasn't injured. 'One of the bullets lodged in a grapefruit,' he said, 'That annoyed me more than anything else. I'd been looking forward to eating it.'

He loved swimming in the nude. A woman accosted him one day and said she was going to report him to the police. He told her he'd go with her – without his clothes on. 'She backed off after that,' he said. One day he went swimming on Christmas Day. It was a particularly cold one.

Helicopters circled overhead. It was the police. They thought he was attempting suicide. The incident made the papers.

Brian gave me a lot of interesting material for the book, much of it concerning Brendan. A man I knew called Gus Smith said he wanted to publish it in conjunction with a film that was due to be made about Brendan. It was going to star Sean Penn. Penn was deeply involved in the project at the time. It was said he'd even had some teeth extracted to look more like him. That was dedication.

He pulled out of the film after I about halfway through the book. Gus said he wasn't able to publish the book because of that. He couldn't guarantee it would sell without the tie-in. I thought to myself: To hell with Penn. He'd ruined my deal. I couldn't feel sorry about his missing teeth. In my angrier moments I thought I'd be only too willing to knock out a few more of them for him.

I found another publisher soon afterwards. He said he wanted to call the book *The Brothers Behan*. I wasn't in favour of the idea. I'd have preferred to call it *The Life of Brian* like the Monty Python film. The publisher preferred *The Brothers Behan*. He thought it had a ring to it like *The Brothers Karamazov*.

The book came out with his title. Brian's name was put in big letters under it and mine in small ones. I'd done 90% of the work but he was a Behan and I wasn't. That was all that mattered.

We launched it in McDaid's pub. It was one of Brendan's stomping grounds. Niall Toibin was the main guest of honour. He'd spent a lot of his life doing one-man shows as Brendan.

He gave a nice speech about it from a corner of the bar. When he was finished I started talking to him about drink. He was trying to get off it at the time. He said to me, 'If you're going to cut down to, say, two pints a night, it's important to have the two every night. Don't just have one on the nights you're not thirsty. It's important not to upset the plan.' Only an Irish person could have thought like that. I was reminded of the joke about the Catholic hippie. He gave up pot for Lent.

Toibin had a drink problem himself. What Irish person hadn't? He wasn't too much younger than the Unblessed Trinity of Behan, Flann O'Brien and Paddy Kavanagh. Between them this trio probably drunk more in McDaids than the rest of the pub's patrons put together. Writing was almost inextricable from drinking in those days. O'Brien used to say any copy submitted to *The Irish Times* without the smell of liquor of it was deemed suspect. It was like John B. Keane telling me in 1980 that I must have been a good writer because I had a stink of porter off me.

Only bad writers were teetotal. 'I'm not a writer with a drinking problem,' Behan said, 'I'm a drinker with a writing problem.' This was a man who had his priorities right.

Behan drank himself to death in the sixties. So did Kavanagh and O'Brien. Such a practice was almost lauded at the time. The Irish branch of Alcoholics Anonymous was said to be an organisation where, if you told them you were planning to sober up, they sent someone round with a bottle of Guinness. J.P. Donleavy said, 'When I die I want to decompose in a barrel of porter and have it served in all the pubs of Dublin.'

Toibin was different. He took the plug out of the jug and lived to a good age. One of his daughters said to his mother one day after he went cold turkey, 'Wouldn't it be gas if it turned out Daddy wasn't an alcoholic after all?'

Toibin overheard the comment. He thought it was hilarious. Nobody in the house had ever mentioned it in association with him up before. The Irish were good at keeping secrets. Denial was a game all the family could play.

Doing the book with Brian was one of the most enjoyable periods of my writing life. He may not have been as well-known as Brendan but he was as funny as him at times. He also had a deep side to him that he kept well hidden.

I only saw it surfacing now and again. One day when we were driving past the Industrial School in Artane he broke down crying. I couldn't believe it. Here was this hardchaw who'd taken on publishers and politicians all his life. Now here he was being reduced to tears simply by passing a building he hadn't occupied for over half a century.

I should have understood. Muredach's had damaged me too. Our childhood never leaves us. He told me he saw a boy being struck so hard in the industrial school one day that he fell over a banister. He never found out how badly he was injured. He could even have died. The next day at lunch his chair was unoccupied. Nothing was ever said.

Sally didn't live long after the book came out. She died the following Christmas Day. It was a shock to everyone because she was so much younger than Brian. Her passing broke his spirit completely. He only lasted two years after her.

Life After Brian

After finishing *The Brothers Behan* I felt a sense of anti-climax. I thought of doing another book along the same lines. For a while I considered writing one called *The Brothers Joyce*. Stanislaus had an interesting relationship with James. Then I thought of *The Brothers Van Gogh*. Vincent's brother Theo kept him going when everyone else turned against him. Brothers were an interesting breed. Alas, such projects came to nothing. They were like so many other ideas I had over the years. Sometimes I thought my best books stayed in my head. Maybe they were better off there.

Instead I wrote a few books for a company called Prion. They were based in London. The first one was *The Cynic's Dictionary*. It was a revamp of Ambrose Bierce's *The Devil's Dictionary*. I'd been trying to get it off the ground for a few years with Chelsey Fox but publishers weren't biting.

Prion's editor was a young man called Andrew Goodfellow. He'd worked in Waterstones before becoming an editor so he had some inside knowledge of the kind of thing that appealed to the public.

He said we needed to give it a bit more authority. Hence the new title. It sold well and went into various editions on both sides of the Atlantic. It also went into a few foreign ones. I bought a copy of the Mexican edition, *El Diccionario de Los Cinicos*. At one point I thought of taking up Spanish so I could read it. Seeing your words in a foreign language is the closest thing an author feels to being God. Unfortunately they weren't my words.

Happy with the way the book performed, Prion now said they wanted me to do more work for them. I was learning how the business worked. Like any other one, if you had a hit you were asked back.

People kept saying I was 'prolific.' It was the word everyone used for authors when they couldn't think of any other way to describe them. I never liked being called prolific. Why was the term applied to authors more than anyone else? Mothers were prolific if they had big families. So were people who cooked lots of meals in restaurants and people who repaired cars or built houses or took in your washing.

Brian Behan said to me one day when I was writing his biography with him in 1996, 'If all the writers in the country died tomorrow nobody would notice but if all the binmen snuffed it, society would collapse.' I loved that quote, especially because it was a writer who'd said it to me. I mightn't have thought it was as good if it was a binman. We all like to protect our corner.

He was right. Writers shouldn't get any more credit for what they did than anyone else. Most of the time we were just massaging our egos.

Mine was dented one night when I got a phone call from Ballina. It was from a girl who said she was entering a quiz in her local school. Each contestant in the quiz had been asked to pick a subject and she'd picked me. I was flattered until I heard the reason: 'I felt you'd be easier to swot up on since your output is so slim.' I thanked her profusely for boosting my morale so much.

I always tried to remind myself that writing wasn't really important in the grand scheme of things. Gloria Swanson claimed she put more effort into her autobiography than into her marriages. Why? 'You can't divorce a book.'

Tom Murphy said *The Sanctuary Lamp* cost him his marriage. He secluded himself away from his wife almost totally while he was writing that play. Food was left on a tray outside his door during the heat of composition, presumably by his wife. Was the finished product worth her alienation? You couldn't divorce a play either.

Prion asked me to do two list books after *The Cynic's Dictionary*. One was on films and the other on books. I had a lot of material for the first one already on hand from my research for *Hollyweird*. It was easy enough to do because of that. I rarely threw anything away. You never knew when it would come in handy.

Andrew told me I needed to get into the modern way of doing things. He was always after me to buy a computer but I kept putting it off. I preferred pottering around with bits of paper that I stuffed into my pockets and transcribed onto a manual typewriter. I enjoyed that way of working. I heard it was the way John Lennon wrote books, and even Woody Allen.

I never got used to the idea of writing books on a computer. The noise of the typewriter was preferable to me. Maybe it brought me back to the days of listening to my father tapping away. We had the same two finger style.

I wasn't too keen on mobile phones either. When Mary got one she put all her contact numbers into a section of it. I advised her to write them out in longhand in case she lost the phone. The Luddite in me always distrusted technology.

My friend Des Duggan wanted me to do podcasts for his magazine *Senior Times*. He ran a successful set of these in conjunction with the magazine. He also wanted me to go on twitter and even Wikipedia. I told him I wasn't the type for any of that stuff.

People said to me, 'Once you get in on computers you'll never look back. They even do spellchecks for you.' I said, 'So what?' Whenever I mis-spelt a word on the typewriter I didn't mind typing it again on a little piece of paper and sellotaping it over the original page. Everyone thought I was mad to do that. Maybe I am but it works for me. Everyone is mad in their own way. I probably sound like the Kerryman sitting in front of his computer screen with a bottle of Tipp-Ex painting out the typos.

Another problem with computers is that they break down. What that happens you have to disconnect all the plugs and bring them somewhere to get them fixed. Anytime I did that I felt I'd forget where the wires went after I got back to the house.

People told me I should do a course on them. That way I'd lose all my phobias. I never went down that road. Maybe I hadn't enough respect for them. I made a decision to learn only as much about them as I needed to get by. Everything else I grudged.

You could also have an accident with a computer. What would happen if you spilled a cup of coffee over one? You could lose a year's work that way if you hadn't saved the file. I had a fair amount of Word documents. What if they got infected? Then there was all the time you had to sit at your desk. I preferred putting my typewriter into the car and whizzing down to Dollymount with it on the passenger seat.

I did a lot of my writing down there. You could park close to the sea. I liked listening to the waves thrashing against the shore. They inspired me. So did a little fox that used to ramble up to the car. I fed him bits of chocolate. Afterwards he toddled back to his covert in the dunes.

I wrote a biography of Ernest Hemingway in 1999. The following year I did *Historic Pubs of Dublin* for Andrew Goodfellow. It involved going into about thirty pubs around the city and asking them for their histories. I'd been frequenting someof them in the eighties when I enjoyed my drinking maybe a bit too much. I fell foul of a few barmen as a result. I wasn't sure if the same people were working in these places now. I got a few funny looks from them sometimes.

Had they seen me acting Jack the Lad? It was possible. There was a night in The Strawberry Beds when myself and another teacher started firing pool balls at one another for a laugh. It was the end of term. That's what happened at the end of term, wasn't it? Now I was behaving myself with a biro in my hand instead of a pint.

English publishers often asked me to do books about Ireland. As well as the Guinness one I did a few anthologies of Irish quotations for them over the years. I must have inherited my father's love of quotes.

Sometimes they were plagiarised by other writers. For a while I thought of taking them to court but I never did. It was practically impossible to prove something like that. I had to just accept it. Because I didn't make up the quotes I had no provenance over them. One plagiarist that I exposed was brazen in her defence. 'I'm just doing what you did,' she said. There was a slight difference. At least I chose the selection. She was copying it.

Now and again I made my own quotes up. I used to put the name of a non-existent person beside them to catch the plagiarists out. If they repeated it I'd know where they got it.

Historic Pubs of Dublin sold well. The publishers organised a television interview for me for it. I'd been asked to appear on TV once before. It was after I wrote *Hollyweird*. A researcher for a Gerry Ryan show had asked me if I'd be interested. I said no on that occasion. This was different. It was already set up.

I hated being on television. It brought up the old chestnut of my name change again. Was I Aubrey or Peter? Thankfully the programme was on at the crack of dawn. I presumed most of the people who knew me as Peter would be sleeping off their hangovers at that time. Mark Cagney was the interviewer. He came out to have a chat with me in hospitality. I told him I didn't like the idea of facing the nation. He was very reassuring, telling me not to worry.

When we went on air I got a blank. No matter what question he asked me I had trouble answering it. It was as if someone else wrote the book. Who was in my head? Who was in my mind?

I resolved never to go on TV again. I needed a drink after the show wrapped. I didn't care if it was in a historic pub or not. Any one would do.

A publisher in Dundrum took out an option on the book the following year. We now had the situation of an Irish publisher reprinting a British book about Ireland. It was ridiculous. I'd put a number of proposals to this publisher over the years without any success. I imagined they'd have turned down the historic pub book as well if I'd suggested it to them in the first instance.

It seemed as if the only way I could get a book published in my own country was to have it published across the pond first. As Charlie Haughey might have said, it was an Irish solution to an Irish problem.

A few years later a company called Powerfresh asked me to write a series of quote books based on the theme of birthdays. One of them was about turning 18. Other ones centred on turning 30, then 40, then 50. It meant dumbing myself down again but I still said I'd do it.

I rarely turned down a contract. A lot of the books I did bored me but I felt they might lead to better ones down the road if I took them on. I liked Michael Caine's quote: 'I always kept acting no matter how bad the parts were. By the time they discovered I couldn't do it I felt they wouldn't be able to stop me. I'd be too famous.'

Whenever I was asked why I went to so many publishers I said, 'Because they're the people who print the books.' It was like Ronnie Biggs being asked why he robbed banks. He said, 'That's where they keep the money.'

Writing the birthday books meant buying as many quotation anthologies as I could find. It was always good to have various sources. As the man said, 'when you borrow from one writer it's plagiarism. Borrow from a lot of them and it's research.'

I didn't expect them to be best sellers. I thought I'd shift a few copies and that would be that. I expected women would be the main buyers. One quote I forgot to put in was, 'Why are birthdays like toilets? Men miss them.'

They sold so well I was flummoxed. How had it come about? 'We advertise big,' the publisher told me.

Writing is as much about publicity as any other business. June told me once that the Irish Permanent Building Society suspended their advertising one year to see what would happen. They lost £1 million as a result.

Whenever I wrote a book I sent review copies to editors I knew. There were a few of these in Dublin. Terry Reilly, the editor of the *Western People*, was always helpful with plugs in Ballina. Since retiring from the Western, Terry has devoted himself to writing books on various themes related to Ballina – GAA, the famine, famous Ballina people and so on. He's the only person I know who's written even more books on Ballina than I have.

I was advised to do more radio and television but I didn't want that. I didn't want people listening to my voice or knowing what I looked like. I knew I was cutting down on my sales by that but it was worth it to me to keep my privacy. Tony Curtis said fame was like Alzheimer's disease: ''You don't know anyone but everyone knows you.'

Powerfresh had a distribution network that went all around the world. They didn't only sell in bookshops but in gift ones too. It was a bit like what happened with *Ryan's Daughter* and *Michael Collins*. The idea was that you went into the shop to buy a card. When you saw my book you took that as well. They were only the size of a cigarette packet. That meant they fitted nicely into the envelopes that had the birthday cards in them.

I earned a lot of money in royalties from these little bundles of rubbish. My more serious books hadn't made much. *Turning 30*, which I wrote one morning before breakfast, outsold my biography of Ernest Hemingway.

It wasn't about quality. It was about getting things to the maximum amount of readers in the shortest period of time. Or knowing the right people. My father used to say, 'Many great men died before Agamemnon but died for the want of a poet to sing their praises.'

Mary had a different angle on it. 'If Joyce was alive today,' she said, 'He wouldn't have been able to get *Ulysses* published without an agent.'

She said I needed to get one but I was reluctant to go down that road. I didn't think I was suited to it. Chelsey Fox found me too impatient. Vernon Futerman was easier to deal with but he didn't have Chelsey's contacts.

To get a good agent I felt I'd have to donate a kidney. In the years since I'd been with Chelsey and Vernon the landscape of writing had changed. The competition was more fierce now. Every second person in the country seemed to be a writer. If you threw a stone in the street you'd probably hit one. (But not hard enough.)

Roddy Doyle lived down the road from me. I often passed him on the street. Sometimes I felt like asking him what his secret was. The fact that he was a good writer maybe?

The people at the tops of the best seller lists usually had something spicy happening in their personal lives to get their books off the ground. Either they were alcoholics or drug addicts or they'd been abused as children or they were sold into slavery in Columbia and spent a few years in a dungeon there before making a miraculous escape back to civilisation.

I started thinking about ways I could beef up my profile. Maybe I could become a Mark Chapman by bumping off some celebrity. I thought of myself standing on the top of the Empire State Building with an Uzi. Then I'd become a household name and everyone would buy my books. It wouldn't be much fun selling them from prison though. Especially if you knew you were never going to get out.

After dropping the assassination idea I started writing poetry. Dennis Greig published a few collections of mine with his Belfast firm Lapwing. Dennis is an idealist. He works outside the mainstream of poetry where people gladhand one another. He's kept the ship rolling along through thick and thin, getting an enormous amount of chapbooks out without much assistance from the government or anyone else.

Don Marquis once said that publishing a book of poetry was like dropping a rose petal in the Grand Canyon and expecting to hear an echo. That was certainly true of my ones. I was hardly surprised. Poetry was never a big seller. That was especially true when you were working with a small publisher.

Tony Curtis – the poet, not the actor – said most people don't care about most poets because most poets don't care about most people. He had a point. The poems I studied at school were from another era. Dermot Bolger once said his ambition in becoming a writer was to be able to put the word 'car' into a poem. He'd never seen it in Yeats.

I could see where he was coming from. We were told about things like pathetic fallacies from Elizabethan sonnets but we hadn't the foggiest what they were. Could someone not have imitated Butch Moore crooning, 'Nobody knows I am cryin', 'cos I'm walkin' the streets in the rain'?

Things are different today. The people who make up the school courses bend over backwards to make the poems on them relevant to their readers. I'm not quite sure what 'relevant' means. Does it mean that instead of immersing themselves in the dubious delights of the Celtic Twilight, children now read poems about deadbeats getting hammered in pubs and then going home and beating up their kids?

At the launch of one of my Lapwing books there were seven people present. I was sharing the launch with another poet. He had four of his friends with him. I only had Mary. The etiquette is that each attender buys a copy of the other person's book. We just had to buy two of his whereas his company had to buy five of mine. I think I did better out of the night than him.

I doubt he or his friends ever read my book. I have to confess I didn't read his either. I wouldn't have blamed him if he threw it into the fire when he got home. Maybe it propped up the leg of a table for him or acted as a doorstop. What can you expect for five quid? Or from an unknown poet?

There are pecking orders in poetry like there are in every walk of life. I've seen the Tweed Brigade with their pipes and their corduroy trousers. They walk down Grafton Street expecting people to genuflect before them. I doubt these writers sell more than a dozen copies of their works. Most of the purchases are probably made from guilt. Or maybe the buyers want the person at their next party. The only poets who make money, as the man said, are those who write ransom notes.

Harry Clifton is one of the most respected poets in the country but I doubt the royalties on an average book of his would net him much more than the cost of a long weekend in Stepaside. It's his lecturing and his administrative work that's helped him keep the wolf from the door.

A few writers have avoided this scourge, like Seamus Heaney.. Winning the Nobel Prize expands your audience. Now you're going to have at least a dozen people at your readings instead of four.

Did he deserve it? I've always felt he was over-rated. Famous Seamus was a lovely man but not everything he wrote was a masterpiece. If he'd written 'Shit' on a cow's backside his fans would have said, 'Bucolic genius.'

Big Brother is Watching

The new millennium came in. I'd now been out of the day job for about ten years and managing to survive. Some years were better than others. There were highs and lows, periods of great activity and periods of doing nothing, just like in anyone's life. When I left teaching I promised myself I'd never complain about anything again. It meant that much to me to get out of it. I was never much good at keeping resolutions but maybe I'd change that for what people started to call 'the noughties.'

In 2001 all our worlds were changed when 9/11 happened. I was walking on Dollymount beach with Mary when the planes went into the Twin Towers. She got a text from one of her friends. Both of us went into a state of shock as we made our way back to the house.

It was a beautiful day. I believe it was beautiful in New York too. A cerulean sky hung over the city. It made the horror of watching the towers fall even worse. It was like being at a film. The thought of somebody jumping out of a building because they were burning to death sent shivers up my spine. Osama bin Laden, previously known only to people in politics, now became as much of a household name as his nemesis George Bush.

It was a long time before people went up in the air again. It was a long time before life became normal. Afterwards we had the retaliations and recriminations. Why did it happen? How were we going to get revenge? Tony Blair joined forces with Bush to save the world and in the process killed more people than Stalin. Blair pretended he was trying to save the world when all he wanted to do was ride on Bush's coat-tails.

What a ghoulish ambition. He'd been one of my heroes during the Good Friday negotiations. Now I felt he should have been indicted for war crimes. How could someone fall so far so fast? Somebody said to me, 'Bush and bin Laden aren't that different.' It made me think.

Life was getting serious. People started talking about nuclear threats, about the fact that in Bin Laden's eyes everyone in the western world was the enemy. You didn't have to be wearing a military uniform to be one of his targets. We all were. What was he going to do next?

I started to involve myself in trivial things, soap operas I wouldn't have watched to save my life a few years before. It was like therapy, the kind of escapism Keith got watching the old movies. I now felt I understood him better.

I developed a fascination for *Big Brother*, a television show that was so dumb it made *Carry On* films look intellectual. It featured people of limited intelligence. They lived with each other in a house in Elstree studios. Every day they told one another they adored each other over chick peas and cheap beer. At a designated time each week they went into a room and voted their new friends out of the house. The last person standing won the show.

Big Brother created an environment that was underlined by similar types of shows that followed it in the years ahead. People sat on sofas with cans of lager in their hands which they only left down to shout at the screen. Nonentities became superstars and in the process laid the groundwork for the kind of world that would create the Kardashians a decade or so down the road. Or *Gogglebox* – a programme which turned the camera on people watching television. we were now watching the watchers. The end of the world had to be near.

It was a Dutchman who thought up the concept of *Big Brother*. I had to commend the intelligence of a man who realised that if you put twenty people into an enclosed space together, no matter how much they professed undying love for one another at the outset, eventually they'd start stabbing one another in the back while giving eminently plausible reasons for doing so. What a noble work of art is a man.

The camera caught their every move. The highlights programme was on at 10 o'clock at night on Channel 4. Huge numbers of viewers tuned into it. It became a talking point on buses, in Darts, in pubs. Was it more important than World Wars? More important than famines and typhoons and global disasters and the fall-out from 9/11? Of course it was. For years I'd been looking for something to match the banality of my own life. Now I'd found it.

I'd been in withdrawal from trash TV since the O.J. Simpson trial ended in 1995. I needed something equally ridiculous to foist my addictive personality on. A show featuring nobodies doing nothing was just about right.

I became hooked on it. I watched the live feed as soon as it came on around noon and stayed with it most of the day. If I had to go out somewhere Id record it. On holidays I'd dart into internet cafes to hook myself up to a computer and find out who'd been evicted each Friday night.

The contestants were a mixed bunch in the first year of the show. One of them liked tofu. Another did Reiki healing. A third liked splashing paint all over her body and then flinging herself up against a wall to create works of art. It was a long way from playing marbles on Arthur Street in Ballina and then going in for lamb chops and spuds.

The show gathered extra momentum about half way through it when a man called Nick Bateman rocked the foundations of the house by telling the other housemates that his wife had died. It was a made-up story to get them not to vote for him to be evicted.

Then he started writing their names on pieces of paper. This was forbidden. It was a strict rule that nobody was allowed to write anything in the house. It wasn't as if he wrote 'Evict Darren' or anything like that. No, he just wrote 'Darren.' We were meant to believe that this was brainwashing of the highest order. As soon as the housemates saw these names they'd be motivated to vote them out by sme kind of subliminal hypnosis.

This was the worst crime in the history of civilisation. It was worse than Hitler and Ceausescu combined.

Bateman became a hate figure right through the country. People worried about what might happen to him when he got out of the house. Would he be tortured? Murdered? Hanging was obviously too good for him. They should tar and feather him and then pull his fingernails off.

I wondered if Tony Blair was going to get involved. He'd intervened about Deirdre Rachid in 1998, hadn't he? She was the woman who was imprisoned unfairly for fraud in *Coronation Street* once. He'd asked Jack Straw, his Home Secretary, to look into it. Wasn't this even more urgent?

Nick was let out the back door eventually for his own protection. I wrote to him after he was released. I had a bunch of insults I'd compiled. I thought they'd be good to put together in book form. They were things like, 'What do you think of a human race? I mean as an outsider.' If I brought them out myself I thought maybe they'd sell about ten copies but if we put Nasty Nick on the cover and let him write an introduction we could make a kill. Unfortunately he didn't reply. It was another brilliant idea down the drain.

Some time later he brought out a book himself called *How to Be a Right Bastard*. I wondered if I'd given him the idea.

In the second year the show was shown live on E4 as well as on Channel 4. That meant you could watch it almost non-stop. It wasn't totally live. The programmes were on a time delay of about twenty minutes. in case someone said something libellous and it had to be edited out. The producers turned the sound off if they had a doubt about something being contentious. It was replaced by birds tweeting or the drone of aeroplane engines. Sometimes I'd find myself watching people nattering away for hours without knowing what they were saying. I imagined them having these big discussions about the meaning of life. They were probably talking about whether they'd have chickpeas for lunch.

There was a contestant called Jonny Regan who intrigued me. Most people talked about Jade Goody. She really came out with some howlers that year. She was a sweetly eccentric fireball but for some reason I was more interested in Jonny. He was a fireman from Newcastle. Every night he kept the other contestants entertained into the small hours.

He formed a strong friendship with Kate Lawlor. She won the show that year. I wondered if he had a romantic interest in her. At one stage the house was divided into a poor side and a rich one. The rich got luxuries and the poor just basic rations. They were separated by a set of bars. One night at a party Kate transmitted beer into Jonny's mouth via a kiss. It was a beautiful moment.

In his outside life Jonny was engaged to an accountant called Joanne Llewellyn. Would his relationship to Kate jeopardise that? There weren't many people in the world who knew about Joanne Llewellyn. You knew you were a genuine fan of the show when you started memorising the names not only of the contestants but of the people they knew on the outside.

I was delighted for Kate when she won but in many ways I felt she owed her success to Jonny. Over the next few weeks I found myself writing to the fire department in Newcastle asking them what was happening to him. I knew he'd had a bit part in a film called *Billy Elliott* in the past. Was he continuing his acting endeavours? Nobody ever got back to me. Years later I surfed the net and discovered he married Joanne. My relief was palpable.

Brian Dowling won the show the following year. He was gay. He appeared in Eason's to sign a book about it. I went in to see him. Life didn't get much better than this. I was seeing this icon in the flesh. Was it really him?

I bought his book. I queued up with all the teenyboppers for him to sign it. Everyone was talking about the fact that he was in the closet when he entered the house.

'I went in to come out,' he said.

A few years later Ray Shah came second. He had Irish blood in him. He lived up the road from me. One day I saw him in a car and I followed it. What was I going to do if he stopped? Hug him? Tell him he was my reason for living?

When Victor Ebuwa was up for eviction in 2004 I was in Wexford. He was my favourite *Big Brother* housemate of all time next to Jonny Regan. I couldn't accept the fact that he might be leaving the house. Things looked bad for him because he'd lost his temper with one of the contestants the previous day. I broke every red light I came to so I'd get back to Dublin in time for the highlights programme of the show and all for nothing. Victor was evicted.

For the first five years of the show I could probably have named all the contestants who appeared on it, including the alternates (the 'newbies'). If I ever went on *Mastermind* it would have been my special subject.

Ray Shah was one of the last Irish people to do well on it. After that the Irish contestants tended to be mostly loopy. I felt it was a concerted policy on behalf of the Brits. They couldn't compete with our wit. That had been in evidence from the first year when Anna Nolan only lost by 2% to a rather ordinary DIY guy from Liverpool called Craig. Brian Dowling won it in its third year. Afterwards the programme planners seemed to get more and more nervous of us, leading them to put in the least attractive Irish contestants they could find. They couldn't leave us out altogether because that would be seen as racist so they did the next best thing: let us disgrace ourselves as a nation.

There was a spin-off show to *Big Brother* called *Big Brother's Little Brother*. It was hosted by Russell Brand, a man who was so funny he was obviously going to go places. He used to tell the audience they were 'a bunch of fucking bastards' if they were talking too loud. I got to know these people really well thanks to Russell.

I should have realised it was time to get worried the night I found myself looking at the show and thinking: I wonder where Barbara is tonight? Barbara wasn't a housemate. She wasn't even a panellist on *Big Brother's Little Brother*. She was an *audience member*.

Whenever I was away on holidays I asked Jacqueline to record *Big Brother* for me. She was my fail safe mechanism in case the places I was going to didn't have the channel that showed it. I used to book holidays with the proviso that they would but you never knew. I couldn't take the risk.

After the show moved from Channel 4 to Channel 5 I had a meltdown. Jacqueline didn't have that station. I was on holiday in a place called Pwllheli at the time. It was in Wales.

The apartment I was staying in didn't have Channel 5. I'd made sure it had Channel 4 but that was no good to me now. I rang the landlord but he couldn't do anything. I told him I'd pay him extra money but he still wasn't interested. What point was there getting the station for a week?

I went into a shop that sold televisions. The man behind the counter said there was something you could do with a connection cable that linked you up to the station. I tried it but it didn't work. I could never master intricate things like that. I ended up in withdrawal for the week. Was there a *Big Brother* Support Group in existence? Sadly no. I sat in the corner of the living room with a wet towel over my head muttering mantras to myself: 'Holiday please end soon, holiday please end soon…'.

When I got back to Ireland I linked up with a guy called Chris Smedley. He ran a video shop in South London. He sold me a DVD of the entire first episode of the show. I offered to send him my entire collection of DVDs if he recorded the current season for me and sent me on the tapes.

'You realise you're insane, don't you?' he said to me.

'Of course,' I said, 'Just don't forget to send on the tapes.'

He did that every week. It meant I was watching the show about a week after it took place. I had to avoid newspapers that had articles on who was evicted. It would have spoiled the surprise.

The show operated on a domino principle. Each week a contestant went out. The same formula was used for *X Factor* and *The Weakest Link*. These two shows had another thing the public seemed to like – rudeness. Anne Robinson bantered cruelly with her contestants. So did Jeremy Kyle. He exploited dysfunctionality in his gladiatorial-style exchanges with guests, sitting smugly on a platform as he told them they were worthless and needed to get a grip. His show had pretensions to rehabilitate his guests – or should I say his victims – but it was really about humiliating them. Robinson's show had money as its goal. Most hosts of money shows express sadness when a contestant fails but not she. When she said 'You leave with nothing' to the runner-up you got the feeling she was delighted.

Simon Cowell's putdowns on *X Factor* seemed to be just as scripted as Robinson's and Kyle's but nobody in the outside world complained. People liked seeing other people eating humble pie in front of thousands on national TV. Maybe they were being insulted in their own lives by a boss or a neighbour or a family member. It could have been their way of feeling they weren't alone.

X Factor was really just karaoke with better lighting. It had various manifestations on both sides of the Atlantic before it went for its tea. I hardly shed any tears about that. The game was up for people who didn't know a hatchet from a crochet. They had their shortcomings camouflaged by special effects. Not everyone could be Subo or Leona Lewis.

By now the public was beginning to realise it was little more than a soap opera. Good Guy Louis Walsh sparked against Bad Guy Cowell and the unfortunate (non) singers were caught in the crossfire. If they were liked they got into Paradise (another week in Boot Camp). If they weren't they were sent packing down the M1 with their out-of-tune voices. Cowell would dismiss them by saying, 'Depart from me ye cursed into everlasting flames' - or words to that effect.

I knew I was watching too much television. It was like a substitute for a social life. Old movies, crap game shows, it didn't matter what was on. I buttonhopped to beat the band. There was a time I used to like going to concerts and sporting events. Now I just watched them 'on the box.'

In 2002 Mick McCarthy dismissed Roy Keane from the Irish team in the lead-up to a World Cup match. He was our best player.

Poor Roy. He was the wrong man to have on the team that year. The rest of the lads knew we weren't going to do any good in the competition. They were mainly there to have a bit of fun and a few beers. The games could be sandwiched in between. It was the Irish way after all, wasn't it? The parties were always more important than the games.

Eamon Dunphy said of Ray Treacy once, 'He got 56 caps for Ireland. Thirty of those were for his singing.' How could Keane fit in with that mindset? Imagine being interrupted in the middle of your pint by him saying things like, 'Fail to prepare, prepare to fail.' It would put you right off, wouldn't it?

Roy called McCarthy 'an English cunt' during a press conference. Nobody could talk about anything else for months afterwards. The soccer became a side issue. More families fell out at this time than during the Civil War. People wondered which part of the insult bothered McCarthy more, being called English or a cunt.

I reached fifty the following year. Where had the years gone? I once interviewed the actor Tony Curtis. He said to me in the course of the interview, 'Yesterday I was born. Five minutes ago I went into Universal Studios. Five minutes later I was sixty.' That's how it felt to me. The minutes may drag in our lives but the years fly.

Mary threw a surprise party for me. Audrey's husband came up from Cork and June's one came over from Ballybrack. I wasn't very sociable to either of them. I didn't like surprises and I didn't like being fifty. It was the age at which people stopped asking you where the next party was and started saying things like, 'How's your prostate?'

Life became practical. I busied myself with sensible middle-aged things. We got the kitchen extended. Then we got the attic converted. The garage was converted into a second living room with a fancy carpet and atmospheric lighting. We called it The Meditation Room.

I even got the furniture in the house revamped for my bad back. Every chair had to be ramrod straight. Upholstery was pulled asunder by a bevy of experts so the degree of hardness in the padding was exactly right. One of them knocked me back almost a grand with all the work I had done on it. Hugo called it 'The Throne.'

Some of these jobs were complicated. Workmen tended to lose interest in them as a result. They said things to me like, 'No can do.' I'd say back, 'If I was Colin Farrell you'd find a way to do it, wouldn't you?' The last step in my sell-out to the values of the Celtic Tiger was getting a 42-inch plasma television screen. That was a kind of watershed. The sofa now owned me.

House jobs become important when you're in the thick of them. You get a hernia if everything isn't done exactly to your wishes. Days are built around trips to DIY shops. There are mega-important phone calls to plumbers, builders, electricians. Then a few months later you look at all the changes and you say, 'What was all that about?' It means nothing.

When lice started to invade The Meditation Room it wasn't much suited to meditation anymore unless you wanted to meditate on the fact that armies of lice were crawling across a very expensive carpet and leaving nasty black marks on it when you stepped on them.

A few months later there was a fire in it. It was an electrical one that started in the fuseboard. When a fireman opened it to investigate it, it exploded and he got thrown across the room. That didn't do much for the carpet either. On the credit side he wasn't killed. For a few seconds I thought he was. So did the other firemen. They were out in the driveway looking in at him with their mouths open. Like me they were probably wondering how foolhardy he was. The walls were black for months afterwards. The smell lingered even longer. We abandoned the room sand returned it to its former status of being somewhere that we dumped everything we didn't want.

Afterwards we got mice in the kitchen. In the old days when we had mice it was easy enough to find how they were getting in. That wasn't the case with the fitted kitchen. I cursed the magic presses, the fridge, the worktop. Nothing could be moved. Then we started to get mice in the attic. And birds.

After my disenchantment with the new attic, the new kitchen, The Meditation Room and the plasma TV I had a kind of catharsis. Maybe, I thought, there was a lesson to be learned from all this. Consumerism was evil. Greed was evil.

I threw 'The Throne' out and went back sitting in a chair I picked up in an old folk's home for twenty quid.

Obsessions

I went through a phase of ordering foreign movies from the internet. It became like an obsession. I kept hitting buttons on the computer. They had a thing where if you ordered a film they sent you details of another one that resembled it. 'If you liked that you might like this' sort of thing. They were unadulterated sales pitches and I fell for them all, hitting the computer keys so fast I was probably in danger of developing repetitive strain syndrome.

I didn't realise how much I was spending because it was online. I wasn't physically parting with money. It was like the time I was in Las Vegas with my gambling chips. They weren't like money either.

A part of me didn't believe digital things were real. When a few magazines I wrote for went online I lost interest in them. Nothing could compare to seeing them on a shelf or having them arrive in the post. Clicking keys on a computer screen to read them didn't measure up. I was like the Doubting Thomas who had to put his finger into Jesus' side to make sure he was properly resurrected. I wouldn't have wanted a virtual Saviour.

After the first few films arrived there was a lull. Had I been pressing the wrong buttons? I contacted a website forum called 'Where's My Stuff?' The reply said they'd all gone out to me.

One day the postman knocked on the door with a particularly heavy thud. When I opened it I saw he had a bag beside him. It was nearly as big as himself. It had all the DVDs in it. There must have been about sixty of them.

'Could you sign for these?' he said. Then he said, 'And when you're finished, do me a favour and throw that fucking computer out the window.'

Marlon Brando died in 2004. I thought there'd be an explosion of interest in him like there was when Elvis died. I even thought his house on Mulholland Drive would become a shrine just like Graceland had been with Elvis.

I needn't have held my breath. They showed some of his films on TCM for a few nights but that was about the size of it.

What was happening? Did people not realise how good he was? His main crime, I concluded, was not to die young. Okay, so Elvis wasn't a spring chicken at 42 but he wasn't 80 like Brando.

James Dean died at 24. He was freeze-framed at that age like an Adonis. Marilyn Monroe was in her thirties when she died. Both of them became iconic as a result. We got key rings, fridge magnets, endless coffee table books featuring shots of them in their prime.

Dean astride a motorbike with that arrogant look on his face. Marilyn in any one of a thousand luscious poses beaming at the camera. Brando didn't get the fridge magnets or the key rings or the coffee tablers. He wasn't 'cool' to the new generation so he was forgotten.

Robert de Niro filled the gap he left for me when he'd lost interest in acting after *Last Tango*. Sadly the same thing had happened to De Niro by 2004. He seemed to make about a half dozen films a year, each as bad as the next. I was reminded of a comment Richard Burton made once: 'I've done the most unutterable rubbish just to have somewhere to go in the mornings.'

I tried to look on the bright side. I'd lost Brando and De Niro but there was still Bob Dylan. I had all his albums by now but they weren't enough for me. Being a completist I went in search of CDs of his concerts.

There were a lot of these. 'You'll find me on a stage somewhere at 91,' he said once. He was on something he called The Never Ending Tour. It felt like it. There was a time when going to a Dylan concert showed you were hip. Now it more likely suggested you'd had a hip replaced.

I went to see him every time he came to Dublin. Some of the concerts were dire but I couldn't risk the opportunity of missing a good one. t was like my father with the horse he kept backing that never won a race in his life.

His connection with audiences was almost non-existent. He didn't introduce his songs and didn't react when we applauded. It seemed like he didn't much care whether we were there or not. He might have been singing to himself.

At one of the concerts he didn't even face us. He stood sideways at a keyboard the whole night. I'd have been as well off listening to one of his CDs at home. In another one he appeared with a hoodie over his head looking like a terrorist. He murdered the old classics that night.

Sometimes I felt like a masochist going to see him. It was like a woman continuing to date a man who constantly abused her. I was like a moth being drawn to a flame.

I never complained about any of this. You paid your money and you took your chance. It was a buzz just being in the room with God.

I was usually well armed with booze on these nights. You were frisked going in. That meant you had to be clever about it. I had an old coat with the lining torn. It provided a number of secret compartments. Before going out I used to store various bottles there. They rattled a bit as I walked in but not too much.

As the concerts went on I guzzled away to my heart's content. The people around me must have wondered where I was getting my supplies from. A pint cost a fortune at the bar in these places and you weren't allowed bring it back to your seat. What good was that?

Dylan's voice got croakier when the new millennium came in. That was saying something. Often you didn't know what song he was singing. Tommy Tiernan said, 'Bob probably doesn't know what one he's singing either.'

I didn't mind. He was Bob Dylan. It was his world. The rest of us just lived in it.

I found a CD dealer in Canada who had bootlegs of nearly all his concerts. He'd done approximately a hundred a year since the sixties. That meant we were probably talking in the region of 4000 concerts. 'I'll take them all,' I told him.

It was a slight exaggeration but I made big orders from this man. They arrived in little envelopes like the old movies I used to order from my movie dealer. He lived in Canada too. God bless Canada.

I brought them up to the attic to play them. Because they were bootlegs they were poor quality but that made me like them all the more. His voice was hard to hear if someone who was beside the person recording the concert made noises.

Sometimes they belched or started laughing. Now and then you'd hear the sound of someone spilling a drink on the floor. Incidents like these became part of the tapes. They made me feel I was at the concerts. I didn't have to leave the house. I just had to put on my headphones and turn the volume up.

When Dylan hit seventy he made albums from old classics of the Sinatra era. If someone told me Bob Dylan would do 'Some Enchanted Evening' when he was singing like a hound dog back in the sixties I'd have told them they were mad. But he made a great job of them.

One year he came to Vicar Street. Tickets were like gold dust. I heard of one girl who flew over from Germany for it. She sat outside the venue with a placard saying, 'Ticket wanted. Any price.'

Nobody was parting with them. The concert was a sensation. Bono even sang at it. I would have sold my soul to be there. Vicar Street was such an intimate venue it would have been like having Dylan in your kitchen.

A few weeks later I ran into my Kerry friend Donie O'Donoghue. He told me he'd been at the concert and fell asleep at it. I couldn't believe what I was hearing.

'I didn't want to go,' he said, 'Someone gave me a ticket so I thought I'd better use it.' He knew I had a big thing about Dylan. 'Why didn't you give it to me?' I said. 'I should have,' he said, 'The thought didn't strike me.' It took me a long time to get over that.

Dylan was a guru to many people in the sixties but I never lost my reverence for him even as he approached eighty. I always had to have that one person to float my boat. It happened with everything in my life, in music, films, even sport.

In golf my man was Seve Ballesteros. In tennis it was John McEnroe. Snooker had three heroes for me: Alex Higgins, then Jimmy White, then Ronnie O'Sullivan. Higgins got me through the seventies and Jimmy the eighties. Then Ronnie O'Sullivan came along and did things they couldn't. I never had pretensions to being comprehensive. I zoned in on individuals.

It was only when Elvis died that I got into Dylan. A few years later Abba came along. Then there was the Saw Doctors. These groups were regarded as middle of the road. I never liked labels. For me there was only two types of music: good and bad. The Saw

Doctors immortalised many things: Red Cortinas, Presentation Boarders and lots of others.

I never bought a U2 album. I realise how good they are but they don't move me like The Saw Doctors do. For me the N17 is more iconic than 'The Joshua Tree.'

In my opinion Abba was the greatest group of the century. I could never hear one of their songs without wanting to dance to it even if I was on my own. I read an interview with Bjorn Ulvaeus once where he said he composed them with forensic precision. That went along with Hugo's idea of music being created mathematically. I didn't mind how it was created as long as it moved me.

Nobody will ever appreciate how brilliant Abba were. Almost every song they recorded was a classic. The standard never flagged over all the years. Music snobs debunked them but what did they know? Snobs never got anything right, be it about music or literature or anything else.

After Abba split up I developed a passion for Bruce Springsteen. He became the new Dylan for me for a time. I listened to him with the same reverence with which I once listened to Dylan.

I was late getting to one of his concerts at the Point Depot one year. The bouncer wouldn't let me in for love or money.

I hung around outside waiting for someone to come out. I used to do that with Dylan. If I couldn't get a ticket for a concert he was giving there was always the chance of getting one from someone who left it early because they weren't enjoying it.

A guy came out. I approached him.

'I'll give you anything you want for your ticket,' I said. He shook his head.

'It's a different system now,' he said, 'They put something on your arm with a machine.'

He rolled up his sleeve to show me. There was some kind of mark on it.

'I'd have to amputate it to get you in,' he said.

'Then do that,' I said.

He went off laughing. Where were all the transplant surgeons when you needed them?

More Books

The years ran into one another. My book-writing went on in fits and starts. The most common word most writers hear from editors is 'No.' I never minded that. The important thing was to keep punching. It was either a feast or a famine but I promised myself I'd never complain about it. It got me away from teaching. I'd always be grateful to it for that.

My disordered life became as normal as my old ordered one. I kept doing books that sold to niche markets. The contracts I got weren't always good. I hardly ever read them so there were times I didn't know that until it was too late.

I got big advances, small advances and often no advances at all. It didn't matter to me. Big advances didn't always mean big sales. Sometimes it worked the other way round. When that happened you tended to get the blame. You weren't used again.

It could work the other way with a small publisher. They had less overheads and less expenses. Sales of a few hundred copies meant the world to them. As a result they were happy to let you do another book. I came to realise I was a product just like in any other business – selling shampoo or toothpaste or bars of soap. You were used when you were wanted and then dispensed with when you weren't.

When Robert Mitchum died I got a phone call one morning at about 6 a.m. It was from a radio person asking me if I'd like to say a few words about him on the air. It was a few seconds before I realised why he was ringing me. Apparently I'd asked for a plug for a book I did on the film *Ryan's Daughter* some years before. He hadn't given me the plug but he'd kept my number. Now he wanted me to do a favour for him to fill a slot. I said no. I also gave out to him for waking me up.

I was sorry to hear Bob was gone. He was one of the last of our two-fisted drinkers. I loved him as an actor. He always looked like he was going to fall asleep in the middle of a performance. Was anyone on the modern screen as natural? I doubted it.

I'd love to have met him when he came to Ireland to make *Ryan's Daughter*. I heard someone gave him a glass of poteen one night and it didn't knock a feather out of him. That was the real test of a drinker. I was given a sip of it one night in Ballina and it floored me.

I tried to keep my focus on why I started to write books in the first place – my fondness for films. That was more important than the things you had to go through to get them published or the bad treatment you got from publishers.

My advance for one book consisted of a meal in a fancy restaurant. The publisher acted as if he was giving me the earth. It was *nouvelle cuisine*. The menu looked so elaborate it could have been done by Michelangelo. Restaurants with elaborate menus usually have lousy food. They give all their money to the printers and have none left for the chefs.

I was presented with a cup of coffee in a soup cup. Why do restaurants do that? So it will go cold quicker? I can't come up with any other reason for the practice.

I got bit of meat that wouldn't fill a hole in your tooth. Beside it sat the tiniest potato I'd ever seen in my life. I gobbled everything up in record time and felt ravenous afterwards. I stopped for a spiceberger and chips on the way home. That was the best part of the night.

I had a few agents after Chelsey Fox but none of them managed to get me contracts. I wasn't sure how hard they tried. I felt like a mealticket to them. I resented giving them commissions on contracts I'd got myself. They were happy to let me do the donkey work as they sat back reading the contracts.

They phoned me now and again and made some points about copyright and percentages in plummy voices. When push came to shove they didn't do much more for me than post out invoices to publishers for my royalties. Then they took their 15%. That's nice work for licking a few envelopes. It was a ridiculous situation. I decided I'd be better off freelancing. Why buy a dog when you could bark yourself?

Some writers found it harder to get an agent than a publisher. They were the new aristocracy. In the film world it was even worse. Agents in Hollywood were harder to contact than producers or directors. If an actor wasn't 'hot' he was blanked by them. The harder he tried to contact them, the more they backed off. Woody Allen said, 'We're not living in a dog eat dog world anymore. It's more like dog won't return dog's phone calls.'

Writers were on the lowest rung of the totem pole in Hollywood. That was Keith's brief in a book he was writing about screenwriters. He was going to call it *Every Picture Tells a Story.* Screenwriters, he said, were the Cinderellas of the film industry.

There was a joke about them. 'Did you hear about the blonde actress? She was so dumb she slept with the writer.'

Maybe writers are the Cinderellas of the book world as well. Publishers do what they like with us. When my biography of Ernest Hemingway came out in 1999 I wasn't even informed about it beforehand. I was sitting in a journalist's office one day when I spotted it on his shelf. He'd got it to review. The publishers had sent him a copy but they didn't bother to send me one. I was 'only' the author.

A few years after that experience a publisher re-published some of my books under another name,

400

that of a non-existent person. My own one had been removed from the cover.

I rang her to ask her was going on. She said, 'Read your contract.' When I did I realised they'd done nothing illegal. The terms protected them. They could re-package my work any way they liked. I hadn't read the contract when I got it. Even if I had I wouldn't have thought 're-packaging' extended to a fictional person's name being put on the cover of a book.

Agents rarely contacted you. One of them apologised for not getting back to me once by telling me he had cancer. Another one went one better. He said he was in the Twin Towers when I was trying to contact him. The date in question was the 11th of September 2001, the day Osama bin Laden had his kamikaze pilots drive into the towers.

I was more intrigued by this man than annoyed by him. How had he survived bin Laden's attack? Had he jumped from a window? Parachuted his way out? With an imagination like that, maybe he should have been writing the books instead of me.

I felt like issuing a flier to all my potential agents saying, 'If any of you out there have any life-threatening illnesses, if you've been kidnapped by terrorists or are in the middle of an earthquake or a tornado or any other natural disaster I won't take it badly if you don't get back to me.' That should have solved any problems of communication.

My experiences in the book world led me to think I should publish a guide to any prospective writers out there. It could have warned them about what to expect from their chosen avocation. I made out some notes about what they should expect. It never became a book but I came across the notes the other day. Here they are:

Novels: The market is good for this genre but only if the novel in question is junk. Bodice-rippers go

401

down well. So do sprawling family sagas with a spicy undertow. For more bolshie readers a post-modern rant on disenfranchisement will work a treat, especially if the lead character gets disembowelled in the last chapter. If your junk novel sells, there's an even better chance your second one will. But only if it's trashier than the first.

Short Stories: There's a glass-blower in Carrigaline who isn't writing a collection of short stories at the moment. Apart from him I haven't been able to find any other people in Ireland who aren't. Check your local grocery shop for details.

Poetry: A writer approaching a publisher with a collection of poetry today is in danger of being shot on sight. Any poetry publisher disposing of prospective writers in this way will probably have a statue built to them. It's the least we can do.

Non-Fiction: Preferred areas here include tarot card reading, books on catamarans, healing, macrobiotic diets, bellydancing techniques among East African tribes and the latest techniques on carpet-cleaning in meat processing factories. All the better if you can link up the themes.

Editors: Editors tend to be in meetings from 9.01 on Mondays to 5.29 on Fridays. They have lunch between 1 and 2. After 2 they're in more meetings. A good time to get them on the phone, I've been told, is between 3.17 and 3.18 on August 18, 2027.

Secretaries: These are people who are paid to keep you away from editors. They generally tell you they're 'doing lunch' or 'indisposed.' Both of these terms are shorthand for getting drunk and playing golf – usually in that order.

Rejection Slips: Every good writer has enough of these to wallpaper their study. Treasure these if you're in the happy position of having a few yourself. You can use them to tell people how difficult your path to fame was when you finally get your novel published. (See *Novels*). If you haven't got one it's either a sign your proposal has gone AWOL in the post or your editor's secretary didn't think it worthy of one. (See *Secretaries*).

Critics: Critics have been described variously as eunuchs in the harem, people who know the way but can't drive the car, and a group of legless men who teach running. All such descriptions are resoundingly true but they're usually only dredged up by writers after they've been savaged by them in the trendy Sunday supplements. If you're one of this breed, buy a dartboard and put a photo of the offending writer on the bullseye. You may not hit it. Being angry, your aim may be off. But it will while away a few hours for you as you contemplate how you'll be viewed by posterity. (See *Posterity*.)

Money: The only books that make money are bad ones. This is mainly because bad books are enormously more difficult to write than good ones. Ask Jeffrey Archer. If you've written a good book, the best thing to do is throw it in the bin. If you've written a bad one, send it off to an editor immediately. (See *Editors*.) No doubt he'll accept it. After it's published, expect to hear gushing words of praise from the critics. (See *Critics*)

Publicity: If your book sells well you'll probably get invited onto the radio and maybe even the telly. Here you'll explain to a bored deejay with a hole in his jumper what Awfully Important Things you were trying to say in your novel (See *Novels*.) At this point he'll nod profoundly before telling listeners that the next item on the programme is the postal quiz or the cut-price offer on bottles of Dettol up in Finglas.

Friends: Your friends will love you if you have a best seller but, being human, they'll love you even more if you have a flop.

Posterity: This, as the man said, is what you write for after being rejected by all the reputable publishers.

403

As the heavy thud of yet another misconceived manuscript hits the floor in your hallway and you read the plummily-worded rejection slip (See *Rejection Slips*) of the silver-tongued devils who deal in such matters, remind yourself that they laughed at Marconi too.

Then blow your brains out. You'll be doing the world a favour.

Identity Crisis

Modern Woman shut up shop in 2003. A different supplement to *The Meath Chronicle* started in its place. Margot Davis stepped down as editor. The circumstances weren't great. She wasn't pleased about the way it happened. It always had a good readership. Now it was being discontinued for no good reason.

It was the *Chronicle* that made the decision. Margot said she didn't think it would be good for me to keep writing for 'The Woman' under the new editor. She didn't need to say that. I wouldn't have written for it anyway.

By now she'd developed eye problems. It was the worst thing that could happen to an editor. I'd damaged my own ones over the years by reading in bad light. I don't know if that was part of Margot's problem. She told me once that she had a detached retina.

She'd had various operations to correct it. Not all of them were successful. The bottom line was that she was without almost 90% of her vision. I felt really sorry for her but it wasn't a subject she liked talking about.

Anytime I tried to sympathise with her she changed the subject. I didn't know what to do. I used to enjoy sending her my books to read in the past. Now I couldn't.

She lost one of her daughters at this time too. 'Tragedies come in threes,' he said. First her eye problems, then the closure of the magazine and finally, worst of all by a mile, the death of one of her beloved children.

I don't know how she kept going. A small consolation was a plaque that was put up in her honour in Navan to acknowledge the great work she'd done for mental health over the years. It lifted her spirits to finally get some recognition for all the functions she'd organised for that cause.

I continued to play bad snooker as Peter Malone. Eventually the team fell apart. We reached our nadir the night we were beaten by a team of wheelchair victims. It gave a new meaning to the term 'walkover.'

Peter became my name outside snooker as well. It rolled easier off the tongue than my real one. People didn't give me a funny look when I said it. The problems started when I had to have my photograph taken as Aubrey. It was too late to change my writing name to Peter. I'd become too established.

The first time I'd encountered the problem was when I was working for the *Evening Press*. The editor had asked me for a photograph of myself that he wanted to use at the head of my columns. I decided to have one taken in a disguise.

I bought a theatrical wig and put on a pair of Groucho-style specs. Then I went into one of those booths that are used for passport photos. I put on as many weird expressions as I could: grimaces, frowns, bewildered looks.

A person I knew appeared as I was coming out. People you know always appear at the wrong times. It was a friend of Mary's. I told her I was appearing in a play. I was trying to get 'in character.' It was sort of true.

I sent one of the photos to the editor. He rang me in an agitated state.

'What the fuck is this?' he said.

I told him it was for the column, that I needed to disguise myself because I didn't like my name and I didn't want anyone I knew outside writing recognising me.

'It would have been easier to change your name instead of your face,' he said. It was a fair point. I told

406

him I didn't think of changing it when I began to write. Now it was too late. He ran the photo grudgingly. People who knew what I was doing thought I was a bit mad but it worked for me.

At least most of the time. I was in the snooker club one night when I saw the man who organised the fliers reading my column. He had his arms folded over it. My photograph was on top of it with my name beside it.

We started talking. He knew me as Peter. Now he was reading my column as Aubrey. I was hoping the Groucho wig was good enough for him not to make the connection.

It seemed to be. Writers usually get a buzz when they see people reading their work. I was no exception but that night I nearly needed a Valium until he turned the page.

The tenants in Viking Road knew me as Peter too. It was awkward when they were paying the rent into my bank account as Aubrey. Some of them thought it was a tax dodge.

I was Peter to my car mechanic too. His name was Frank. One day he came up to the house and asked me if he could borrow my car. His own one had broken down. We'd been friends for years so I didn't mind giving it to him. It was a mistake.

He arrived at the house again the next day. He looked distressed.

'The cops caught me going through a red light,' he said, 'I have to go down to the station with the insurance documents.'

They were in my name. When I showed them to him he got a fright.

A few weeks later I was up in his house for something or other. His mother came to the door. 'I heard you on the radio last night,' she said. I'd been doing an interview for one of my books.

407

Her attitude to me was different after that. I became a writer rather than Frank's friend. I was relieved when she sent me a Christmas card that year addressed to Peter rather than my 'real' name.

Then again, what's real? Is Bob Dylan 'really' Robert Zimmerman? Was Kirk Douglas 'really' Issur Danielovitch? Isn't the message of existentialism that you can be anyone you want?

Another person who said they heard me on the radio one time was the man who did my photocopying.

I hadn't given him my name. He must have recognised my voice. I didn't feel like getting into a discussion with him about writing. 'It wasn't me,' I said. Afterwards I transferred my business elsewhere. It bothered me when my two worlds collided like that. It spoiled both of them.

I hated talking about writing. Maybe most writers did. I read somewhere that Proust met Joyce one night. They had nothing in common. Proust said to Joyce, 'Do you like truffles?' Joyce replied, 'I do.' That was it. Both of them did well that night. I think I'd prefer to talk about truffles than writing.

My problem was that I attracted attention to myself by my dual identity. It was all right for people to have pen names but I had a 'life' name. My writing name was my real one.

Frank's mother continued to send me Christmas cards every year. She addressed them to Peter Malone.

I appreciated that just as much as I appreciated it when the girl who did my typing for me, Debbie, addressed items in the post to Peter Malone. Some of these were transcripts of my books with my 'real' name on them. Maybe I should have been psychoanalysed for having a crisis of identity.

Most of the problems with my name centred around photographs. When I published a book about the funny side of dating in 2002, a journalist from the *Evening Herald* interviewed me about it. The interview went well but then he said he wanted a photograph of me.

I sent one in to him but he said it wasn't 'high res' enough. I said I'd send him another one but he wasn't happy with that. He said he was sending a photographer to the house.

I panicked when I heard that. How was I going to disguise myself? I put on a pair of glasses and a beanie. When the photograph appeared I looked ridiculous but I didn't care. The book was quirky. I could be quirky too.

A few years after the dating book I did a guide to Harry Potter books. It wasn't my idea. I'd never read a Potter book in my life. A friend of Des Duggan's saw it as an investment opportunity. His daughter was big into the books. He said he'd pay me a fee to do it. We were going to share the royalties.

'Harry Potter is one of the things you can't lose money on at the moment,' he said. The other two were *The Da Vinci Code* and Sudoku. Someone said, 'I'm writing a best seller. I've decided to call it *Harry Potter and the Da Vinci Code of Sudoku.*'

It was the first book I wrote on the computer. I had to be in the house because we were having it done up at the time and the builder needed me to be around. He was using a Kango hammer to drill through a wall. It never seemed to stop. The noise deafened me all day every day. I resolved never to use the computer again for a book.

After I finished it I sent it off to HarperCollins and they took it. They got a woman who'd done some kind of a thesis on Rowling to fact-check it. She went through it with s fine toothcomb before it was published.

Even then it didn't measure up to the standard of the Potter trainspotters. They took it apart on the internet. Most of them were teenyboppers. No matter how much of a Hogwarts expert you were you'd never know as much as a twelve year old. But we did well out of the book. What we earned wouldn't have been more than pocket money to Rowling but it tore strips off most of my other books as far as royalties went.

The only bugbear about it concerned my old problem with photographs. The features editor of the *Irish Independent* rang me one day and told me he was doing a feature on Harry Potter guide books. Rowling had just sued someone who'd done a guide like mine.

He wanted to know if I was worried. 'Would you like to do an interview?' he said, 'I'll send someone out to take your photograph.'

I did the interview but when a photographer rang to say he was on the way out to the house later that day I told him to do a U-turn. I didn't give a reason other than to say I was camera-shy. I'd spoken to the editor for over an hour about the book but when the interview appeared it was reduced to a few lines.

I rang him and asked him why. 'My boss wasn't impressed with your coyness,' he said.

My name caused another kind of a problem when a woman called Anna Malone from Tucson hacked into my email account one day when she was trying to get into her daughter's one. She was worried about the friends she was making and wanted to keep tabs on her.

Her daughter's name was Aubrey. It was a girl's name in America.

Suddenly I knew how the character felt in Johnny Cash's song 'A Boy Named Sue.' He tries to kill his father towards the end of it. He only stops when his father tells him he gave him the name to toughen him up.

I wasn't sure if it had that effect on me. Maybe it had. Maybe when I was mixing around with all those hardchaws in the snooker halls in my teens I was subconsciously trying to break out of the Edwardian environment my father mapped out for me by calling me Aubrey.

I thought of other 'tough guys' who had Christian names that weren't exactly macho – Norman Mailer, Humphrey Bogart, Sylvester Stallone, Arnold Schwarzenegger. Even Ernest Hemingway.

Did they over-react too? Philip Larkin's famous lines came into my head: 'They fuck you up, your mum and dad.' In my case it was just my father.

It was six months before I got the account back from Anna Malone. By then about 400 emails had come in. The header on the first one said, 'Oops, I Accidentally Hacked Into Your Account.'

She should have told me. She could easily have given it back to me if she wanted. Why didn't she? Mary suggested emailing my account from her one to see what would happen but I didn't want to do that. If I did I thought she'd be hacked as well. There were reports in the media about the Russian Mafia doing a blitz on people around that time.

We'd also been getting a worrying amount of phone calls at 8 in the morning from a man who called himself Malcolm. He said there were irregularities in my bank account.

He didn't sound like a Malcolm to me. He sounded more like an Abdullah. And I didn't think he was calling from London as he said. More likely it was somewhere like the Philippines.

The first time your email account is hacked into it's a shock. Not only because you've lost your account but (at least if you're me) you haven't kept a list of your contacts. You start thinking mega-important messages are coming in for you that will change your life - and you can't see them.

Did Penguin email me to say I'd been nominated for the Booker?

Was there a tax error in my favour that just netted me ten grand?

Afterwards you get more savvy. You prepare back-up lists. But the first time you lose your account it's like losing an arm or a leg. That's how attached to technology we are.

Cruising

'The sun shone, having no alternative, on the nothing new.'

Hugh Kenner said *Waiting for Godot* was a play in which nothing happens twice. Nothing seemed to happen in my life many more times than that. I felt the way Dave Allen said he felt about John Major: If I was drowning and my life passed before me, I wouldn't be in it.

Work is hard, as they say, but not working is harder. I missed the routine of having to go into school. When you had nobody cracking the whip you had to crack one yourself. It wasn't always easy. Motivation became a problem. It was too easy to become a couch potato, to soak myself in mindless books and mindless movies.

What will I do today, I asked myself. Scrub down the worktop? Iron my shoelaces? Contemplate the meaning of existence?

Every morning I rolled the boulder up the hill like Sisyphus. Some days I found it difficult to wake myself up. My idea of exercise was having my breakfast in bed.

To adrenalise myself after getting up I took to putting on the radio at full blast. Sometimes I put the television on as well. I let them fight it out as I stood between them trying to get energy from somewhere. I sat at my typewriter but nothing came out. I wasn't suffering from writer's block but rather writer's apathy.

Some days the voice I heard during the day was that of the weighing scales in the bathroom. It was a very nice one, I have to say.

There were phone calls from America at all times of the day and night. Sometimes I couldn't think if it was morning or evening over there when I picked up the receiver. Maybe they weren't sure what time it was in Ireland either. Or else they knew I was a night owl.

There was a time Basil and Jacinta might phone once or twice a year. That was usually at birthdays or Christmas. Now they were on much more frequently. It was great to hear from them but I never really had any news for them whereas they had loads for me. Occasionally I even got a call from Ruth. That was like getting a call from The Pope because Ruth was even more of a recluse than I was. She hadn't been to Ireland since my mother died. That wasn't because she didn't want to come but because she wanted it too much. The loneliness of going back would have been too much for her.

Any form of connection with the outside world knocked me out of my rhythm. I tried to get into a space where I could create a parallel universe on the page. This was something the 'real' world interfered with. Or was my writing the real world?

I kept watching *Big Brother* to fill in the time. It had gone steadily downhill since the early years but I was still addicted to it. Sometimes I thought of applying for the auditions. I'd have been good drawing up a menu for chick peas - and talking rubbish for twelve hours every day.

All you needed to get in was to have a tattoo in an unusual place. And some eccentric characteristic, like, say, the fact that you thought you were God. Or the reincarnation of Louis Quatorze.

It also helped if you mis-spelt your name. If you were Roger you should write it as Rodger or Rodgyer. If you were Billy you should write it as Billie or Billye. I could write my name as Aubree or even Awbree. Maybe I'd say I had a sex change as well. Or that I was kidnapped by Martians as a child.

The show was supposed to be about ordinary people in an extraordinary situation. It gave rise to a spin-off one called *Celebrity Big Brother*. That was supposed to be about extraordinary people in an ordinary situation. Except they weren't extraordinary. In fact they weren't even celebrities. Many of them were has-been soap stars desperate to get their faces back on the telly. My father had a phrase that came back to me when I watched the show: 'When everybody is somebody, nobody is anybody.'

Both shows lost their credibility when the lines between them became blurred. We weren't watching ordinary people in an extraordinary situations anymore or extraordinary people in ordinary ones. We were just watching boring people in boring ones.

After my fascination with *Big Brother* ended I looked for a substitute for it but I couldn't find one. Maybe I was better off. I was watching too much television and eating too much bad food. My doctor told me I needed to go on a fat-free diet.

'You have a sweet tooth,' he said.

'All of them are sweet,' I told him.

I ate because I had to be doing something. That was the problem about being hyper-active. I bit my nails until they bled. Then I plastered them so they wouldn't bleed any more. As a child I'd been prescribed something called Stop 'n' Grow. It was to try and make me curb the habit. You painted it on your nails with a little brush. 'It's a foul-tasting substance,' the doctor said. Over time I developed a taste for it. Then I went back to my chomping. Maybe I was a cannibal in a previous life.

Being hyperactive didn't mean I was busy. I just had to keep moving. I saw a film called *Magic* once. Anthony Hopkins played a magician in it. He had the same problem. His manager asked him one day to stop moving for a few seconds. He thought it was a laughable suggestion but when he tried to do it he couldn't. I wondered if I was a bit like that.

I tried to write creative literature. Sometimes I succeeded and sometimes I didn't. I went through a phase of writing plays. I sent one of them to Hugh Leonard to see what he thought of it. He was the man who wrote 'The Kennedys of Castleross.'

He'd done dozens of plays since. He wrote back to say, 'God help you, I think you might be a playwright some day - but not with this. Send it to the Abbey with my recommendation that they reject it.'

I had to scratch my head over that one. Was he saying he liked it or that he didn't? What would be the point of sending it to them for them to just return it to me? I decided to save myself a stamp. I stuck it in a drawer somewhere instead.

When my playwriting bug passed I looked for other ways to keep the process of blackening pages going. For a time I became a letter-writer. I wrote letters to everyone I could think of. Most of them were about sport.

I wrote to the manager of the Mayo football team to tell him the team needed to tighten up on their marking. I wrote to the manager of the national soccer team to tell him my ideas about the best way to qualify for the World Cup. I wrote to Eamon Dunphy to say he was wrong about his view that Michel Platini wasn't a good football player. I wrote to Arsene Wenger and told him not to worry about the fact that Arsenal didn't seem to be able to beat Manchester United.

'The problem,' I told Arsene, 'is that Ruud van Nistelrooy keeps diving in the box.' I got a letter back from his assistant saying, 'Arsene is out training the squad at the moment but he appreciates your comments.' I was disappointed not to hear from the man himself. I was hoping he'd tell me he'd be keeping an eye on van Nistelrooy from here on so he wouldn't get any more soft penalties.

The best letter I wrote was to Bill Clinton. It was when he was getting a lot of grief over his relationship with Monica Lewinsky.

I told him I felt sorry for the way they were trying to get him impeached and how I hated Kenneth Starr for hounding him from pillar to post. I told him I agreed with Barbra Streisand in her view that a person's private life had nothing to do with their ability to govern a country. I can't remember ever agreeing with Barbra Streisand on anything before this.

I got a nice letter back thanking me for my good wishes. It probably came from a machine but so what. I felt reassured that the impeachment proceedings would be derailed. Bill could show Starr my letter. It would open his eyes to how the western world felt about him. He'd be loved by people again.

After I ran out of people to write to I went back to my short stories. Most of these went nowhere. I had the odd ones published in obscure magazines that I imagined about ten people in the world read. It seemed pointless. Why did I work so hard for so little reward? I saw other writers of my age with their reputations already made. Why wasn't it happening for me? Had I chosen the wrong career in life?

I went on long walks trying to sort my head out. Sometimes I thought I should have stuck at the teaching. I'd never known what I wanted to do since childhood. Teaching wasn't ideal but at least it got me through a few difficult years. Now the stakes were higher. I was nearing middle age. It was time I got sense.

I cruised the malls of Coolock and Donaghmede looking for something to stimulate me. I drove to indeterminate locations – Howth, Sutton, anywhere I could think of to get some thought processes going. I parked the car beside beaches, gazing out at the horizon as I nurtured vague dreams of visiting the places I took for granted when I was younger. I'd got to a lot of them almost without thinking. Now the idea of going anywhere at all was a challenge. I felt like Sisyphus rolling a boulder up the same hill year in and year out. Life became a glorified form of *Krapp's Last Tape.*

I thought the problem was lack of routine. Maybe I needed something with a timetable.

I applied for a job in a college off Clyde Road in Dublin 4. It was fine for the first few days, like most things in life, but then I realised I'd made a mistake. Before the week was out it was made blindingly clear to me why I'd got out of teaching. It was doing my head in.

The college was posh. The pupils were so precocious they thought they knew more about life than I did. I found them insufferable. They were the new Belvederians, the X generation, the millennials. They didn't need me to teach them. Maybe I needed them to teach me.

They looked about four years of age but spoke like middle-aged men. I remembered the old joke about two kids in an Oxford kindergarten. Pupil One says to Pupil Two: 'There's a contraceptive behind the radiator.' Pupil Two says: 'What's a radiator?'

I fell back into my old habit of watching television non-stop. We got a digibox that had about fifty channels on it, each more worthless than the other. I button-hopped till I was blue in the face, not even knowing what I was looking for. My fingers seemed to have a life of their own as they went from programme to programme.

Sometimes I found a football match or a documentary that diverted me for a few minutes. One day I happened on to an American channel that featured people being asked about unique experiences they had. I couldn't make up my mind if they were mad or not – or if I was. They said things like 'I'd love to make love to a penguin.' 'My mother is a telephone box.'

The Celtic Tiger continued to roar from the midnineties through the new millennium. For the past decade or so Ireland had been the style capital of the world. We weren't the country of the IRA anymore. We were from the country that created Riverdance. Dublin had morphed from a rebel stronghold to Disneyland with superpubs.

Property prices went through the roof. A horsebox in Ringsend sold for a million euro. There was a time you'd be ashamed to say you owned it. Now queues were ten deep on a Saturday morning to try and secure an interview with an estate agent. The website advertising such properties was appropriately called DAFT.

I thought of selling Viking Road. Its value had increased a lot over the years. People were now queueing up to move into it. I put up the rent and nobody complained. I was working my socks off at my books but they weren't making any money. All I had to do to make money from Viking Road was sit back and do nothing. It didn't make sense but then what did in life?

I didn't even need to put in ads for tenants anymore. The ones who were leaving always knew someone. If you offered them the keys they'd nearly bite your hand off.

That hadn't always been the way. There were years when I couldn't rent it for love or money. Some tenants used to make me feel they were doing me a favour even by looking at it. I rented it to some disreputable tenants in those days just to have it inhabited. Now I could tell someone they weren't suitable for any sort of reason.

I felt sorry for a lot of them. Some of them were in dire straits. I tried to take in people who needed the house rather than those who had other options. It made me feel good to give it to someone on welfare, a hard-pressed family who'd probably end up in a hostel somewhere if I didn't take them. Would I go for the safe option or the hard luck case? It was a hard balance to get.

One couple I felt sorry for turned out to be nightmares. The woman was a depressive and her husband was an alcoholic. They had a young daughter. I heard a rumour that the man was abusing her. He lost his job afterwards. They stopped paying rent. I told them they'd have to move. They didn't say anything to that. Then they started harassing the neighbours. I got many calls from the police in those days.

Eventually they moved out but only as far as the other side of the road. One night soon afterwards I was in the house doing some renovating for the new tenants when I heard screaming.

I looked out the window. The man was at the door of the house. He was shouting at his wife to let him in. 'Open the door or I'll kill you,' he was saying. She was afraid to. The shouting got louder. Then he broke a window. He climbed in through it. A few hours later a cavalcade of police cars arrived.

The people living in the surrounding streets weren't aware of these kinds of scenarios. They didn't realise affluence and poverty lived tooth in jowl with one another. I wouldn't have been aware of that either if I hadn't been put in the position of seeing it at first hand. There were two Irelands, official and unofficial. I saw both from my eyrie in Dublin 7.

Temple Bar wasn't far away. It used to be nothing in the old days. After it was done up it became the most talked-about area in the city. Once the refuge of stragglers and hobos, it was now where all the trendies went. A meal there could set you back a week's wages.

People flew in to Dublin by the bucketload for stag parties in Temple Bar. Some of them just flew in to make eejits of themselves. Thanks to *Fr. Ted* they knew that word now. And feck.

Ireland became rich for a few years. Anyone with a few bob in the bank bought second houses. Some of them went to New York for the weekend. People whose ancestors fought for the clothes on their back were now shopping for designer wear in the best stores. Even poor people became rich. Suddenly every Tom, Dick and Harry was buying an apartment in Andalusia.

We became vulgar but it didn't suit us. We were like someone who won the lottery and didn't know what to do with the money.

In 2008 we became poor again. The economy collapsed like a house of cards. We should have seen it coming. What went up had to come down. It was the way of all things since the dawn of time.

Businesses closed down. You couldn't walk down the street without seeing somebody with a cup in their hand asking you for a coin or two. People who'd been on the pig's back a few short years ago were now on the breadline. There was a high suicide rate among the most unlikely professions – dentists, taxi drivers, psychiatrists.

Ireland became ruled by the troika. They came over from the EU and told us what to do. If we didn't accede to their demands, we were told, the country would come to a standstill. We wouldn't even be able to get money out of ATM machines.

We obeyed them to the letter. Even though we had the reputation of being a nation of rebels we did everything we were told. Maybe it suited us better than prosperity. The famine mentality was still in our DNA.

A lot of people went into negative equity. Many lost their homes. They threw their house keys into the letterboxes of auctioneers and started living on the streets.

Disaffected husbands went back to live with alienated wives. Disaffected wives went back to alienated husbands. Kids went to McDonalds to have vanilla milkshakes and try to bond with parents they only saw once a week.

Would we ever crawl out of it? Someone said the only light at the end of the tunnel was a train coming the other way.

Eddie Hobbs was more positive. Eddie knew everything about money. He was a kind of God for us. David McWilliams was another one. David used a lot of big words. He was like the guy in your class at school who always had his hand up. People listened to Eddie and David as if they were the new Maharishis. Our country was in pain. We needed gurus to lead us out of it to some Promised Land.

We found them everywhere. A man called Conor Faughnan became famous because he told us to drive safely and join the AA. That stood for the Automobile Association. I thought he'd be better off telling us to join the other AA, Alcoholics Anonymous. It seemed to be a more reliable way of ensuring safe driving, at least for an Irish person.

Billy Connolly said there was an organisation somewhere called AAAA: 'If you get elephants they tow you home.'

The unemployment figures rose to a ridiculous level. Men who'd told their bosses to eff off a few short years before because they were going to New Zealand to start an ostrich farm with their Serbian girlfriend were now going back to them with their tails between their legs looking. They were looking for their old job back in the haberdashery shop in Boris-in-Ossory.

Enda Kenny told us we had to keep practising austerity. Angela Merkel was cracking the whip from

Germany. Her ancestor Adolf Hitler had cracked it in a different way. This was dictatorship from the distaff side. She wasn't attacking us with tanks but rather bank balances. The pen was just as mighty as the sword. We listened to her just as we listened to the troika.

More beggars appeared on our streets. Homelessness became rampant. So did hospital queues. People on trolleys were afraid to go to the toilet in case they came back to find them gone.

We got the message. This was hard core poverty. We stopped buying apartments in Andalusia and Gucci shoes in New York. We even started paying house rates. Angela Merkel said we had to.

She said we'd have to pay water charges as well. Enda agreed. All the other countries in Europe had them, he told us. He had Corporation workers dig up our streets so they could put counting machines outside every house. He said we couldn't turn on taps without monitoring how much we'd be using. Children started saying to their mammies and daddies, 'Can I flush the toilet after I go to the loo?'

It got too much for us. We told Enda and Angela what to do with themselves. House charges were bad enough. The water rates were a bridge too far.

Brian Lenihan, our Minister for Finance, tried to hammer out a money deal with the EU. We were asking for a lot of it. They said they'd give it to us if we paid megabucks interest on it. We asked them to reduce this. Would they take pity on innocent little Ireland? The short answer was no. We were going to be poor for a long time.

Brian had cancer. He was on his last legs and we still made him haggle with Angela. Then he died. It was like what happened to his uncle. He was called Brian too. He had a liver transplant in the Mayo clinic. The Lenihans always seemed to have bad health.

423

The drug wars on our streets got worse. People shot one another in the heads in bars. Every other day the corpses piled up. We gave them cuddly names like something out of Walt Disney. There was even a television programme that glorified them. It was called *Love/Hate*. A character called Nidge developed a cult following no matter how vicious he acted. It was as if Quentin Tarantino had come to Dublin.

Instead of becoming distressed by the bloodbaths unfolding around us we turned a blind eye to them. We watched soap operas and silly films and filled our days with trivia. It was like Nero fiddling while Rome burned.

We wondered if we'd have a good song in the Eurovision. I wasn't sure why. So we could be humiliated again? That had been happening with disconcerting frequency in recent years. We'd won it 2704 times in the old days. Johnny Logan was responsible for 1187 of these. Now Eastern Europe was having its day in the sun. Suddenly we were the bad guys. The new world was getting its revenge on us.

We entered Dustin the Turkey one year. Either we were trying to amuse the judges or annoy them. I wasn't sure. Whatever our motive was it didn't work. Eastern Europe wasn't amused and still didn't vote for us. Countries we'd never heard of usually won now. They sang atrocious songs you'd pay *not* to hear.

Another year a transgender woman won. Her name was Dana. She was a long way from our own very prim and proper Dana, a lassie who wouldn't say 'Shit' if her mouth was full of it.

Graham Norton commentated on the show for the BBC. He referred to England as 'we' instead of 'they.' His predecessor Terry Wogan used to do that as well.

Norton was from Bandon and Wogan from Waterford. Had they forgotten their origins? 'When in Rome, do as the Romans' was okay as a precept but did they have to *become* Romans in the process? Maybe they had to renounce their birthright to preserve their sanity. Marty Whelan used to say commenting on the show made him lose the will to live.

Outside the never-never world of Eurovision there were horror stories. Everywhere you looked you saw people being turfed out of their homes, being murdered, being mown down on motorways. Hospitals suddenly didn't seem to be places you went if you wanted to be cured anymore. Instead they gave you infections, vomiting bugs, MRSA.

Unemployment figures reached an all-time high. Someone told me a story about a man who jumped into the Liffey one day in an attempt to kill himself. Another man swam towards him and pulled him out. 'It's nice of you to save my life,' the man said, 'but your heroism is misplaced. I want to die.' The other man said, 'I'm not trying to save you. I just want to know where you worked.'

Mary told me I should stop watching news programmes. She preferred to soak herself in Jeremy Kyle, Steve Wilkos, Judge Judy. She said too much reality was bad. I reminded her of Peter Finch in that film where he said he was as mad as hell and wasn't going to take it anymore. I told her I thought Finch was an optimist.

She liked a programme called *Say Yes to the Dress*. It involved a bride-to-be visiting a bridal store and choosing between various dresses she might wear on her wedding day. The climax came when she found one she liked.

The proprietor of the store asked her the pivotal question; 'What do you say to the dress?' To which she replied, 'I say yes to the dress.' At this point her family, whom she'd brought with her, broke into applause – and often tears. After seeing the excitement generated by such moments I concluded that society would probably be much happier if we did away with grooms and replaced them with wedding dresses. In all my years watching the show I never saw a woman divorcing a dress. They also seemed to bring them much more happiness than men did.

Mary tried to domesticate me by giving me jobs around the house. I was tasked with dealing with the problem of mice. They'd been coming in for years without showing any evidence of an entry point. I put down poison and traps. I preferred the traps because of *habeas corpus*.

The poison was just as lethal. I saw a mouse on top of the curtains one day that was shivering. It was summer at the time. I deduced it was because of something in the poison. The man who sold it to me told me it did something to their nervous system. I felt mean. Was there any other way to deal with the problem? Eventually I came to a 'peaceful coexistence' solution. I boarded up all the areas behind the presses. They could scurry around in there as long as they didn't come into the kitchen itself. They seemed happy with that.

The second step in Mary's domestication of me concerned an attempt to teach me how to use the washing machine. That was never going to happen. I preferred taking my clothes down to laundermats to be cleaned by other people. I wasn't good with machines. It was difficult to know which switch to press for the different garments. The New Man was nowhere to be seen.

I'm of average intelligence. I'm sure if I put my mind to it I could probably make a fairly good fist of learning how to work the washing machine. Unfortunately I don't want to. I've always believed that if you give your mind over to things like that there'll be less room in it for more interesting things. That's my excuse anyway.

Every now and again Mary told me the windows were dirty. I was able to do the downstairs ones easily enough but I didn't have a ladder to get to the top ones. She said if I didn't do something about them she was going to get a man in. I didn't see the point of paying someone 500 euro for a half hour's work so I got down to business, sellotaping a brush to the top of the kitchen broom and swishing away. I stood on the roof of the car to get at the high bits.

Whenever I tried to paint a wall I was even worse. My handiwork looked a bit like Picasso from his cubist period. I got the nickname 'Slob It On Milosevic.'

The grass was another headache. It was about the size of a tennis court. I kept breaking lawnmowers in my attempts to keep the grass down. I got a man to put some substance over it to stop it growing. Then he put a thing he called a membrane over it. He added pebbles to complete the job. He seemed happy with his work but I didn't like it. I thought it looked like a car park.

'Let's plant things,' Mary said in an optimistic voice. It was as if you could just flick your fingers and lovely things came up. That might have been the way in an ideal world. In the real one, everything I planted died.

I decided I'd have to do something about the grass. I put in paving stones and planted some red robins around them. They grew so fast the garden came to resemble a jungle.

I added some other plants afterwards. I was never a 'green fingers' but when I started something I tended to become consumed by it. I remembered looking out at the gardener in the school in Clonsilla one day when the pupils were giving me a hard time. I said to one of the other teachers, 'I wish I was him.' Now I was. Be careful what you dream for.

One advantage of gardening was that it got me away from books. Exercise revived me whenever I felt my head was about to explode from all the reading I was doing.

Dollymount beach was my favourite place to get away from that. Whenever I felt up to it I walked as far as I could with the wind in my face, driving out all the cobwebs. The beach became my substitute for Enniscrone. It was like an unofficial gym.

I had exercise equipment in the house but I didn't use it. I bought a treadmill one year but I rarely stepped up on it. I convinced myself if I looked at it long enough I'd lose weight by some kind of osmosis. When that didn't work I turned it into a clothes horse. My wardrobe wasn't big enough for all my jackets so it came in handy to drape them across it.

I used every excuse I could think of to avoid exercise. Nature provided me with the best one of all when it gave me an Achilles Heel problem in my left leg. It put me out of commission for months. I couldn't walk anywhere now. I went up to the doctor to find out what caused it.

'You're walking too much,' he said.

'I thought walking was good for you,' I said.

'It depends on your age,' he said, 'You're over sixty now.'

'So why hasn't the other foot got it?' I said, 'That's over sixty too.'

I had a different theory about how I got it. For years I'd been wearing shoes that were too big for me. My horror of having anything too close to my skin extended to footwear as well. Sometimes my feet were practically swimming in shoes I wore. I had to stop buying big ones now. Pain made us all ditch our preferences.

How many women spent their youth squeezing their feet into sexy stilettos so they looked well and then cursed themselves in old age? I could empathise with them from the other extreme.

I was fitted with a surgical boot that acted like Plaster of Paris. It meant your foot didn't move when you walked. You weren't supposed to drive with it on but I did. Try hitting the brake wearing one and then changing gear a second later. It's not easy.

I got laser treatment from a man in Stillorgan but it didn't work. Afterwards I went to the Sports Clinic in Santry. A doctor who was working there took some blood from my arm and injected it into my foot. I couldn't understand how that would do any good. 'It's the same blood,' I said, 'What's the point?' He told me circulation wasn't generally good in people's feet.

I wondered why that was. I remembered the old Groucho Marx joke about blood rushing down to the feet, taking one look at those dirty feet and then rushing back up to the head again. Maybe he was on to something.

That didn't work either. Then I heard about a retired surgeon in Hume Street. He was supposed to be able to work miracles on people like me. He gave me an injection too and this time it worked. The pain went away. When my foot got stronger I was advised to take the surgical boot off and use a walking stick instead. I bought a fancy blackthorn one with a carved handle.

I felt like my father swanning around Ballina with his umbrella as I walked down the street. Then one night the stick was stolen from my car. By now I was nearly better. I didn't miss it. Good luck to the person who robbed it, Maybe they had an Achilles problem too.

I promised myself that if I stayed pain-free I'd never complain about anything again. I'd walk ten miles every day to show how grateful I was. Of course we never honour our promises. As soon as I took it off I was back to my old habits – eating junk food, drinking too much and driving twenty yards to shops to buy things because I was too lazy to walk to them.

Later that year Garth Brooks said he was coming to Ireland to do five concerts in Croke Park. I had to pinch myself. *The* Garth Brooks? Surely not.

The residents of the area started kicking up. They said the shows would create too much noise. Too much noise, too much litter and too much hooliganism. They'd had their fill of that kind of thing from other concerts. The City Council needed to step in.

It did. A gun was put to Garth's head. They said he could only do three concerts. If there were going to be any more they'd have to be matinee ones.

Matinees? For the great Garth Brooks? How could he deliver the full force of his special effects in the daytime? No way, José. It would be heresy.

He pleaded with the Irish people to let him go ahead with the five. That was the number that had been agreed on by the promoters back in January. He even pleaded with our Taoiseach, Enda Kenny. Could he not pull some strings with people in high places – or low places?

Garth went down on his knees to him. If Tony Blair could get Deirdre Rachid out of jail, surely Enda could get Garth up on that stage for five concerts. We had the Guildford 4 and the Birmingham 6. Now it was time to help the Croke Park 1.

Garth was left to rot in the end. Enda failed to rouse himself to the challenge his country put to him. He stayed in America and his loyal following cried into their stetsons in Clontarf.

Some of the spleen directed at Enda eventually trickled down to Garth. Ireland became divided down the middle. Whose side were we on – Garth's or the Angry Residents of Dublin 3?

It was like the Civil War all over again. Was it for this the wild geese spread their wing on every tide? Forget Padraig Pearse. Forget James Connolly. Get out your gun and fight for Garth. That was what real patriotism meant.

I don't know how people didn't die over the cancelled concerts. I don't know how blood wasn't spilt on the streets of Drumcondra. Did people get coronaries? Did they erect effigies of Garth? I needed to know.

By the end of July we had to accept the fact that he wasn't coming to us. In fact there was a very real prospect that he might never grace our shores again after the way we'd treated him. Could we live with the prospect of such a calamity?

I got my mind off him after a few months by writing another book. I called it *To Hell With the Diet*. It was meant to be an anti-slimming project. I saw so many books on the subject in Easons I thought a corrective was needed.

It was inspired, if that's the word, by a book I'd seen in Waterstones one time called *How to Take Up Smoking*. There were dozens of books on how to give up the habit. Who needed another one? For the same reason, who needed another diet book?

I thought a collection of quotes telling you to eat more instead of less junk food and spend more instead of less time lounging on a sofa watching TV would be more fun.

Unfortunately the reading public didn't agree. It didn't sell. I felt part of the reason was the fact that the publishers put a well-heeled lady on the cover. That made it look as if it was a guide to *haute cuisine*. We'd have been better off pitching the idea to the McDonald's audience.

To Hell with the Diet was my third book in a row that under-performed sales-wise. It made me think maybe I should stop writing them. For all my hard work in compiling these things I felt I was peeing against the wind.

I didn't blame myself as much as my publishers. For this title they totally revamped its style. I wrote it as an A-Z of dietary concerns like my book *The Cynic's Dictionary* which had sold so well some years back. One of the reasons for its success, I thought, was that each letter only had one or two quotes attached to it. For reasons best known to themselves the publishers of the diet book changed it into about a dozen chapters with a half dozen quotes in each. That totally changed the focus and made it much more boring.

They then had the gall to ask me for £500 towards the cost of publication. I nearly fainted when I heard that bombshell. When you got a contract weren't you supposed to get money from your publisher instead of giving it to them?

'Everyone is struggling in the industry today,' a sweet-voiced editor informed me when I rang to ask what was going on. She then said, 'We're going for shared responsibility.'

Whenever a publisher talked to me about 'shared responsibility' I learned to decode the expression in my mind. It meant: 'You pay for everything.'

But I gave in. Anything for a peaceful life. And at the end of the day it was another book on the shelves. Maybe this one would become a best-seller and make me rich.

It didn't work out like that. In fact it sold so badly it was remaindered in no time. As if that wasn't bad enough, I then got an email one day to ask me if I'd like to buy 141 of the remaindered copies for £2 each. Again I almost fainted.

'I paid you £500 already,' I said, 'Are you trying to bankrupt me completely?'

Eventually I agreed to give them £141 for the 141 copies. I was wondering if I had 141 friends I could give them to. Did I even have 41 friends? Or 21? Or even 1?

Maybe, I thought, I could go down to McDonalds and exchange them for 141 Big Macs. I felt sure a book extolling the merits of junk food would go down a bomb on the McDonalds counter.

Unfortunately, like most of my other 'bright' ideas, this one was an epic fail. I was left crying into my chocolate milk shake over yet another project that went belly-up.

Why were my books not selling? There seemed to be a different problem each time. It was hard enough finding a publisher. Anytime I did, they took the wrong approach in marketing them. Why could I not get someone who was pro-active, who'd take a gamble on me and run with the ball?

Everything seemed to be going pear-shaped in my life. It wasn't just the books. It was the whole direction of my life. First the move away from Ballina, then the decision to do the B.Comm when I hated the whole idea of it, then all the problems in teaching. There was also the end of the *Image* column, the closure of the *Evening Press* and the unnecessary NUJ membership.

Maybe that was where everything started to go wrong. I joined a union I didn't want to be in. Maybe I deserved every bad thing that happened to me after that.

Where could I turn to now? I kept looking for work in journalism in the following months but that didn't work out either. . It was hard come by after *Modern Woman* went bust. Creative writing fulfilled me more than journalism but there was no money in it so what was the point? I could write masterpieces up in my attic that nobody would ever read. Suddenly I knew how Van Gogh felt.

I resisted the temptation to cut off my ear but some hard truths had to be faced. I hadn't been able to make it as a playwright or a novelist or a short story writer and now I wasn't even going to be able to see Garth Brooks. It was as if there was an Indian sign over me. What else could go wrong?

I told myself that if Dolly Parton had triplets I'd probably be the one on the bottle.

Exits

Keith died in 2015. His son Derek gave me the news over the phone one morning. He was so upset he could hardly speak. They'd become very close in Keith's last years. He'd contracted Parkinson's disease a decade or so before. He couldn't understand why he got it.

He'd lived a healthy life. He never smoked and only drank now and again. He also ate all the right foods. He thought that entitled him to be healthy into his old age. It definitely increased your chances but which of us have those kinds of guarantees?

He really battled it and never gave in. In one sense the disease brought peace into his life. He suffered a lot with it but I'd seen him cope less well with smaller problems he'd had over the years. He had some troubled times as a younger man. Where did his strength come from?

Jacinta often said, 'God never gives us anything we can't bear.'

I wasn't too sure about that one. If it was true, why did so many people end up in psychiatric homes or taking their own lives?

But it seemed to be true in Keith's case. At the end of his life he was almost like a mystic. He was an example to all of us. Everyone spoke fondly of him at his funeral. The church was thronged. Joe Cahill even came up from Ballina for it.

He died in his sleep so he didn't suffer, at least as far as we know. Derek told me that the night before he died he tidied his room in a way that was unusual or him. Maybe he had a premonition.

He'd been weak for many years with the disease, so weak sometimes he wasn't even able to watch his beloved films. He'd stopped going downstairs for any length of time many years before. The huge TV he watched them on was idle now. He only had an average-sized one in his bedroom. It didn't have a remote. I watched him changing stations one day with the butt of a snooker cue.

I was up with him one day shortly before he died. He asked me to watch a cowboy film with him. He was a great fan of cowboy films, even ones with people like Roy Rogers and Gene Autry.

I stopped watching these when I got into my teens but Keith stayed with them all through his life. This one starred Dale Robertson. He watched it for a few minutes and then asked me to turn it off. That was very unlike him.

He took a copybook from his locker and started reading it. He'd transcribed key speeches from some of his favourite films into it – *Shane, Gone with the Wind, Casablanca, Double Indemnity*. He read them in the voices of the stars as he'd always done, capturing them to perfection, especially Humphrey Bogart and Clark Gable.

Afterwards he took out a mouth organ and played a song on it. That was something he'd developed an interest in over the past few months. I hadn't heard him on it since the days in Ballina when he played the theme song from *Shane* on it. He'd also started putting bets on snooker matches. I found that amazing too. I'd never managed to get him to show any interest in snooker over the years.

Even more amazing was the day he told me he was thinking of writing a book on Hollywood producers. I asked him what was going to happen to his screenwriter book, the one he'd spent the last 25 years writing. 'I'm taking a break from it,' he said.

You never knew what was going on in his mind. Had he abandoned it because he was finally coming around to the idea that it was unpublishable in its present form? He'd started it when he left Unidare, the Finglas firm where he'd worked all his life. He'd taken early retirement in 1990 to embark on it.

I wondered if he ever intended it to be on a shelf. Often it seemed more an end in itself, something to fill in the long hours of the day when he wasn't working. He'd got a good severance sum when he left Unidare but obviously it wasn't going to last forever. Maybe he felt guilty about leaving the job when it ran out.

He never needed to have. Nobody worked harder than he did over the years and he always provided for his family. When he left Unidare he cut his cloth to suit his measure. It's nice to get out of the rat race, as someone said, but you have to make do on less cheese.

He didn't even take one holiday for the last quarter of his life. He went to Jersey on his honeymoon but I never remember him being out of the country after that except for a brief trip to London to do research for the book.

I tried to persuade him to bring it to a publisher. I'd been doing film books for a company called McFarland in South Carolina. I mentioned his one to them one day. They expressed an interest in it but after they saw a sample of it they said they wanted amendments.

He'd used a lot of quotations from people. He needed to edit these down or even cut them out altogether. He was unwilling to do that. Hugo offered to paraphrase them to solve the problem but he didn't seem interested in that either.

Basil took up the baton then. He emailed McFarland and got more details on what they wanted. During this time Clive was transcribing Keith's words onto a disc in his office in Zambia. He was also fitting them around the many illustrations Keith had in the book. In effect he he'd become his typesetter.

437

Keith had done some of this in Ireland already. It was very detailed work. He said to me once that he thought his Parkinson's could have been caused by all the intricate fitting in of pieces of text into small spaces for hours on end.

Hugo and Basil kept offering him suggestions for how to get the book published. Ruth and Jacinta gave him moral support from America. June and Audrey expressed their wonder at his achievement as they read through the book any time they were up to him on a visit.

I was often a discordant voice. As someone who knew a bit about the inner workings of publishing I felt he'd used too many quotes to sidestep the 'fair use' clause publishers had. I also thought he could have been sued for using some of the photographs he intended to use.

He had hundreds of these. I helped him collect some of them. He often saw a book in a shop that was too expensive to buy. He'd ring me up and ask me if I could get it for him from the publisher.

I was in the habit of ringing publishers for books to review. I didn't have to pay for them. They'd send them to me and I'd write a few words on them for the places I did book reviews for. When I did that first I didn't realise he had little or no interest in the books in question. All he wanted was the photos.

He asked me to get a biography of Alfred Hitchcock for him once. It was a gigantic tome of over 600 pages. When I gave it to him he went straight to the illustrated section. He carefully cut out a photograph that was about the size of a matchbox. Then he handed the book back to me.

'What are you doing?' I said.

'Giving you your book back,' he said.

I asked him why he didn't want to read it.

'I wouldn't have the time,' he said.

When I saw all the photos he planned to use without permission I told him he was entering dangerous waters. He never expressed much interest in conversations like that.

Clive had a copy of it printed after he died. He gave it to Jacqueline. It was a lovely gesture. He'd spent so many years working on it, it would have been a travesty not to see it in print. The bound copy made up for everything. Keith said to me once, 'Even if I only sell one copy of the book it will justify all the years I spent on it.' Now he had that.

If it was mass produced it could have sold in the quantities it deserved. Keith was a great writer but he never had enough confidence in himself. He thought the books he was reading for his research were written better than his was. That was why he used so many of their quotes.

I didn't agree. I found a lot of them dull. He had better ones of his own but he didn't put them down on paper. We heard them when he was talking to us about films over the years. For some reason he didn't seem interested in transferring his opinions onto paper.

He regarded talking and writing as two completely different activities. I saw them as the same thing. If he could have brought a conversational aspect into his book it would have been more readable.

He would have been bringing himself into it. Readers would have got to know the boy who fell in love with films all those years ago when he was being brought to the Estoria by our father when he was hardly old enough to walk. That's where his love affair with Hollywood started and where it should have continued.

His book never ended up on a shelf but I don't think any the less of it on that account. Maybe I think more of it.

What makes a book superior to a person? Keith was its embodiment. It got him through 25 years of retirement. How many people take to drink and drugs when they leave their job? *Every Picture Tells a Story* was Keith's drug but it was one that improved his health rather than damaged it. He could have done a lot worse.

After he died I thought of all the sayings he immortalised in his impersonations of the stars over the years. James Cagney's 'You dirty rat!' Humphrey Bogart's 'Here's lookin' at you, kid,' Clark Gable's 'Frankly my dear I don't *give* a damn.' He had these people on pedestals right through his life. Now he was with them.

Every time we watched an old movie we thought of him. Mary was just as distraught as me. She'd got on brilliantly with him over the years and he thought highly of her as well. She could never watch 'The Chase' after he died. It was a TV show he liked. Whenever it came up on the screen she hit the remote to get to another station.

What I missed most about him was his simplicity. He never had any luxuries in life but that didn't bother him. Listening to him describe the experience of having a pint of Guinness you'd think he was dining on caviar and champagne. A week in Butlin's was his Marbella.

Just as my family dispersed after my father's death, so did Keith's after his. Stephen moved to Leitrim after getting married. David went to Thailand with his wife and children.

Derek moved down to Westmeath with his partner Daragh. Up to now I'd always associated Derek with bricks and mortar. In Westmeath he indulged his passion for photography. He was excellent at it and produced many stunning shots. He also produced a daughter, Dayna, that he doted on.

Another person I knew well went out of my life after Keith. Donie O'Donoghue died in Portugal. He hadn't been in good health for a number of years. He'd put on a lot of weight from eating the wrong kind of foods. 'It makes me more like Elvis,' he used to joke. I remembered how he impersonated him at June's wedding. We'd had lots of great chats since then.

He died on his birthday. Somehow that made it seem even more tragic. I thought of other people who'd died on their birthday – Shakespeare, Ingrid Bergman, the painter Raphael. He was cremated as it would have been too expensive to fly his body home from Portugal. At the funeral his wife Mary said, 'It's hard to think of such a big man in such a small box.' I felt the same. Donie had been larger than life in all senses.

A classmate of mine from Muredach's also died around this time – Pat Curley. He was one of the people I used to play soccer with in Belleek. My parents lived beside him on Convent Hill before we bought Norfolk.

He was one of the first people from Ballina I met after we moved to Dublin. It was in O'Connell Street outside the GPO. He'd just done an interview for a job in the Civil Service. He was excited about it.

'I think it went well,' he said, 'They asked me where could you walk a mile and end up at the same place. I knew the answer. It was the North Pole.' It was just like him to know something like that. I remembered him burrowing into books in Ballina – encyclopaedias, car magazines, anything he could get his hands on.

Pat was a dynamo. He never lost his boyish quality and was always in good form. The last time I met him he told me a joke about Basque extremists getting stuck in a revolving door. The punchline was, 'Don't put all your Basques in one exit.' The joke was typical of him. He giggled at it in that boyish way he had.

He died of a massive coronary. It reminded me of my father and Paddy Dillon-Malone and Elvis. Sudden exits from life seemed to define larger-than-life characters. Not for them the hospital bed.

Made in Cheshire

Donald Trump became president of America in 2016. Hillary Clinton had been 1/3 to beat him. Americans went for the good ole boy, the sexual predator, the man who made the dollar his god. Why? Maybe because he had a better personality than Clinton. He represented the common man even though he was filthy rich. Maybe that was what the common man fantasised about. Oh, and he didn't need notes, like Hillary, to make his speeches.

Did he win the election or did she lose it? Maybe it was a bit of both. We were told she was hated, that America had had enough of the Clintons just as it had enough of the Bushes.

It also had enough of poverty. They knew Trump was a good businessman. He'd run the country like a shop. The forgotten people in the small towns felt they'd do well by him.

I stayed up all night watching CNN the night he was elected. As he swept through state after state I thought I was seeing things. Hillary was dead and buried against all the odds. It was true, as Abraham Lincoln was once reputed to have said, that anyone could become president of America. That was the problem.

As soon as he got in he sacked everyone who looked sideways at him. He was more in the tradition of a dictator than a president. Then he started his silly talk, sniping at people in the most childish language he could think of. Was this a president or the guy on the barstool next to you in your local dive?

I relaxed. He wasn't a madman, I told myself, which was my first opinion of him. He wasn't even a simpleton. That was my second opinion. My third one was more clear-cut. He was just a bastard.

Ireland's economy recovered. Slowly but surely we got back on our feet. Leo Varadkar took over as Taoiseach. His voice made him sound as if he was two thousand leagues under the sea. He was Indian and also gay. Well done Ireland. We were shaking off homophobia and embracing multi-culturalism in the one go. But would he be any good? Could the coalition of Fianna Fáil and Fine Gael save us from more desolation? Not many people felt they could. They were seen as two cheeks of the one arse. Sinn Féin could, maybe, if it could shake off the shadow of the gunman.

Gerry Adams stepped back as leader of the party. Mary Lou McDonald took over. She had less of a whiff of cordite about her. It was a pity she ruined it by saying 'Tiocfaidh ár lá' at an Ard-Fheis. It seemed like a Freudian slip. The gunman's shadow was still hovering over her party.

Britain voted for Brexit. Like the election of Trump it was seen as a victory for the small man. It was another result the bookies got wrong.

By now I'd become a betting man. I'd have got a nice treble on Trump, Brexit and Ronnie O'Sullivan to lose in the World Championships at Sheffield. Which was the most important part of the treble, I asked myself – the world's economic future, its political future or a game of snooker? It was a no-brainer. The game of snooker.

Ronnie didn't get beyond the second round, losing 13-12 to Barry Hawkins. Hawkins hadn't beaten him since 2002. Strange things were happening.

Theresa May failed to deliver Brexit. Maybe she didn't believe in it deep down. She'd been an anti-Brexiteer in a previous incarnation. Sometimes it showed.

Boris Johnson was seen as a better bet even though he was anti-Brexit in the past as well. He blustered his way through his speeches like an overgrown schoolboy. Horrors like Nigel Farage and Michael Gove were delighted. Boris assured the populace Britain was in good hands. Its sovereignty would be maintained.

He sounded good on the surface but there was a faultline in his rhetoric. It wasn't quite Churchillian no matter how many big words he used. Polysyllabic language couldn't camouflage that bovine look in the eyes. I liked what Frankie Boyle said about him: 'The Labour Party must really be in trouble if they can lose control of London to a fat albino with Down Syndrome.'

He reminded me of Prince Charles, another man with a silver foot in his mouth. A graduate of Eton, he spoke in the same plummy tones as Charles. If he hadn't gone there I imagined him as someone who'd be cleaning the spark plugs out on my Yamaha twin. Maybe he was like Charles' idiot nephew. Didn't members of the royalty always have an idiot nephew tucked away somewhere? Somehow this one blustered his way out of the closet leaving all the other skeletons behind.

Johnson got Brexit 'done' after humming and hawing for what seemed like an eternity Maybe deep down he didn't believe in it either. But he was a good actor. He made you think he did. Now it just needed to be signed into the constitution so the British could finally tell all those European bullies what to do with themselves. God help them, I thought. they're digging their economic graves. I only hoped they wouldn't bring us down with them.

It wasn't all doom and gloom across the pond. In 2018 I started sending my fiction to a man called Ken Clay. He ran Penniless Press, a company in Cheshire. I liked the name. It sounded romantic in a kind of Dickensian way. Ken was a writer too. He'd published a lot of funny stories and a collection called *Nietzsche's Birthday*. I always felt more comfortable dealing with editors who were writers. They knew how fulfilling the process was – and how tough. They'd been up there and down there.

Ken was always excited by new ideas. He was the first publisher I ever knew who didn't say, 'What's in it for me?' He reminded me of a gentleman farmer. He took great care over how he produced his books but he didn't stay awake all night worrying about how they performed.

He has a repertory of writers that he allows to flourish both inside and outside Penniless Press. Few of them, including yours truly, are in the flush of youth. Angry Young Men have become Angry (or funny) Old Men. They create the aura of workshops. None of them seem too interested in fame or fortune. Their style of writing reminds me of everyone from Alan Sillitoe to Barry Hines. They have names you'd never hear anywhere else – Lykiard, De Nemethy, Birtistle. I imagine them as dishevelled eccentrics, smoked salmon socialists living in mansions on the edges of industrial estates in the Black District, being waited on by butlers as they patrol the grounds of vast estates, blackening the pages of labyrinthine manuscripts about characters as wacky as themselves that will never see the light of day.

Either conventional publishing has passed them by or they've passed it by. It doesn't matter. Ken presides over them like a falconer ministering to a flock of birds with broken wings. When they're healed up he lets them fly off to whatever eyries they might find elsewhere. There's always another Troy to burn, another forgotten gem to unearth.

Penniless Press is like a literary orphanage. Ken is happy to release his writers to their adoptive parents if and when the time comes to spirit them off to their arcane Valhallas. The agreements he makes with them aren't manufactured by documents or even handshakes. His word is his bond. Everything moves

446

with the kind of smoothness that's anachronistic in the mechanised environment that passes for publishing today.

Ken also edits a quarterly magazine called *The Crazy Oik*. It features many of these personages in their various guises, reminding you just how so many quirky voices (including his own) need to be heard by the wider literary establishment. It's illustrated with an array of vintage photographs with Pythonesque captions applied to them by him. He recently put many of these photographs into a book. It's called *Detournements* and it's a howl.

In many ways Ken is like an avuncular film director. He's a Svengali figure who likes to watch other people flower while he stays in the background. Often his own writing is done under a pseudonym (or three).

He's technically gifted. You can see that from the cover of this book. He designed it in a day – or more probably an hour. I think of him as a one-man army. He produces eclectic books at a time when most publishers are running scared of anything approaching creativity. As well as being a nurturer of talent he's a bibliophile. He ferrets out lost gems in dusty bookshops down side streets in small villages. Sometimes he re-prints them.

By the time I encountered him I'd given up thinking my fiction would ever be published anywhere. It was my first love but I'd abandoned it after the David Marcus days. I had to. A living had to be made. Journalism was where the money was. I often churned this out to editors who didn't care too much about the finer points of how I said something. It was a case of, 'I don't want it good. I want it Tuesday.'

I wasn't submitting much stuff to places now. After years of sending things off and either having it printed or returned to me – or, in some cases, neither

– I was adopting a wait-and-see policy, letting editors to come to me with proposals rather than vice versa. The competition was too fierce for any other course of action. I was pitting myself against teenagers with laptops. They had more Facebook connections than you could shake a stick at. Facebook was everywhere. You were nothing if you weren't on it. Many nerdy types had hundreds of friends on it. The only problem was, they didn't know who they were.

Andrew Lloyd Webber was once asked, 'Which comes first, the words or the melodies?' He replied, 'First comes the phone call.' I abided by that dictum. It meant you knew what people wanted. Otherwise you were whistling in the dark.

Moving from journalism back to fiction was like leaving a mistress to go back to a wife. Ken published some of my poems as well. I'd stopped writing poetry after my last book with Dennis Grieg. He was the Belfast publisher who'd done three of my collections with Lapwing. Now I started again.

Many of them were about Ballina. I felt like Hemingway when he wrote *A Moveable Feast* in his fifties. As we get older we go more into the past. It becomes more real to us than the present. In that book he re-visited the Paris of the 1920s when he was a young man. There was a treasure trove of memories there. His life was falling apart after two plane crashes and God knows how many electric shock treatments. He found solace tripping down Memory Lane.

Ken published two of my novels after the book of stories and poems. Both of them were set in Ireland. I hadn't got much interest in them from Irish publishers over the years. Now they were going to be published across the water by The Auld Enemy. It was a bit like what happened with my historic pub book - and my Guinness one. Both of these were originally published in England. I was falling into the tradition of everyone

448

from Brendan Behan to *Fr. Ted*. After being let down by Ireland I was being adopted by England. Behan was a sensation on the West End before he became famous in Ireland. *Fr. Ted* was taken up by Channel 4 before RTE bought it.

No man is a prophet in his own country. I'm far from a prophet but the point still stands. Familiarity often breeds contempt. My father used to say, 'No man is a hero to his valet.' Maybe if I went away from Ireland for a few years I could come back like Jesus on Palm Sunday. People would throw flower petals at me. Or would it be rotten tomatoes? Ask James Joyce.

By this stage I'd also published a biography of Maureen O'Hara, Ireland's most famous actress from the Golden Age of movies. A university press in Kentucky asked me to do it. To this day I've never seen a copy of it on sale in Ireland. I have to be content with the 44 million Irish-Americans in the States buying it. It continued the tradition of me being adopted by other countries after being ignored by my own one. So what's next for me – a book on Finn McCool for McGraw-Hill? A biography of Bono for Penguin? Maybe nobody can be a prophet in their own country. 'The Irish are my raw material,' Brendan Behan said once, 'but that doesn't mean they're my audience.' James Joyce would no doubt have agreed.

I got the contract for the O'Hara book as a result of emailing the University Press of Wisconsin one day to ask them if they'd be interested in publishing a book I was writing about friction between actors in Hollywood. I'd called it *Star Wars*, not to be confused with the George Lucas film. My email was answered by a man called Patrick McGilligan. He said, 'Tell me more about your book.'

I recognised the name immediately. He was one of Keith's heroes. He'd done the Hitchcock biography

449

I'd got him sometime before. His special subject was screenwriters. He'd interviewed everyone from George Stevens to Katharine Hepburn. I wrote back, 'Are you *the* Patrick McGilligan?'

He was gratified to know his name was known in Ireland. He said he wasn't interested in the *Star Wars* project. Instead he wanted me to do the biography of O'Hara. I liked Maureen O'Hara but she was never one of my favourite actresses. I didn't tell him that. You didn't always have to adore your subject. I remembered what happened with Harry Potter. Maybe she'd grow on me the more I learned about her.

I said I'd do it. The process was arduous. I had to a proposal and a synopsis and then various chapters to 'blind peers' - the famous *'saumple chaupters'* Chelsey Fox swore by all those years ago. The peers were people who vetted what you wrote but didn't identify themselves. I had to re-do the proposals time and again before they were happy with them.

I spent over three months on them. By the time I got the contract I was spun out. I was tired as I approached the writing of the book. It probably suffered as a result of that. I was reminded of a story I once read about the film *The Countess from Hong Kong*. Everyone on the set hated the film but they had a brilliant wrap party. Before they went home someone said, 'I have an idea. Let's dump the movie and release the party.' I said to Pat, 'Let's dump my book and release the proposal.' He wasn't too amused at my joke.

Anytime I voiced anything even vaguely negative about O'Hara it was struck out of my text. I felt I was being censored, that it was going to be targeted to a middle-of-the-road readership rather than an academic one. I told Pat this wasn't what I signed up for.

'You have to suck it up,' he said.

Suck it up. Was this the man Keith idolised, the man who was such a wonderful biographer, who met all the greats? 'University presses are dying on the vine,' he told me. If that was their philosophy of writing, I thought, I wasn't surprised.

I didn't interview Maureen for the book. That fact came against it when it was reviewed on Amazon. I'd made an attempt to contact her after I got the contract but I didn't follow it up. I never felt comfortable writing biographies of people I was in contact with. It worked with Brian Behan because he was so self-deprecating but he was an exception. I didn't contact Jimmy White when I did a biography of him in 2008. I wouldn't have felt comfortable asking him, 'Do you have any idea why you lost six world finals?'

Neither did I contact Tom Jones for a book I did on him for a Welsh publisher a few years later. It would have been even more uncomfortable saying, 'Is it true, Tom, that you slept with over 100 women while you were married?' I knew Maureen, like most film stars, was thin-skinned and would want to go through everything I wrote with a fine toothcomb. That would have made the book even more obsequious than my editor wanted. It would have handcuffed me totally in what I wanted to say about her.

After I had my two novels published with Penniless Press, Ken Clay said he didn't mind me running off some copies for myself if I wanted. I found a digital printing firm in Rathcoole called Sprint Print. It was run by a man named Gerry Kelly. Gerry was as capable and talented as Ken. He made a great job of printing them. He's a perfectionist with a long history in publishing. He goes back to the time I worked with Colour Books though I didn't know him personally then. He produces work of high quality with a speedy turnaround.

One of the novels I published with him was the autobiography of a Cork nurse. I called it *A Nursing*

Life. It was written in her voice. I liked taking on voices. It freed my hand up. I'd done it for Elvis and also for Brian Behan. Now I was doing for a woman. Maybe it was the failed actor in me. I imagined Brendan would have been impressed. 'We're all ambi-sextrous,' he said once, 'not ambidextrous.'

I wrote *The Nursing Life* on my computer. I don't expect to do any future books on it. I'll continue to use my typewriters as long as they're functional. I don't know how long that'll be. Every year or so the thermal head burns out on one of them. I have about twenty of them in the attic with the heads burned out. A head is only about the size of your fingernail but there's nobody to repair things like that nowadays. My ribbons are nearly gone too. I once had nearly a thousand of them. These days I bid for them at exorbitant prices on eBay. The typewriters sometimes go for less than the price of a ribbon.

I didn't expect the bookshops to be interested in my novels. I wasn't a big enough name. Why would a corporate book chain open an account for someone who was only going to sell a handful of books? It didn't matter if they were well written or not. All that mattered was whether something moved off the shelves. It was an assembly line.

Chicklit was everywhere now. You couldn't go into a bookshop without tripping over one of these tomes. Some of them seemed to be as big as phone books. They were stacked ten or twenty high. I didn't read them. I climbed over them. I don't want to sound snobbish about chicklit. Some of them are well written. They fulfil a need. But they're rarely what we might call 'literature.'

I contacted a man from the HSE who expressed an interest in distributing *A Nursing Life* for me. He lived in Enniscorthy. There was a function coming up that was going to be attended by hundreds of nurses there. It was a good opportunity for me to get the book circulated and for him to make some money for a charity at the same time. The idea was that the nurses would buy the book on the way out of the function, paying as much or as little as they wanted for it. His wife came up to the house. I gave her a few hundred copies.

I gave some copies to the charity shops as well. They weren't always happy getting numerous copies of the same book. It's an awkward feeling giving someone something for free while being aware they don't particularly want it. Sometimes I just left them on the counter without talking to anyone. I think this is what's known as being a maniokleptic – going into shops and leaving things.

It wasn't the first time I'd done a book for charity. Some years ago I answered an ad in a newspaper for a man looking for someone to write his life story. It turned out to be a retired surgeon called Malachy Smyth who'd pioneered important research into back pain. He'd spent most of his life in America and was now retired in Monaghan. Over many phone calls and some meetings we got the book done. We called it *Killing Pain*. I wanted to call it *Painkiller* but he thought that was dramatic. 'I'm not a killer,' he said. At least part of the pun was preserved. The profits from it went to a wheelchair association in Monaghan.

My contact with the HSE resulted in a strange coincidence. The person who answered it turned out to be a past pupil of mine. Not for nothing had Brendan Behan once termed Dublin 'the largest village in Europe.'

Coincidences were always happening to me. Later on in the year I heard from another past pupil by email. She tracked me down from one of the magazines I wrote for. She'd left the school as far back as 1985. Her father had got a job in, of all places, Zambia. Not only Zambia but the university where Clive worked. What were the chances of that? How far was Zambia from Clonsilla? 5000 miles? One day the man in question passed Clive's office. He saw his name on the door and knocked. When Clive answered it he said, 'You wouldn't be related to Aubrey, would you?' They ended up becoming good friends.

It reminded me of something that happened to me in the 1970s when I was on one of my trips to America. I was having a drink in New York with a police sergeant who was the brother of my car dealer in Dublin. I told him I'd arranged to meet the brother of my brother-in-law later in the day. His name was Michael. While we were drinking, another brother of a brother-in-law of mine walked in. He was also called Michael. I hadn't even known he was in the country. I was blown away. The sergeant couldn't understand why. 'Is he the brother of your brother-in-law?' he said. I said he was. 'Is his name Michael?' Again I said yes. He said, 'So what's your problem?' It was too complicated to explain to him.

Another coincidence happened on a day years later when Mary and myself were driving through Salthill on one of our trips to Galway. We found our path blocked by a dog that seemed to be ailing. After getting out of the car we noticed it had a band around its neck. There was a phone number on it. When we rang it the owner said she'd meet us at a playground. She arrived half an hour later. It turned out to be one of my favourite Irish instrumentalists, Sharon Shannon.

Another coincidence happened to me one night when I met Uncle Louis son Stephen for a drink one Christmas when he was home from England, where he lived. When I asked him where he drank in England it turned out to be a pub run by our friend Sean McDonnell. Both of them were living in Poole.

What were the chances of that? He hadn't even known him when he lived in Ballina.

Sean was part of a more recent coincidence as well. It was related to the distribution of my books into the charity shops. One day earlier this year I got an email from a woman who ran the Irish Wheelchair Association shop in Listowel. I hadn't been down there since Writer's Week in 1980. She said, 'Your friend Sean MacDonnell was in here today. He bought all your books.' I hadn't seen Sean for over a decade.

The woman from the shop had my number so she gave it to him. He rang me the following day. Even though many years had elapsed since we talked, he acted as if it as yesterday. I often found that about people I knew from Ballina. It was one of the things I liked most about them.

We talked about all the things that had happened in our lives since we'd seen one another last. He remembered the names of everyone in my family and asked about all of them. He was sorry to hear Keith had died. People always spoke so warmly of Keith even if they'd only known him slightly.

I asked him about his own family. His brother Joe had studied art at college. In one of the frequent coincidences that happened in my life, he'd been renting the house where I met Mary on Bird Avenue. We used to joke that it was well named. His sister Maureen had been in Audrey and Jacinta's class in Ballina.

I wanted to know what he was working at now. With Sean you never knew. He changed like the weather. 'I'm in pest control,' he said when I asked him. He told me he had to go to a house to get rid of some bats the following day. 'Don't let them get into your hair,' I said. He said, 'I don't have any anymore.' Alas, what time does.

I sent some more boxes of my books to charity shops around the country in the following weeks. They only got a few euros for them but it was better than nothing. It felt good being able to short-circuit the traditional system of distribution. I'd always wanted to be a publisher. I saw this was a form of being one.

I was lucky enough to be able to survive financially without royalties. I'd just reached pension age so I had a few pounds to spare. Like most businesses, publishing was driven by money. When you took that out of the equation you could do anything you wanted. Charles Bukowski used to say Norman Mailer had to write to feed his ex-wives. He said, 'Alimony has him chained to the typer.' How many authors had to write to eat? Bukowski did it himself when he was starting out.

Self-publishing in the digital era isn't like the old days. In former times people ended up with binliners full of novels in their garages or under their beds. They got more moth-eaten and dog-eared as the years went on.

Self-publishing had a stigma attached to it when I started writing books. It was seen like a woman joining a dating bureau because she was afraid she'd be left 'on the shelf.' That term applied almost literally to books.

Dating bureaus were trendy now with the phenomenon of sites like Tinder. We were living in a world where people created their own universes in matters of love and everything else.

What's Another Year?

If 2019 was a good year, 2020 was the year of death. It was only a few days old when Marian Finucane died. A week later Larry Gogan, another one of its best-known broadcasters, was gone. He was the man who asked a contestant on his quiz show one day what Hitler's Christian name was. He got the answer 'Heil.'

Neither of them were young but neither was expected to die either. Nobody knew Larry's age. I tried to get it when I was doing my Guinness book back in 1996. The editors wanted dates for all the people featured in it. I rang his son David and asked him. 'I can't tell you,' he said, 'It's a State secret.' Larry was the only person in the book with a question mark after his birth date. Some things are beyond sacred.

The following month Keelin Shanley died. She was another RTE broadcaster. She was only 51. Was there something in the air that was decimating the staff of our national TV station?

It was a good few years now since it had been rocked by the passing of Gerry Ryan. I'd listened to his radio show almost every morning when I was doing the courier work. I remembered the time his team had asked me to go on TV for *Hollyweird* and me saying no.

I met him at a function once with Margot Davis. He was surrounded by two scantily-clad ladies who were endorsing some beauty product. It was after Gay Byrne retired. I told him I thought he'd be a great replacement for Gay on *The Late Late Show*. I don't know if he agreed with me because he wasn't interested in talking to me that night. He was too busying eyeing up the scantily-clad ladies.

He didn't get the job as things worked out. They went for Ryan Tubridy instead. Gerry only hosted *The Late Late* once. One of his guests was a man I'd interviewed earlier that day, the actor Tony Curtis. It was one of the most enjoyable interviews I ever did. You can see how friendly he was from the photograph of him with me on the cover of this book. He made me feel as if I was the celebrity instead of him. That kind of old world gentility is gone from Hollywood today.

There were a lot of similarities between Tony and Gerry. Chief among these, I think, was the fact that neither of them ever grew up. In going for Tubridy, RTE evinced their well-known penchant for a safe pair of hands. I don't think it's a good working principle. Gerry put his foot in it on a few occasions but he was larger than life. Tubridy is the consummate professional but I find him boring. He's too middle of the road. People who walk down the middle of the road get knocked down.

Gerry died not long after being passed over for the *Late Late* slot. He'd been on a diet of booze and cocaine. These were seen as the main causes of his death. I didn't think they were. You have to look beyond these things. You have to ask why he was abusing himself in this way. I think it was because of depression over not landing the *Late Late* gig. He wouldn't have needed the other drugs if he had that one.

Caroline Flack was another casualty of 2020. She was the host of the show *Love Island*. It pulled in all the audiences *Big Brother* lost when it fell out of favour with the public. People suddenly weren't looking for the kitchen sink anymore. They were looking for fantasy. They liked gawking at women sitting in a firepit with their latest squeeze. And using the word 'connection' a lot.

Big Brother appealed to people who had little in their lives looking at people who had even less. *Love Island* appealed to people who were looking for love and thought they'd find it in bronzed bodies with fake boobs and tattoos. It was Mills & Boon in 3D.

The contestants were all Beautiful People - at least on the surface. When they took off their warpaint some of them were ordinary enough. Even Maura Higgins, the Irish contestant who found fame on the 2019 series of the show after using terms like 'fanny flutters' in a midlands brogue.

Love Island was supposed to be about finding love but what it was really about (like *Big Brother*) was finding fame. If a relationship went on for any length of time at all after the show ended it became news. Anyone who stayed together longer than a month was regarded as Romeo and Juliet. I was reminded of the old Bob Monkhouse joke, 'They said the marriage wouldn't last but they left the church together, didn't they?'

Every night there was a new twist in some romantic triangle that was unfolding. Would A team up with B or would C gum up the works? Had D a secret obsession with E, who'd just dumped F to be with G? As I watched the sexual musical chairs unfolding I thought of the lines of a Dorothy L. Sayers poem: 'As I get older and older/ and totter towards the tomb/I find that I care less and less/Who goes to bed with whom.'

Love Island candidates started killing themselves after a few years. They weren't well cared for by the producers. It wasn't only viewers of it that were being sold down the river but the participants as well. On the drab Mondays of its aftermath when they went back to their grotty bedsits in Romford, they found their Instagram followers had departed. It was time to turn on the oven. Their fifteen minutes of fame were up.

Caroline killed herself too. It was after a domestic incident with her boyfriend. She hit him with a lampshade one night when she read some texts on his phone. They suggested he was seeing someone else. Blood gushed out of him. He rang the cops.

'She's trying to kill me,' he said, or words to that effect. When they got to the apartment she was still in a rage. One of the policemen had a secret camera on him. He filmed her. The footage was going to be used in evidence when the case came to court.

Caroline never got a chance to tell her side of the story. The #MeToo people turned against her. They thought they were being fair when they said, 'This case must go ahead. We have to be seen to be treating men and women equally. When a woman uses violence against a man it's just as serious as when a man does it against a woman.'

Right in principle, of course, but Caroline wasn't a principle. She was a person. Political correctness had gone mad once again. The #MeToo movement always picks the wrong people to target.

The media got on her case. They branded her a bunnyboiler. Another term started being used in connection with her too, 'lamped.' One article about her said, 'She *lamped* her boyfriend.' Wasn't the writer of that one very witty? It reminded me of when I was labelled a corpse-thief after I did my Bukowski book.

We were told she died because of bullying from internet trolls. That was only part of it. We'll always have internet trolls with us. It's how we react to them that defines us. I ignored them. Caroline was tortured by them. She set her standards too high for herself. When she fell below them, and her nose was rubbed in that fact, she couldn't take it. Part of the problem was in herself. Trolls can only kill you if you let them. None of us are perfect but perfectionists like Caroline (who won *Strictly Come Dancing*) think they have to be. We need to accept something less than perfection in ourselves to survive in an imperfect world.

The programme planners got worried after Caroline died. Not so much about the girl herself, or the other tragic cases who'd been sent to their graves by scurrilous journalists, but about the fact that the show was in danger of being axed. Jeremy Kyle's one had recently been taken off the air after one of his guests, Stephen Dymond, committed suicide. They didn't want to be seen as another catalyst of misery brought on by their seedy purveying of dreams.

I was obviously sad for Mr Dymond but I was glad to see the end of Kyle. For years he'd abused guests who were troubled, playing into the mob mentality of his audiences over 'that all-important DNA test' if the theme was paternity or a lie detector one if it was infidelity. It was the latter in Dymond's case. He failed the lie detector test and Kyle exploited the situation to insult him. Dymond crawled across the floor of the studio trying to escape his barbs but found it locked. The audience booed him. Kyle egged them on with comments like, 'I wouldn't trust you with a chocolate button.' The poor man struggled to breathe as he made for the exit on all fours.

A few weeks later *The Jeremy Kyle Show* became *The Jeremy Kill Show* after Dymond took a morphine overdose and died. It was the end of Kyle's routine of parading dysfunctional lives of vulnerable people before us, people who poured their hearts out on live TV for the delectation of the mob. It was a new form of confession now that the official version of it had largely disappeared from society. A counsellor was on hand to offer solace. Society was growing counsellors like potatoes to soak up the anxieties of people who'd been let rot by society until someone like Kyle felt they'd make good circus animals.

Margot Davis also died in 2020. She hadn't been well for a long time. I'd watched her turn from a fun-loving person to a sad woman beset by health problems. It was heartbreaking to see her retiring from life when she had so much to offer. She died of blood poisoning brought on by flebitis.

The biggest shock of the year was the death of my brother-in-law John Davis. He was Ruth's husband. I hadn't seen him for many years but we'd kept in touch through emails and the odd phone call. I always got on well with him. He was one of the few quiet Americans I'd ever met.

He actually asked my father for Ruth's hand in marriage when he was dating her in the seventies. It was a custom that had gone out long before that. John came from the era where you questioned the pop before you popped the question.

It was so sad to see him falling into bad health. He'd always taken great care of himself. He bore his illness bravely and did everything he could to fight it. In the end it proved too much for him. Nobody could help being relieved that he was out of his pain.

Another fatality of the year was Tom Wills. He'd been at many of our nights in the Villas in the seventies. His death was different from that of John or Caroline Flack or Margot Davis. He died from a disease we'd been hearing of for a few months. It came from a city in China called Wuhan. Someone said it sounded like the name of a villain from a spy film. It was called Covid-19.

Tom was a friend of Hugo's from the days when he was in the seminary. He had a twin brother called John. The three of them left the seminary at the same time. They all got married soon afterwards. It made me wonder about the point of celibacy. They would all have made good priests too. Vocations were at an all-time low in Ireland by this time. The celibacy rule had robbed the church of three vocations in Hugo,

462

Tom and John. When was a Pope going to come along and get rid of it? Not that celibacy was the only reason they left. They had problems with the authoritarianism of the church too. But all three of them felt marriage should be an option for every priest.

Weren't some of the apostles married in the Bible? It sounded freakish for too many men to be together all their lives without a female presence. I remembered Gabriel Byrne's pronouncement about seminaries being breeding grounds for perversion. If people's natural urges were stunted it seemed logical to think they could get derailed. How many priests were turned into child abusers as a result of not being allowed to fulfil their natural sexual instincts?

Hugo started to spend more time with John after Tom died. He often played tennis with him in Belfield. They'd first played there over fifty years before when they were doing their B.A. It was a great testament to their hunger for activity that they were still running around a court at their age. Hugo was now older than my father when he died and struggling with a back problem. I couldn't imagine my father running around a tennis court in his seventies. I couldn't even imagine him running around one in his twenties.

Hugo and John reminisced a lot about Tom during their meetings. Both of them were more talkative than him. Tom was a great listener. Sometimes he was so good you felt he was too polite to tell you if you were boring him. He didn't talk much unless you got him going on the work he was doing. That was usually something technical. He could take a watch apart and put it back together exactly as it was.

He fixed cars for people with John when they weren't working on their boats or building houses. They were geography teachers by trade but their real work was for their friends. They'd get up in the

463

middle of the night to do a favour for someone. It didn't matter what time it was. They never charged. I got to know both of them well in the seventies. They used to fix my motorbike for me anytime it broke down. All they asked for in return was a cup of tea and a jam sandwich. They'd come in from the little laneway at the side of our house in Iona Villas reeking of oil but never spilling a drop on the floor. I don't know how they managed that. Neither do I know how they managed all the complicated repair jobs they did.

They did lots of jobs for Hugo's other friends over the years as well, especially Liam and Michael Hogan. Both Liam and Michael were dead by this time. Michael lived to a good age but Liam died young from a rare disease. It was so unfair. He'd placed a huge emphasis on health all his life. He ate all the right foods and exercised regularly.

Sometimes you can put too much of an emphasis on doing the right things. I've often gone into health shops and seen the most malnourished-looking people behind the counter. Vegetarians in particular always look very fragile to me. I'm a carnivore and something of a junk food addict and I'll take my chances with that. Maybe that's just an excuse to over-indulge in the wrong things but it's the way I feel. My father broke all the rules of nature and was never sick a day in his life before checking out at 72. I'm not saying that's the way it always works but too many people obsess about health today. A lot of them end up with psychological problems if not physical ones.

Neither Liam nor Michael married. That was a pity. Both of them would have made fine husbands. They loved the company of women but they were afraid of commitment. Somebody told me their father hadn't got on with their mother, that he warned them away from marriage. I don't know if that was true or not. I was reminded of the old Spike Milligan joke, 'I'm a bachelor at heart. It's my father coming out in me.' I never knew two people who enjoyed the company of women more than they did and yet they never entertained the idea of marriage.

Michael seemed to view women like porcelain vases – creatures of beauty to be admired from a distance. Liam engaged more with them but he was equally reluctant to go to the altar. Either he was terrified of losing his independence or he was influenced by his father's belief that most of them became a different breed when they changed from girlfriends to wives.

Tom and John Wills married soon after leaving All Hallows. So did Hugo. It happened often with ex-seminarians. Deprived of the company of women for so long, they embraced the idea of matrimony. It was like a liberation.

Everyone told stories about Tom's kindness after he died. I had a few of my own. I remembered one incident that took place on the day I was due to do my motorbike test in the early seventies. I'd gotten a puncture on the way to the test. It seemed to be always the way life worked. Accidents happened at the worst possible times.

I was near his house when I got the puncture so I brought the bike over to his house to ask him if he could fix it. He said the time was too short for him to do that. Instead he gave me another bike and changed the number plates. That meant I did the test on the wrong bike.

The examiner was in a car. He drove down the road and asked me to follow him. He got out at a corner and stood there. He told me to go round a circuit a few times where he could watch me.

The bike leant to the side. Tom said he'd got it from a scrapyard for a fiver. To stop myself falling off I had to tilt my body a bit. I was hoping the examiner wouldn't notice. I tried to make it look intentional.

Tom refused to stop helping people even when Covid struck. He reminded me of Paula Cafferkey, the Scottish nurse who contracted Ebola in Sierra Leone when she was treating a patient. She survived but Tom didn't.

The virus meant he didn't have a proper funeral. Margot Davis hadn't either, for different reasons. It didn't seem right for Margot. She collected crowds around her like bees around honey. Tom was more subdued so maybe it fitted him more. He reminded me of his mother in many ways. I felt himself and John got a lot of their qualities from her. She was a saintly woman who looked a bit like Mother Teresa and acted like her as well.

White Silence

Covid-19 reduced us to prisoners in our homes as the lockdowns came into force. You left you were living in a parallel universe, an Arctic world. Postmen left parcels in the porch and departed like ninjas. It was the same with the shopping. We ordered it over the phone and had it delivered. You'd hear the bell ringing. When you answered it all you'd see would be boxes and a car driving off at speed.

Some countries practised lockdowns better than others. Fun-loving nations like Italy and Spain were hit the hardest. Maybe they didn't like being told what to do. But then Germany was hit hard too. That surprised me. Germans were good at obeying orders, weren't they? And the French were usually obedient too. How come they got it so bad?

Covid didn't discriminate. It came to us all eventually. We were all going to be Covidified.

Donald Trump said the whole thing was a hoax at the outset. In Britain Boris Johnson told the people not to change their lifestyles in any shape or form. Life was to go on as normal. He even let the Cheltenham races go ahead. Then he came down with it. It seemed like poetic justice.

A man called Tony Holohan spoke to the people of Ireland every night on a TV programme. He was from the HSE, a kind of Dr Kildare figure crossed with Walter Kronkite. In gentle tones he told us what we had to do to stay safe.

Italy was the first epicentre. Then it was Spain, then France, then the U.S. In New York people were dying every six minutes but Trump was still saying he wanted to get the work force up and running again. When I watched him on CNN I saw his face growing more and more worried. Not because people were dying but because of all the dollars that were disappearing from the American economy.

It was ironic. He got into the White House because he was good with money. Now he might have to leave it if the economy collapsed. Maybe God was pulling the strings after all.

Trump claimed to be pro-life. It was why some of his critics put up with his racism and with his misogyny. Some holier-than-thou folks could forgive you everything if you were pro-life.

Except he wasn't. He was just anti-abortion. There was a difference. How could anyone say they were pro-life when they supported capital punishment and the NRA? And when they wanted to send Covid-19 victims back to work in the middle of the pandemic? I had a vision of him going into an ICU. He approaches an old man with about twenty tubes hanging out of him. Hepulls him out of his bed and goes, 'Hey, man, you're doin' good! You'll be back to work in no time!'

He told us the virus would be gone by the summer. Brilliant. So where was it off to? Barbados for the holidays?

My age meant I was in the group that was being cocooned. I saw that term as being more patronising than protective. Most people stepped aside gracefully when I passed them on my walks. They entreated their children to do the same: 'Give the man some space, Abigail!'

I saw resentment in young people's eyes. They saw oldies like me as being responsible for the curb on their freedom. It was like, 'We can't go out because we could give the virus to him.'

It wouldn't bother them if they got it. They could shake it off. Maybe some of them felt there were too many geriatrics around. We'd had our day. Maybe God should call us home.

A lot of people became depressed. Some of them became violent. Others tried to find ways out of the situation. A man in Fermoy showed films to his neighbours on the gable of his wall with a big projector.

Some weird exercise routines were trotted out on TV programmes. Children started painting stones and leaving them under trees for passers-by to view. They had messages like 'Be Happy' on them. It sounded like good advice.

Some of the stone designs were elaborate. Maybe they'd become artists sometime in the future. Maybe this was their first exhibition.

The weather got warm. I thought of the summers of my youth. There was only rain now and again. Was that because the ice caps weren't melting anymore? We were developing a new-found care for the environment.

I walked down streets where people were playing bingo. They sat outside their doors in chairs, even wheelchairs. Some of them were wrapped in blankets. They were aged from nine to ninety. I admired them. They acted as if it was nothing unusual to be sitting across the road from their neighbours marking cards. A man with a microphone barked out, 'All the threes, thirty three.' The heads went down.

There weren't less deaths on the roads, there were more. People always loved to speed. Now there was nothing to stop them.

I felt I was in a dystopian film. It would have been shot after Armageddon. The only difference was that in dystopian films you got to see the enemy, at least if they weren't directed by M Night Shyamalan. Here it was invisible. It wasn't The Blob or The Thing. It was in the air.

That's what made everything so surreal. On the surface life looked normal. There were no tanks on the streets. You didn't hear air raid sirens. There wasn't fear on people's faces, just bewilderment. They looked at you as if to say: Why are we behaving so weirdly? Who's making us do it?

I made my way to the shops for things it was awkward to order over the phone. You had to stand in line like when you were back in school. You observed a social distance from the people before and behind you. Irish people didn't like queues. We liked to ramble around lines that snaked all over the place. Until now.

A lot of places were closed. I felt sorry for women who couldn't get into hairdressers, especially the ones who weren't admitting to using dyes. People would have said to them over the years, 'Your hair looks so natural!' They'd reply awkwardly, 'That's because it is.' But now the truth was out.

I'd let my hair go grey years ago. I didn't care about things like that. When I was asked what kind of shampoo I wanted in chemist shops I replied, 'Any kind.' It was the same with most of the things I bought during Covid. The main thing was to get out of the shop ASAP.

'What kind of bread would you like, sir?'

'Any kind.'

'Any kind.'

'What kind of milk?'

'Any kind.'

Let's extend this line of thinking to health. A man goes into hospital for a heart transplant. He's asked what kind he'd like, that of a teenager or a ninety year old man. 'Any kind!' he replies.

Which reminds me of a joke about a man who's about to go into hospital for such an operation in pre-Covid times. The surgeon tells him he has two options – the heart of a 20 year old athlete or one belonging to a 70 year old lawyer. He goes for the latter, which bewilders the surgeon. The patient explains, 'I want one that hasn't been used.' My father would have enjoyed that joke.

The 'any kind' ethos affected all of us. Even the people who used to obsess about 300 different varieties of Mocha coffee and Americano and skinny lattes in the good old days were now becoming victims of it. I was never into that. Coffee didn't agree with me. Any time I suggested meeting people 'for coffee' I'd have tea. It was just an expression.

The only thing I discriminated about was beer. Not if I was in an isolated cell in Sing Sing would I drink Bavaria. Even Corona sooner than that. There was a brand still going by that name and even a musical group. Mary Black's son was in it. I didn't think he'd be selling many record.

I stopped using money. Notes and coins were only for the lower orders. I felt like Elvis. The same five euro note sat in my wallet for over three months. I was surprised there weren't cobwebs growing out of it. Eventually I got rid of it. That left me with no hard cash on me at all. I didn't know how I was going to deal with beggars on the streets. What would I say to them if they looked up at me imploringly and I had nothing to give them? 'Do you take Visa?'

The streets were so quiet they were like the streets I saw in cowboy films when I was young with tumbleweed blowing through them. When you looked down them all you saw was white silence.

Many of them doubled as graveyards. A disease that started in a city nobody ever heard of in China took over the world and filled it with coffins. There wasn't a thing we could do about it. It didn't matter if you were the Pope or the president of America. You were still a target. It relegated everyone to the same status as the hobo lounging in a sleeping bag on a street corner. It could claim your life while you were looking around you if someone sneezed or coughed in your direction. It could claim it if someone breathed on you.

It changed the way we lived. We heard expressions like 'self-isolating' and 'flattening the curve.' They were a novelty for a while. Then they kept getting repeated. We got fed up listening to them. Anytime people asked me how I was coping I said, 'I've been isolating since about 1958.'

We washed our hands until they almost fell off. We bought toilet rolls with the kind of excitement we used to have when we bought Gucci. We opened parcels with the caution of bomb disposal experts, wearing surgical gloves as we cut the wrapping. We even sanitised the scissors afterwards. For a while in April I actually stopped biting my nails. I couldn't get at them because of the gloves.

The precautions were new to my generation. We hadn't been through a war. The closest we got to hardship was having to queue for petrol in the eighties. That was when there was a crisis in the Middle East. This was much closer to home.

Social distancing suited some nations more than others. I thought of the George Mikes quote: 'An Englishman, even if he's alone, forms an orderly queue of one.' Maybe that didn't apply anymore. It certainly didn't to the ones who came over here for rugby matches.

We were told not to talk to anyone for too long because the virus hung in the air. Conversation was even more dangerous if you were in an enclosed space like the Dart. I didn't think that would be a problem. The last time I remembered anyone talking on the Dart was about ten years before - unless it was to their phone.

Every day the death toll rose. It was like the march of a genocidal army. We cocooned ourselves in our homes, coming out under cover of night for tabulated walks. We prayed for a vaccine to be found. All we could do until then was try to recover the values we'd lost when we sold our souls to Gucci.

Religious people told us Covid was God's punishment on us. They said he was annoyed with us for the way we'd destroyed the planet. He seemed to have a bad temper all right. The virus was like something from the Book of Ezekiel.

I thought his annoyance could have gone back to Brexit. He gave Boris Johnson the bug to stop him talking about it. Okay, Boris, he was telling Britain, you've got your sovereignty back but I'm afraid you won't really be able to enjoy it. Because you'll be, er, dead. Any God that stopped Boris Johnson talking about Brexit got my vote.

Post-Covid Boris was a different animal. He said he regretted Cheltenham now. He urged the public to wash their hands regularly and wear masks. Hindsight was 20/20. Hindsight was 2020.

Britain became another epicentre. It was hit even worse than Italy. When I was growing up, people used to say, 'If Britain sneezes, Ireland reaches for its handkerchief.' That was all changed, changed utterly. When Britain sneezed now we ran a mile.

The disease put manners on us, reducing us to the kind of lifestyle we might have scoffed at a few months earlier. We didn't go to the boozer anymore. We didn't hold wild parties. 'Early to bed and early to rise,' we said, 'made a man healthy.' We didn't put in the 'wealthy and wise' bit anymore.

Most of the people I knew started working 'remotely.' That was a fancy term for working from home. It was nothing new to me. I'd been doing it since 1993.

They crawled downstairs to their computers in their pyjamas at unearthly hours of the morning. Sometimes they spent all day in them. Or at least in their pyjama bottoms. They had to look good from the waist up in case their boss zoomed them. They were like Elvis in the fifties when the guardians of morality censored his pelvic gyrations on 'The Ed Sullivan Show.'

'Zoom' was another trendy word we learned. We filed it away in our minds to put alongside curve-flattening, social distancing, contact tracing, hand hygiene and PPE.

What did it mean? Basically it meant you were showing off your library. I wanted to give a prize to anyone I saw on zoom that didn't have a bookshelf behind them.

Eco warriors had pots and plants. Twee types had painting by Renoir and Manet. Most people had bookshelves. If you looked carefully you saw there were some seriously intellectual titles there. You weren't looking at chicklit or penny dreadfuls or the last Jeffrey Archer howler. No, it was Solzhenitsyn and Banville and Goethe and Lorca and the collected stories of Cesare Pavese.

Often the people who were talking didn't look like serious readers. You imagined them saying to their wives an hour before the broadcast, 'Darling, get rid of all those Jacqueline Susann novels you've been reading. And the Danielle Steeles too. I'm going to be on the telly. See if there's any of that pseudo-intellectual crap down in the cellar that I used to read in college.'

Remote workers missed the craic at the office. They missed nipping out for coffees, shooting the breeze with colleagues. What they didn't miss was taking abuse from their bosses. But some bosses gave them even more shit than usual from afar.

The main advantage of working remotely was that you could pig out on junk food while you were working and nobody could say a word to you. Some people said they'd never go back to the office even if the virus went away.

Our world perspective changed. We didn't look up to anyone anymore and we didn't really look down on anyone either. We were too busy just trying to get through the day.

Celebrities fell from their thrones. We didn't want to keep up with the Kardashians anymore. That show was once said to have changed the way we lived. Now all it changed was the way we hit the remote to turn the TV off.

People who used to talk down to us were now where we were. I thought of the old phrase: 'If you sit at the edge of the river, sooner or later you'll see the bodies of your enemies floating by.' This was no time for *schadenfreude*. Survival was the best revenge on those who betrayed us in the past. Everything evened out – like in the Bible.

Matt Damon rambled into Dalkey. He was making a film – or something. In normal circumstances we'd have been genuflecting before him. Now it was more like, 'There's yer man from the Jason Bourne films.' Someone took a photo of him at the local Spar with a grocery bag in his hands. He looked like someone trying to put a few euros together to buy a bag of spuds.

I felt I was living in a Samuel Beckett world. It was like the time after I left teaching. Nothing made sense anymore because everything was turned on its head. Maybe I should have gone out and stood in the bin for a few hours like the characters in *Happy Days*. It sounded like as good a place to be as anywhere else. At least it got you out of the house.

That was the great thing about Covid. Nobody cared what you did or didn't do anymore. We were all in the same boat. All we were hoping was that it wasn't the Titanic.

Social graces went by the board. It was a relief to pass people on the street that I used to feel I had to stop and talk to. Before the virus I'd have jumped under a bus to avoid some of them. Now I didn't have to. I just chanted 'Hello' from a distance and moved on.

I wondered what the future would be like. Would children remember what a handshake was? Would they ever hug anyone? I imagined the new Catechism going, 'Who made the world? God made the world. Who destroyed it? Covid.'

When was it not the first item on *The News*? When would it not be? Would that day ever come? Covid wasn't in our world. We were in Covid's world.

An unseen enemy from an unknown Chinese city continued its devastation. Some people said it was like 9/11 all over again. An older generation thought of the Spanish Flu. Those of us who hadn't experienced either of these travesties moaned about having to stand two metres apart from one another in convenience stores as we queued for our six-packs and our toilet rolls.

There were compensations. We became more spiritual. Global warming was halted. Worship of the Golden Calf of consumerism stopped. We heard birds singing again. They had the sky to themselves now. There were no aeroplanes getting in their way. Maybe they didn't want a vaccine to be discovered.

We didn't see juggernauts belching smoke into the atmosphere quite as much. The sky was blue. We looked up at it and marvelled. We enjoyed nature again. We became united by staying apart. Greta Thunberg was well pleased.

How could we avoid becoming infected? By doing nothing, we were informed. It didn't sound too difficult. If someone told you that you could avoid cancer or heart disease by doing nothing you'd have said, 'I'll take it.' We didn't have to go into bunkers to avoid being bombed like someone in a war. All we had to do was go down to our basements armed with a six-pack and a box of Pringles. There you could get blotto.

Some people went wild under it. There were incidents of domestic violence, suicide, bleeding-hearted liberals giving grief to the police for the withdrawal of civil liberties. John Waters even launched a court action about it. Children were being home-schooled by day drinkers. Where were the statistics for stuff like this?

England hid their nursing home deaths for a while. So did Northern Ireland. They were cited as natural deaths, not Covid ones. Everyone was afraid of being seen as having a high tally of fatalities. Nursing home clusters accounted for 60% of Irish deaths. The oldies of my generation had always been seen as lucky. Seventy was the new sixty and eighty was the new seventy. Not anymore. Now anyone over the biblical span was a target for the virus.

Dogs raced around the streets without anyone to stop them. There were clips on the news about other animals parading through empty towns – sheep, flamingos, even a crocodile.

Clive sent a video from Africa. It showed a group of lions walking from a nature reserve onto a road and just sitting there. Any motorists that came by stopped in shock. The drivers looked terrified but the lions didn't seem to want to attack anyone. They were just enjoying their day out.

The world was upside down. In former times people talked about going to the zoo for the day. Now the zoo was coming to us. Mary's brother-in-law had been in a film a few years before about a lion that rampaged through the streets of Fairview in the fifties. He had to be shot dead. Maybe he wouldn't have to be if it happened now. There'd be nobody to attack because the streets were so deserted.

When everybody stopped talking about the medical aspect of the virus they started talking about other things – money, mental health, obesity, suicide – the collateral damage of a recession that was as bad as anything the world had experienced since the Great Depression. I remembered my father telling me of businessmen that had jumped out the windows of their apartments in New York after the stock market collapsed.

Every night on *The News* we saw people making pleas to the government for grants, pleas for help to get their businesses up and running again. My relative Gina Murphy came on a few times. I stayed in her B&B in Ballina once. She was now running a salubrious restaurant in Merrion Square. Well-heeled politicians and members of the entertainment industry went there. When her restaurant was closed down she felt victimised as she'd adapted the seating for the virus. She didn't think restaurants contributed as much to its transmission as was believed by the HSE. The people infected by it didn't fall much after their closure. Every time she appeared on television she seemed to be more angry. She'd been entertaining celebrities for years. Now she was the same as the rest of us.

Pubs were closing down. So were factories and hotels and airlines and universities. Many of them would never open their doors again. The only people making money were doctors. And undertakers.

We were told we were all going to be poor. It would be like the troika all over again. I thought to myself, if that's the case, why don't we just cancel every National Debt on the planet? Let all the countries of the world start their own private mints. Then they could make as much money as they needed to get them through the crisis. There'd be no poor or rich countries anymore. Everyone would have exactly the same amount. Karl Marx would have been pleased at the idea even if Paris Hilton wouldn't.

The government offered 305 euro a week to anyone who'd lost their job as a result of the outbreak. It was generous. Many people wouldn't have been earning that much in normal times. We lived in a good country. I couldn't imagine Korea or Singapore offering people 300 quid for sitting on their arse. Covid dole beat ordinary dole. Bring it on.

After a while we got complacent. Seismologists registered more footfalls on the streets. We didn't just go down to the deli for essential items anymore as we were advised to.

At the beginning it was, 'Come on, Covid, give us your best shot.' We were rabbits in the headlights. Then we started to think we had it on the run. We got brave. We've beaten you, bad guy, we thought. Leo Varadkar said this kind of thinking was a mistake. He didn't want to wave a big stick but if we disobeyed the restrictions he told us the lockdown might last longer.

Donald Trump told us we should try injecting disinfectant into ourselves to avoid the virus. Dettol killed it on the kitchen worktop. We all knew that. Why not extend the logic to other areas. It was a no-brainer. Flu? Cancer? Who had the needles?

Was Donald being serious? Hell, yes. He'd dropped some tulips on us before but this was in a different league. The world's headlines carried his comments but he didn't seem too bothered. Should he have been?

He'd escaped being impeached on the Russian business. He'd cheated the tax man and got away with it. He'd come back from bankruptcy when his casinos collapsed. He'd been captured on camera talking about grabbing women between the legs. Everything ran off him like water off a duck's back. How weird it would be if Dettol did him down.

Was this man really the president of America or were we all just having a bad dream from which we'd one day awake? Robert de Niro said he never thought he'd end up living in a country where the president and the village idiot were the same person. The inmates were running the asylum.

I thought of a film I saw once with Peter Sellers. He played a gardener of limited intelligence. Due to some bizarre circumstances, he was elected president of America. Any time he made some pronouncement about flowers, people took a metaphorical interpretation out of it. He became a guru, a prophet. If he told someone to jump out of their window they'd probably have done it. I felt some of Trump's supporters were loyal enough to do that too.

Sellers played an equally inept president in *Dr. Strangelove*. That film ended with a nuclear holocaust. Nuclear war was my first fear when Trump was elected. When he didn't press the button I felt everything afterwards was a bonus.

I could see the frustration on his face growing daily as Covid spread its tentacles. No matter how many times he told us he was combating the virus I saw his face belying his words.

From the day he was born he was used to getting his way. Covid-19 wasn't interested in being bullied. It wasn't interested in the fact that The Most Important Man In The World was telling it to go away. It carried on regardless.

People's frustration eventually gave way to a kind of black humour. After a certain stage, probably after the surge was reached, they started to think: I'm fed up of being afraid. At this point the jokes started. The Irish were always good at gallows humour. A man was pictured hiding on a desert island hiding from a luxury liner, terrified the captain would spot him.

A man entered a bank with a balaclava on him. 'Hands up,' he said to the teller, 'This is a robbery.' 'Thank God,' the teller said, 'I thought you had the virus.'

Jesus was even brought into it. Someone posted a cartoon of him rising out of the tomb on Easter Sunday. St. Peter is standing a few metres away. He's saying, 'Don't even think about it.'

We needed a break from our minds. Every now and then I picked up a novel and tried to read it. It was difficult. My mind kept wandering. I was doing well if I got past a few pages.

There was a programme on the television on Tuesday nights called *Normal People*. It was about two university students falling in and out of love. The whole country became addicted to it. They exchanged meaningful glances with one another for hours on end, occasionally breaking into monosyllables about the depth of their passion for one another.

'I love you,' Connell said to Marianne. 'I love you too,' Marianne replied. In later episodes they started to develop problems. They drifted apart. Then they got back together again. It kept going on week in week out, this see-saw of emotions.

I loved it. It became like a drug for me, a drug that stopped me thinking of Covid. There was a world out there where people thought of something else besides the virus. I wanted it to go on forever. For a while it seemed it would. 'I love you, I love you not.' I envisaged the two of them saying these words to one another when they were ninety. I wouldn't have minded if it went on that long.

A lot of people agreed with me. Viewers went into withdrawal when it ended. Death from Covid was bad but what was going to happen to Connell and Marianne? What were we going to watch on Tuesday nights? Would RTE recycle *Love Story*? *Romeo and Juliet*? *Jane Eyre*?

In the end the programme was replaced with an Australian drama called *The Secrets She Keeps*. It was about this woman who went batty after losing a child. She kidnapped someone else's one and then started killing people. It was tame stuff in comparison to the love agonies of Connell and Marianne.

At the end of May something of more significance took place. A black man called George Floyd was murdered in Minneapolis. A policeman by the name of Derek Chauvin pinned him to the ground. He stood on his neck for nine minutes, thereby blocking off his supply of air. Three other policemen stood by, accessories after the fact. He was being arrested for a minor misdemeanour.

'I can't breathe,' he said. It was like a metaphor for Covid, a metaphor for all the people who were asphyxiated in ICU wards around the world. He then said, 'I'm dying.' Even at this point Chauvin refused to remove his knee from his neck. I thought of a name for the incident: Wounded Knee. Blacks were like the new Indians.

Chauvin was casual about the murder. He even had one of his hands in his pocket as he watched George Floyd take his last breath.

Riots ensued after the incident. It was captured by someone on a camera phone. If a police officer was capable of doing something like that in broad daylight in full view of dozens of onlookers, what might he do in secret?

The riots were reminiscent of the ones that took place in L.A. in 1991 after the Rodney King beating. People charged down streets brandishing weapons They started screaming. The caution they practised during the lockdown was thrown to the wind.

A crowd gathered near the White House. Trump got the National Guard to quell them. Tear gas and rubber bullets were used. Once again he showed himself to be more in the tradition of a despotic tyrant than the president of a democracy. He even invoked a 19th century law on insurrection to justify his use of force.

With his large gait and his square shoulders I imagined him as one of those kings of Third World countries who had epaulets streaming from their uniforms. An American Idi Amin maybe. If he was officiating over some country like that, the people he fired from the White House would have been shot. It was the same scenario at play. Saddam Hussein used to get 100% of the population to vote for him in Iraq. They knew the score if they didn't. 99% would have looked better to the outside world but it wasn't good enough for Saddam. I saw Trump in that light. I could see him wanting to put anyone who didn't vote for him up against a wall.

'George would be happy knowing the economy is doing well,' he said. Was he insane or appealing to the insanity of his fans? Some of them looked as mentally ill as he was. At least he'd be gone by November. The thought was a small consolation for the murder.

For three of the four years of his presidency he'd had a virtual honeymoon. The economy had improved and there was hardly any Isis activity. He looked like a shoo-in for a second term before Covid. He disgraced himself with that and even more with the murder of George Floyd. The American tree was mad at the top.

Would anything be done to Chauvin in the long term? He was arrested on a charge of manslaughter and second degree murder but that was only the first step. Would he be convicted? My mind went back to Martin Luther King. It went back to black victims Bob Dylan had immortalised in various songs - Medgar Evers, Hollis Brown, Hattie Carroll. I remembered Hugo singing Dylan's 'Only a Pawn in the Game' in our kitchen in Iona Villas in the early seventies, 'A bullet from the back of a bush took Medgar Evers' blood...' he sang.

What would Dylan think now? Had anything changed since the sixties? Would anything ever change? There would be a few months of anger before the legal process took over. The murder charge would be dropped and he'd be convicted on manslaughter instead. He'd serve a few years and that would be that. He'd go into hiding somewhere and get on with his life. For the family of George Floyd it would be a life sentence.

Covid went on. People talked about the tragedies in care homes, in ICU units. They talked about the plight of doctors, nurses, shopkeepers, the disenfranchised, the unemployed, the unemployable, the homeless.

Lady Gaga raised millions for the World Health Organisation at the beginning of the virus. She roped musical legends together like Bob Geldof had for Live-Aid. They gave their services for free. I didn't know too much about Lady Gaga except for the fact that she'd recently been in the remake of *A Star is Born*. When I saw it advertised I thought: Why make the same film three times?

She said Trump was a disgrace. Things were beginning to fall apart from him. If the election was held now instead of in November I didn't think Joe Biden would have had any trouble beating him. Amazingly, Biden's ancestors were from Ballina. Laurita Blewitt was descended from him. She'd met him in the White House when he was vice-president to Obama. There was a mural of him in the Market Square. I was aware of the Blewitt family growing up. Mary Robinson had put Ballina on the global map. Now it was there on an even bigger scale. One night Laurita was even interviewed on CNN.

Covid stopped being the main item on *The News* around the middle of June. By now another black man had been shot in cold blood. His name was Rayshard Brooks.

In Roscommon a policeman had fifteen bullets pumped into him by a drunk man on a motorbike. It was a freak incident. He had mental health problems. The policeman was shot with his own gun after having had it snatched off him by the man. I tried to make an analogy between the two incidents in my head. In America the policemen were too tough. In Ireland maybe they weren't tough enough.

At the end of June Trump held a rally in Tulsa to kickstart his re-election campaign. Any kinds of large gatherings had been banned for months but he didn't care.

By now all the medical experts were advocating the wearing of masks. We'd seen them in Wuhan as far back as February. We laughed at them at that stage. Even the epidemiologists told us they probably wouldn't help stop the infection then. Now they'd changed their tune. In some countries they were mandatory on public transport. I even saw ads for designer ones – Levi masks, leopardskin ones. Maybe we'd get a Gucci one yet. Trump could buy it for Melania. To go with her handbag.

He was still refusing to wear one himself. The thinking was: Masks were for wimps. Would John Wayne have worn one? Hardly. Trump was like a political version of Wayne.

There were about 100,000 people at the rally. They had to sign a waiver saying they wouldn't sue him if they got the virus. Did they seriously think they'd all escape it? The human capacity for delusion was infinite. These were probably the kind of people who put Trump into the White House in the first place. I thought of the guy in Waco years before who brainwashed his followers. Eventually he killed them. This wasn't Waco. It was just wacko.

He didn't get the turn-out he expected. Some people bought tickets online to create the illusion there'd be crowds there. They never intended to turn up. Something similar happened the year before in Ireland when the Pope came here.

It was good news for me - and for Biden. It was also good news for the people whose lives were saved by not having to be in a mass gathering. But Donald wasn't happy.

He loved crowds. His life was about numbers just as it was about money. He reminded me of King Midas, a man who turned everything to gold. Midas wasn't happy because he couldn't eat golden food. That was his Achilles heel. Trump's Achilles heel was Covid. He didn't seem to mind if everyone got it at Tulsa – including himself.

By now I was more concerned with politics in America than in Ireland. A new Dáil was about to be formed but I didn't pay much attention to it. Irish politicians were too ordinary. I preferred listening to a madman like Trump. By now my TV set was almost permanently switched to CNN.

He held another rally on the eve of Independence Day. It was in Mount Rushmore. Looking at his face framed in that rictus grin I could see him fantasising about being up there some day with Lincoln and the rest of them.

The turn-out was bigger than it was in Tulsa. Again there were few masks and no discernible social distancing. By now I thought it was time for someone to arrest him for being a danger to public health. The most powerful man in the world was now the greatest threat to its survival. CNN reported that some deranged people in the U.S. were holding parties where you got prizes if you contracted the virus. Maybe Trump should have been at them. Maybe he was throwing them.

To try and save my sanity I went away from CNN. The BBC started showing retrospectives of classic soccer games on *Match of the Day*. There were re-runs of World Cup finals, European Cup finals. They were important matches in their time but they held no interest for me now.

Games I would have given my right arm to see when they were happening meant nothing. The here and now was all that mattered. The boring present rather than the thrilling past. I realised I got more excited looking at Scunthorpe United thrash it out with Stevenage on a waterlogged pitch in Division 4 of the reserves than seeing Maradona beat five people to score a mind-blowing goal.

On RTE there was news of road accidents, drownings, violent deaths. These were different types of tragedies to the ones we'd been hearing about since March. Suddenly we weren't living in a Covid world anymore. It wasn't so much the New Normal as the Old Abnormal. It didn't feel any better. It just felt more familiar. We were being brought back to the way life – and death – used to be.

I couldn't empathise with these reports as much as I should have. As I watched them I found myself becoming wrapped up in trivial thoughts. Sharon Ní Bheoláin would be talking about an earthquake in Ecuador and I'd be looking at her thinking: That necklace is totally wrong for her dress.

Men and women found it difficult to meet one another. I thought of a good chat-up line: 'Nice mask.' Afterwards things could be difficult. How could you socially distance when you were locked in an amorous embrace with your partner? Could you observe a 2km distance from someone when you were sleeping with them?

Sofa So Bad

When June passed into July I stopped thinking about Covid. I had something else on my mind now that was much more important. My sofa.

We'd gotten rid of my old one a few weeks before the virus broke out. Now we had nowhere to sit. Just before the shops were shut down I made a commando raid to Bargaintown. Lucky me – I got one of the last ones in the shop. Unfortunately I didn't have time to vet it. It was a display model. The man who sold it to me said he couldn't take it back if it didn't suit. The legs looked a bit wonky. Probably as a result of all the customers plonking themselves down on it.

He asked me if I wanted it delivered. I didn't want someone with the disease coming to the house. He was also looking for fifty euro for the delivery. I thought that was a bit much. I said I'd put it onto the roof of the car and drive it home myself.

'I see you don't have a roof rack, sir,' he said as he came out to have a look at my vehicle.

'Ah,' I said, 'You noticed.'

I hoisted it up. It sat nice and snug. I put it upside down in a V shape. He gave me some rope to tie it. I rolled the windows down. Various ropes were wound in and out through the dusty windows.

I couldn't open the door so I had to climb in one of them to drive home. When I got there I had no scissors to cut the knots so I had to climb out again.

I was watching TV later that evening when one of the legs collapsed. I nearly fell into the fire.

The other legs looked a bit shaky too. The only solution in the long term was castors. Lenehans of Capel Street had great ones but they were closed because of the lockdown. When would they open again? Christmas? In ten years time? Anything was possible. Fuck Wuhan.

The previous sofa was prehistoric but at least it had good legs. Why had we picked the Covid year to get rid of it? It looked ridiculous standing there with three legs.

I went looking for a heavy book to prop it up. I found one in the attic. It was a commemorative volume on the film *Some Like It Hot,* the 50th anniversary edition. I'd bought when I was writing a biography of Tony Curtis a few years ago. Marilyn Monroe looked up at me smilingly from the cover.

I propped it under the sofa. It seemed to stabilise it for a few days. Marilyn's face put me into good form every morning when I came down for my breakfast. Covid had its good points. But I kept banging my leg off the book. I had to wrap it inside a pillow cover eventually. After that I couldn't see Marilyn's face. There's always a catch.

Then one of the other legs broke. I went up to the attic again to see if there were any more heavy books up there. I finally found one with Ingrid Bergman on the cover. She looked lovely but not as lovely as Marilyn. Even so, I put her under the leg. This time I didn't bother with a cover.

Meanwhile the death toll from Covid kept rising. People broke down crying at all hours of the day and night. I met them on my walks. We exchanged a few words from a respectable distance.

Leo Varadkar eased the restrictions. Ireland started to open up more. Suddenly it was like the virus never happened. There were more people on the streets. It was the same all over the world. In America the beaches started to be thronged. It was like at the start of *Jaws* when everyone wanted to get out for the Fourth of July despite the shark threat. This shark wasn't in the water. It was in the air.

Had people forgotten how many died? Were they not afraid of a second wave of the virus? The one thing we learn from history is that we do not learn anything from history.

'Don't get smug,' Leo said, 'We're still in the inferno.'

Tony Holohan stopped giving broadcasts. His wife was in palliative care. He was replaced by a younger man, Ronan Glynn. Epidemiologists like Luke O'Neill and Sam McConkey appeared on our television screens almost every night. We didn't know these people from Adam a few months ago. Now they were like blood brothers to us. There was a time I wouldn't have watched programmes like these if you paid me. Now they were like the highlights of my day – *Prime Time*, *The Tonight Show*, documentaries on frontline workers, sufferers from Covid, people in danger of losing their jobs.

The disease had made us all pragmatic. Suddenly the idea of watching a *film noir* with Barbara Stanwyck or Kirk Douglas was a luxury you couldn't afford. No matter how good it was you couldn't get immersed in it. Afterwards you went back to Matt Cooper, David McCullough, Miriam O'Callaghan. You thought about what things were like in the real world. How many patients had been admitted to Intensive Care since the film started? How many had died?

Trump still wanted to get the economy kick-started. He also wanted to win the election in November. Many religious people voted for him because of his stance on abortion. 'Let's open the churches,' he said. He was probably thinking most practising Catholics had one foot in the grave. He didn't mind spiriting them off to their reward on a Covid chariot as long as they gave him a vote before they shuffled off the mortal coil.

By now he was taking a drug more usually used by malaria sufferers. Things were getting even more surreal than they had been a few months ago.

Suddenly I didn't want him impeached for reckless endangerment of people's lives anymore. I thought: Let's keep this guy in the White House. He's too entertaining to kick out.

The football season reached its climax. Liverpool were so far ahead on points there was no way they could lose the Premiership. They'd been my team ever since the eighties when I developed an obsession with the goal-scoring skills of Ian Rush.

I'd witnessed their ups and downs, their agonies and ecstacies. I cried when they lost and exulted when they won. In recent years that wasn't as frequent as it should have been. There were an uncanny amount of times when fate seemed to conspire against them winning matches. I'd screamed at the TV screen when decisions went against them, when they hit the crossbar, when their goals were disallowed, when they got yellow cards, when they got red cards. It was almost like a collective conspiracy.

I pined for the day they'd win the League again. It was thirty years ago now, wasn't it? They came close in the 2013-2014 season but it wasn't to be.

Then Jurgen Klopp arrived. He transformed them from Nearly Men to winners. No longer were the shots going wide. No longer did a deficit in a match preclude a comeback. No longer were goals being disallowed.

In the 2019-2020 season they won so many games in a row it looked like they'd forgotten how to lose. At one stage they were so far ahead of the pack you felt they'd have the title in their hands by Christmas. They even made Man. City look ordinary.

Covid-19 struck when they were just a few games away from holding the title aloft. Klopp said, 'Football isn't important. What's important is people's health.' We didn't believe him. We remembered what his predecessor Bill Shankly had famously declared: 'Some people think football is a matter of life and death. I assure you it's much more serious than that.'

The team was forced to wait for the ultimate accolade. Forced to wait until the FA let the players back on the pitch again to wrap things up.

When the games began again months later they were without audiences. It took the gloss off their achievement. Poor Jurgen. What evil deity dreamt up such horrific timing? Was it the same one who'd kept them waiting thirty years for their hour of glory?

When they were finally crowned champions, the fans went mad, thereby setting Britain back about a month in its recovery from Covid. Nobody batted an eyelid. It was soccer after all. More important than life or death.

Kenny Dalglish said he wouldn't have believed it if someone told him in 1990 that Liverpool would have to wait thirty years before they won another Premier League. Neither would I. Kenny retired from managing the team when they were in the ascendency. His reason? Pressure. I could never get my head around that one. The team were beating all around them at the time. Yes, Kenny, it's tough at the top but it's even tougher at the bottom.

Another anomaly took place in the same week. Fianna Fáil formed a government with Fine Gael and Labour. Mícheál Martin became Taoiseach. Like Liverpool he'd been chasing fame for a long time. Now he had it. Another outsider was coming in from the cold. It was as if the disease was giving people who'd spent most of their lives in the shadows a chance to shine.

The celebrations were muted. It seemed appropriate. Big winners won big, small winners won small. It reminded me of a night I won the weekly snooker competition in my local club on a rainy night when most of the players stayed home. There were only eight entrants. I only had to win two matches to be in the final.

The only other time I remembered winning anything on the green baize was a day years before that when I won a record player for winning a pool game in a dilapidated hall opposite the Plough Bar. My opponent was Jim Barclay. He was appearing in a play in the Abbey at the time. He was also in the TV series *Tolka Row* and later *Fair City*. The record player was almost as big as the radio we had in Ballina. I still have it. Like most of the family I suffer from the disease of being unable to throw anything away. For twenty years it lay idle after vinyl records went out. Now it's probably fashionable again.

The Covid debates switched to the subject of summer holidays. Travelling out of the country was dangerous, especially if you were going to a country where the virus was rampant. What if you'd booked a holiday to the Algarve back in February and now that the airports were open, Michael O'Leary wasn't going to give you a refund? Did you just grin and bear it> Fork out new money for a 'staycation' in Ireland? Bundoran in the rain?

It was a tough call. At this point Ireland was almost Covid-free. That was good news but England and America weren't doing well. Even so, their airports were still open. Should we let people in or close our borders *a la* Trump? The Australians were making visitors to their country self-isolate for a fortnight. What if you only got a fortnight's holiday? Would you not be better off staying at home? The Aussies knew what they were doing.

We got the infection rate down to almost nothing but then it started to rise again. This time it was young people who were getting it. The deaths were low but how long would that last?

We postponed opening the pubs but tourists were still coming in on flights from other countries.

Adopting the Australian model wasn't practical. Clusters started to grow at the isolation centres. There seemed to be no answer.

A new word was coined: 'Fakecation.' It was when you pretended to be holidaying in Ireland but secretly went to the Seychelles. Traitor.

Politics started to get a bit strange. Barry Cowen was sacked as Minister for Agriculture after an old drunk-drive ban reared its head. He was hardly a wet day in the job. Now he was gone.

Different kinds of problems surfaced elsewhere. Tragedies were happening that had nothing to do with Covid.

John Travolta's wife died of cancer. Elvis Presley's grandson shot himself. Could he not live with the fact that he wasn't able to sing like Elvis? Or be loved like Elvis? He'd been given a music contract but did nothing with it. He was 27, the same age as so many other ill-fated music stars – Amy Winehouse, Janis Joplin, Jimi Hendrix, Jim Morrison, Brian Jones, Robert Johnson, Kurt Cobain. Everyone knew it was a dangerous age in music if you had particular habits. These people became known as members of the 27 Club.

We got a second spike of the virus in August. It was inevitable. Pub owners griped that their openings were put on hold because of it. They said house parties were more dangerous than pubs. As Mandy Rice-Davies might have said, 'They would, wouldn't they?'

Trump argued with Dr Fauci and with Doctor Brix. Trump argued with everyone. Things were suddenly looking good for Joe Biden. Trump said he wouldn't accept the election result if Biden beat him. Hadn't he said something similar when Hillary Clinton was running against him four years before? After he beat her, needless to say, he shut upabout electoral anomalies.

494

He was low in the opinion polls. It was time for some drastic action. He started telling the people of America all the good things he'd do if he got in again. There were going to be tax breaks, guarantees for renters, the works. Dammit, he was even going to roll out a Covid vaccine for us. That would be on November 3,' the day after the election. It was like, 'If you vote for me I'll save your life.' Where was this bleeding heart back in February or March? People were sick then too.

Joe Biden chose Kamala Harris as his running mate. A black woman ticked two important boxes for the voting public. Nice move. Trump fumed. Now he had someone else to hate on the Democratic ticket besides Sleepy Joe.

He said vile things about Harris but you felt he'd have dumped Pence in a heartbeat to get that double whammy. Dammit, it was almost as good as having Michele Obama in your camp.

I thought back to Bill Clinton's comment when Hillary was running against Obama, 'When I was young I wondered if we'd ever have a black president or a female one. Now they're competing with one another.'

He started a birthing debate about Harris. It mirrored the one he'd started against Obama some years before. This time his racism was buffeted by one of his other main characteristics - misogyny. And maybe a little bit of desperation as well. It didn't matter that his innuendoes had no evidence behind them. He operated mainly on corrosive asides in matters like this. They didn't have to be backed up by facts.

What was Biden heading into - an America that was bankrupt? Every country in the world seemed to be on its knees. In Ireland we faced a collapse in the economy that made the recession we'd come through some years back look like a minor hiccup.

Companies were desperate for business. I got emails from hotels I hadn't stayed in for years making me offers that were too good to resist. They were offering residencies for half nothing with perks thrown in. I waited for the day they'd actually *give* me money to stay with them instead of asking me for it. It looked like things were heading for that.

September approached. People started asking what was going to happen about the schools. Should they open now that we were heading for a second spike? Hell, no. We were all going to be broke. Why shouldn't we be ignorant as well?

Ronnie O'Sullivan won the world snooker championship for the sixth time. He played most of his matches in an empty auditorium. The sport's great showman said that helped him. He didn't like crowds. They put too much pressure on him to perform.

He won £500,000. An interviewer said he should use the money to buy up all the tickets for the following year's event so the auditorium would be empty then too.

The front fender came loose on my car. I patched it up with a piece of rope. Afterwards the bonnet wouldn't close. I had to loosen a panel. How long would that get me? I decided to put up with it. I didn't want to catch Covid from a mechanic.

My watch strap broke but I didn't want to replace that either. Too dangerous going into a jewellery shop. I super-glued it so tight it stuck to my hand. I had to wrap a towel around it in the shower.

I imagined there were people like me all around the country. People with dodgy cars, dodgy watch straps, dodgy everythings.

A lot of them had dodgy bodies too. They didn't want to go to the doctor with 'ordinary' illnesses anymore, just Covid-related ones.

'Irregular heartbeat? Don't worry about it, sir.' 'Pain in your chest? No problem, it's not Covid.'

'Legs giving out? It could be worse. You could be in the ICU struggling to breathe.' 'A filling fell out of your tooth? Put a pebble into the gap and superglue it.'

Superglue became my 'go to' substance for every problem. An arm fell off a chair. I superglued it. A door came loose on a kitchen press. Same solution. If I lost my leg in an accident I had visions of myself asking a surgeon to superglue it onto my calf.

People started to re-visit old hobbies. Jigsaws that hadn't been used since childhood were brought down from the attic. Scrabble sets came out. We even played Connect 4.

Some of us tried a bit of carpentry to maintain our sanity. Not all of it was commendable. I felt like launching a campaign for the cancellation of any home 'improvements' carried out during the Covid epidemic. I wanted to say to all DIY enthusiasts: 'Be honest. The shelves you put up that wet Sunday are bockety. They'll fall apart before the year is out. Admit it. You bought them in a state of high tension. Your mask probably wasn't on right. Your fingers shook as you tapped your Visa card. You ran out of the shop like a man possessed.'

The same could probably have been said of any garden furniture purchased during this period. It's probably rotting as I write. As for the Home Cinema Units some film fans installed at this time...No Comment. All they ended up seeing was snow. They could only watch *White Christmas*.

Dara Calleary resigned from the government. He'd breached the regulations regarding numbers when he attended a golf event. There were eighty guests at it and you were only allowed fifty.

The country became enraged. People had been cancelling weddings. They'd been going to funerals where there were only six attendants. They'd sacrificed saying goodbye to dead people to protect the living. And now this. To make things even worse he was from Ballina. The incident became known as Golfgate.

Calleary was Barry Cowen's replacement as Minister for Agriculture. That meant two ministers from the same department were gone within a month. I had visions of Mícheál Martin shouting out the windows of the Dáil, 'Anyone interested in being Minister for Ag? You don't have to be a politician. Just give me a shout and you're in.'

Some nutcases thought the government was being too restrictive. 500 of these protested in Dublin against the 'unconstitutional' nature of having to wear masks. I had to pinch myself to believe what I was seeing. This wasn't Trump's America. It was my own country. Sometimes I was ashamed to be Irish. Was dying unconstitutional?

The singer Jim Corr was among them. Jedward called him a 'Cov-idiot.' He replied, 'Get a brain between the two of you.'

Was it not Jim that needed the brain? Jim also believed swine flu was man-made, and that the U.S. military had a secret tectonic weapon that may have caused the 2010 earthquake in Haiti. What made him so batty? Had he spent too many years looking at his unbelievably beautiful sisters? Yes, that could scramble your brain all right.

There was nonsense on the television about something called herd immunity. I thought, hello, let's get rid of the disease before we start discussing fancy intellectual things like that. Another thing that got me was the number of people who said, 'We knew nothing about this disease six months ago. We know a lot more now.'

Correction. We only knew two things. One was that if you stayed away from it, it would die. The second was that if you didn't it could kill you.

Ireland faced the possibility of a second lockdown but it still insisted on opening the schools. I had visions of *Apocalypse Now*. When were we going to get the message?

The schools involved a million pupils. My advice to their parents was: Keep them at home. Who was going to remember in five years time whether little Johnny got his Junior Cert or not in 2020? What they'd remember was if his granny died.

Businesses were closing down every day of the week. Many pubs would never re-open. Was Covid laughing up its sleeve at our ignorance? It set out its stall in February. In September we still hadn't got the message.

The optimistic pronouncements of our genial epidemiologists suddenly appeared to be too moderate for me. I preferred the Malthusian tones of people like Kingston Mills and Gerry Killeen. They knew the score. We were heading down a dark road. Again.

Someone once said, 'The first big war was fought with bows and arrows. The second one was fought with tanks and the third with nuclear power. The fourth one will be fought with bows and arrows.'

I didn't shed any tears about the absence of the conglomerates. Maybe it would be nice to get back to a time of simplicity, a time when you went down to the shop on the corner for a loaf of bread and some messages.

There were over 24 million cases of the disease in the world. It was a frightening statistic. I got an idea. You couldn't get the disease twice. Let's give it to 24 more million. Put them into meat factories. Let them all get it, or at least all the young healthy people who don't have underlying conditions. After they recover they won't be able to kill us oldies.

I watched the U.S. Open tennis tournament. Novak Djokovic was kicked out of it for hitting a judge in the neck with a ball he fired in anger. It was after being defaulted on a point. A joke went the rounds: What's the difference between Djokovic and Trump? Answer: Trump is having more rallies.

Trump got the virus. More jokes started to circulate. One of them had him being given Domestos through a drip. I found it hard to laugh at this kind of humour anymore. Too many people were dying. But Trump didn't die. It's hard to kill a bad thing.

Brexit talk started up again. Johnson tried to screw Ireland with the backstop. There was the usual guff about him not wanting to be bullied by Europe. England knew all about colonial bullying. We felt their pain.

Ursula Von Der Leyen said he wasn't going to get away with it. So did Nancy Pelosi. Europe and America were running to our aid against our neighbours. It was like during the Famine. Didn't the Red Indians help us then? Didn't Europe? Britain let us die.

I looked at the map of our two countries. We were probably united once. That would have been millennia ago. We broke away from it in all senses. Now it crouched over us. Geographically, culturally, economically, it would always be The Enemy.

The numbers continued to rise. By late October they were back to over 1000 a day. We'd learned nothing since March. There was another lockdown. What was it going to achieve?

Europe went crazy with infections. Ireland wasn't far behind. There was talk of a dozen new vaccines coming onstream. When would we get them? Next month? Next year? In a decade? Everyone said something different.

'The time lag isn't unusual,' an epidemiologist said, 'We haven't even found a cure for the common cold yet.' You couldn't argue with him. We'd put a man on the moon but we couldn't cure colds. Life was absurd.

The American election was held on November 3. Before the official voting day a record 94 million postal votes had already been cast. That was three-quarters of the entire votes cast in 2016. Obviously everyone was taking this election much more seriously than the Trump-Clinton one.

I thought Biden was going to walk it. In the end he did, winning by some seven million votes. That was a big margin but not as big as I expected. The fact that Trump got seventy million votes was unfathomable to me.

His main fans were the riflemen, the religious, the rich and the racist. He gave the riflemen their guns. He made out he was religious by doing things like standing outside a church with a Bible in his hands (upside down.) He put money into rich people's pockets by reducing their taxes. He made racist ones feel better about their racism by being one himself. How could so many people like such a contemptible human being?

The eventual result came down to the mailed-in votes in seven key states. Trump hadn't allowed them to be counted until after the other ones. They were the votes of those who hadn't attended his rallies. They were afraid of picking up the virus. Sane people, in other words.

He disputed them, calling them fraudulent. Or at least some of them. Votes for Biden were illegal. Votes for himself were legal. In a Trumpian world, life was that simple.

He accused the Democrats of vote-tampering. What else was new? He'd been making this accusation for months. It was as if he saw the deadlock coming. 'They're trying to steal the election,' he said. But there was only one man trying to do that. He was like a child losing a football game who decided to run home with the ball.

Biden was declared the winner on November 7. It was thirty years to the day since Mary Robinson was made president of Ireland. Two presidents from our little town of Ballina. Not bad going.

Apart from the fact that I couldn't stand Trump, the election meant a lot to me in other ways as well. It meant less Irish immigrants would be sent home from America because their papers weren't in order. It meant America would re-join WHO and the Paris Climate Accord. It meant work would stop on Trump's famous wall. And it meant the backstop would be preserved in Northern Ireland.

Boris Johnson wasn't going to like that. It was obvious Johnson had no interest in Ireland. He wouldn't have had a problem throwing us under a bus any more than Trump would. You could see the pain on his face when Biden was elected. He knew he'd have to draw in his horns with the EU now.

I continued to watch CNN. Every night we were treated to the sight of Trump telling us the election was rigged. It was rigged just like Covid was rigged by the Chinese and the Hillary Clinton election was rigged by the Russians…until he won.

Everything Trump didn't like in life was rigged by someone. 'I don't like to lose,' he said. His eyes narrowed as he said it and his teeth gritted. In that moment you could see how he'd become so rich, how he'd become so corrupt.

He kept talking about 'fake news.' It was a term he coined. This was ironic considering he was the main purveyor of it on the planet.

Rioting broke out on the streets. Trump loved riots. He loved anything negative about life. Biden said he'd do his best to heal all the divisions. He was going to have his work cut out for him.

Peter Sutcliffe, The Yorkshire Ripper, died from Covid on November 13. It was a Friday. The idea of a brutal serial killer dying on Friday the 13th seemed somehow appropriate. Before he died he said he knew he was going to heaven. I hoped it kept fine for him. I wondered if he was going to bring his ball pein hammer with him to get past St. Peter. Maybe I shouldn't judge him. My father used to say, 'The devil himself doesn't know the mind of man.'

In America the death toll from Covid continued to rise. It was over 240,000 by now. The incidence rate passed 11 million. When Pfizer said a vaccine was on the way he all but claimed credit for discovering it. Good old Donald. A medical guru as well as everything else.

He was still appearing at rallies. It was as if nothing had happened. He was still president because he physically occupied the White House. Was he insane? No, he was just addicted to the aphrodisiac of power. He didn't drink or smoke. Adulation was his drug.

He refused to release funds for the transition of power. It wasn't enough for him to be responsible for the deaths of over 240,000. He didn't care how many more of them choked to death. I felt he should have been arrested for mass murder.

People were encouraged not to go home for Thanksgiving. It would only cause another spike, How many of them would obey the injunction? 'Better a Zoom Thanksgiving,' said CNN, 'than an ICU Christmas.'

The outside world watched in horror as Trump pursued his legal challenges. If any of his team said the election was fair they were rapidly dispensed with. One of them was sacked by tweet. A climate of fear was created in others not to follow suit.

His associate Rudi Giuliani looked like a panto villain as he ranted on about voter fraud. Hair dye ran down the side of his face as he fulminated. 'I have the evidence,' he roared. But where was it?

People were finally beginning to realise what a Pandora's box it had unleashed by letting Trump loose in the corridors of power. Now he wouldn't leave. Was he going to have to be dragged out feet first? Someone said the locks on the White House should be changed when he was out playing golf. He did that one day out of every five that he spent in that building.

It's a pity he didn't spend all five of them there. Then the country mightn't be in such a state.

I wanted to be in Washington. I would have gone up to him and said, 'You're fired' like he used to do to people in *The Apprentice*. I wanted to see him carried off to Guantanamo Bay in leg irons and a boiler suit.

Part of the blame lay with his followers. Hitler couldn't have had the influence he did if anti-semitism wasn't so rampant in Germany in the thirties. Trump fed off a similar type of hatred. Over 70 million people voted for him. Many of them now rioted against the 'injustice' of the election result. A few Republican senators came out against him but most of them stayed in the bunker. Anyone who got 70 million people to vote for him was a dangerous enemy to have, especially if he ran for president again in 2024. There was speculation he would.

He said he was accepting the transition to the Biden administration just before Thanksgiving. With this man, even that seemed like a big deal. Was he finally coming to his senses? Anthony Scarmucci, his former Communications director (and another man he fired) said, 'He's nuts, but clever.' It was important to add that bit. Nonsense made sense if you were as smart as Trump. He could make the most outlandish claims sound sensible because of that way he had with crowds.

He was still muttering about corruption in the voting. I knew by now he'd never stop. He set up a fund to which those of a similar belief could donate. It brought in over $200 million. Were there really that many deluded people out there willing to collude in his Faustian pact with the devil?

I wondered how much of the money would go to his investigations and how much would be kept for himself. There was talk of legal actions pending against him for his tax and other irregularities. Would Melania divorce him? She'd never looked happy in the White House. If he tried to get back into it in 2024, $200 million would come in handy with or without her.

When Biden fractured his foot playing with his dog, Trump send him a 'Get well soon' tweet. Was he being sarcastic?

The Argentinian soccer genius Maradona died the day after Trump gave the green light to the transition. It was fifteen years to the day since George Best passed on. In two days we'd lost a devil and an idol. Or rather a devil and a flawed idol. No more than Best, the 'little bull' with the massive talent was beset by demons.

It always seemed to be the case. The greatest among us had the greatest personal problems as well. Did God arrange it like this? Did he say to himself, 'I'll give these people God-like qualities but the price they'll pay is that they won't be able to live with them'? Would the rest of us mortals accept a deal like that if it was offered to us?

By now a second and third vaccine had arrived along with the Pfizer one. They were beginning to resemble Dublin buses – nothing for ages and then three at once. Would they work? We kept our fingers crossed as their various merits were teased out by epidemiologists.

Ireland reduced its Covid restrictions from level 5 to 3 as we got into December. The country opened up again as it had done in late August. With one difference. In August the incidence rate was down to single figures. In December it was roughly 200 a day. Were we mad? The government caved in to pressure from the retailers, the shoppers, the party animals. It was obvious what was going to happen. The numbers were going to shoot up again exponentially.

Oh well, at least I could still go to the pictures in the meantime. I hadn't been in a cinema since February. Restaurants were open too. It would be nice to sit down somewhere instead of getting the old McDonald's takeaways from the car. Theatres, sadly, didn't get the nod. Too many people. Could they not put on a Beckett play somewhere? Nobody went to those things as we all knew. The cast would be okay too. Nell and Nagg would be safe in their dustbins in *Endgame*. They'd have automatic social distancing, at least if they pulled the lids up.

Christmas approached. When I was ten years old I put a letter up the chimney asking Santy for Scalextric. Sixty years later I wanted to send him one pleading with him for the vaccines to work.

'It's the season to be jolly,' Boris Johnson said, 'but it's also the season to be careful.' The line sounded too good for him to have made up himself. He said he was locking London down for Christmas. Well done, Boris. It only took you ten months to get the message.

Macron got the virus. Our numbers shot up to nearly 500 a day but the government still wouldn't close the schools or the shops. The madness continued.

Mayo played Dublin in the All-Ireland a week before Christmas. They lost again – inevitably. They scored a goal after 15 seconds. That probably said it all. Mayo only had one shot at goal in the match. It came in the 77th minute, seven minutes into injury time. After so many bruising defeats over the years, by now I'd become tired shouting for them. They were probably the best thing that ever happened to Dublin. I don't think Dublin would have won as many All-Irelands if they met other teams in the final. Mayo had an uncanny ability to falter at the last hurdle. I was annoyed with them not because they weren't a great team but because they were. The problem was in the head.

Someone sent me a video of Donald Trump saying, 'The match was rigged. Mayo won.' Just this once I wished he was right.

A lot of revellers brought the virus around Belmullet by bingeing in pubs and at parties around the wilds of the Céide fields, the last place in the world you expected it to get to. For a while Belmullet was the world capital of infections. Eat your heart out, Wuhan! We Irish always celebrate more when we lose. So Dublin didn't only deny us another All-Ireland, they caused us to infect ourselves as well. Thank you, Dublin.

I needed consolation from somewhere. It came from an unusual source.

A Star is Born came on the television. It totally wiped me out. After seeing it I thought: How could I have missed this in the cinema? It was one of the best remakes I've ever seen. Lady Gaga sent shivers up my spine with all those torch songs she did. I was also blown away by the incredible expressiveness on her face, right up to the final frame where she looked at the camera as if to say: What just happened? That was a stroke of genius on Bradley Cooper's part. He directed it as well as appearing in it. How often did we see films ending by having characters look at the camera?

The story of the film was beautiful. It was the story of a woman who didn't want to be more famous than her husband because she loved him so much. They were both singers. He was more famous than her when they met but then he developed alcohol problems and her career outstripped his. He killed himself at the end. Her success meant nothing to her now.

I recorded it and watched it four nights in a row. I would have burned the television out with it if I could. It got me through Christmas just like *Normal People* got me through spring. The last song she sang pinned me to my seat with emotion. It was like watching an opera.

I'd been aware of the name Lady Gaga for years but I knew nothing about her except for the fact that Basil's daughter Shali had roomed with her sister when she was in college. The only song of hers I knew was 'Poker Face.'

After seeing her in *A Star is Born* I made it my business to get everything she ever did. I bought her CDs and DVDs. I remembered Keith's son David being similarly fascinated by Madonna in the eighties. He watched her videos all day long. I liked Madonna but not as much as David did. Now I knew how it felt to be consumed by someone.

After Whitney Houston died I thought nobody could ever equal the power of her voice. Now I knew someone could. That's the thing about life. Once an icon dies another one comes along with the baton for a new generation.' When I listened to Lady Gaga singing 'I'll Never Love Again' at the end of *A Star is Born*, in my mind I was hearing the reincarnation of Whitney Houston singing 'I Will Always Love you.' Nobody could jump octaves like these two women. Lady Gaga sings the song from three different sides of her throat: the top, the bottom and the back. Who else ever did that?

Back in the real world, Covid cases hit the thousand mark per day. Then they went beyond it. The third spike was worse than the second one. Once among the lowest countries in Europe for infection rates, we were now among the highest.

We opened the country up for Christmas. Over 54,000 people came from England for the holidays. Did we really expect them not to bring the virus with them? It was on tour.

We were inviting disaster with open arms. Leo Varadkar said, 'The safest place for you to be is at home on your couch.' Obviously he hadn't seen the legs on our one.

I tried to prop my spirits up by thinking of Christmas. Were people going to put up trees? Were they going to go mad with their loved ones after the year they'd been through? How long were the new restrictions going to last? When were we going to get the vaccine?

Never mind. Santy was coming. A message came up on my computer saying Micheál Martin had designated his trip from Lapland to be essential travel. Yippee.

This year the feminists were ensuring Mrs Claus was going to be with him. It was only right. Why should she stay home washing the dishes with the elves? There was also a practical reason. Apparently last year his sleigh had been clamped in Temple Bar when he stayed beyond his parking time. She could now keep an eye on that.

I expected Christmas under Covid to be quiet. There would be no surprise visits from people you hadn't seen for the past 364 days and no useless presents you had to fake excitement over. I'd send a few cards and speak to people over the phone. Then it would be over-eating, over-drinking and over-bingeing on the useless TV programmes that were foisted on you at this time every year.

It didn't quite work out like that. First I got a puncture in the car. Then I set the bin on fire from not checking some hot ashes. Then the drains got clogged. Then the kettle shorted, blowing practically every socket in the house. And then the cooker broke down.

Someone started kicking the door just before midnight on Christmas Eve. I went upstairs and looked down. It was three lads with hoodies and mobile phones. They started rattling the letterbox. After a few minutes a stone went through the glass of the door. Then one of them smashed the windscreen of the car with a whiskey bottle.

We called the guards after they went off. They caught one of them but couldn't pin anything on him without CCTV footage. He wasn't arrested. In the Dublin of 2020 it probably went down as a minor incident. We were told it was related to drugs. I knew they were in the area. Sometimes I saw pairs of tennis shoes thrown up onto telephone wires. That was always a sign. A lad in the area had been chopped up by drug barons some months before. We were small fry in comparison to things like that. I got a new windscreen put on the car. A man from Tallaght put a new pane of glass onto the front door. Life returned to normal – sort of.

At midnight on New Year's Eve we waved goodbye to the year just gone. Or rather good riddance. It was probably the worst one in most people's memory. I hoped 2021 would be better. How could it be worse?

On the credit side it saw the end of the Kardashians. Covid did some good things. There was hope for the human race yet.

The new year had hardly begun when Trump was in the news again. He'd been taped on a phone call trying to put pressure on the Secretary of State in Georgia to find 12,000 votes that would give him victory over Biden. Biden had won Georgia by 11, 789 votes. 'I need 11,790 more votes,' Trump said, 'I won Georgia. Everyone knows that.'

The *Washington Post* released a tape of the call. Trump immediately said he'd sue for breach of confidence. He was too clever not to have known the call would be recorded and most probably released to the public. He wanted his millions of followers to hear it, to hear him talking so plausibly about Biden having won by forged votes. Apparently his lawyers had found two. That meant there were only 6, 999,998 to go. It had to be only a matter of time.

By now his exploits were making those of Nixon in the seventies look minor. I couldn't figure out why he wasn't arrested by the FBI. Or impeached. Or indicted for perversion of the course of justice.

Someone told me he'd had threats of being assassinated but I couldn't see that happening. It was usually idealists that were assassinated rather than mediocrities like Trump. That was the pattern all the way from Abraham Lincoln to John F. Kennedy. John Hinckley tried to shoot Ronald Reagan in the eighties. That was an exception but he failed, even though Reagan 'forgot to duck.' It was hard to kill a bad thing.

On January 6, under Trump's incitement, his supporters invaded the Capitol building. It was like a coup. They broke windows and entered the building, terrorising the politicians inside. The incident must also have made China and Russia smile. ('Is this all we have to invade to take over the world?').

Trump must have watched it all unfold with glee. His attitude seemed to be, 'If I'm not going to be in that building next year, I don't want anyone else to be either. Burn it down. Maybe I'll build another Trump Tower in its place.' It was like Samson in the temple. He'd tried the law courts and got nowhere. This was the next step.

Five people died in the incident. The religious right were still calling Trump pro-life. I saw him as a murderer.

Nancy Pelosi's office was invaded. A man sat on her seat. He put one of his feet on her table. Things were getting surreal. He wrote on a note, 'We won't back down.' Someone else said, 'We're coming for you.' A sign on a car parked outside the building carried the message, 'Pelosi is Satan.'

A noose was put around a scaffolding. A man applying it said he wanted to hang Pence for going against Trump.

Some of the police seemed to be letting it happen. One of them even posed for a 'selfie' with a rioter. I tried to figure out what was going on. Most riots that took place in countries were against the establishment. This one was being endorsed by it. It was a right wing riot.

Robert de Niro said he was living at a time when America's president and the village idiot were the same person. Maybe he could now say Guy Fawkes and the American president were the same person. Would that be an insult to Fawkes?

The police waited on orders from him to attack the rioters but such orders were never going to come. It was a bit different to the time when the Black Lives Matter protestors congregated at the same place. These people were teargassed for their troubles. Trump posed outside a church with a Bible.

If George Floyd had broken a window on Capitol Hill you felt sure he'd have been shot on the spot. Here the glass was knocked in as casually as my own window had been broken five nights before. I live in a suburb of Dublin 5, not in a place occupied by The Most Important Man in the World.

He waited until all the damage was done before he told the rioters to go home. It was left to Mike Pence to call in the National Guard. Trump was enabling anarchy. It was the last sting of a dying wasp.

One of the rioters said to a policeman, 'You didn't move us. We moved ourselves.' That's what made it all so surreal. The last time I saw such reticence from the police force was during the O.J. Simpson car chase down a motorway in 1995. That seemed to be almost in slow motion. Was there collusion? Was it an inside job?

Rudi Giuliani, a man who advocated zero tolerance for crime when he was Mayor of New York, said, 'This is combat. Bring it on.' Trump called the protestors patriots instead of scumbags. His daughter Ivanka echoed his sentiments in a tweet.

She deleted it after there were calls for Trump's impeachment. The tide was turning against him at last. Maybe the insanity of the past four years was finally coming to an end.

George Bush condemned him. So did Mitt Romney. These were two Republicans. I grew up thinking Republicans were the bad guys and Democrats were the good guys. In those days my delineations weren't any more nuanced than that. It was like heroes and villains in gangster films. Maybe it was time for me to grow up. His own party were denouncing him.

I wasn't really worried about Trump. I was worried about the malevolence at the core of the psyche of Middle America. He couldn't have brought this on without that sickness being there in the first place any more can Hitler could have got away with the holocaust of World War II without a similar sickness in Germany.

Hitler was mad. That was how he managed to whip up such hysteria in his followers. I didn't think Trump was mad. He was just power-mad. There was a difference. He didn't want to take over the world. He just wanted to take over America. Phew.

What was the secret of his attraction to so many? He was just a businessman. Businessmen didn't usually have charisma, did they? Maybe it was his corruption they loved. Corruption recognised itself. If one was minorly corrupt as a yellow vester or a neo-Nazi, their role model was one who was majorly so. Enter The Donald.

Many of the protestors had blank faces. They were the kind of faces I'd been used to seeing on CNN over the past few months when types similar to them were asked why they thought Biden had stolen the election. 'Because he did,' they said. Then there was silence. They had nothing to add. Facts weren't important. evidence wasn't important. His victory was simply 'fake news.'

They reminded me of a definition of America I once heard: 'A land of wide open spaces surrounded by ears.' How different it was to when I went there in 1972, in 1973, in 1980, in 1981. What happened in the meantime?

Donald Trump happened. Maybe that was all that needed to be said. He could still push the button in his last fortnight and wipe us all out. It would be like the end of *Dr Strangelove*. I found myself wishing Stanley Kubrick could be resurrected to make a sequel to it. *Dr Trumplove*. His relationship to Putin was reminiscent of Peter Sellers talking to 'Dimitri' in Kubrick's film.

Nancy Pelosi called for his impeachment under the 25th Amendment. Trump got nervous. In a panic he made a politically correct speech condemning the rioters. He promised an orderly transition of power on January 20 even though he wouldn't be attending it. It was the most unDonald Trump-like speech I'd heard in four years. Like many politicians with a talent for being Houdini he was able to speak out of the two sides of his mouth at the same time. It must have stuck in his craw to say those words.

He talked about the horror of the virus. It was the first time I'd heard him mention it in a month. Everyone knew he didn't care about Covid or how many people it killed.

He didn't care about the rioters either. 68 of them had been arrested by now. Many others had been captured on CCTV footage. They were being sought in various states.

The coup hadn't worked. Now he was selling them down the river. He'd let them rot in jail if and when they were found. He fired them up to create havoc and then deserted them. It was the same way as he deserted so many others who supported him when he started to feel the heat.

The threat of impeachment loomed closer. He employed Rudi Giuliani to defend him. Giuliani? He was asking the man who'd cried 'Combat!' to plead his case. It was a bit like Don Corleone asking John Gotti to be his advocate. Someone sent a video of him in prison, He was saying to a jailer, 'I demand to phone my lawyer.' A voice comes from the next cell saying, 'I'm here.' It's Giuliani.

Pence was asked if he was going to invoke the 25th Amendment. He said no, that he'd save it just in case Trump became 'more unstable.' Would he be convicted? Maybe it didn't matter. At least he was silenced. That was enough for me for the moment.

I watched the impeachment proceedings. A Congressman said one of the windows that was broken in the coup still hadn't been fixed yet. If I had the phone number of the White House I'd have told him I knew a man in Tallaght who'd sort it out for him.

Back in Ireland we had different kinds of problems. The number of people who got Covid surged to 8000 on January 8. Despite such a statistic there were still people complaining about their places of work being closed down. Did they have death wishes?

Every day after that the numbers were staggering. The death toll, the hospitalisations, the ICU patients. We knew January was going to be a 'keep the head down' month but not like this. The curve was flattening but not in a horizontal way. It was flattening vertically.

Frontline workers were getting breakdowns as the hospital service reached surge capacity. It was getting to the point where discussions would have to be had about who should live and who should die. Lifeboat-style discussions.

We'd been hearing the word 'exponential growth' about the virus for ten months. Now we finally knew what it meant.

The Department of Education announced that the schools would be closed for the month of January. Some pupils said they wanted them to be kept open so they could study for their Leaving Certs. Come again? If I was 17 and I heard the schools were closing I'd have done a jig of delight. The modern student was a different breed. Did they want to be educated or to die? Take your pick. I was glad I wasn't teaching anymore. I might have forgotten to pack my oxygen mask along with my cheese sandwiches.

Nero fiddled while Ireland burned. Sometimes I thought my father was right, that dictatorships sometimes worked better than democracies. If I was running Ireland during Covid I'd have ordered a curfew from six o'clock every night. Anyone on the streets after that time would be put into a paddy wagon and carted off to jail. Forget your level fives and level threes and level three and a halfs. It was time to get real.

I had a vision of myself as the Minister for Education. I'd have issued this manifesto to the children of Ireland: 'As of today, an automatic Leaving Cert is being granted to each and every one of you.' It would be like when I got my driving licence back in the seventies. When there was a backlog in testing.

I would have felt validated in my decision. Let all the dummies loose into the universities. They'd probably make more sense than a lot of the students I sat beside in the seventies. And they'd be alive. That was important too.

January went on in its crazy way. Each day a new emergency. In the middle of it all, the report on the Mother and Baby Homes came out with a different kind of shock. Thousands of babies had died at birth and had been buried secretly in the decades gone by. Another despicable chapter in Ireland's history to add to people like Ann Lovett, Joanne Hayes, Eileen Flynn and the Magdalene Laundries. I was reaching a surge capacity of my own.

The night before Joe Biden was inaugurated he held a dignified tribute to all those who'd died from Covid at twilight in front of the Lincoln Memorial. Looking at him standing there quietly beside his beautiful wife Jill I felt the surge of elation I always got when a Democrat was elected president, a surge that went back to John F. Kennedy and continued through Carter, Clinton, Obama.

Trump said he wasn't going to attend the ceremony. I was glad. I'd probably have vomited having to look at his ugly puss even for another second.

Pat Stacey wrote in the *Evening Herald*: 'Today it finally ends. Mid-morning our time, early morning in Washington. Donald Trump and his ghastly wife Melania - a worthless First Lady to a worthless Commander-in-Chief – leave the White House, bringing a gaudy gold curtain down on the worst presidency in American history. Sour, spiteful, infantile, envious, needy, nasty and narcissistic to the very end, Trump won't be attending Biden's inauguration. In a pathetic bid to steal his successor's thunder there'll be a farewell ceremony at Andrews Air Force base, a send-off that would be more appropriate for a winner than the seditious loser Trump is, not that he'll ever admit he lost.'

'A few hours later Biden will be sworn in in front of the Capitol Building. It's currently surrounded by barricades, razor wire and seven-foot fences. These are the stark reminders television viewers will see of the carnage Trump inspired and leaves behind as he and Melania – bounced back to the status of just another trophy wife and one probably destined for a trade-in very soon – head back to Mar-a-Lago in Palm Beach, Florida.'

The ceremony was highlighted by an inspirational speech from the new president. He promised to heal the divisions that had riven the country in recent times. Listening to him speaking I felt as if a four-year cancer had just been ripped out of America, leaving it open to the healing that had to take place if it was going to survive. I felt as proud listening to his words as I did reading the 1916 Proclamation.

This was the true spirit of America, the spirit of the Statue of Liberty, of the 'United' States. It was the America I'd visited in the seventies and the eighties, a country for all people, all colours, all creeds and none. And who better to sing the National Anthem than Lady Gaga? Could things get any better?

Biden spoke about racism, about the climate crisis, the economic one, the surging virus. He even mentioned enemies of truth, though without mentioning Trump's name.

He was gone. Only now did the fact sink in for me. Ding dong, the witch was dead. Without a rouser, where would the rabble be? Did better times lie ahead? None of us knew for sure. There were too many variables.

The virus started to mutate. There were variants from Britain, Brazil, South Africa. Would the vaccines stop them? Were we involved in a race against time? And yet there were still people going on holidays to Lanzarote. Jesus wept.

I thought of the world as it used to be, the world I'd known from 1953 to 2020 before everything went crazy. A world where students hated school and presidents accepted defeat in the White House with dignity. A world where people didn't turn a blind eye to a disease that could kill you.

I thought of a world where people who attacked your house on Christmas Eve would be treated as serious criminals instead of casual offenders. A world where people who stormed a government building were stopped instead of enabled. A world where you didn't have to put on plastic gloves to handle something because of a virus. A world where you didn't have to wash your hands 100 times a day. A world where things around you looked normal without being the 'new' normal. A world where you saw people on the street who didn't look like they were about to rob banks.

A world where Lenehans hardware shop opened its doors on Capel Street and let you in to buy new castors for your sofa.

Memory is the Only Friend...

The recollections I've featured in this book aren't meant to be verbatim. If they were it would be a book of history rather than one of reminiscence. Our minds aren't panes of glass. They're prisms. That means our memories are reflected in different ways depending on who we are or where we're at in our lives when we have them.

I don't remember events in sequence. They come to me as isolated incidents – looking out a window one day at a donkey being beaten by a farmer, watching the sky turn from day to night, being in a cot in the kitchen as a young child and having someone spill marbles over my toes when I had chilblains. The cot had railings on it. It's interesting that I remember that. So many of my early memories involve captivity of some sort or other. My first memory of Primary School is railings too. For years during my adolescence I had a recurring dream about being put into a concentration camp by Hitler. In later years teaching became like another form of captivity. Maybe that's why it meant so much to me to finally get out of it.

Other members of my family remember things differently to me. Maybe they're more accurate. Then again, what's accuracy? My father used to say that whenever he had a court case involving a car accident he might get a dozen different eye witness accounts of it from people who saw it happening. If that kind of discrepancy is going to be the way for something that just happened, you can multiply it by a hundred or maybe even a thousand for things that happened years or decades ago.

One memory that comes back to me from my youth may not have happened at all. It has me being ambushed by three boys as a young child coming

520

down Convent Hill on my way home from school. They said they were going to beat me up and then kidnap me. I haven't been able to get this out of my mind over the years. If it happened, surely I'd have had marks on me. If they kidnapped me I'd have been missing. Maybe my imagination conjured it up. But why have these thoughts lingered in my head? Where did they come from?

If I had my life to live over again I think I'd be more outrageous. People say, 'It's better to be sorry for what you didn't do than what you did.' I used to think that for years but now I think it's cowardly. Better to be sorry for what you did than what you didn't do. You never know till you throw.

Early to bed and early to rise makes a man healthy, wealthy and wise, or so they say. It also makes him very boring. Most of the best things in my life happened after midnight and so did some of the worst ones. As the song says, 'You can't have one without the other.' I might have had a more stable life if I went to bed every night at nine o'clock but it would also have been a much more unfulfilled one. I'd have been like one of those golfers who always sent their drives down the middle of the fairway and putted for par.

Most people think they have a licence to misbehave after midnight. Not many of them look into the fridge for yoghurt at that hour. Our defences are down and our demons come out. It's as if we think we deserve some kind of reward for having got through the day. We don't want to let it away with anything.

Norfolk is a community centre now. I feel my parent's presence in it whenever I'm there. One of the rooms holds monthly meetings for AA. My father would have been amused by that. He never trusted people who didn't drink but he'd probably have made an exception for reformed ones. He was one of them himself. I commend him for the way he struggled with that problem and finally overcame it. It went along with the financial struggle of trying to raise nine children on an inconstant income. Somehow we all came through that.

People in the town always said, 'The Malones are so united.' We've had our falling-outs but they usually don't last too long. Not all large families are happy. Sometimes I think our one was too much so. An unhappy childhood can be a better preparation for life.

One time when I was on a visit to Ballina a friend told me his brother had been sent out of the family home to live with a relative when he was young. It didn't sit well with him. In fact he never forgave his parents for doing it. Something similar happened to Nora Barnacle. At the age of two she was sent to live with her grandmother. Her father was a heavy drinker and her mother couldn't cope. This kind of practice was quite widespread at the time.

In an age where we've lifted the lid on Magdalene laundries and various other types of abuse in our country's past, maybe this is an area yet to be explored by historians. It left deep feelings of bitterness in the rejected children. I say 'rejected' because that's what it must have felt like to them. It wasn't always the result of their parents not loving them. Sometimes it was caused by economic necessity. Whatever the reason it left a deep wound. Such a wound often continued into the time when the children had families of their own.

Most of my siblings have married and reproduced. Keith was the first to go up the aisle. He had three sons with Jacqueline. They'd have loved a daughter but it wasn't to be. Jacqueline's brother Paul had three daughters. It would have been nice for both of them to have had a mix but that's not the way life works.

I heard of a woman in England recently who aborted her child after seeing her ultrasound because it wasn't the gender she wanted. What was next? Hitting a child over the head with s hammer because it had bad features? Smothering it in its cot because it had the wrong colour eyes? This is the world we're living in. At times it seems to come close to Hitler's idea of the Master Race.

I'm reminded of Janey O'Hora with her seven sons and no daughters. One night her son Peter, the projectionist in the Estoria, showed *Seven Brides for Seven Brothers*. It must have had a particular resonance for him. To my knowledge they all got brides. A man Mary worked for had eight daughters and no sons. Some people think you aren't a 'real' man unless you have a son. That kind of thinking goes back to Henry VIII. Muhammad Ali once said, 'I have two sons and seven mistakes.' By 'mistakes' he meant daughters. He was joking of course. He doted on his daughters but he had a lot of chauvinistic attitudes. People accepted this from him because he was so loved.

Ernest Hemingway had three sons. He'd have liked a mix too. As he aged he called almost every young woman he met 'Daughter' – or at least the ones who attracted him. He wasn't very subtle about what they represented for him.

June and Pat had a daughter called Joy. She lived up to her name. She lives in London now. She became a huge success in business. She has no bother at all giving lectures to large groups of CEOs.

Ruth and John had three children. Their daughter Fiona visited us one year and proved to be a real charmer. The first thing she said as she got off the plane was, 'Mom never stops talking about Ireland.' The comment made me think of James Joyce, a man who spent more time thinking about Ireland than most of the people who lived in the country. Did Ruth love it too much? Did that stop her giving America a chance to make her happy? I wasn't sure. She hadn't been in Ireland since my mother died. When she left in the seventies, she said, she fully believed she'd never see either her or my father again. I thought of something my father said often, 'In every parting there's the image of death.'

Fiona's brother Colin came over more recently with his wife and children. We have yet to see Brendan, their third child, at least as an adult. He came to Ireland with Colin when he was very young but my memory of that visit is hazy.

Hugo and Kathleen formed a close bond with their two children, Lorna and Patrick. Lorna has two children of her own now.

Basil has a son, Barry, and a daughter, Shali. He lives for their visits to him to his home in Syracuse. Barry's wife Kira recently gave birth to a son, Brennan. We see him developing in leaps and bounds on the photographs they send us.

I've never heard a bad word said about any of Audrey's family. She has five children: Gordon, Robbie, Lauren, Dawn and Ralph. They're so mannerly it's almost unbelievable in today's world. A few of them live in Australia now. The youngest, Ralph, recently had a baby with his partner Jennifer. They called him Lochlann. Audrey was lucky enough to see him on a visit to Australia just before the Covid virus broke out. The visit coincided with Robbie's marriage. Jacinta went with her. She was celebrating her birthday at the time so there all sorts of things happening.

Jacinta never stops doing things for people both inside and outside her family. As well as working hard at her job she visits troubled people in prisons and helps them on their faith journeys.

She has four children and adores them all. Two of them, Darren and Ryan, have children of their own and have become devoted husbands and fathers. She tries to see them as much as possible no matter how inconvenient that might be for her geographically. Her third son, Bobby, is a gentle and soft-spoken boy. He's adopted but she never made him feel any different from the others. If anything she's given him even more love because of that. Her daughter Julie-Ann is travelling around the world as I write, exploring it as only she can with the great energy of her personality.

Mary and myself haven't been blessed with children. Whenever we're asked if we have any I give the Brendan Behan answer, 'Only one – me.' What's wrong with being a child at my age? Growing up is something I never really aspired to. It's been done before.

I don't know how I'd have been as a father. Being 'in loco parentis' was fine for a few hours every day as a teacher but I doubt I'd have coped well in the role for 24 hours a day. Pat Ingoldsby worked with children a lot in his TV programmes. He loved doing it but was equally happy to go home alone after the programmes were finished. He said he got all the fun without any of the responsibility. I saw his point. Maybe Tina was a bit like that too. She never married despite having lots of offers.

Mary would have made a brilliant mother. After she left her job in the solicitor's office she decided she wanted to work with children. A very kind lady called Louise Smith arranged for her to become an assistant teacher in a crèche.

She couldn't wait to get into work every morning to see the kids. They couldn't wait to see her either. She only has to look at one and they fall in love with her. It's like hypnotism. I advised her to stay away from teaching after my experiences in classrooms but she still went in for it. My advice to her on most other things is usually off-target too. Thank God she doesn't listen to me.

Sometimes I wonder how any children we might have had would have turned out. Mary says I'd have spoiled them. I probably would. She would have too. We'd have made the same mistakes our own parents made. Maybe every parent does. How many parents are equipped for the job? There's no training you can do for it like you can for other jobs. Often the best candidates for it are childless. If we had children they'd probably be middle-aged by now. That's a scary thought.

I'm 67 at the moment but I don't feel it. To quote Bob Hope, 'I don't feel anything till noon. Then it's time for my nap.' Why can't we age backwards? Wouldn't we all like to be Benjamin Button?

When my father was my age I was 18. I used to go to him for advice. What advice could I give to an 18-year-old? Crawl back into the womb?

Most of us in the family are now older than my parents were when they died. Both of them lived beyond the Bible's 'three score and ten.' Maybe we should re-define what it means to be old. Seventy, as they say, is the new sixty. Basil sometimes says that when he was young he wondered how anyone could be as old as Aunt Florence. She was probably a young enough woman when he thought that, at least by today's standards. When I visited Siobhan McKenna in 1972 I thought of her as being ancient, a relic of the old Abbey almost, and yet she probably wasn't even fifty at the time.

Cloris Leachman died earlier this year. I thought of her as ancient when she played the cougar to Timothy Bottoms in *The Last Picture Show* but she was only forty when she made that film. Age is different for men and women in Hollywood. Liam Neeson said he's thinking of retiring from action films this year. That's nice of him. He's 69. I can't imagine

Sigourney Weaver jumping off airplanes at 69. Or Uma Thurman.

When I look back at my life I see it as being like a game of Snakes and Ladders. All too often it was one foot forward and two steps backwards. I was always trying to improve myself but I rarely did. I kept making the same mistakes. That's the thing about life. It's like Groundhog Day.

There are many things I never learned to do. Cooking is one. I probably inherited this from my father. He was rumoured to have said to my mother once when she asked him to make her a cup of tea, 'The kettle is making a noise. What do I do now?' His mother ruined him and my mother ruined me. Mary has continued the process, failing to direct me towards the cooker in thirty years of marriage. I know where it is – to the left of the fridge – because I cooked beans on it once to put onto a slice of toast. The trick is not to let them fall on the floor as you're applying them to the toast. It's a skill I'm still working at.

I left Muredach's College fifty years ago. There was supposed to be a reunion last year. In 2010 the Past Pupils Union of Belvedere had a similar one. It was to celebrate the fortieth anniversary of my class doing the Leaving Cert. A representative from it pursued me to attend. I wasn't just contacted once or twice but many times. They went to some trouble to locate me, tracking me down from one of the places I wrote for.

I didn't go. I wondered why they were seeking me out now when they'd made me feel like a misfit forty years before. I felt like a nobody that year. I wasn't exactly famous in 2010 but I was better known than a lot of the people in the class who'd done little with their lives. Was that why they were looking for me? I remember being intimidated by a lot of them in the last months of 1969. Was I getting revenge now? I hoped I wasn't that petty. The reason was probably simpler. I was always going to be a bogman.

The Muredach's reunion was cancelled because of the virus. That disappointed me. I was looking forward to seeing people I hadn't met for half a century. Maybe God took a hand. Maybe he was afraid I'd burn the place down.

How would they look now? I have a photograph of them all standing on the steps of Muredach's. It was taken in 1964. I'm not in it. I mustn't have been at school that day.

I still remember them as they were. Maybe I'm better off not seeing them again. Time can do strange things to us. They might have lost the bright look in their eyes that's in my photograph. They might have lost their happiness, the happiness we all had at the beginning of that exciting year before life caught up on us.

Maybe I'd think they looked ancient. That's what happens when you haven't seen someone for a long time. It's different with ourselves. We only see small changes when we look in the mirror every day. Maybe they'd think I look ancient too.

I've met one or two of them in Ballina on my trips back to it over the years. Occasionally I meet Mícheál Leonard for a drink. He calls himself Mick now. I said to him one night, 'I can't see you as Mick.' He said, 'I can't see you as Peter.'

When I look at him I find it difficult to match him with the person I knew when we were both at Muredach's. Can it really be fifty years since I cycled up that rambling avenue as the gentle currents of the Moy flowed behind me?

Inside ourselves we think we're ten years old even if our bodies give us startling reminders of the fact that we're not.

Our minds can do that too. I was in a DVD shop one day looking for a Julianne Moore film called *Still*

Alice. I said to the man behind the counter, 'Have you got that film Julianne Moore won an Oscar for?' He said, 'What's it about?' I said, 'It's the one where she gets Alzheimer's Disease.' He asked me what the name of it was. I said, 'I can't remember.'

Being born last in the family always gave me the illusion that I was younger than I am. I forget the fact that it's all relative. At my age I'd be the eldest of a lot of families. Mary knew a woman who was called 'Baby Higgins' into her eighties. She was the youngest of his family and the name stuck. Such curiosities can be reassuring but they can also be deceptive.

I got a fright one day some time ago when I was at my local cinema in Coolock. When I was asked if I wanted the senior rate I was shocked. If you're ninety and you don't get offered the senior rate you're delighted. It's the only time in life where you're glad to pay extra. Cinema cashiers shouldn't offer ninety-year-olds the senior rate.

The only time I wanted to be seen as older than I was recently was when I was waiting for my Covid jab. Older people were getting them first. I was thinking of applying some Tipp Ex to the age box on my birth cert before heading up to the vaccination centre.

I got another fright recently when I had to have my photograph taken for a free travel card. It didn't come out well. I looked like I'd been run over by a truck. The lighting in the booth was bad. That's my excuse anyway. The photo of me on my passport wasn't much better. Whenever I looked at it I thought of the old joke, 'If you look like your passport photo you're too ill to travel.'

I don't do much travelling nowadays anyway. A few jaunts down the country every few months and a trip across the pond in the summer is about the size of it. That was before Covid. Things have changed since the virus struck. Travel now means going for a walk out the back lane – if you're allowed.

People slow down as they get older. When I hear about the children of my brothers and sisters going half way around the world for a wedding or some other reason it makes me sad. Even without the virus I could never have done that.

I've always kept my watch ten minutes fast. I don't know why. Maybe it goes back to an insecurity about being late for school. If someone in the street asks me for the time I have to subtract ten minutes from it. If they see the watch they say, 'Why did you give me the wrong time?' They don't understand that sometimes the wrong thing is right. It's like the man who couldn't understand I wanted paint on my snooker cue.

I've reluctantly become a part of the modern world. I use the computer more than I used to and I buy most of my books online. This has advantages and disadvantages. The advantage is that you find what you're looking for quicker. The disadvantage is not having the surprise of finding something you weren't looking for.

I miss going into dusty old shops like Greene's of Clare Street and browsing through what they have. I miss having a book fall down on top of my head from some shelf above me and realising it's a masterpiece that I must have.

I read something every day - and every night. John Major used to say he liked going to bed with a Trollope. He might have been better with a curry - and I don't mean Edwina.

Books help you wind down. And wind up. The fact that they're unfashionable today probably makes them more desirable to me. Are people too lazy to turn pages? When I was writing journalism back in the nineties an editor said to me one day, 'If you're doing an article for me I don't want it to be longer than a page.' That seems to be the limit of readers' concentration today. It's why so many things come to us as soundbites. God forbid that someone should have to suffer Page Two of an author's ruminations. Proust would probably be shot on sight if he was reincarnated.

My life is simple these days. I get the paper delivered to me every morning. If I'm not listed in the obituary page I get up. Then I mooch around the house for a few hours until my brain comes to life. Sometimes it doesn't.

I never found out what 'ufungtatistical' meant, or 'skymuggledy blossom.' Neither did I ever discover what was in Auntie Nellie's room behind the wallpaper.

I try to stay positive. It would be nice to believe in Santy Claus and the tooth fairy and people who married for love and films that ended happily and viruses that didn't wipe our half the planet and presidents who governed instead of inciting riots. Life doesn't always work out that way.

One of the neighbours dropped in recently. The only thing she wanted to talk about was the number of people along the road who'd died. There's only one way to deal with people like that. Reverse psychology. After letting her ramble on for a few minutes I decided to tell her a bit about my new favourite subject of cannibalism. I went into the details of how Jeffrey Dahmer and Hannibal Lecter chopped up their victims and then froze their vital organs, storing them in the frozen food section of their fridges for tasty dinners. She didn't stay long.

The school I used to teach in has over a thousand pupils now. Children are happier going to school than they ever were. Why shouldn't they be? Everything is done to help them.

There were no facilities for 'slow' children when I was a pupil and not much for them when I was a teacher either. They were just regarded as the tail end of the class. Now we classify them as autistic or dyslexic or having ADHD.

Pupils today don't have to suffer depressing poems like 'Gray's Elegy' or writers going back to the 17th century like Shakespeare. Instead they have people you wouldn't normally associate with a curriculum. Christy Moore is even on it now. Is this a step too far? He told me to fuck off one night in a pub on Dorset Street when I was talking too loud and he was trying to sing a song. I can't imagine Shakespeare doing that.

I still watch old films and I still listen to old songs. I enjoy them but it's not the same as it was when I was doing these things in the old days. The past is always receding from us like a tide. The more we try to grasp it the farther it goes away.

I found another Radio Luxembourg. It's called Sunshine Radio. You get it on 106.8 FM. No matter what time of the day you turn it on you get music. It's like having a juke box in the house.

I've decided I prefer listening to people singing than talking. We've been talking to one another for thousands of years and what has it achieved? My father used to say, 'Talk is cheap.' He was right. Maybe we should start singing to one another instead. I feel confident it would improve the state of the world. It might even stop wars.

I go back to Ballina as much as I can. Every time I see it there's something different about it. A building I knew has disappeared or some new housing development is starting. That happens in every town but it strikes you more forcibly when it's your one. I got a fright the first time I saw a child with a mobile phone in Arthur Street. I expected him to have a yo-yo.

Neil Armstrong stepped on the moon the year we left Ballina. It was like a thunderbolt. Today if there's

532

a moon landing it hardly even gets first spot on *The News*.

The last time I was there I met more people than usual. On most of my visits before that I was more like a tourist than someone who'd lived there.

I called up to Michael Courell's house first. He was in to be a priest for a while but left to get married. He opens the cathedral every morning now so he keeps that side of things going. He has the keys of the kingdom. More importantly, he continues to believe how essential it is to 'Keep playing football.'

Joe Cahill is still waiting for Clive to pay him the shilling he owes him from 1951 when he got the straight flush and Clive went off to the Estoria with Keith. He's confident the seventy years that have elapsed since the incident will have caused it to appreciate substantially. Arrangements are being made to have the money transferred to his account by the Zambian government in association with the relevant Jesuitical authorities. Joe is looking forward to spending the rest of his life in a luxurious penthouse in the Balearic Islands.

One night I met Marty Walsh for a drink. He's Tina's brother. He had lots of great stories from the past. He's retired now but he keeps himself busy. He plays in the local band and writes the odd poem as well.

His wife Mary was with him. She used to work in a hotel my father drank in. She told me she got a tip of a ten shilling note from him once. I tried to remember what ten shilling notes looked like. It must have been thirty years since I saw one.

Tina is in a nursing home in Boyle now. She's happy there but it's sad to think of her having had to leave her 'little house on the prairie.'

I visited Mickey O'Hora in his house off the Killala Road. He talked of our family with fondness. His brother Padraig was with him. It was strange to hear him speaking with an English accent. So many of the O'Horas went to England in the fifties. Padraig remembered firing plastic bullets from our front room at the old school across the road one day. 'Why would I have wanted to do that?' he said. I told him I could think of many reasons.

After spending a few days in the town I went down to Enniscrone. I stood on the beach watching the waves of the Atlantic lashing against the shore. The Valley of Diamonds looked small in the distance. So did Bartra Island.

The beach was deserted. As I walked along the strand I felt like Robinson Crusoe. Its expansiveness transfixed me in a different way than it had when I was a child. I'd taken it for granted then. Now it was an unexpected blessing.

Leonard Cohen spent most of the sixties in the Greek island of Hydra. He said after leaving it, 'Once you've lived in Hydra you can never live anywhere else, including Hydra.' I knew what he meant. I feel the same about Ballina. It's a luxury I can't afford. The memories are too idyllic. They gave me a springboard to an ideal and then whisked it away from me. Maybe I was destined to pursue a dream like F. Scott Fitzgerald's Gatsby and run away from it when the reality of it got too close.

There was a time I thought I might like to move to America. I couldn't entertain that idea now. How could I live in a country where I was older than the architecture? It would be too embarrassing. Is this what's called an Edifice Complex?

Neither would I feel comfortable living in a country that elected Donald Trump. Or acquitted O.J. Simpson. Or assassinated John F. Kennedy and Martin Luther King. Or gave an Oscar to John Wayne. I'll always have great memories of the summers I spent there but that America doesn't exist anymore. Individualism is being sucked out of it by

Starbucks and Walmart and McDonalds dads and neo-Nazis. In the next generation I expect it to be Kardashianised again.

In Dublin I'm left with my memories. I don't want to blot them out but neither do I want them to take over my life. I don't think the children of the next generation will have anything like the same kinds of memories though. Will they look back on their past and wish they were back there? Will the events of the years gone by mean anything more to them than something that happened yesterday?

I still say, 'Sorry about that, chief,' when I'm apologising to someone about something, drawing on a line from a fifty year old comedy show. I can't imagine lines from shows that are being aired today having that kind of longevity.

There are very few characters left in the world today. They've gone out of politics, showbusiness, music. We don't even have them in sport. There's no Nastase in tennis, no Eric Bristow in darts, no Lee Trevino in golf, no Bill Werbeniuk in snooker. Rock stars don't drive their Jaguars into swimming pools in hotels anymore. They just ask for room service.

I worry about the next generation. Everyone is going to be on Twitter and Facebook all the time. They'll forget what real living is like. They won't be able to add two and two because they'll be so used to their calculators doing it for them. Neither will they be able to spell 'cat' because it's easier to look it up on Google. They'll procreate through Virtual Reality and raise families of clones.

Or will there be such things as families? Maybe such phenomena have become outdated in our politically correct age. The word 'wife' has almost become an anachronism today because everyone has their 'partner.' If you're married you feel almost embarrassed.

Neither can you refer to women as 'housewives' today. You have to say 'home maker.' To me a homemaker is a builder.

The PC strain infects everything. You're not allowed have gollywogs today because they're regarded as racist. Hello? We had them in Ballina. We weren't racist. A woman in England was prosecuted recently for having one in her window. In the same month in America a black man was shot in cold blood by a policeman who got away scot free. Apparently you're only allowed kill black people today but you're not allowed to have any representation of them in your window. In fact you're not even allowed refer to them as black. You have to say 'African-American.'

I wrote a book about gay cinema a year or so ago. It's called *Queer Film in America*. I said to the editor when she told me about the title, 'When I was growing up, calling gay people "queer" was regarded as homophobic.' She said, 'Well it isn't now.'

That's another thing that gets me about political correctness. It's so arbitrary. Will 'queer' become homophobic again in the next generation? Should we check our noticeboards for updates?

The idea of referring to a bride and groom as 'man and wife' in a marriage ceremony is rightly regarded as sexist but for some reason the feminists have no problem with someone saying, ''Hello guys' to a man and woman in a pub or on the street. Who decides these things? I think we should be told.

There's a new version of Dennis the Menace on CBBC these days. He's not the one I grew up with. For one thing his catapult has been taken away from him. Neither does he bully that guy Walter in the schoolyard who was so much fun to read about in *The Beano*. The CBBC people saw this as 'homophobic' because Walter was effeminate. The new victim isn't quite so soft. He stands up to Dennis. He looks a bit like the Tory MP Jacob Rees-Mogg. Now there's someone we'd all like to bully.

The programme isn't even called Dennis the Menace anymore. It's called 'Dennis and Gnasher.' Has the term 'Menace' also been deemed politically incorrect? Oh, and Gnasher has had his teeth straightened. All these amendments, the producers tell us, are in the interests of 'inclusivity.' For which read 'terminal boredom.'

The Things That Are

Writing has continued to be a hobby for me even in the time of Covid. Or especially so. Mark Lawrenson once said, 'When I was a child I had two dreams – to join a circus and to play football for a living. With Liverpool I got to do both.'

Writing was a bit like that for me when I started it. It was like getting paid for not working. As the old saying goes, 'If you find what you want to do in life you'll never have to work again.'

There's some truth in that but it's not true all the time. Every activity has routine attached to it. There are also long periods where you're doing nothing between commissions. Steven Spielberg once said about film-making, 'It's not the time it takes to take the take that takes the time.' A lot of our lives are spent waiting for Godot.

It amuses me when people say writing is my passion. Maybe it was once. These days it's more like drudgery. Lawrence Kasdan said being a writer is like having to do homework every day of your life. When you do something all the time it loses its romance. It becomes a job. You grudge the time you give to it. Tidying the sock drawer becomes a more attractive alternative.

There's not much money in it either. I once read a quote from Karl Marx: '*Das Kapital* didn't even pay for the cigars I smoked when I was writing it.' Poor Karl. But wasn't he supposed to be a communist? Why should he have been interested in money?

I'm not the only person in the family who likes to blacken pages.

Keith wrote up until the last day of his life. Clive has written two religious books and edits various magazines in Zambia. Hugo has written a number of plays and is having a book of poetry published shortly. June's husband Pat has even joined the writer's club with his recent publication *Hidden Dimensions? From Ancient Greece to Modern Physics.'* It's a book of great erudition but being as ignorant as I am about physics it was 'Greek' to me in all senses.

Basil has just finished a book called *The Last Smoker on Earth.* He's really on fire in it, giving James Joyce a run for his money in the stream-of-consciousness department. It's a picaresque enterprise, a smorgasbord of recollections about his eventful life and the many famous people he's met. It's also a dystopian parable about where our politically correct universe is leading us.

I think it's his best book. I wish he'd bring other ones he's written to fruition as well. They deserve to be on bookshelves. For the moment we have to make do with projects like the compilation volume *30 Life Journeys,* an anthology of mini-autobiographies of his engineering classmates from 1968. He edited this and also contributed a chapter. The people from the class have always kept in touch. That's largely down to Basil's talent for getting people together and making things happen.

The girls in the family haven't been bitten by the bug, the lucky things. If they wanted to I'm sure they could out-write any of us from what I've seen of letters they've composed over the years. I'm often tempted to think book-writing is a matter of inclination rather than talent.

Liam Hogan said to me once, 'If I put my mind to it, I could do everything Denis Donoghue did.' I'm sure he could have. I've always thought I became a writer because I didn't think I'd be able to do it. I'm still trying to prove to myself that I can compose a school essay without my father's help. The fear of failure is still driving me on.

The most recent book I did was a study of *Shane*. Things end as they began. It was my first cinematic love. Maybe it should be my last one too. I'd intended to do it in 2001, the fiftieth anniversary of the making of the film.

A man called Walt Farmer made a documentary on it that year. His wife was good enough to send me the CD-ROM of this. It was a great help in writing the book. So was a biography of Brandon De Wilde written by a lady called Patrisha McLean.

I hadn't any luck finding this on Amazon so I wrote to Patrisha directly. It was a writing group in Maine that published it. Imagine my surprise when she said she was the wife of the singer Don McLean. She met him on one of his tours when she was a young reporter.

Despite being told he was doing no interviews she found her way into his dressing room during a concert and hid there until he walked in. He fell in love with her at first sight and they married soon afterwards.

After I got the book from Patrisha I emailed her to thank her for it. She said she was coming to Dublin with Don for a concert he was doing here in the near future. She promised to look me up when she got here.

That was a number of years ago. Sadly, since then the couple have parted acrimoniously. In fact Patrisha has taken Don to court for spousal abuse. She later set up a society for women who've been victims of this. She called it Finding Our Voices.

I can't think of a more unlikely man to abuse a woman than Don McLean. Patrisha also seemed very easy to get along with from any contact I had with her. They had a happy marriage for 29 years. Don even wrote a love song for her.

She once said of Don, 'He can't stand seeing someone in a position of power stepping on a little guy.' How can two people who were in love for so long become so bitter towards one another? They lived in a rambling mansion in Maine for nearly three decades before their break-up.

Don didn't dispute her allegations because, he said, he wanted their two children to be protected from the publicity. He settled for a plea bargain instead. He's now living with a woman who used to be a *Playboy* model. He's 74 and she's 25. What strange turns life can take.

Don is obsessed with cowboy films. Maybe this was what impelled Patrisha to write her biography of De Wilde. Little did I know when I started it that it would lead me away from a Wyoming cowboy to a Maine singer.

Researching a book takes some of the mystique away. When *Shane* appears on television these days I don't watch it with the same devotion I used to. I wonder if this is the way with everything.

I stopped watching Jimmy White after writing a biography of him. The same thing happened with Tony Curtis.

Does this mean that during the years I was watching them I was storing up notes on them to use in my books? I don't think so. If I was it was subconsciously.

Nietzsche once said, 'We only speak about that for which we've lost respect in our hearts.' The artist J.M.W.Turner expressed a similar idea when he said, 'Every time I paint a portrait I lose a friend.'

One of the strange things about memoirs is that we write them to get painful things about the past out of our system but in the process of doing so we dredge them up again.

That's one of the contradictions of regression therapy. Maybe it's also the price we pay for putting things on paper. It's like when we say a photograph 'captures' a scene. Maybe scenes shouldn't be captured. Maybe they should be allowed to roam free like wild horses.

So many people are using Cameraphones today we're in danger of losing the essence of experience. When you see everything you see nothing. The best things in life are mysteries. The future and the past are more interesting than the present.

People I meet sometimes ask me if I remember when some important event happened in my life. Usually I don't. It's the trivial things I remember. Or are they trivial? Who can define importance?

One of my novels was called *The Things That Were*. It was a nod to my father's love of the past – and a nod to my father. The title was a quote from his beloved *Lasca*:

> '*And sometimes I wonder why I do not care*
> *For the things that are like the things that were...*'

Such words come back to me every time I think of him. They come back to me whenever I see a computer instead of a typewriter like the one he had with the black and red ribbons. They come back to me anytime I see rows of shelves in a supermarket instead of the sawdust on Jimmy Geraghty's floor. They come back to me whenever I go into a faceless multiplex to see a film and in my mind's eye I think of Saturday afternoons in the Savoy when we were jumping over seats and clobbering one another with rolled-up newspapers.

A few months ago I came across a copy of *Lasca* in a drawer. It was written either by my father or Uncle Louis. On the first page it said, 'Monologue, *Laska*.' *Laska* was crossed out and re-written as *Lasca*. As I read the words I found myself becoming nostalgic:

It's all very well to write for reviews
To carry umbrellas and to keep dry shoes
To say what everyone is saying here
To wear what everyone else must wear.
But tonight I'm sick of the whole affair
I want free life and I want fresh air
I long for the canter after the cattle
The crack of the whip like shots in the battle
The melee of horns and hoofs and heads
That wars and wrangles and scatters and spreads
The green beneath, the blue above,
And a dash and danger and life and love
And Lasca...'

The writer was given as Fred Duprey. This was also crossed out. It was replaced with 'Frank Desprey.' On the back of the page I saw the words, 'Louis Dillon-Malone, Clongowes Wood College, Sallins, Co. Kildare, 1910-18.'

That made me think it must have belonged to Uncle Louis. It meant my father probably got it from him. It's the only evidence I have of any connection between them. There must have been many more of them over the years. They were connections I would have been too young to witness.

I'm interested in Uncle Louis because he was my father's brother but I can't bring myself to look up anyone else in my past that I didn't know. There's a programme on the television called *Who Do You Think You Are?* It has people travelling vast distances to research their ancestors. I could never do that. If I haven't had a direct contact with someone they don't mean much to me. *Who Do You Think You Are?* deals mainly with people's circumstances rather than their personalities. To me that's like the way history was taught in Muredach's. I couldn't get into it because it had the tyranny of fact.

That attitude spilled over into everything I did in later years. When I'm reading a book or watching a film I find it difficult to involve myself in the plot. For me plots are nothing more than necessary evils. They're pegs you hang characters on. That's why I can enjoy a book or a film by starting in the middle. Maybe I should have been born in China. Don't they read things backwards there?

The other memento I kept of my father was his diary. He made an entry to it on the day he died. Among other things it said, 'Aubrey gone to town.' He put in the most trivial of events. The pages were almost as long as A4 ones but he managed to fill them every day.

At the end of the page he used to write down how many people were staying in the house that night. It was as if it was some kind of boarding house. It was amazing how much the numbers changed day by day with all the traffic going in and out.

I lost the diary. The only memento I have of him now is an old Gold Bond Benson & Hedges cigarette packet with his writing on the inside of it. I can't make out any of the words. They're just as indecipherable as most of the other things he wrote in his life.

I think he saw this as an example of erudition. It was like doctors were supposed to have unreadable handwriting, the kind we cursed when we were trying to read their prescriptions. Uncle Louis was different in that regard. His writing was as straightforward as his life.

The only memento I have of my mother is a letter she wrote to me when I was in Denver. It's written in her familiar stream-of-consciousness style. She never used capital letters or full stops, just dashes between every sentence. Nora Barnacle wrote that way too. I often think Molly Bloom's soliloquy from *Ulysses* was inspired by this style. Women are more spontaneous than men. They often don't bother much with grammar, regarding it as an annoying irrelevance to getting their message across.

Of course I also have photographs of my mother and father. I look at them sometimes and try to remember what I was doing when they were taken. Was that the Saturday I was looking forward to watching The Monkees on television? Was it the day I lost my bicycle? The day it rained in Belleek and our football game had to be cancelled?

I don't know why such things matter but they do. They're in me as much as my DNA, as much as the air I breathe.

I still miss 'the town I loved so well,' as Phil Coulter put it in his song. I miss getting up on one of those thousand mornings in Ballina not knowing what the day might bring. I miss playing games that seemed to have no end and no beginning. I miss the films in the Estoria, I miss going up to the font and turning left where the crazy paving leads into Bury Street and walking down by the post office and across the road to the Hibs where for a few hours every day I turned away from the world called Reality.

People sometimes say to me, 'If you feel like that you should be living there.' Maybe I should. On the other hand, distance lends enchantment to the eye. Ballina today isn't the town I left.

Time has made me accept that fact. I was brought to Dublin because there were more opportunities for a future here. It was like going from a shop to a supermarket. I stayed in it for convenience, like someone might stay in a bad marriage. That doesn't mean I like it.

I never became Dublinised. I didn't get the accent or have coffee at eleven in Bewley's or meet anyone under the clock at Clery's or shout for the Dublin team or even go to the Dáil or the zoo. I live here but that's it. I'm a Dulchie.

The past is more real to me than the present. It comes back to me in my mind's eye. I re-visit it in the films I go to and the songs I listen to. and the books I read- and write.

I see my mother hanging clothes on the line. She has a clothespeg in her mouth. My father is in his dressing gown in the front room. He's swearing in a client as he signs a document for him over a copy of The Bible.

It's a fair day. Donkeys honk in the street. There are cowpats everywhere. Farmers spit on their hands as they make deals beside malnourished cows. The rest of us are scuttling around the letterbox outside the front door of Norfolk. We're in our ragamuffin clothes swapping comics and playing marbles. Time stretches before us like an eternity.

Children don't play much on the streets today. Their parents would be afraid they'd never see them again. My parents didn't have that kind of worry. There were no Madeleine McCanns in those days. There were no paedophiles, no curfews, no quarantines, no lockdowns.

Most of my life passed by me in a haze. It amazes me when people remember things I don't. I often remember things they've forgotten. Sometimes something that happened twenty years ago comes back to me as clearly as something that happened yesterday. That's the way it is with a lot of people. But we don't remember everything that happened twenty years ago. That's the point.

I go back to what I said about the importance of mysteries. Can you imagine what it would be like if we had an image of Lee Harvey Oswald as he pulled the trigger on John F. Kennedy? Or if we could see the supposed other shooter that day? Or the other shooters? How many conspiracy theories would that kill off?

What wouldn't we pay to be a fly on the wall listening to Adolf Hitler plot the invasion of Europe. Or seeing Madame Curie inventing radium. Or stepping on Mars to see if it was inhabited. Or having some way of seeing how the world looked when dinosaurs roamed around it.

What would we pay to see the moment of *homo sapiens* or the Big Bang? It's our uncertainty about events that drives us on rather than our knowledge of them.

Ignorance is more exciting than knowledge. Sometimes I think it must be boring to be God.